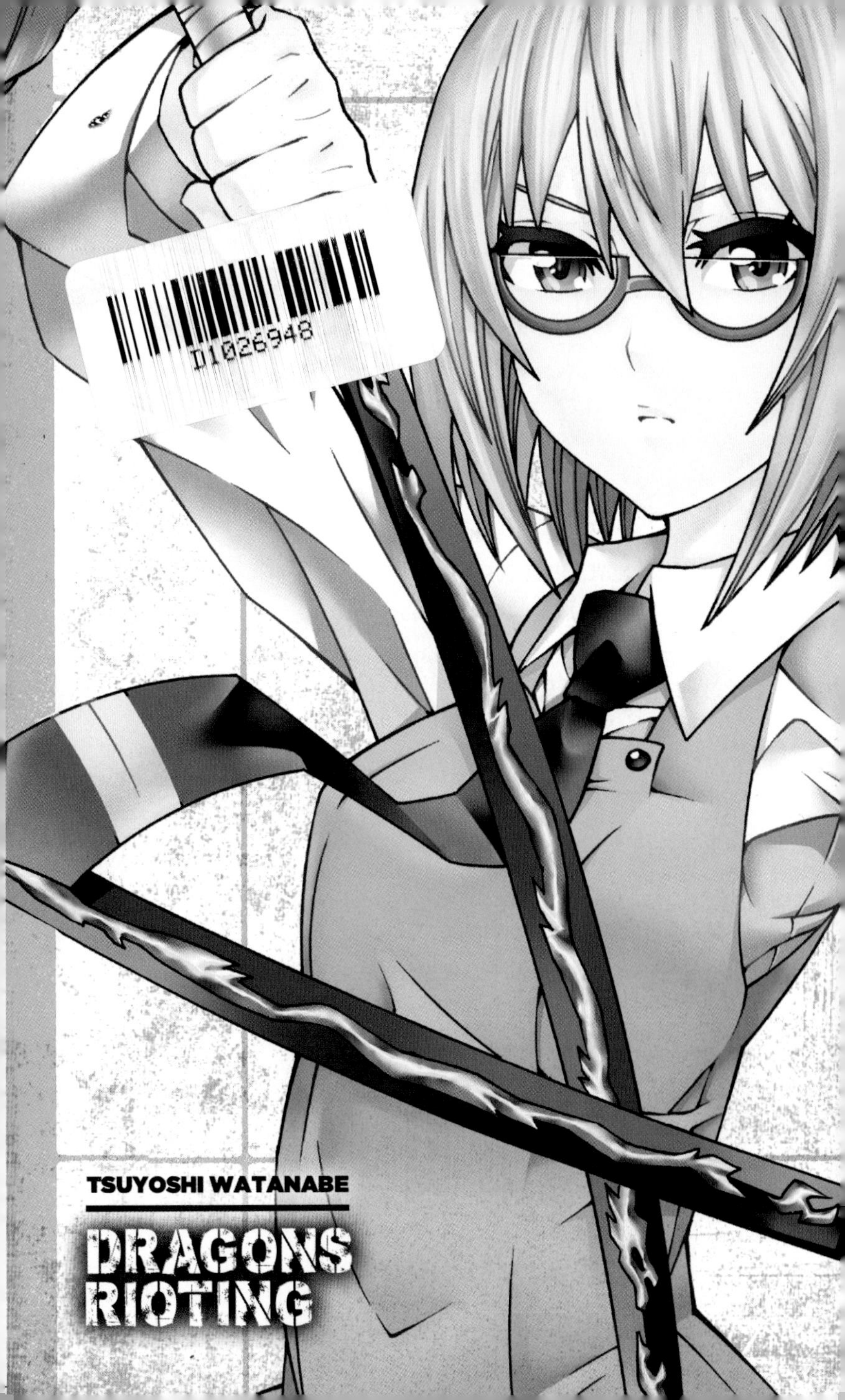
D1026948
TSUYOSHI WATANABE
DRAGONS RIOTING

男獄煉

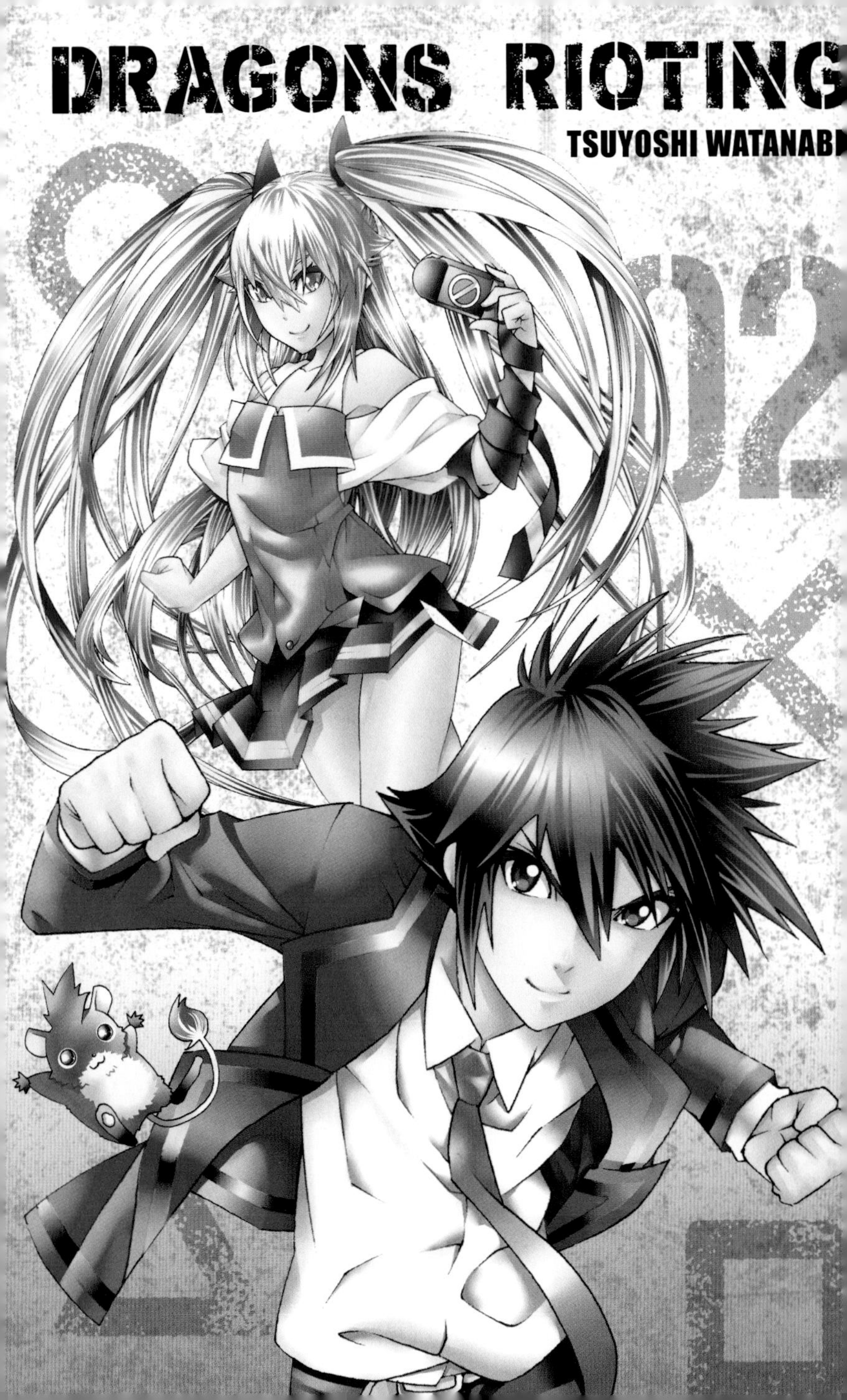
DRAGONS RIOTING
TSUYOSHI WATANAB
02

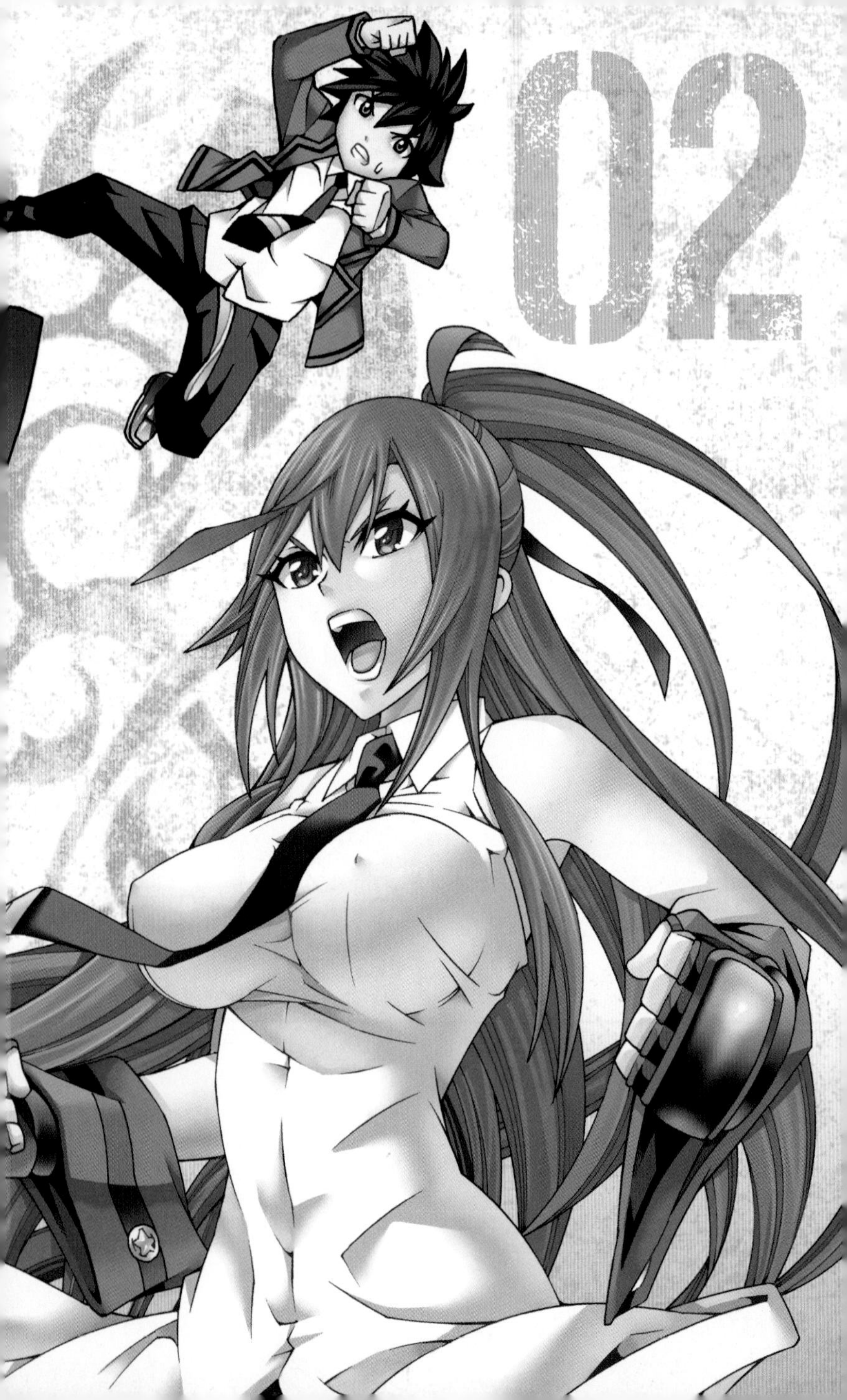
02

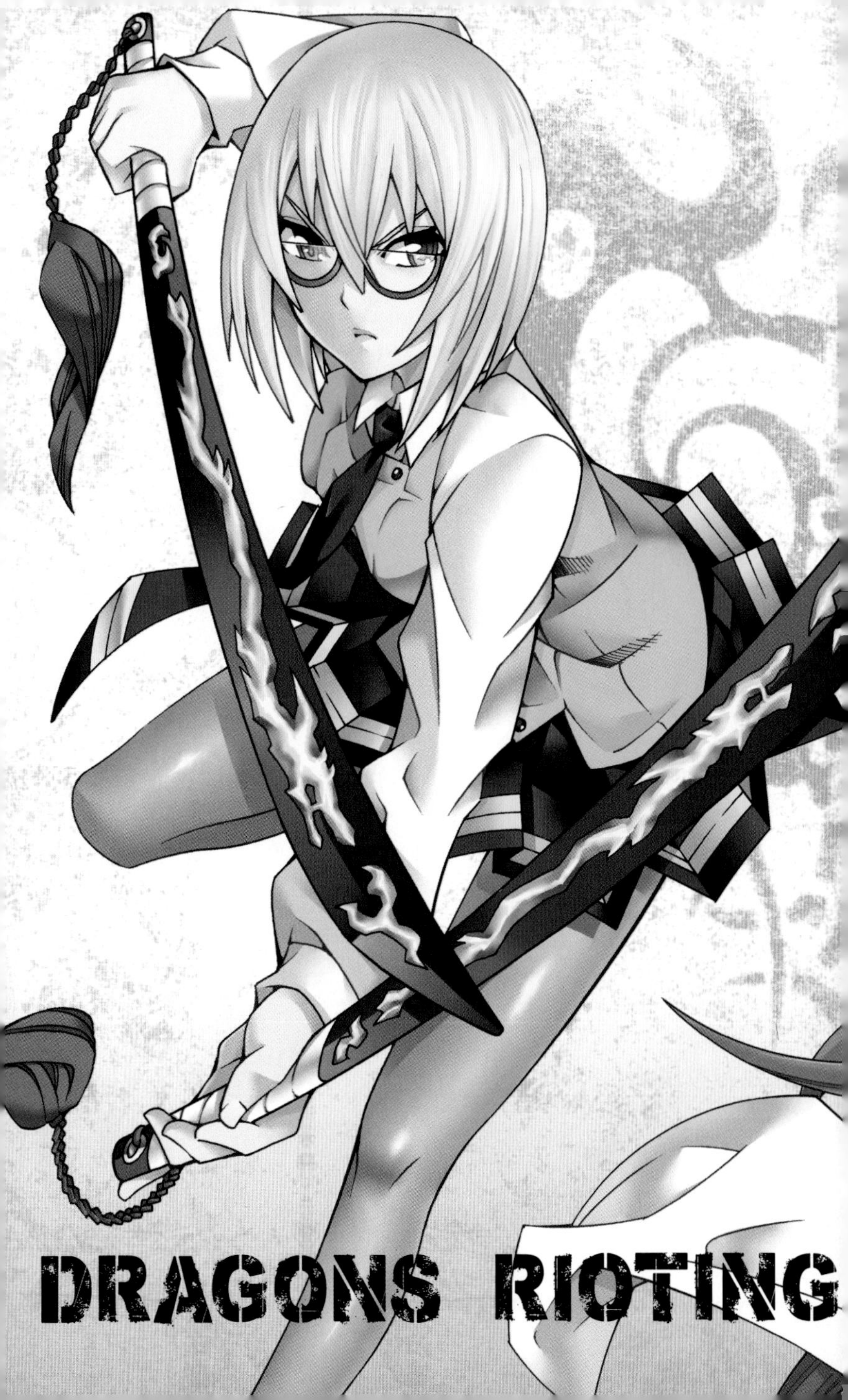
DRAGONS RIOTING

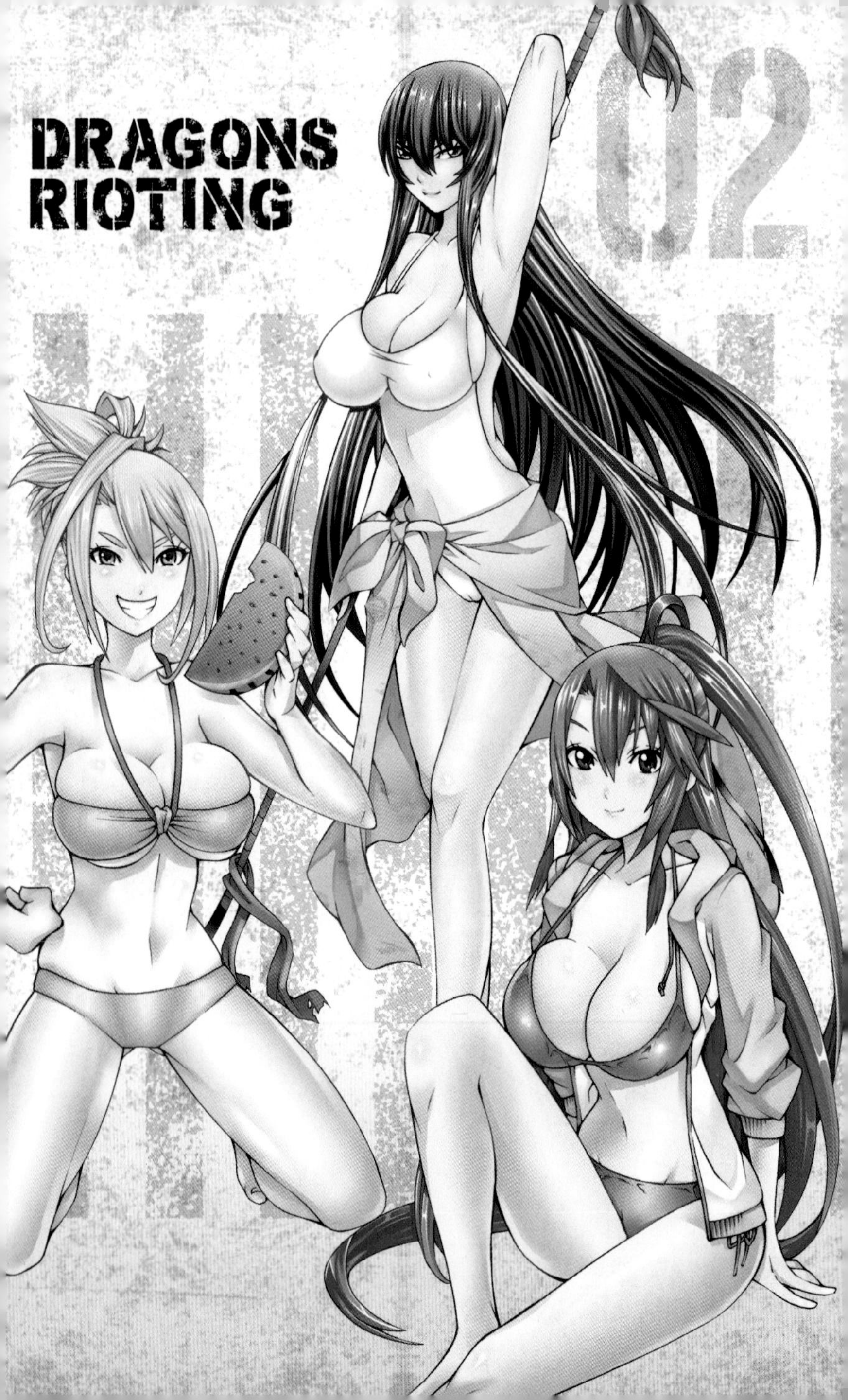
DRAGONS
RIOTING
02

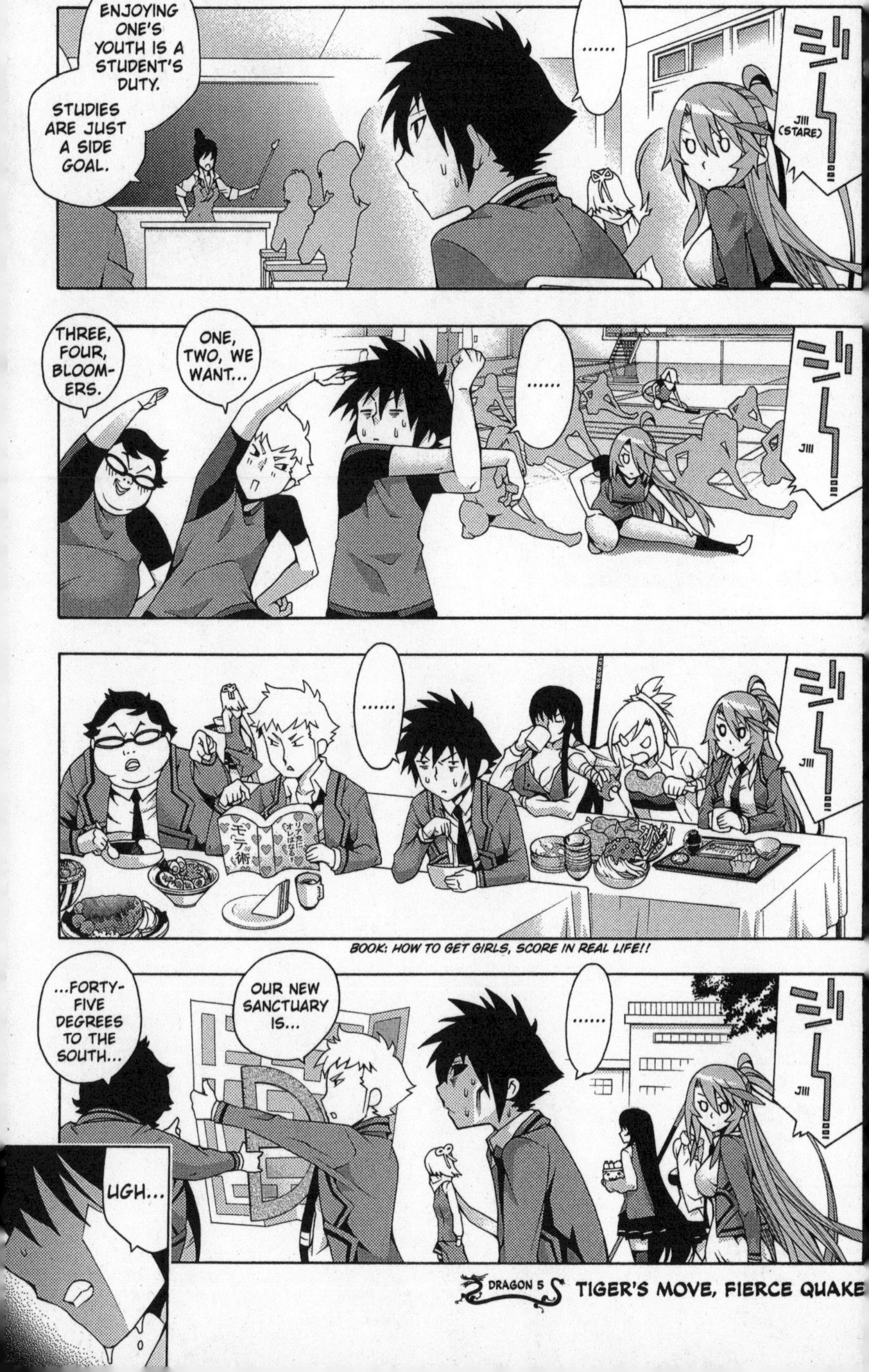
JIII (STARE)
......
ENJOYING ONE'S YOUTH IS A STUDENT'S DUTY.
STUDIES ARE JUST A SIDE GOAL.
JIII
......
ONE, TWO, WE WANT...
THREE, FOUR, BLOOMERS.
JIII
......
BOOK: HOW TO GET GIRLS, SCORE IN REAL LIFE!!
JIII
......
OUR NEW SANCTUARY IS...
...FORTY-FIVE DEGREES TO THE SOUTH...
UGH...

DRAGON 5 TIGER'S MOVE, FIERCE QUAKE

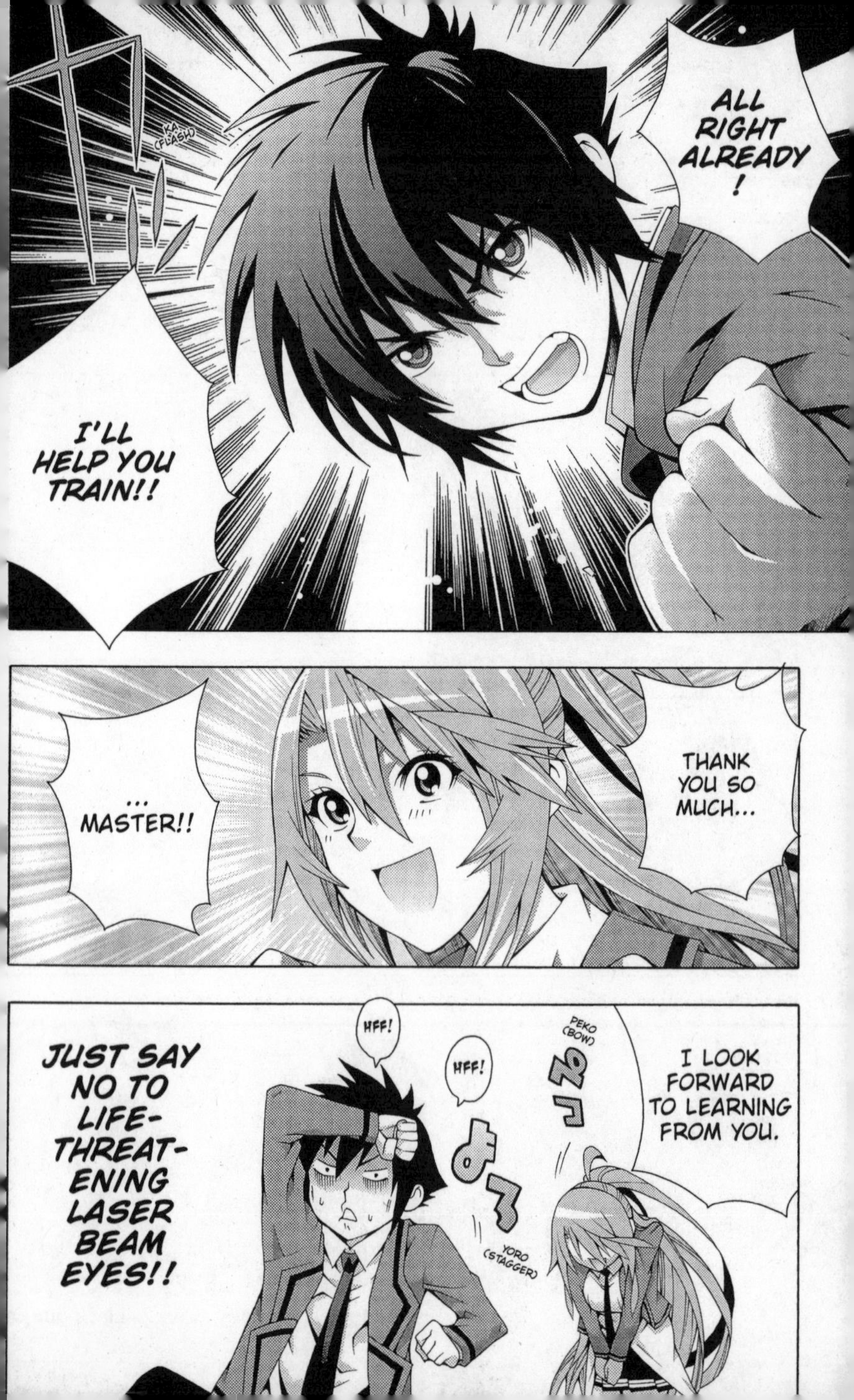
ALL RIGHT ALREADY!
KA (FLASH)
I'LL HELP YOU TRAIN!!
THANK YOU SO MUCH...
...MASTER!!
I LOOK FORWARD TO LEARNING FROM YOU.
PEKO (BOW)
HFF!
HFF!
YORO (STAGGER)
JUST SAY NO TO LIFE-THREAT-ENING LASER BEAM EYES!!

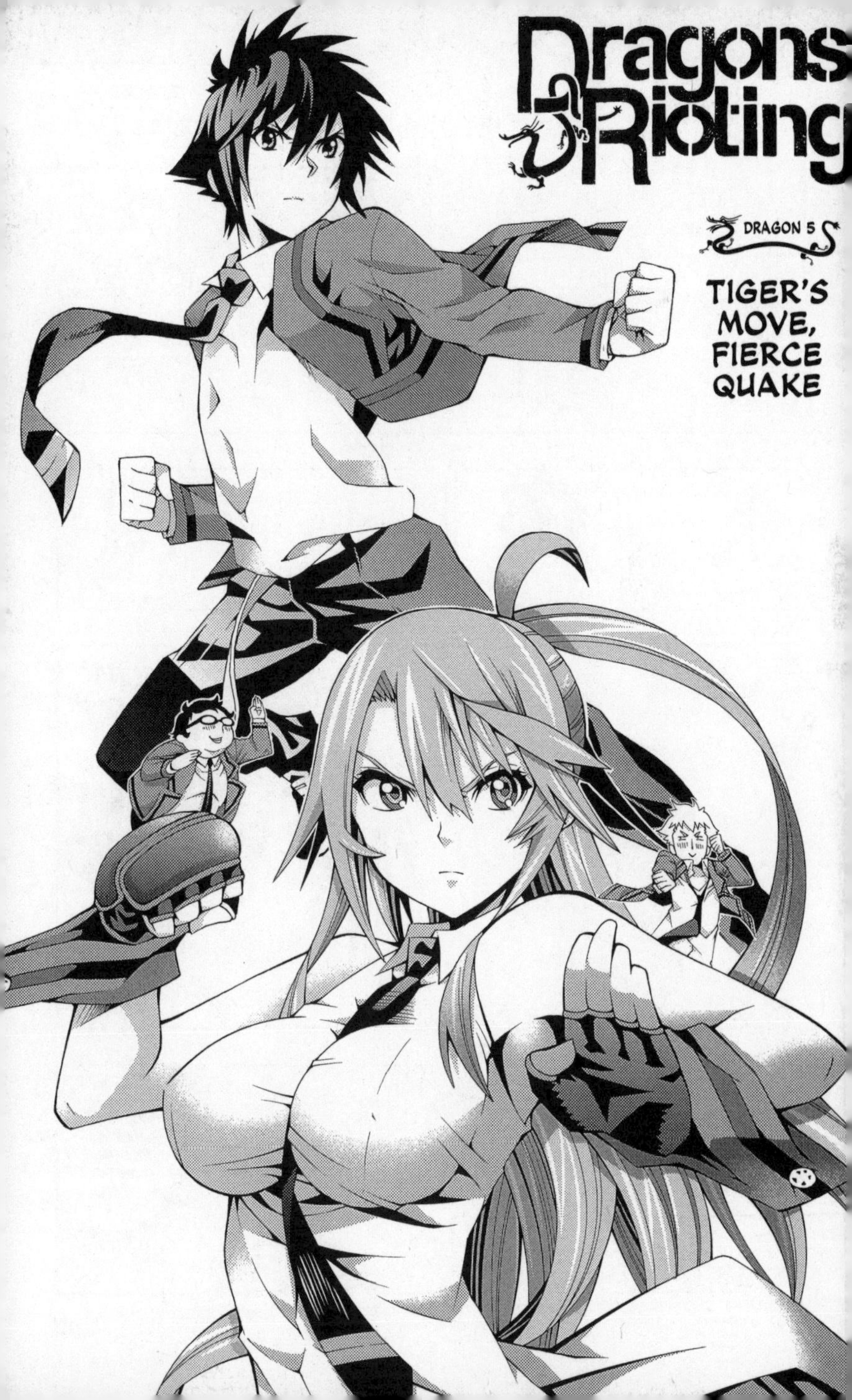
Dragons Rioting
DRAGON 5
TIGER'S MOVE, FIERCE QUAKE

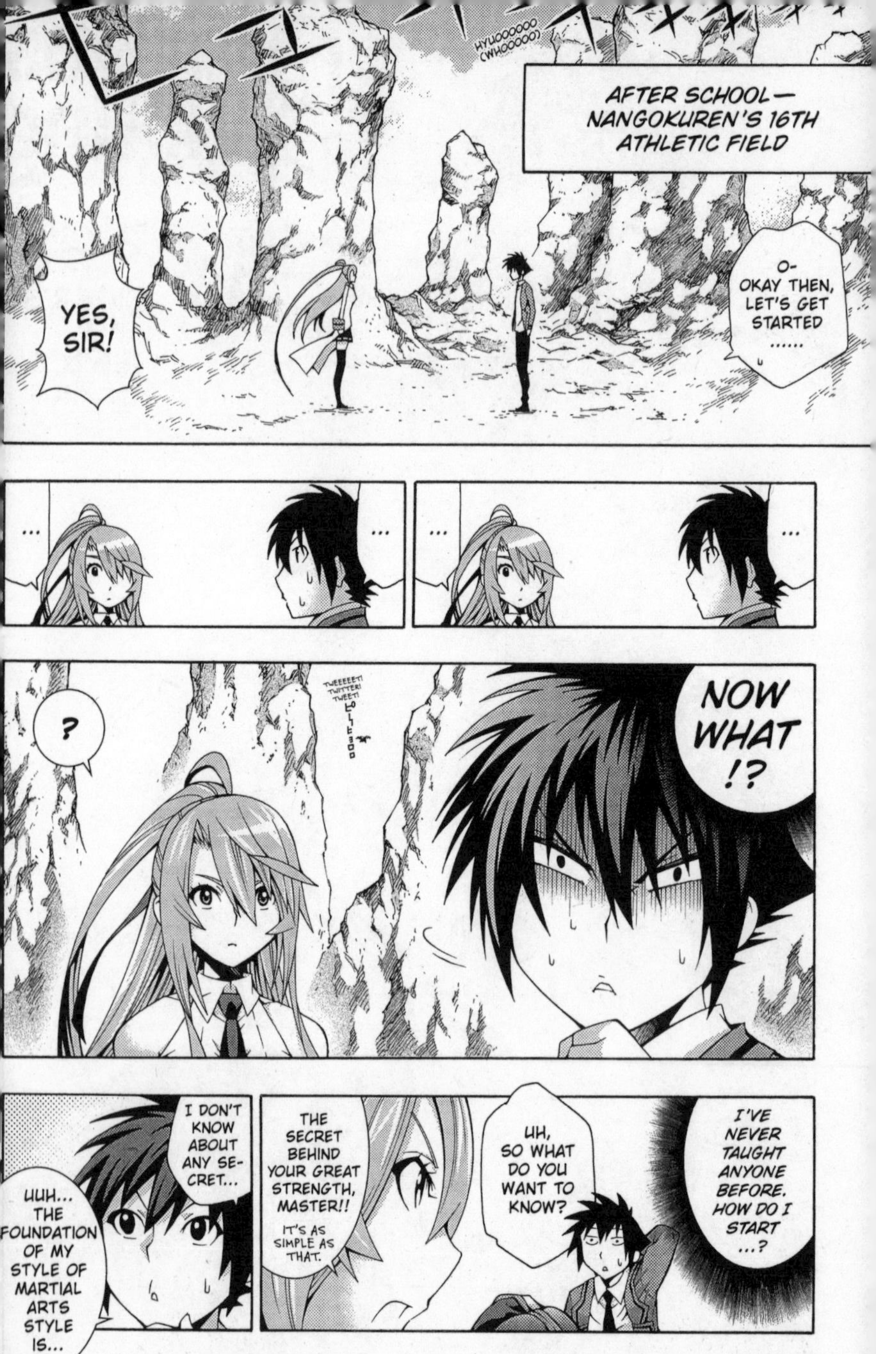
AFTER SCHOOL—NANGOKUREN'S 16TH ATHLETIC FIELD
HYUOOOOOO (WHOOOOO)
O-OKAY THEN, LET'S GET STARTED ......
YES, SIR!
...
...
...
...
NOW WHAT!?
TWEEEEET! TWITTER! TWEET!
?
I'VE NEVER TAUGHT ANYONE BEFORE. HOW DO I START ...?
UH, SO WHAT DO YOU WANT TO KNOW?
THE SECRET BEHIND YOUR GREAT STRENGTH, MASTER!!
IT'S AS SIMPLE AS THAT.
I DON'T KNOW ABOUT ANY SE-CRET...
UUH... THE FOUNDATION OF MY STYLE OF MARTIAL ARTS STYLE IS...

LABEL: KEEP IT UNDISTURBED LABELS, RIGHT TO LEFT: SOUL, SKILL, BODY LABEL: CLEAR THE MIND

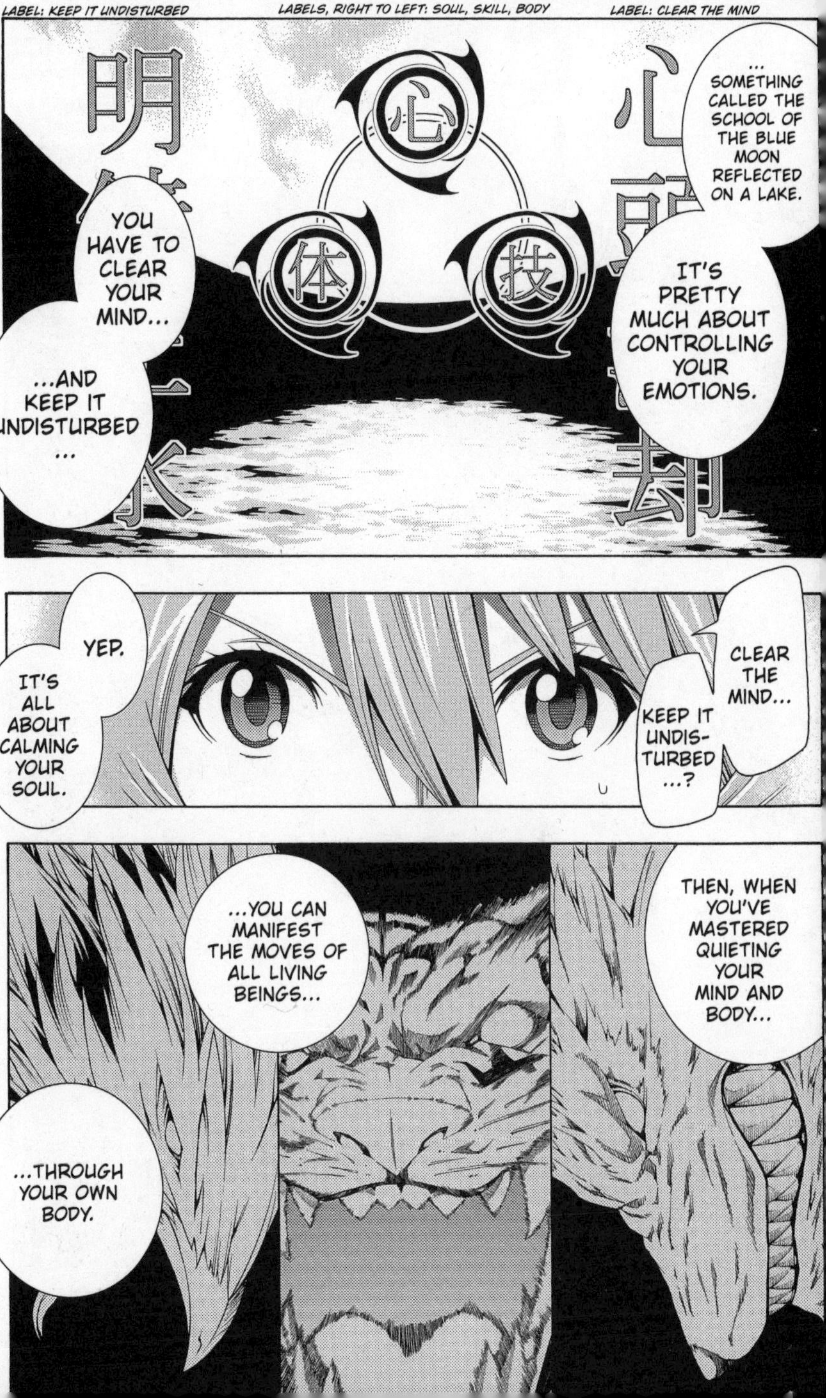
...SOMETHING CALLED THE SCHOOL OF THE BLUE MOON REFLECTED ON A LAKE.
心
技
体
IT'S PRETTY MUCH ABOUT CONTROLLING YOUR EMOTIONS.
YOU HAVE TO CLEAR YOUR MIND...
...AND KEEP IT UNDISTURBED...
CLEAR THE MIND...
KEEP IT UNDIS-TURBED...?
YEP.
IT'S ALL ABOUT CALMING YOUR SOUL.
THEN, WHEN YOU'VE MASTERED QUIETING YOUR MIND AND BODY...
...YOU CAN MANIFEST THE MOVES OF ALL LIVING BEINGS...
...THROUGH YOUR OWN BODY.

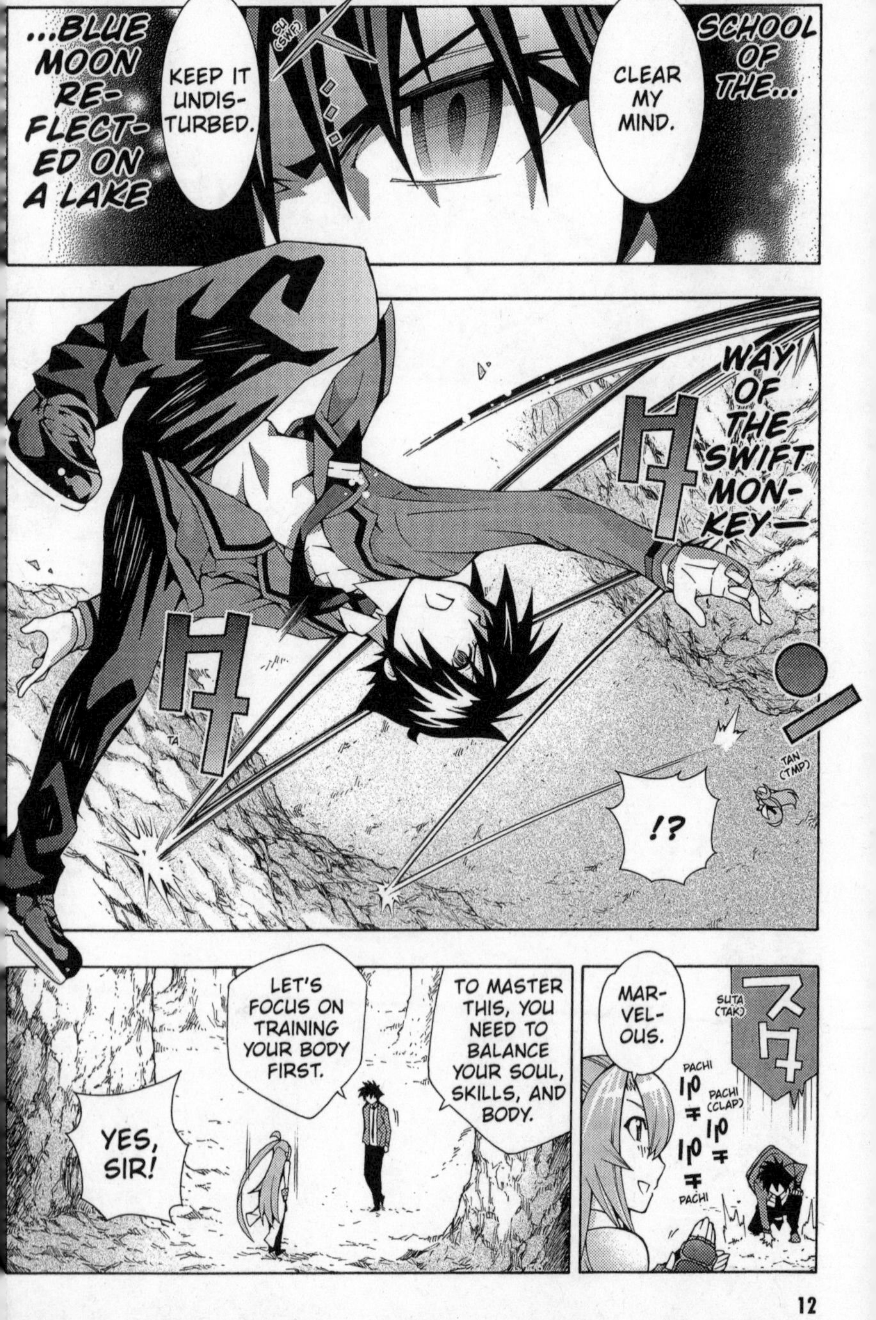
SCHOOL OF THE...
CLEAR MY MIND.
SU (SWP)
KEEP IT UNDISTURBED.
...BLUE MOON REFLECTED ON A LAKE
WAY OF THE SWIFT MONKEY—
TAN (TMP)
!?
TA
SUTA (TAK)
MARVELOUS.
PACHI
PACHI (CLAP)
PACHI
TO MASTER THIS, YOU NEED TO BALANCE YOUR SOUL, SKILLS, AND BODY.
LET'S FOCUS ON TRAINING YOUR BODY FIRST.
YES, SIR!

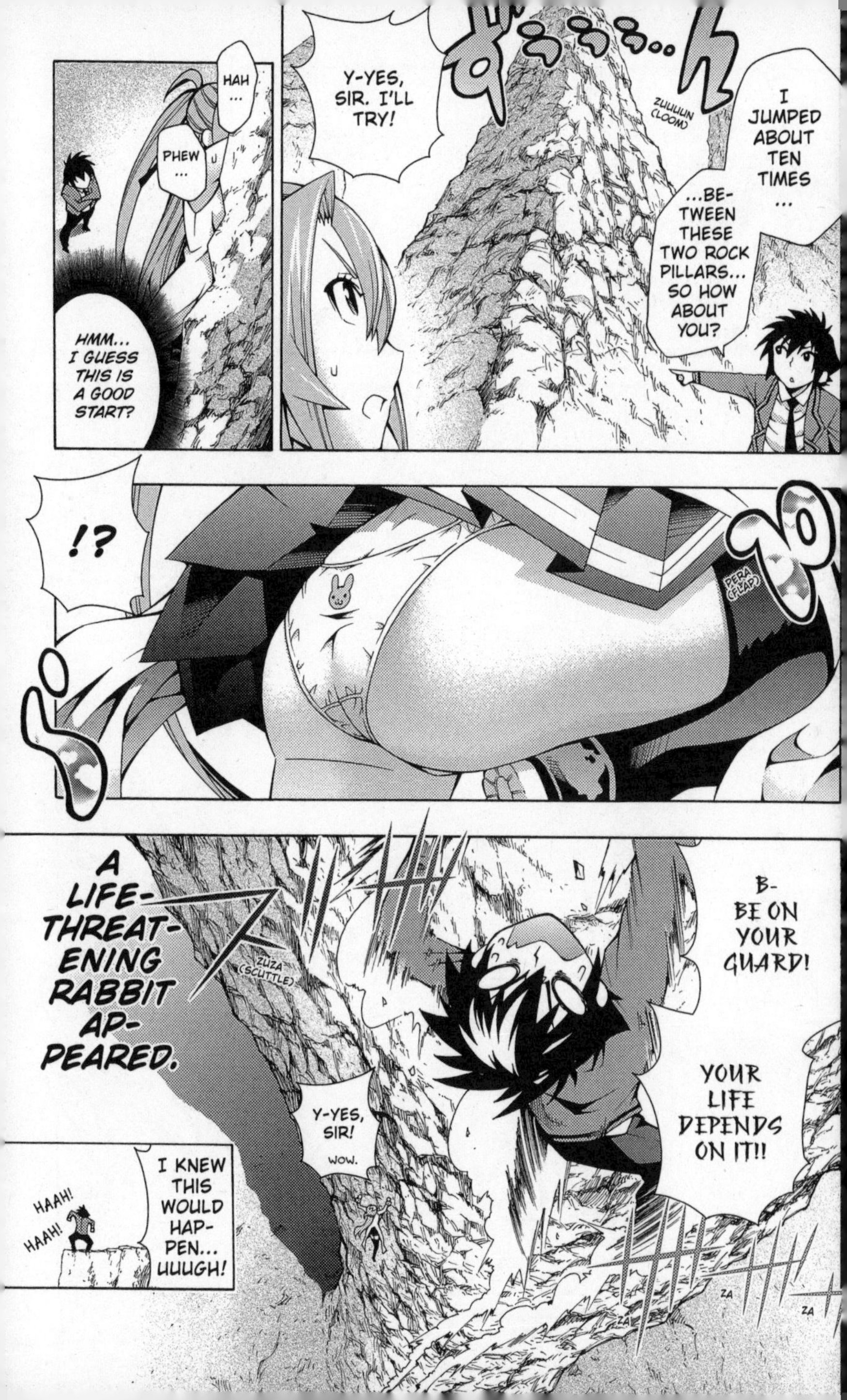
ZUUUUN (LOOM)
I JUMPED ABOUT TEN TIMES...
...BE-TWEEN THESE TWO ROCK PILLARS... SO HOW ABOUT YOU?
Y-YES, SIR. I'LL TRY!
HAH...
PHEW...
HMM... I GUESS THIS IS A GOOD START?
PERA (FLAP)
!?
B-BE ON YOUR GUARD!
YOUR LIFE DEPENDS ON IT!!
A LIFE-THREAT-ENING RABBIT AP-PEARED.
ZUZA (SCUTTLE)
ZA
ZA
ZA
Y-YES, SIR!
WOW.
I KNEW THIS WOULD HAP-PEN... UUUGH!
HAAH!
HAAH!

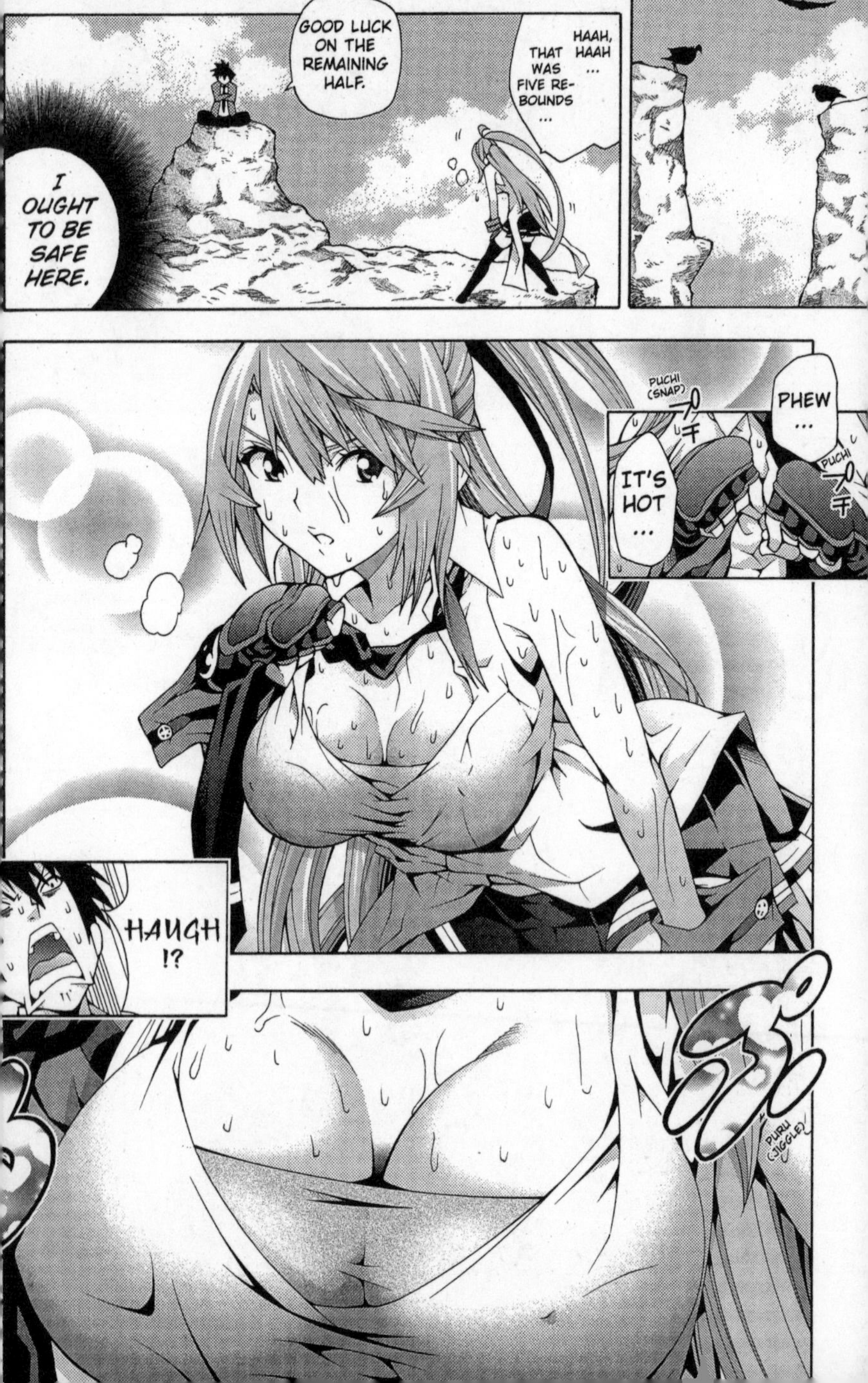
HAAH, HAAH ... THAT WAS FIVE RE-BOUNDS ...
GOOD LUCK ON THE REMAINING HALF.
I OUGHT TO BE SAFE HERE.
PUCHI (SNAP)
PHEW ...
PUCHI
IT'S HOT ...
HAUGH !?
PURU (JIGGLE)

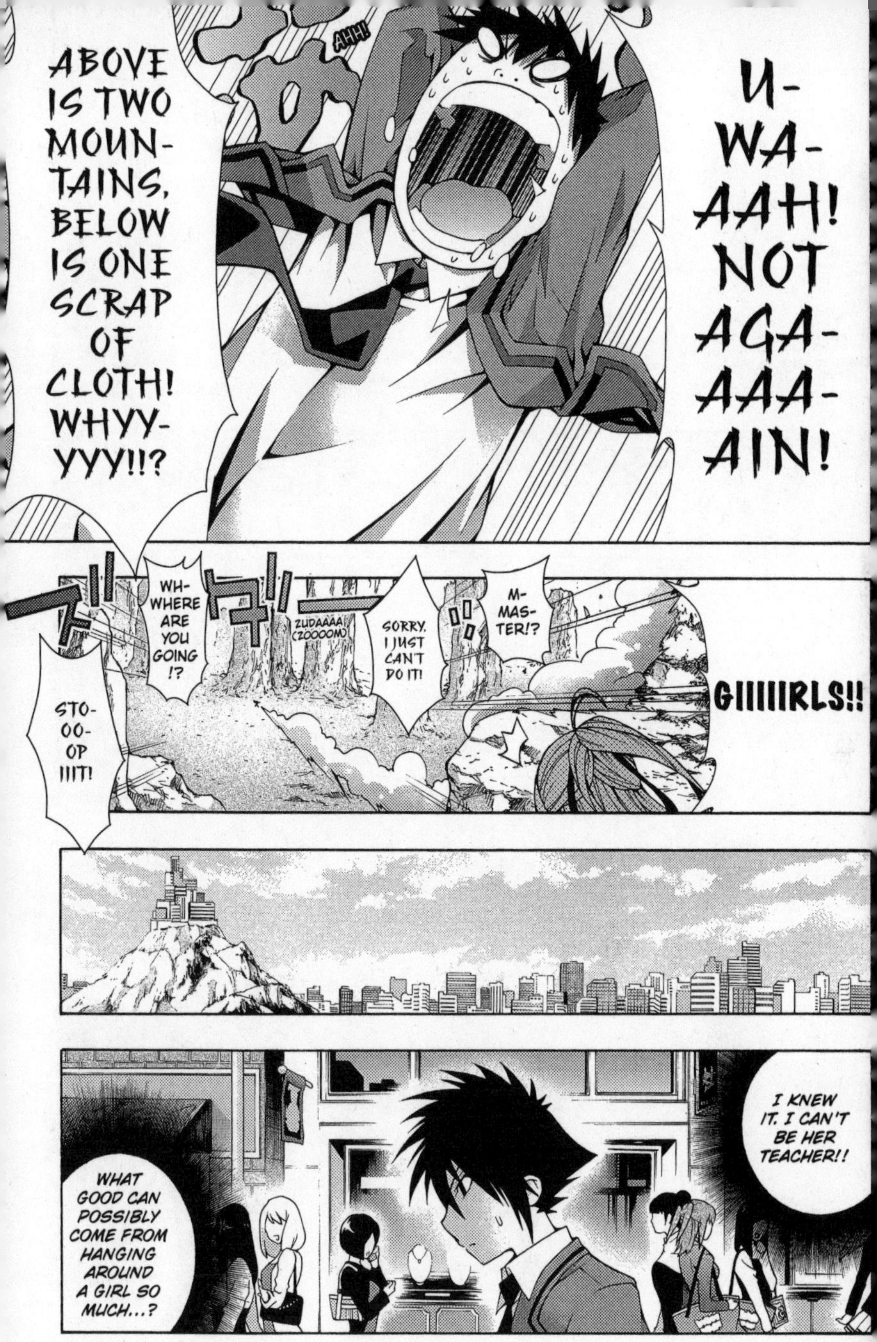
U-WA-AAH! NOT AGA-AAA-AIN!
AHH!
ABOVE IS TWO MOUN-TAINS, BELOW IS ONE SCRAP OF CLOTH! WHYY-YYY!!?
GIIIIIRLS!!
M-MAS-TER!?
SORRY, I JUST CAN'T DO IT!
ZUDAAAA (ZOOOOM)
WH-WHERE ARE YOU GOING!?
STO-OO-OP IIIT!
I KNEW IT. I CAN'T BE HER TEACHER!!
WHAT GOOD CAN POSSIBLY COME FROM HANGING AROUND A GIRL SO MUCH...?

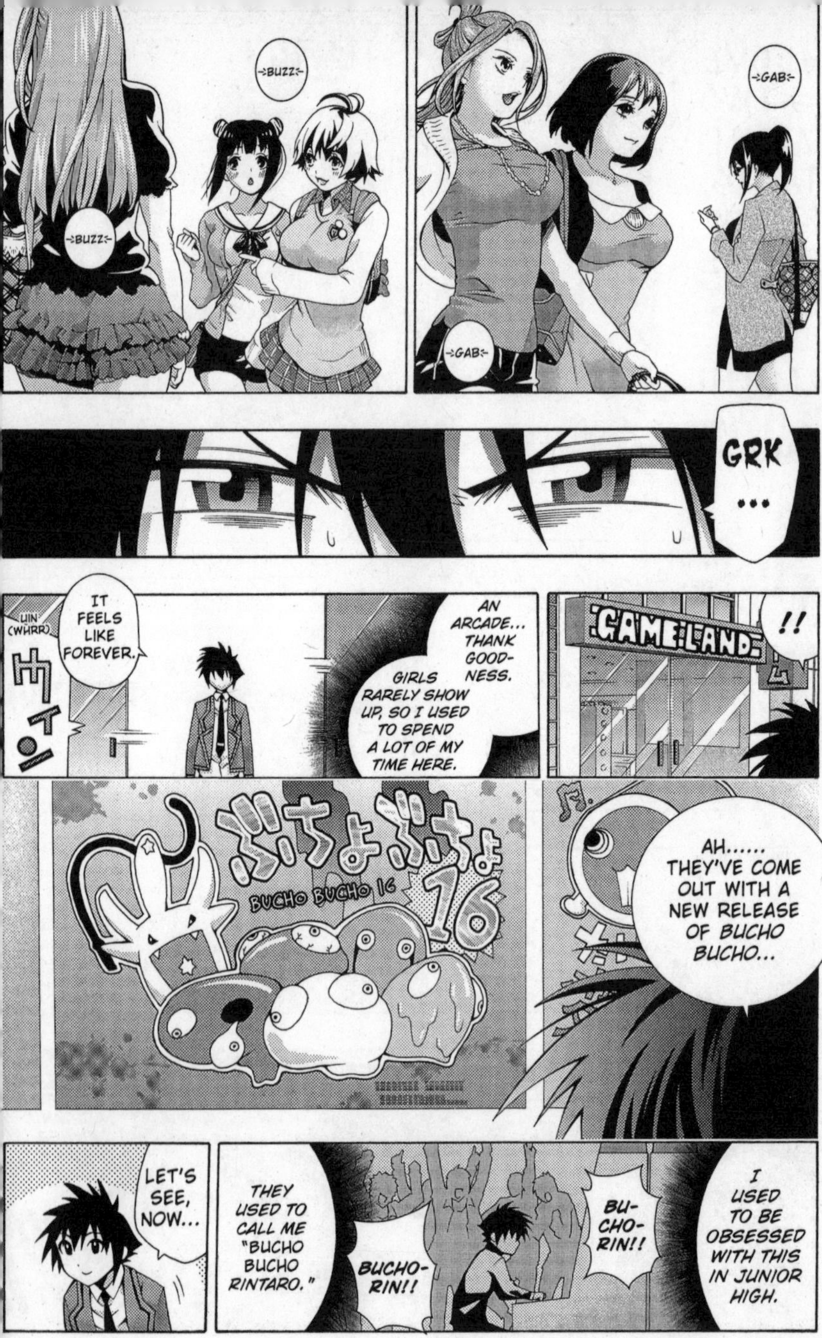
GAB
GAB
BUZZ
BUZZ
GRK ...
!!
AN ARCADE... THANK GOODNESS.
GIRLS RARELY SHOW UP, SO I USED TO SPEND A LOT OF MY TIME HERE.
IT FEELS LIKE FOREVER.
UIN (WHRR)
GAME LAND
AH...... THEY'VE COME OUT WITH A NEW RELEASE OF BUCHO BUCHO...
ぶちょぶちょ 16
BUCHO BUCHO 16
I USED TO BE OBSESSED WITH THIS IN JUNIOR HIGH.
BU-CHO-RIN!!
BUCHO-RIN!!
THEY USED TO CALL ME "BUCHO BUCHO RINTARO."
LET'S SEE, NOW...

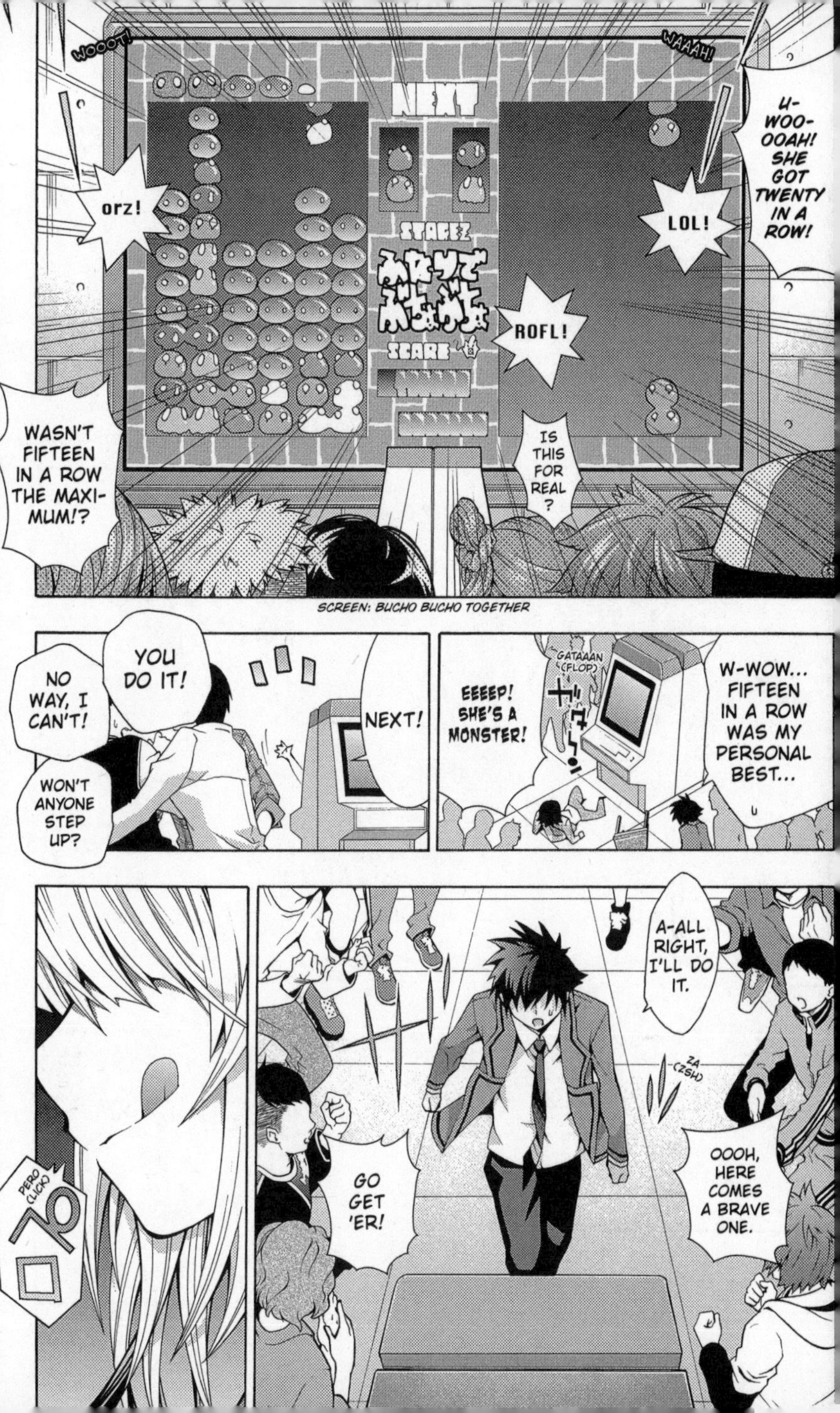
WAAAH!
U-WOO-OOAH! SHE GOT TWENTY IN A ROW!
LOL!
ROFL!
IS THIS FOR REAL?
NEXT
WOOOT!
orz!
WASN'T FIFTEEN IN A ROW THE MAXI-MUM!?
SCREEN: BUCHO BUCHO TOGETHER
W-WOW... FIFTEEN IN A ROW WAS MY PERSONAL BEST...
GATAAAN (FLOP)
EEEEP! SHE'S A MONSTER!
NEXT!
YOU DO IT!
NO WAY, I CAN'T!
WON'T ANYONE STEP UP?
A-ALL RIGHT, I'LL DO IT.
ZA (ZSH)
OOOH, HERE COMES A BRAVE ONE.
GO GET 'ER!
PERO (LICK)

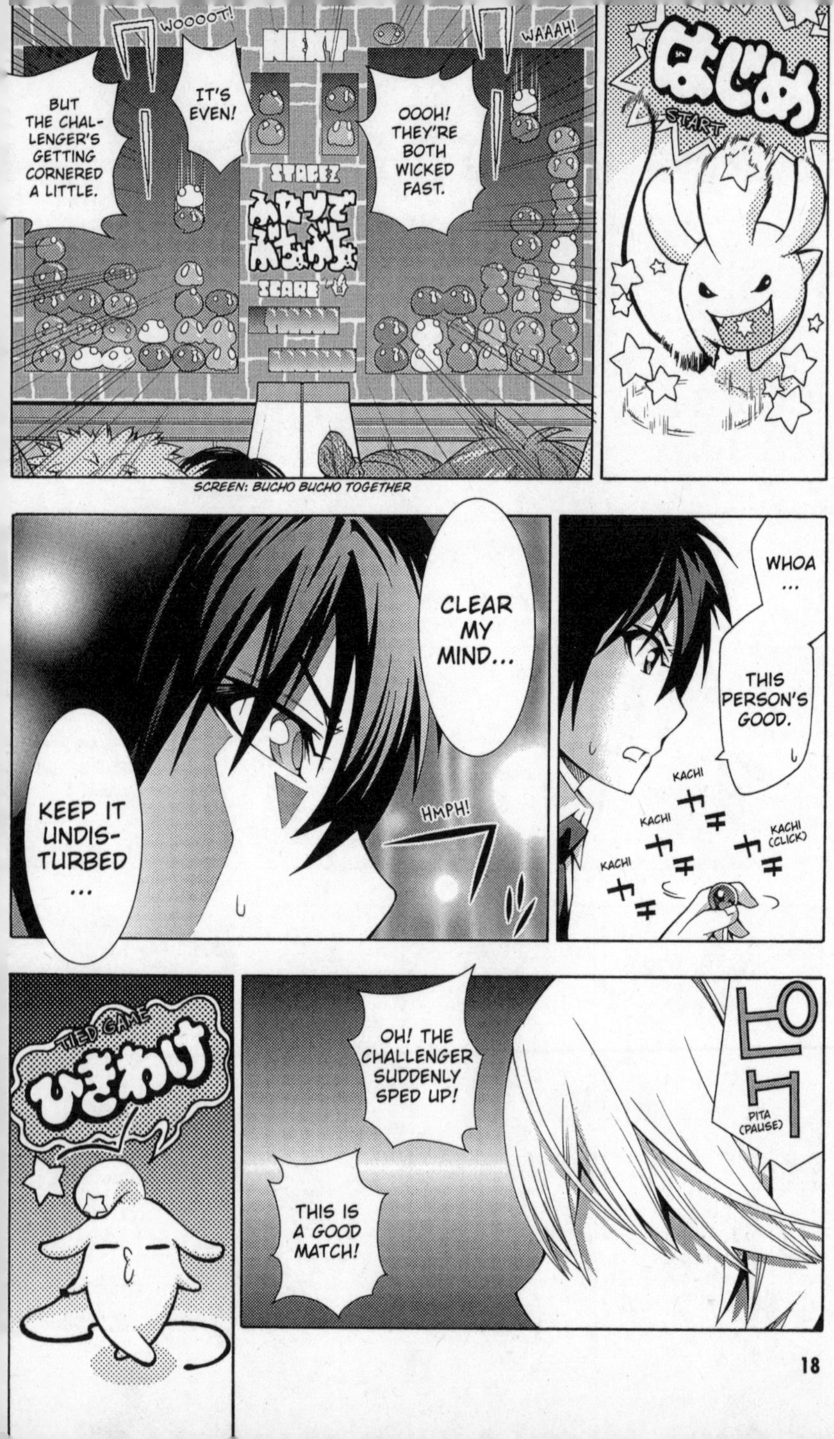
はじめ
START
WAAAH!
OOOH! THEY'RE BOTH WICKED FAST.
NEXT
WOOOOT!
IT'S EVEN!
BUT THE CHALLENGER'S GETTING CORNERED A LITTLE.
SCREEN: BUCHO BUCHO TOGETHER
WHOA...
THIS PERSON'S GOOD.
KACHI (CLICK)
KACHI
KACHI
KACHI
CLEAR MY MIND...
HMPH!
KEEP IT UNDISTURBED...
PITA (PAUSE)
OH! THE CHALLENGER SUDDENLY SPED UP!
THIS IS A GOOD MATCH!
TIED GAME
ひきわけ

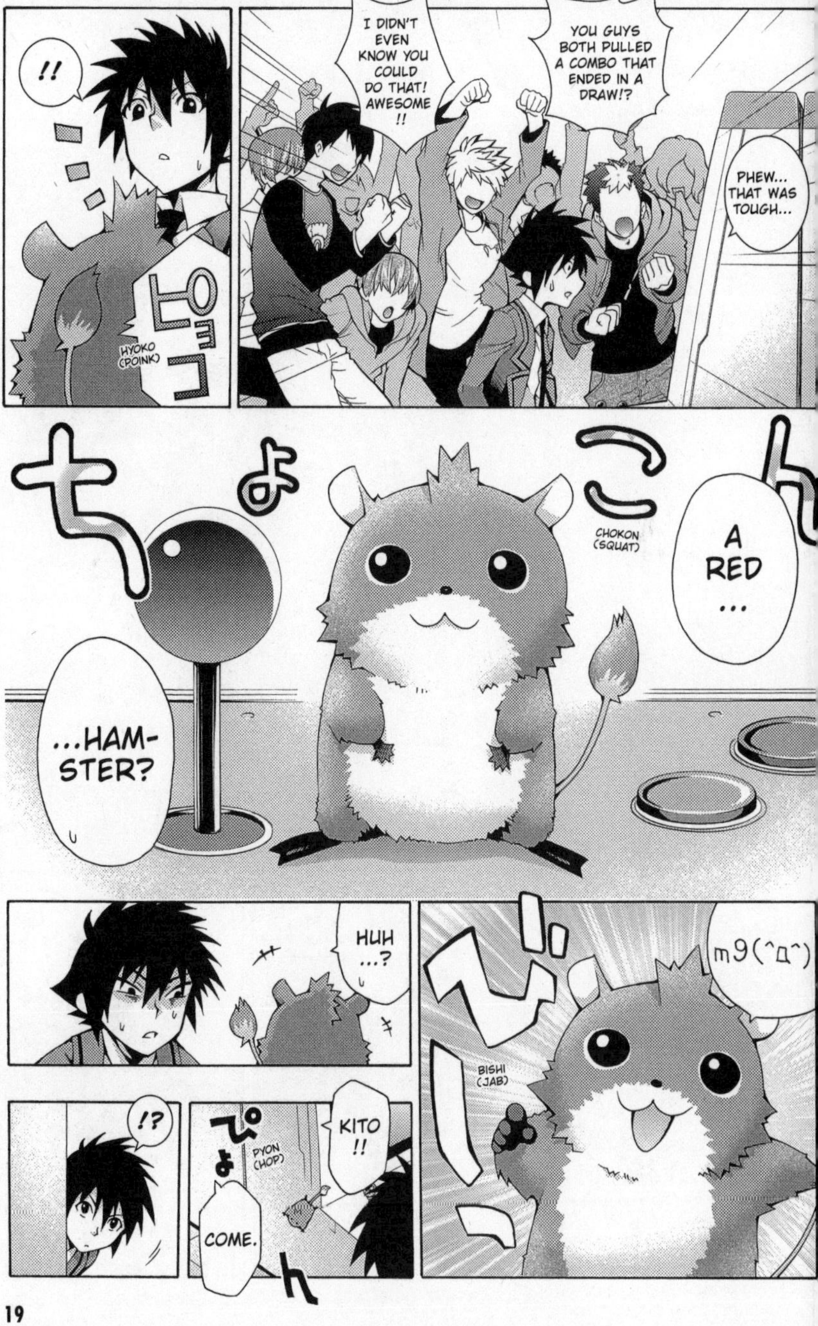
YOU GUYS BOTH PULLED A COMBO THAT ENDED IN A DRAW!?
I DIDN'T EVEN KNOW YOU COULD DO THAT! AWESOME !!
PHEW... THAT WAS TOUGH...
!!
ピョコ
HYOKO (POINK)
ちょこん
CHOKON (SQUAT)
A RED ...
...HAM-STER?
m9(^Д^)
BISHI (JAB)
HUH ...?
KITO !!
ぴょん
PYON (HOP)
COME.
!?

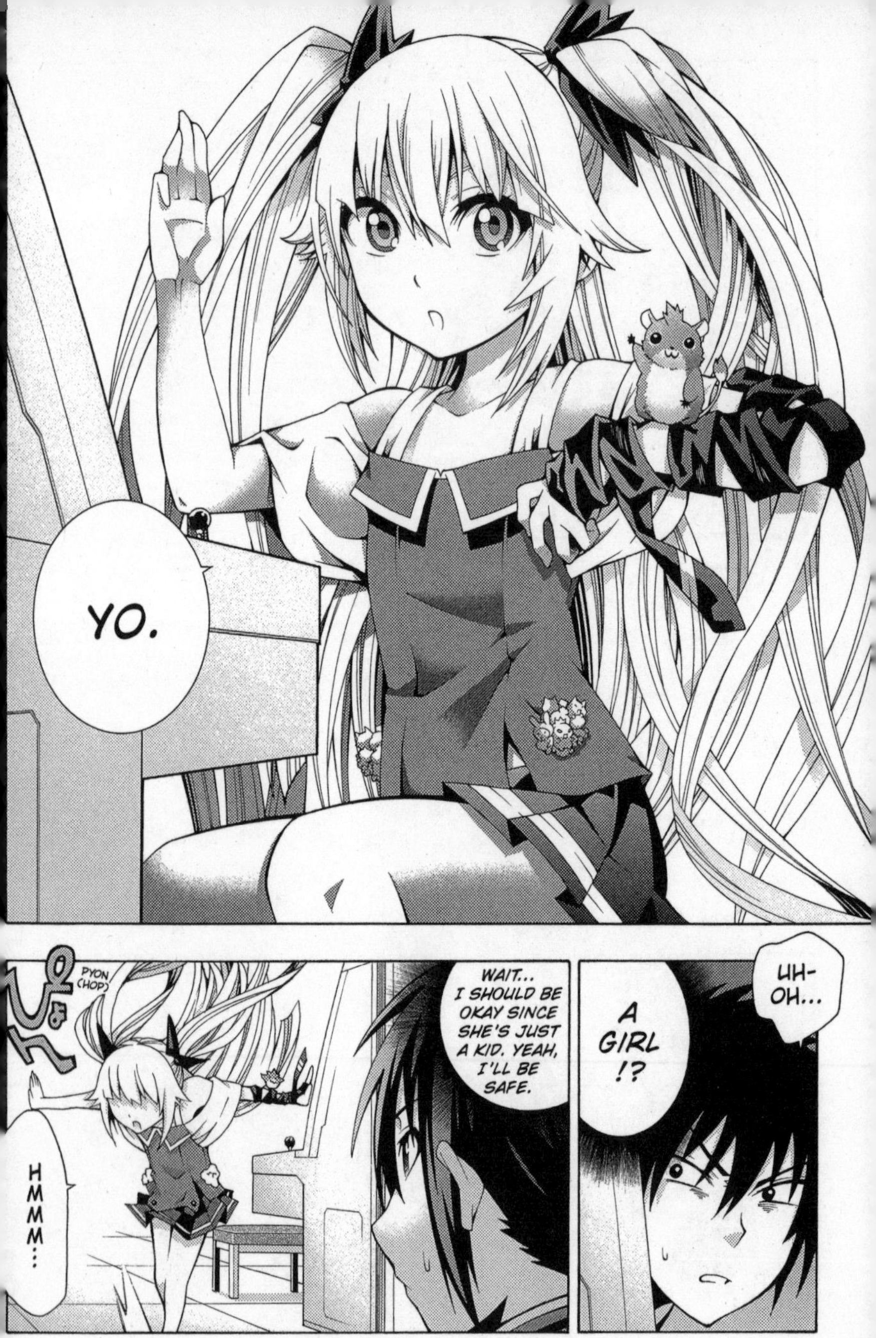
YO.
UH-OH...
A GIRL!?
WAIT... I SHOULD BE OKAY SINCE SHE'S JUST A KID. YEAH, I'LL BE SAFE.
PYON (HOP)
HMMMM...

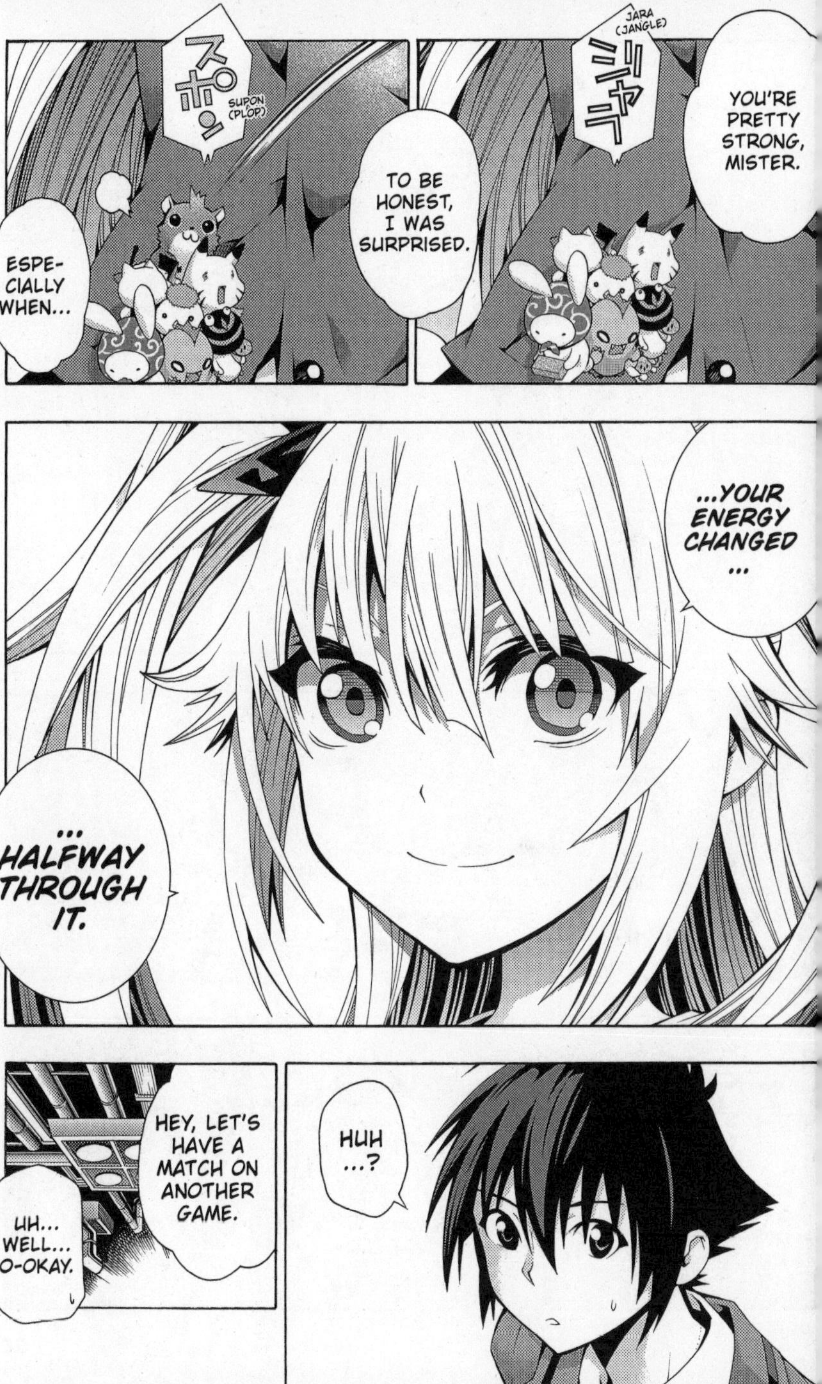
JARA (JANGLE)
YOU'RE PRETTY STRONG, MISTER.
TO BE HONEST, I WAS SURPRISED.
SUPON (PLOP)
ESPE-CIALLY WHEN...
...YOUR ENERGY CHANGED...
... HALFWAY THROUGH IT.
HUH...?
HEY, LET'S HAVE A MATCH ON ANOTHER GAME.
UH... WELL... O-OKAY.

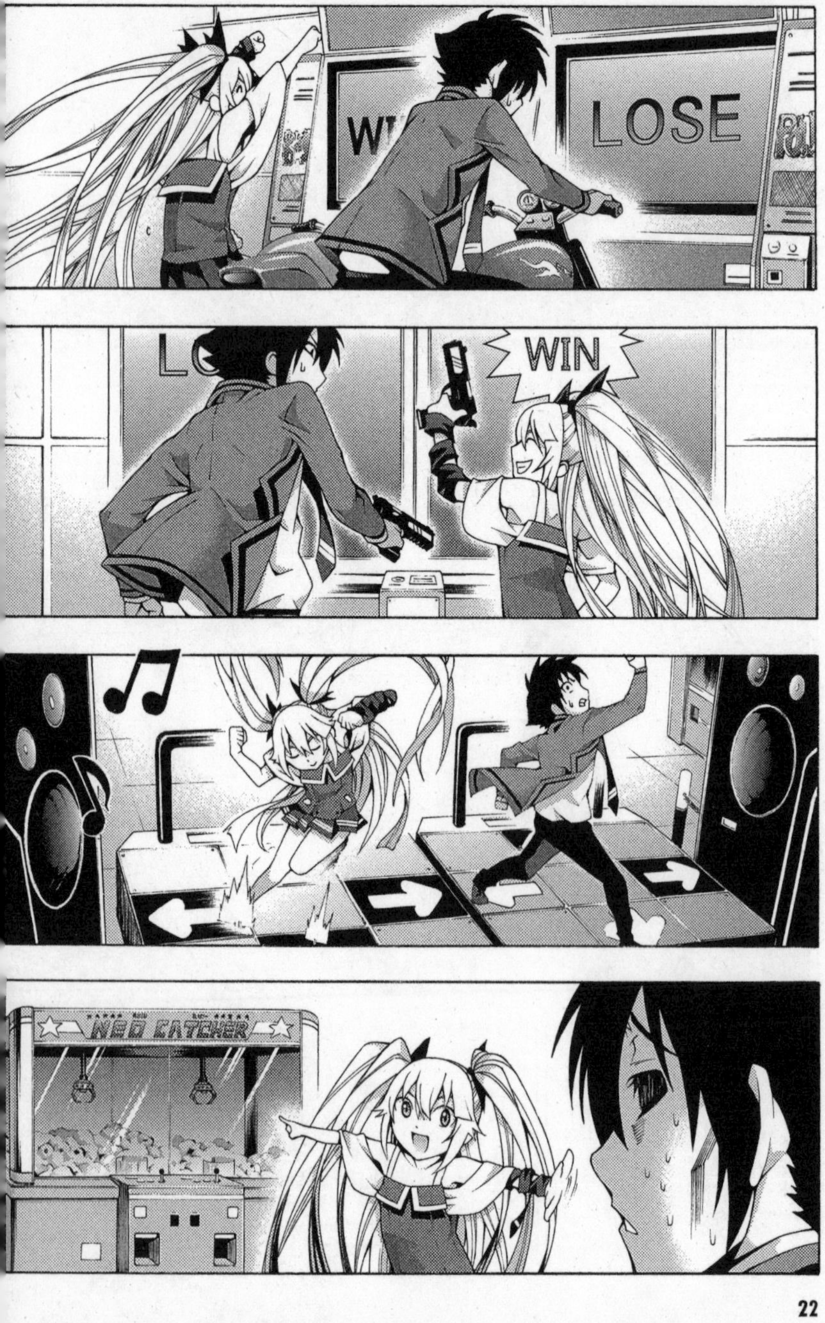
LOSE
WI
WIN
L
NEO CATCHER

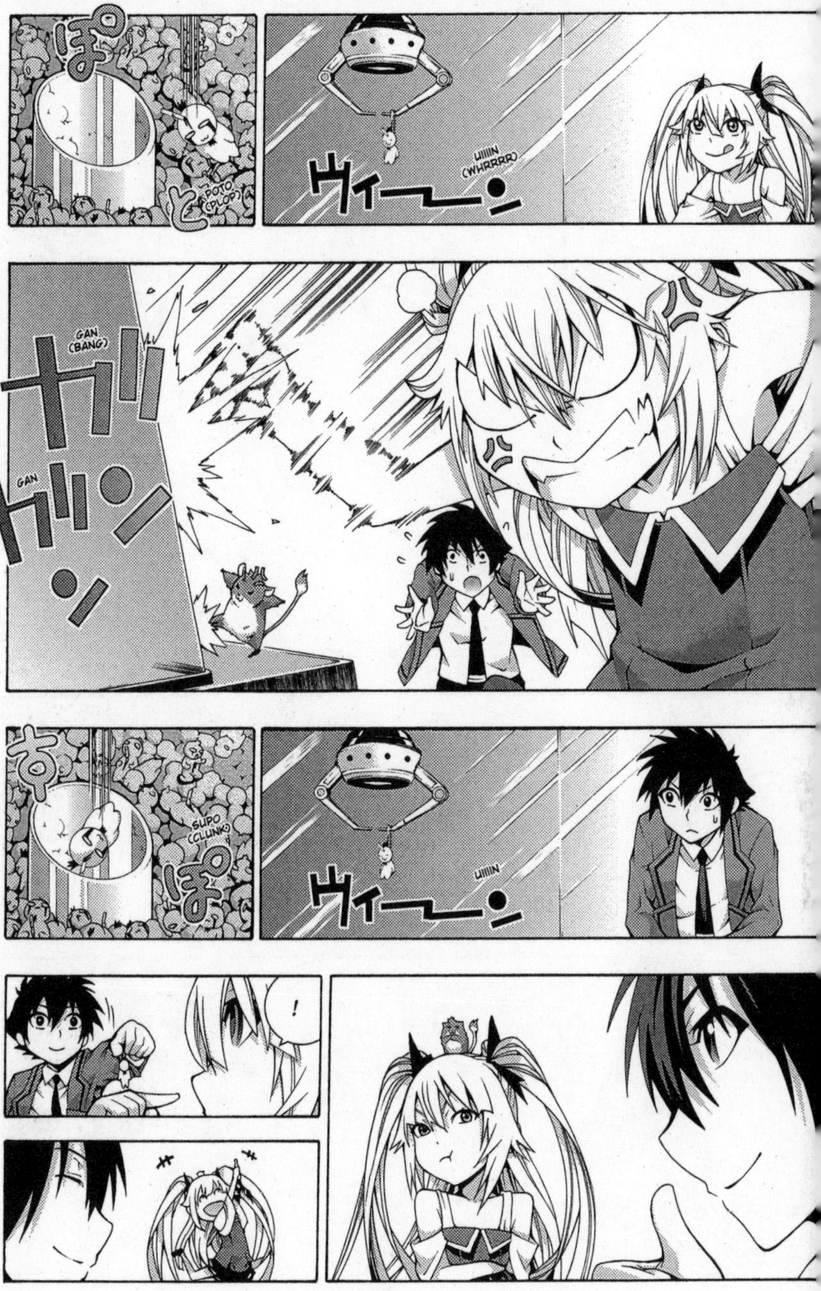
UIIIIN (WHRRRR)
POTO (PLOP)
GAN (BANG)
GAN
UIIIN
SUPO (CLUNK)
!

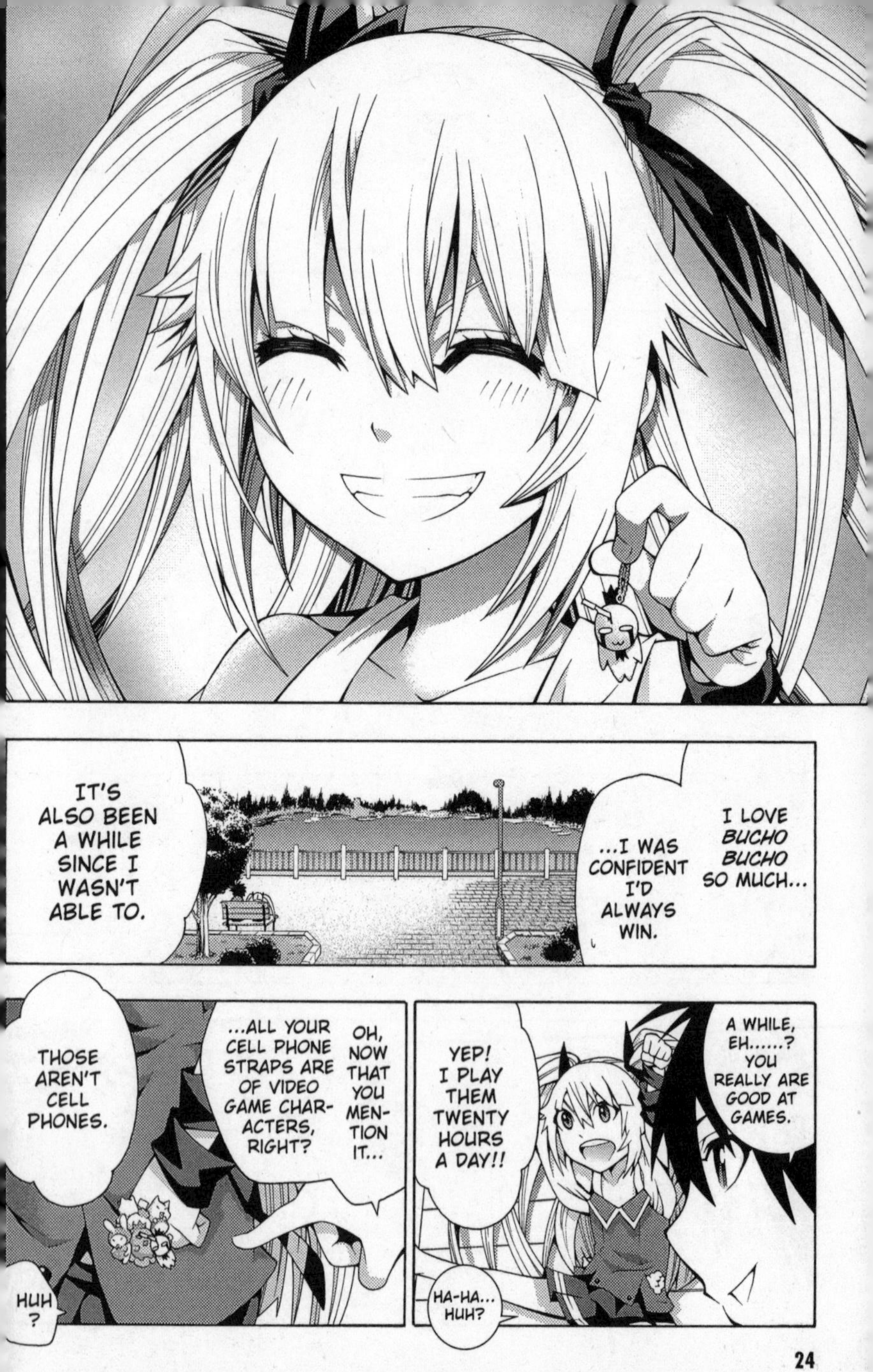
I LOVE *BUCHO BUCHO* SO MUCH...
...I WAS CONFIDENT I'D ALWAYS WIN.
IT'S ALSO BEEN A WHILE SINCE I WASN'T ABLE TO.
A WHILE, EH......? YOU REALLY ARE GOOD AT GAMES.
YEP! I PLAY THEM TWENTY HOURS A DAY!!
HA-HA... HUH?
OH, NOW THAT YOU MEN-TION IT...
...ALL YOUR CELL PHONE STRAPS ARE OF VIDEO GAME CHAR-ACTERS, RIGHT?
THOSE AREN'T CELL PHONES.
HUH?

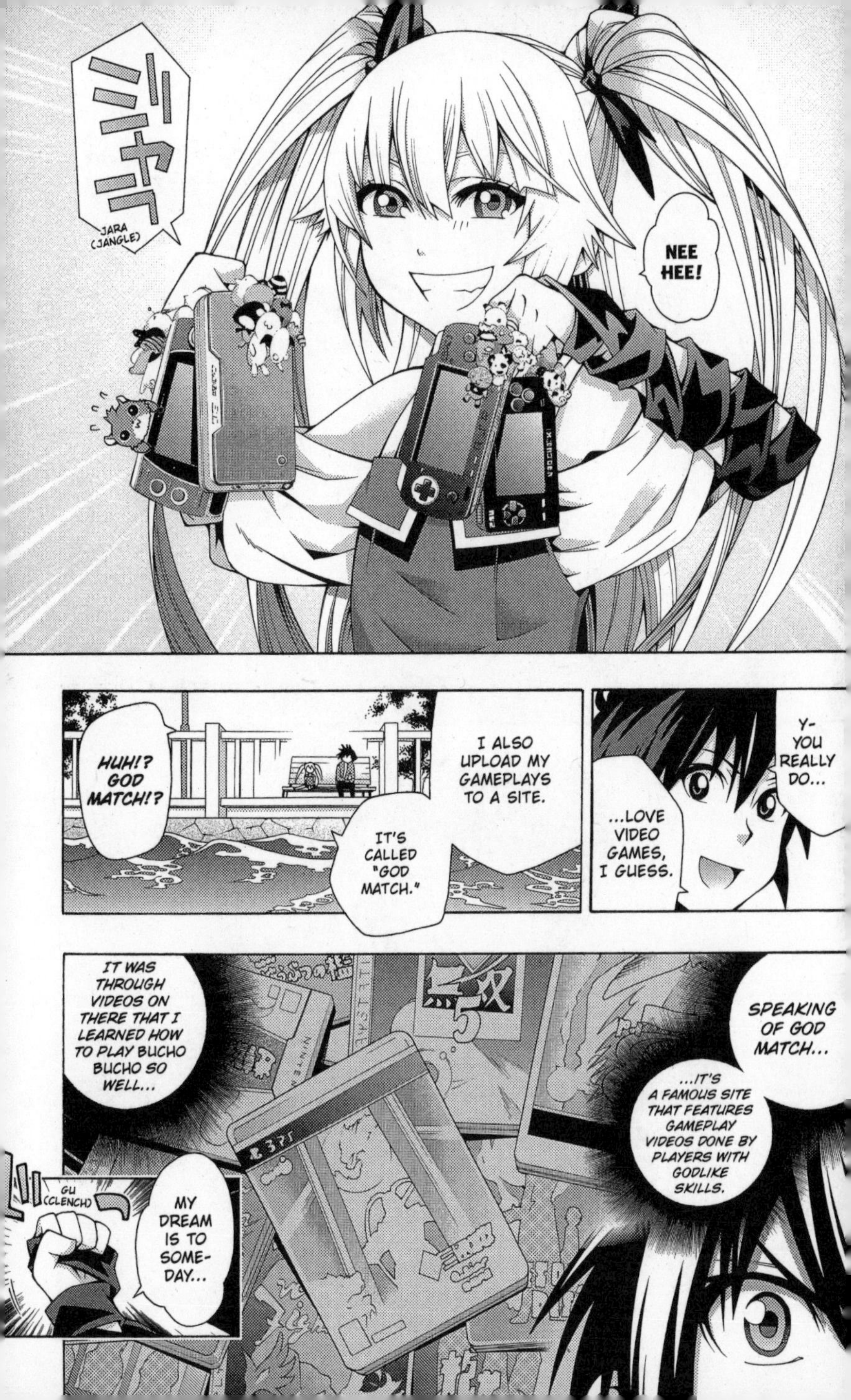
NEE HEE!
JARA (JANGLE)
Y- YOU REALLY DO...
...LOVE VIDEO GAMES, I GUESS.
I ALSO UPLOAD MY GAMEPLAYS TO A SITE.
IT'S CALLED "GOD MATCH."
HUH!? GOD MATCH!?
SPEAKING OF GOD MATCH...
...IT'S A FAMOUS SITE THAT FEATURES GAMEPLAY VIDEOS DONE BY PLAYERS WITH GODLIKE SKILLS.
IT WAS THROUGH VIDEOS ON THERE THAT I LEARNED HOW TO PLAY BUCHO BUCHO SO WELL...
GU (CLENCH)
MY DREAM IS TO SOME-DAY...

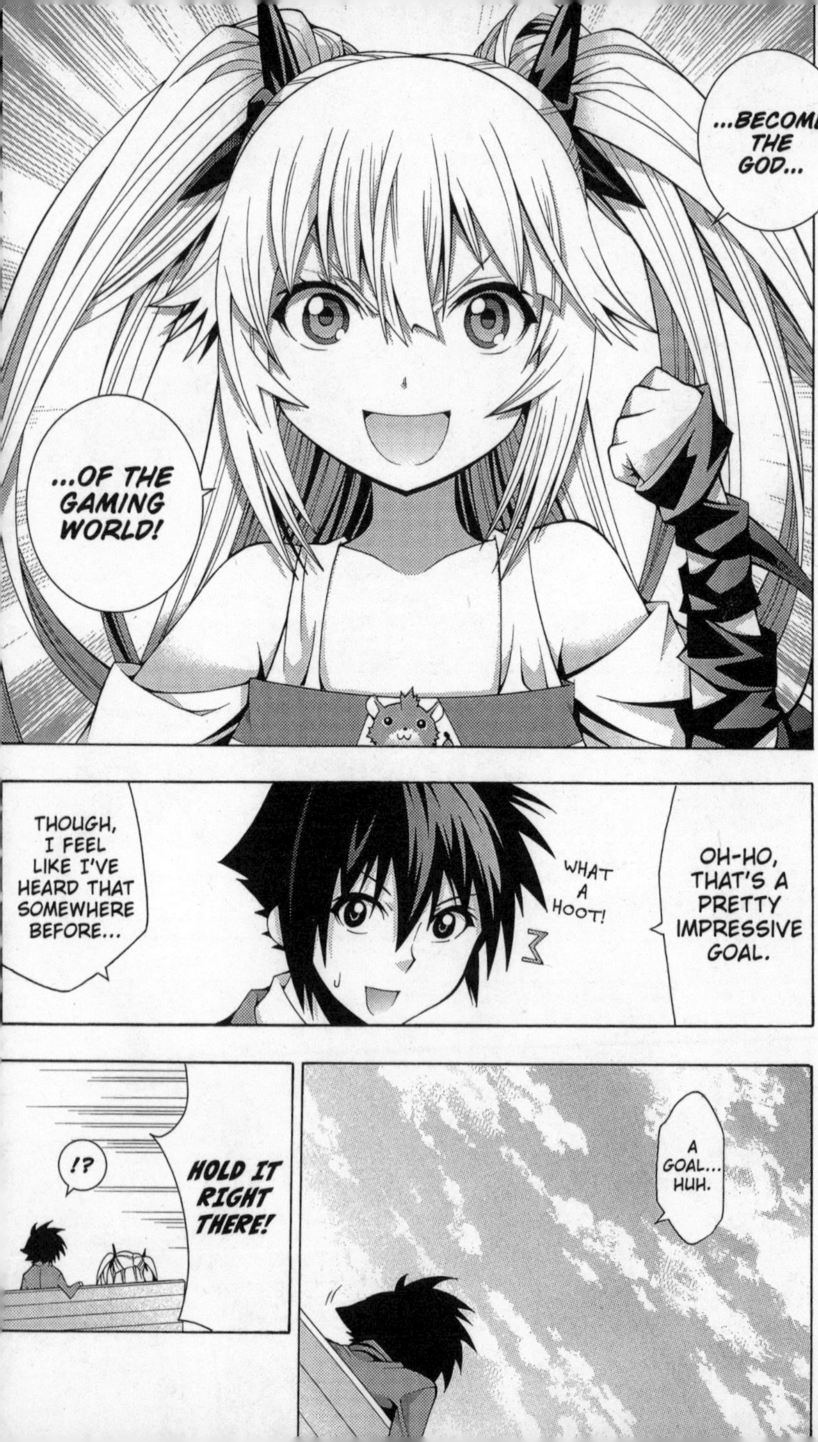
...BECOME THE GOD...
...OF THE GAMING WORLD!
OH-HO, THAT'S A PRETTY IMPRESSIVE GOAL.
WHAT A HOOT!
THOUGH, I FEEL LIKE I'VE HEARD THAT SOMEWHERE BEFORE...
A GOAL... HUH.
HOLD IT RIGHT THERE!
!?

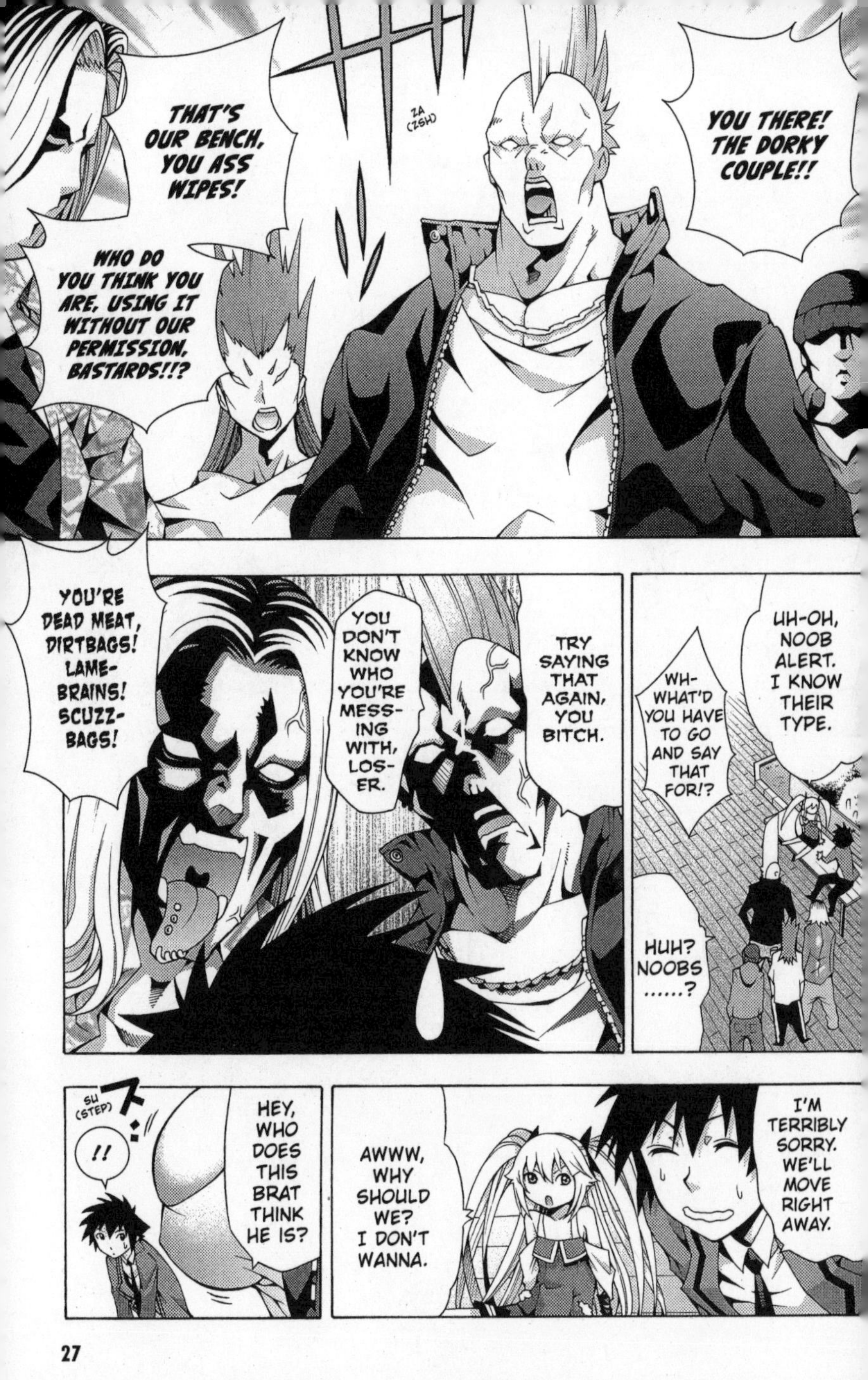
YOU THERE! THE DORKY COUPLE!!
ZA (ZSH)
THAT'S OUR BENCH, YOU ASS WIPES!
WHO DO YOU THINK YOU ARE, USING IT WITHOUT OUR PERMISSION, BASTARDS!!?
UH-OH, NOOB ALERT. I KNOW THEIR TYPE.
WH-WHAT'D YOU HAVE TO GO AND SAY THAT FOR!?
HUH? NOOBS ......?
TRY SAYING THAT AGAIN, YOU BITCH.
YOU DON'T KNOW WHO YOU'RE MESSING WITH, LOSER.
YOU'RE DEAD MEAT, DIRTBAGS! LAME-BRAINS! SCUZZ-BAGS!
I'M TERRIBLY SORRY. WE'LL MOVE RIGHT AWAY.
AWWW, WHY SHOULD WE? I DON'T WANNA.
HEY, WHO DOES THIS BRAT THINK HE IS?
SU (STEP)
!!

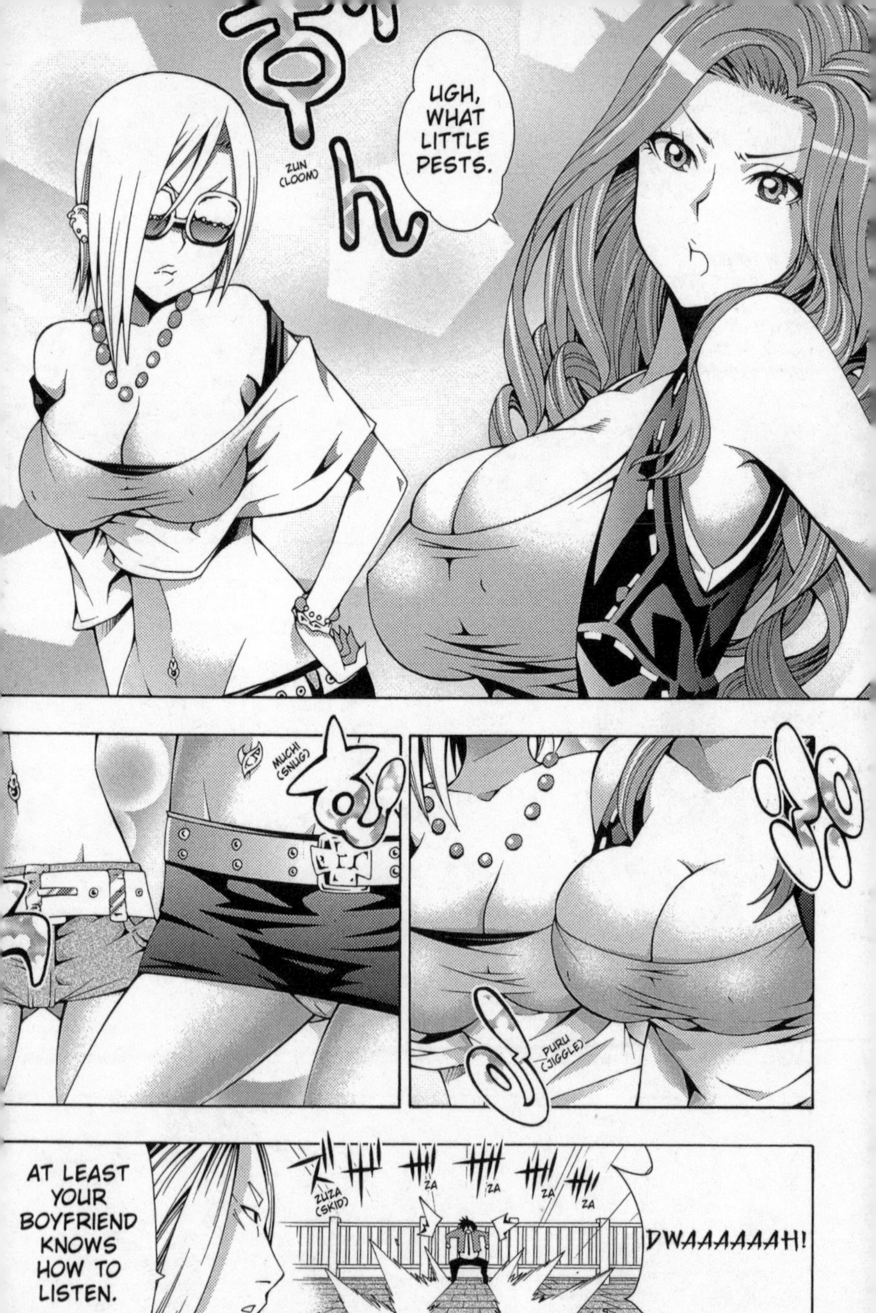
UGH, WHAT LITTLE PESTS.
ZUN (LOOM)
PURU (JIGGLE)
MUCHI (SNUG)
DWAAAAAAAH!
ZA
ZA
ZA
ZA
ZUZA (SKID)
AT LEAST YOUR BOYFRIEND KNOWS HOW TO LISTEN.

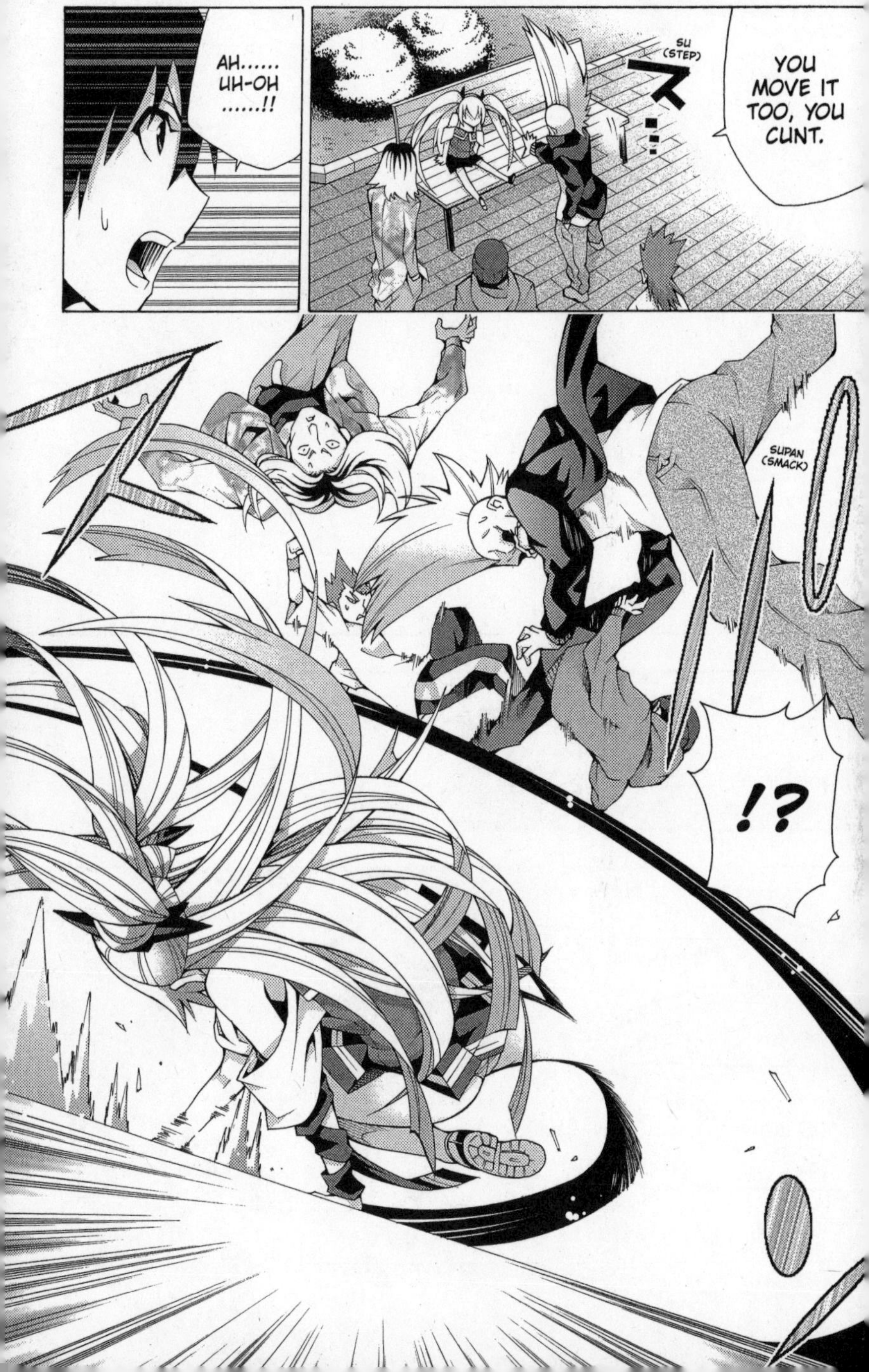
YOU MOVE IT TOO, YOU CUNT.
SU (STEP)
AH...... UH-OH ......!!
SUPAN (SMACK)
!?

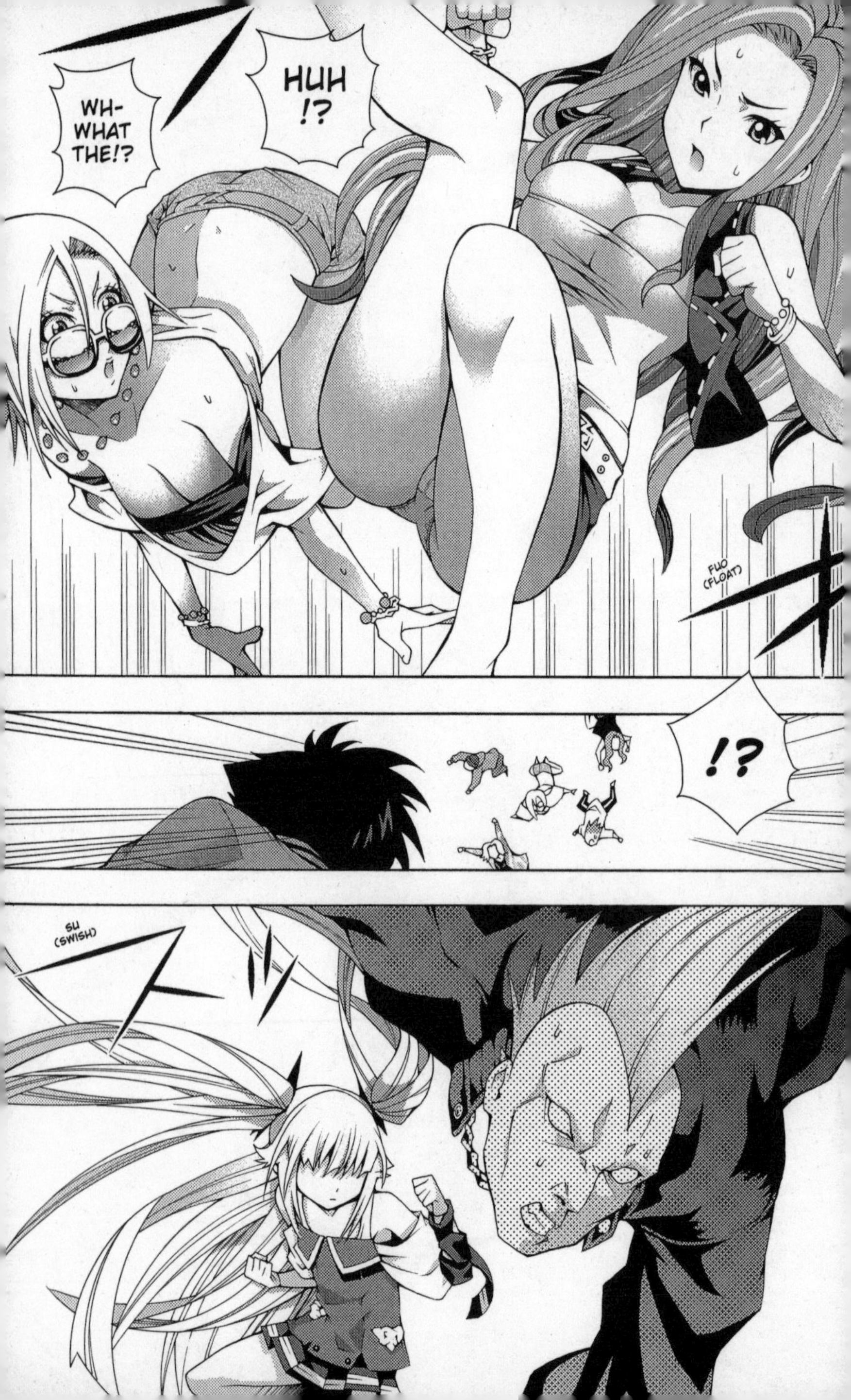

HUH !?
WH- WHAT THE!?
FUO (FLOAT)
!?
SU (SWISH)

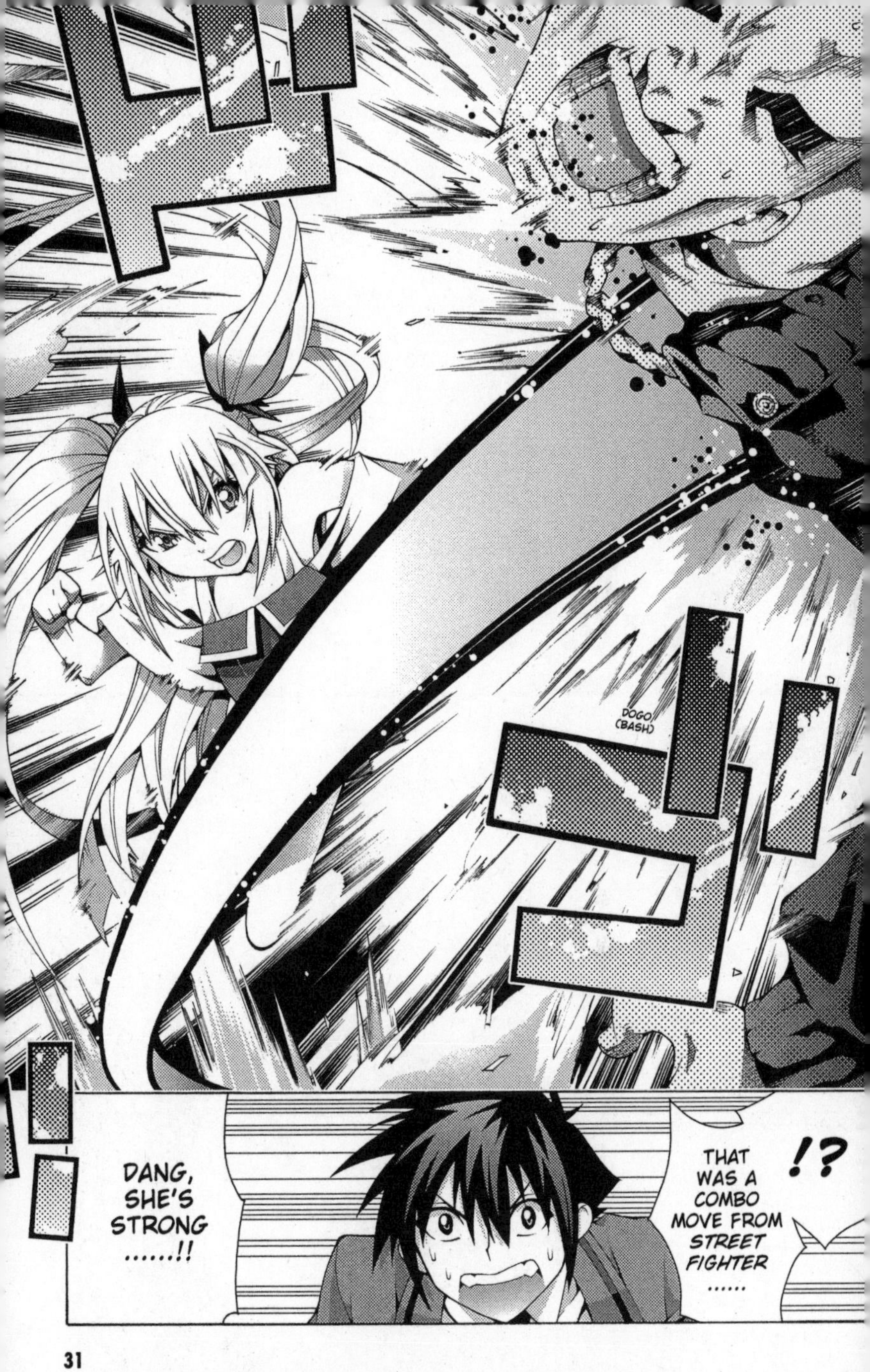
DOGO (BASH)
!?
THAT WAS A COMBO MOVE FROM STREET FIGHTER ......
DANG, SHE'S STRONG ......!!

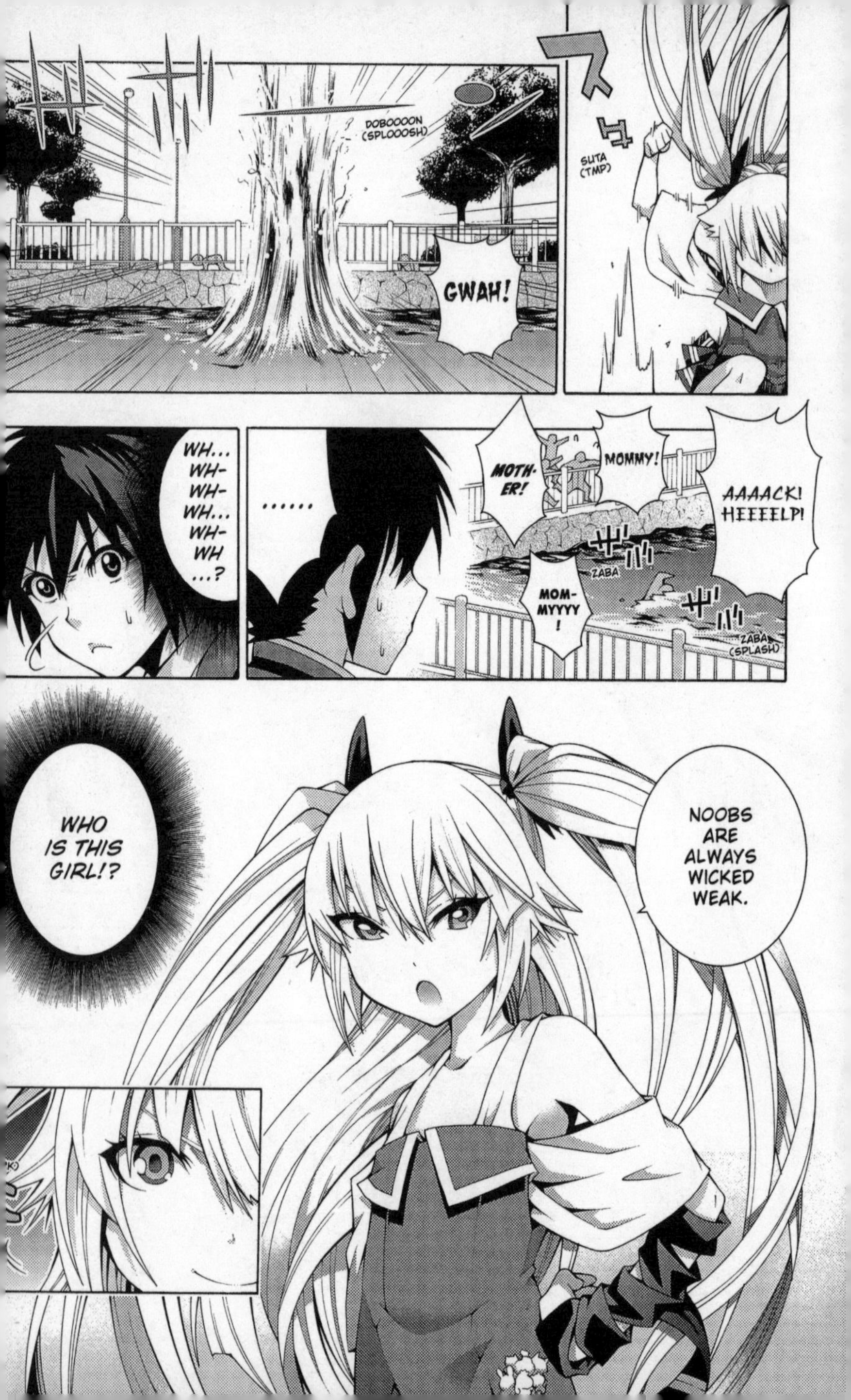
SUTA (TMP)
DOBOOOON (SPLOOOSH)
GWAH!
AAAACK! HEEEELP!
MOMMY!
MOTHER!
ZABA
MOM-MYYYY!
ZABA (SPLASH)
......
WH... WH-WH-WH... WH-WH...?
NOOBS ARE ALWAYS WICKED WEAK.
WHO IS THIS GIRL!?

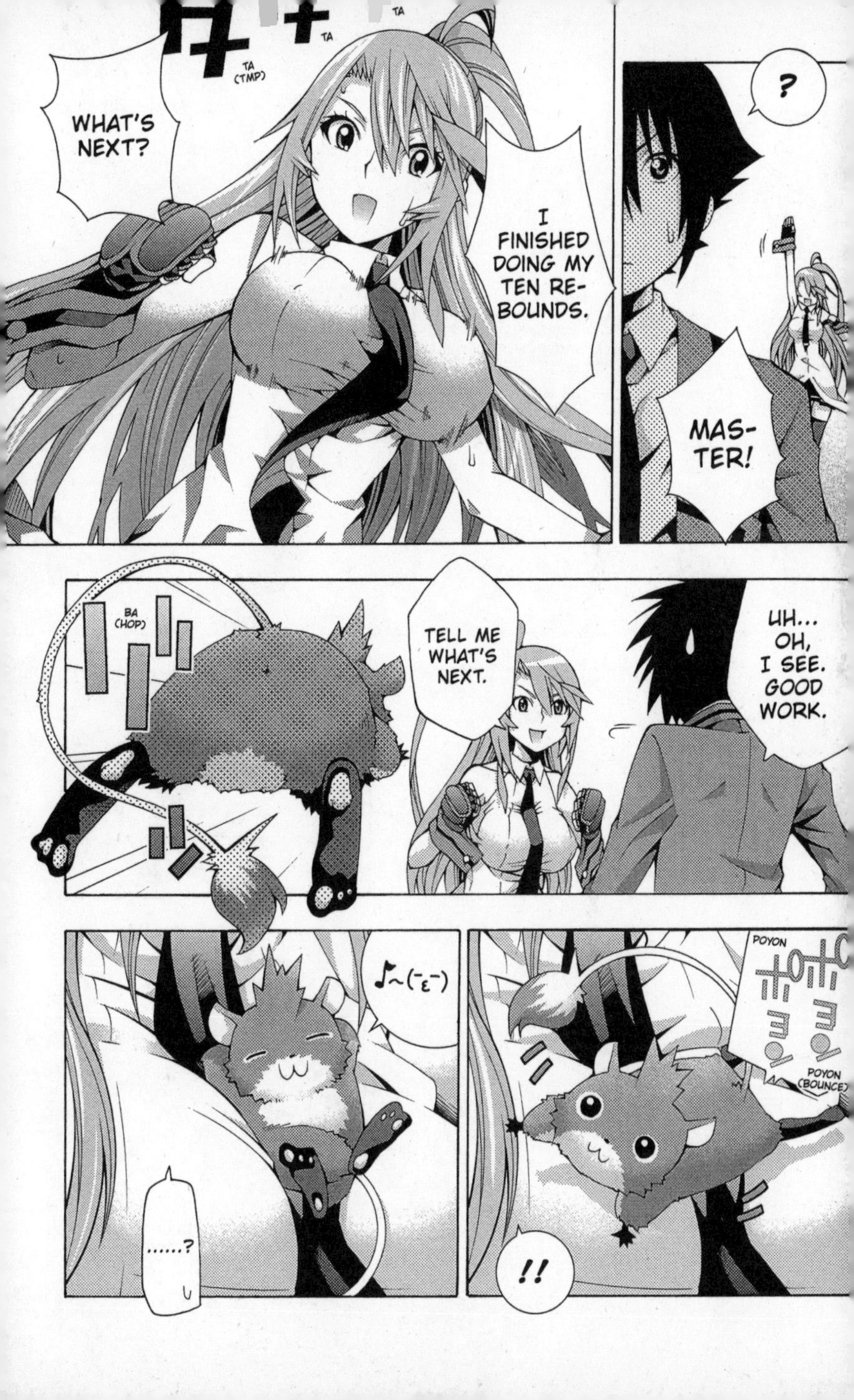
?
MAS-TER!
TA TA TA (TMP)
I FINISHED DOING MY TEN RE-BOUNDS.
WHAT'S NEXT?
UH... OH, I SEE. GOOD WORK.
TELL ME WHAT'S NEXT.
BA (HOP)
POYON
POYON (BOUNCE)
!!
♪~(¯ε¯)
......?

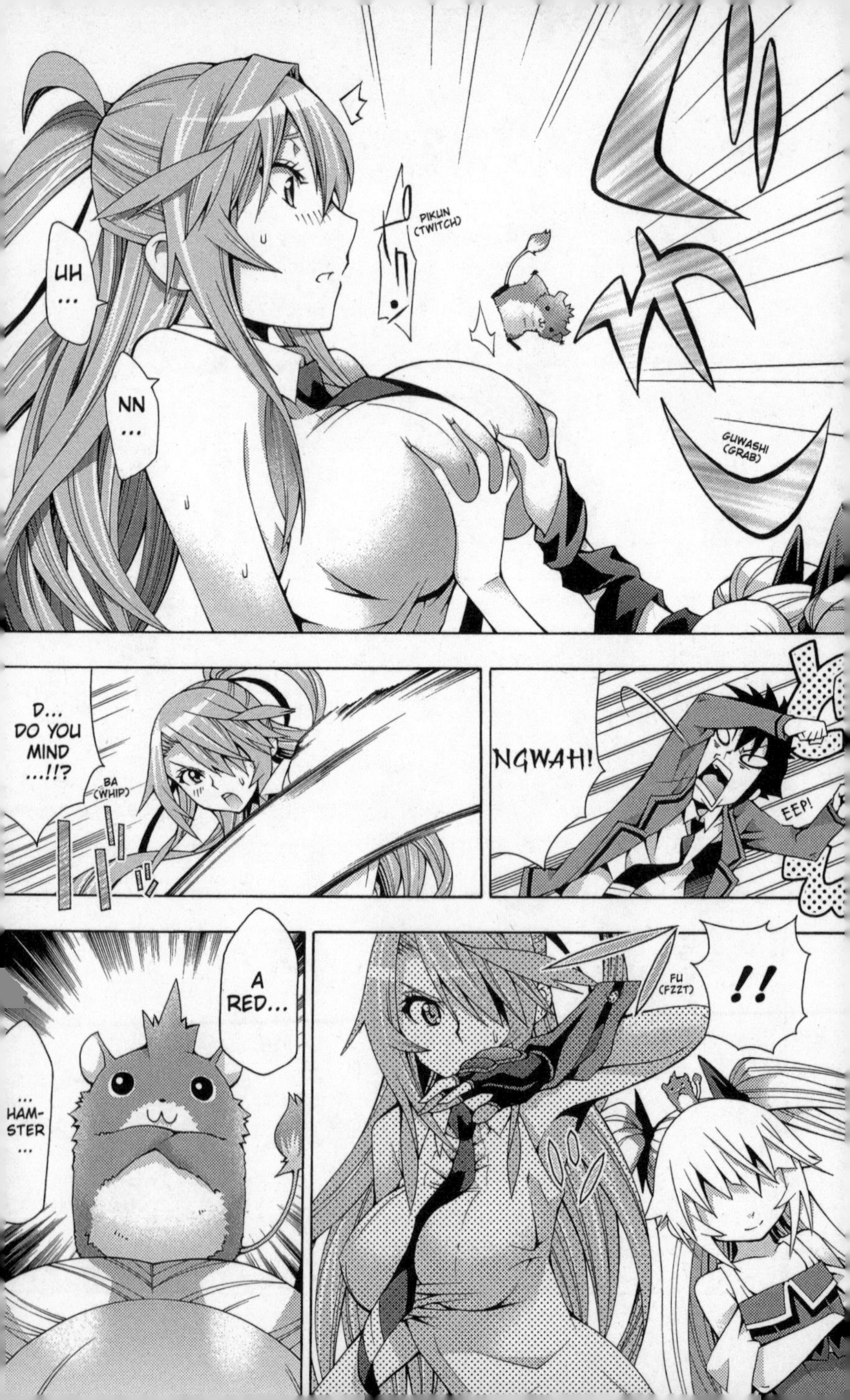
GUWASHI (GRAB)
PIKUN (TWITCH)
UH ...
NN ...
NGWAH!
EEP!
BA (WHIP)
D... DO YOU MIND ...!!?
!!
FU (FZZT)
A RED...
... HAM-STER ...

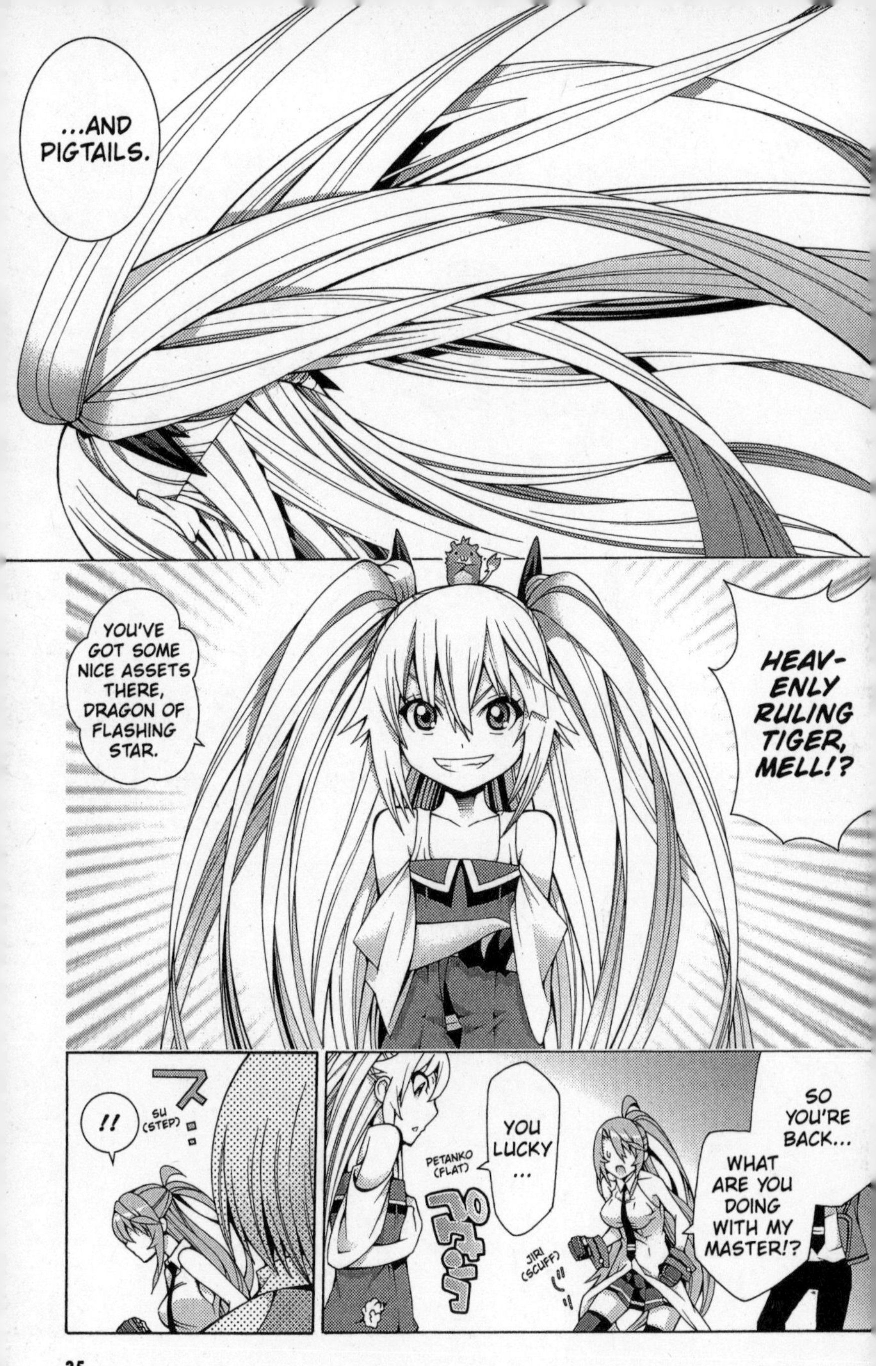
...AND PIGTAILS.
HEAV-ENLY RULING TIGER, MELL!?
YOU'VE GOT SOME NICE ASSETS THERE, DRAGON OF FLASHING STAR.
SO YOU'RE BACK...
WHAT ARE YOU DOING WITH MY MASTER!?
JIRI (SCUFF)
YOU LUCKY ...
PETANKO (FLAT)
SU (STEP)
!!

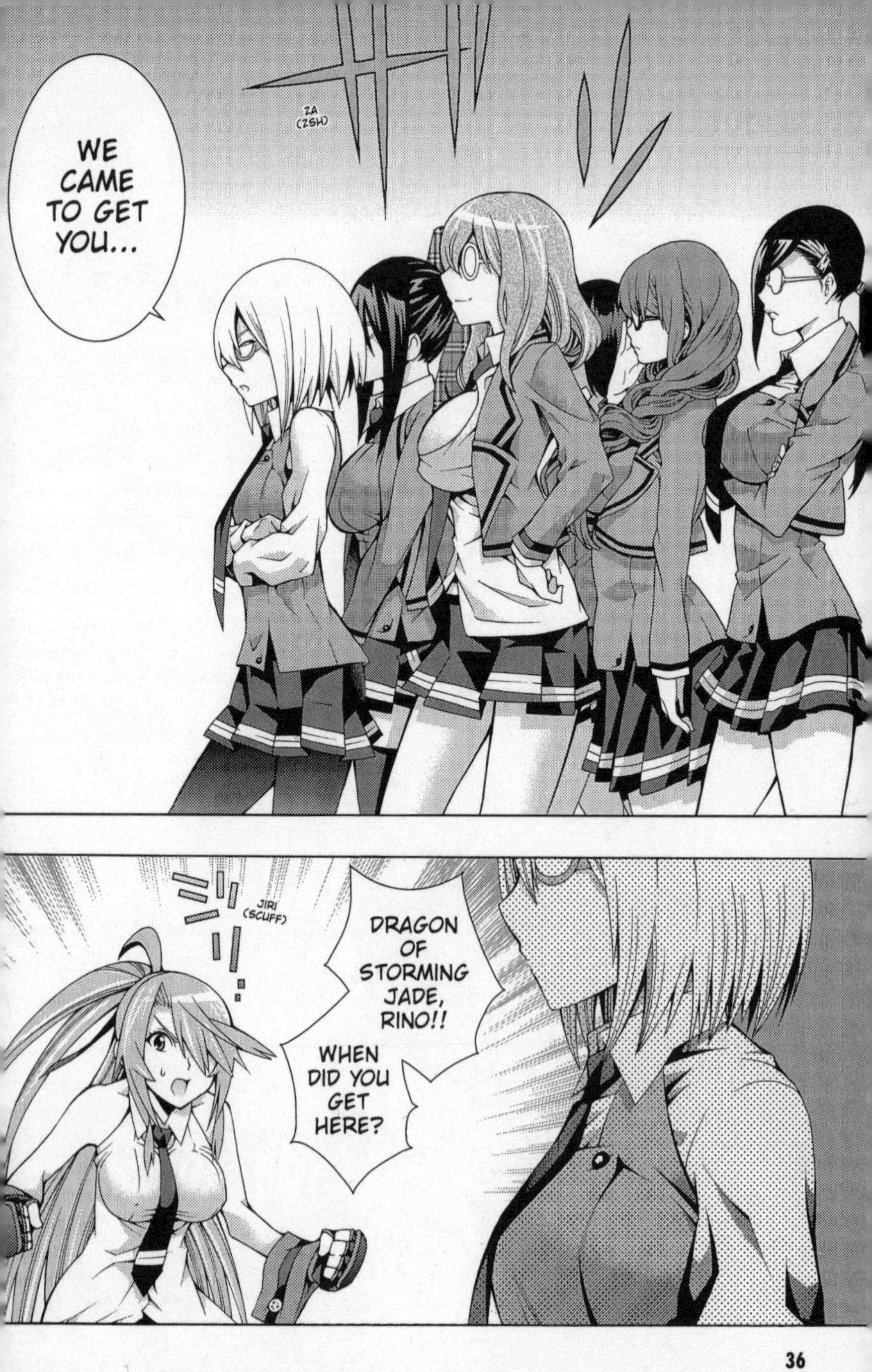
ZA (ZSH)
WE CAME TO GET YOU...
JIRI (SCUFF)
DRAGON OF STORMING JADE, RINO!!
WHEN DID YOU GET HERE?

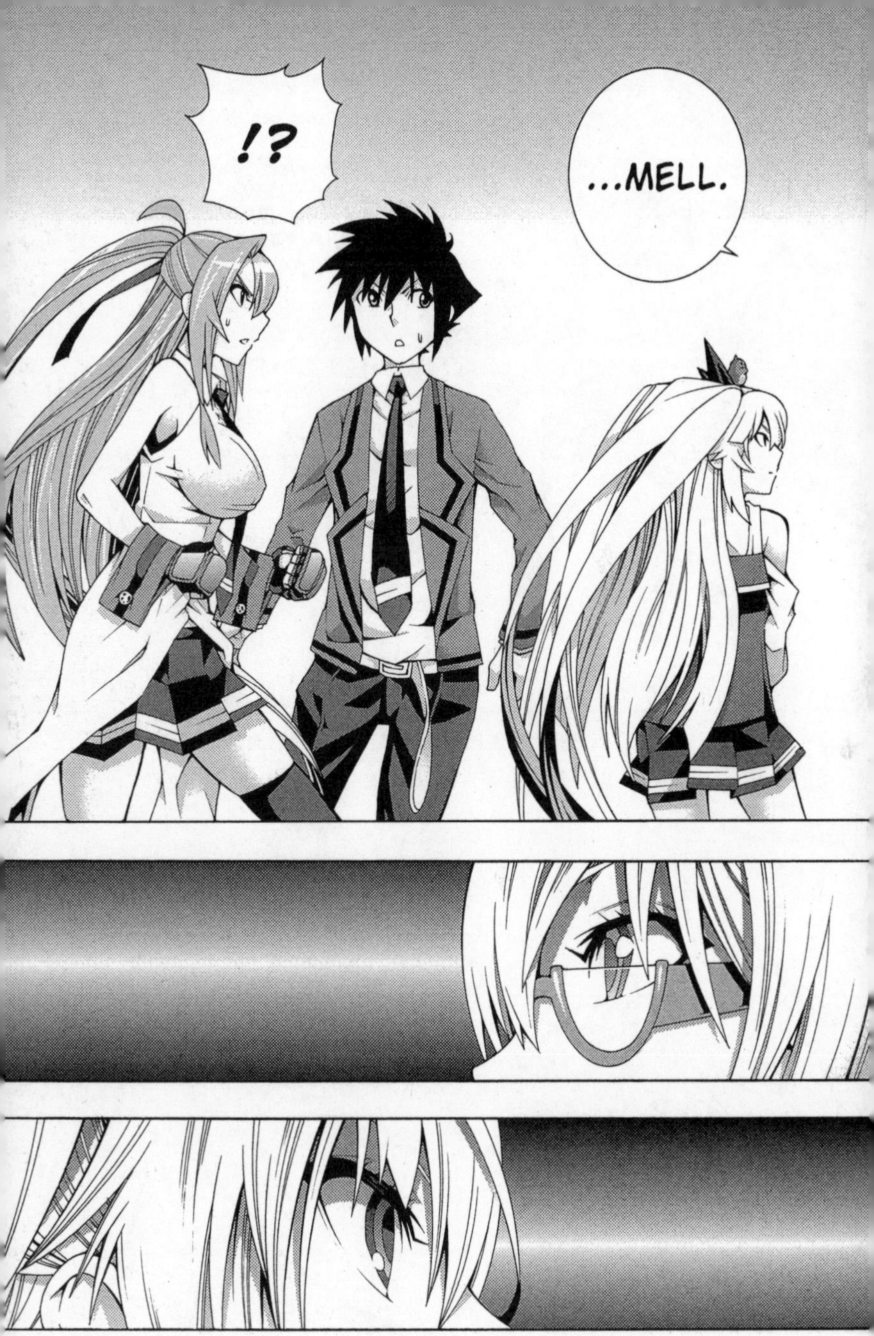
...MELL.
!?

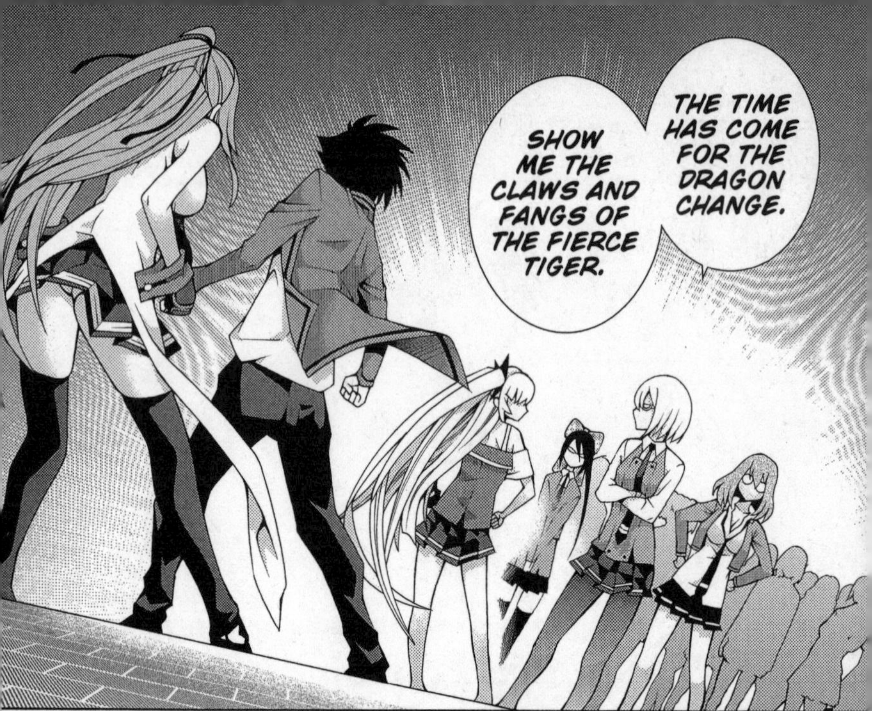
THE TIME HAS COME FOR THE DRAGON CHANGE.
SHOW ME THE CLAWS AND FANGS OF THE FIERCE TIGER.

THE DRAGON CHANGE: WHEN A HERO OR OTHER SUCH SUPERIOR PERSON TAKES ADVANTAGE OF THE TIDE OF THE TIMES TO APPEAR AND TAKE ACTION

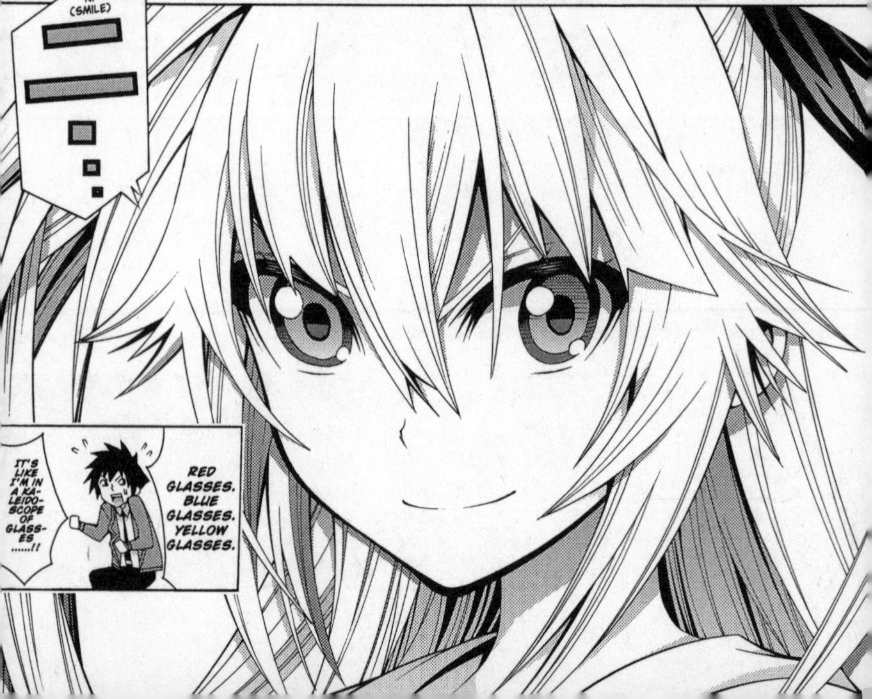
NI (SMILE)
RED GLASSES. BLUE GLASSES. YELLOW GLASSES.
IT'S LIKE I'M IN A KALEIDOSCOPE OF GLASSES......!!

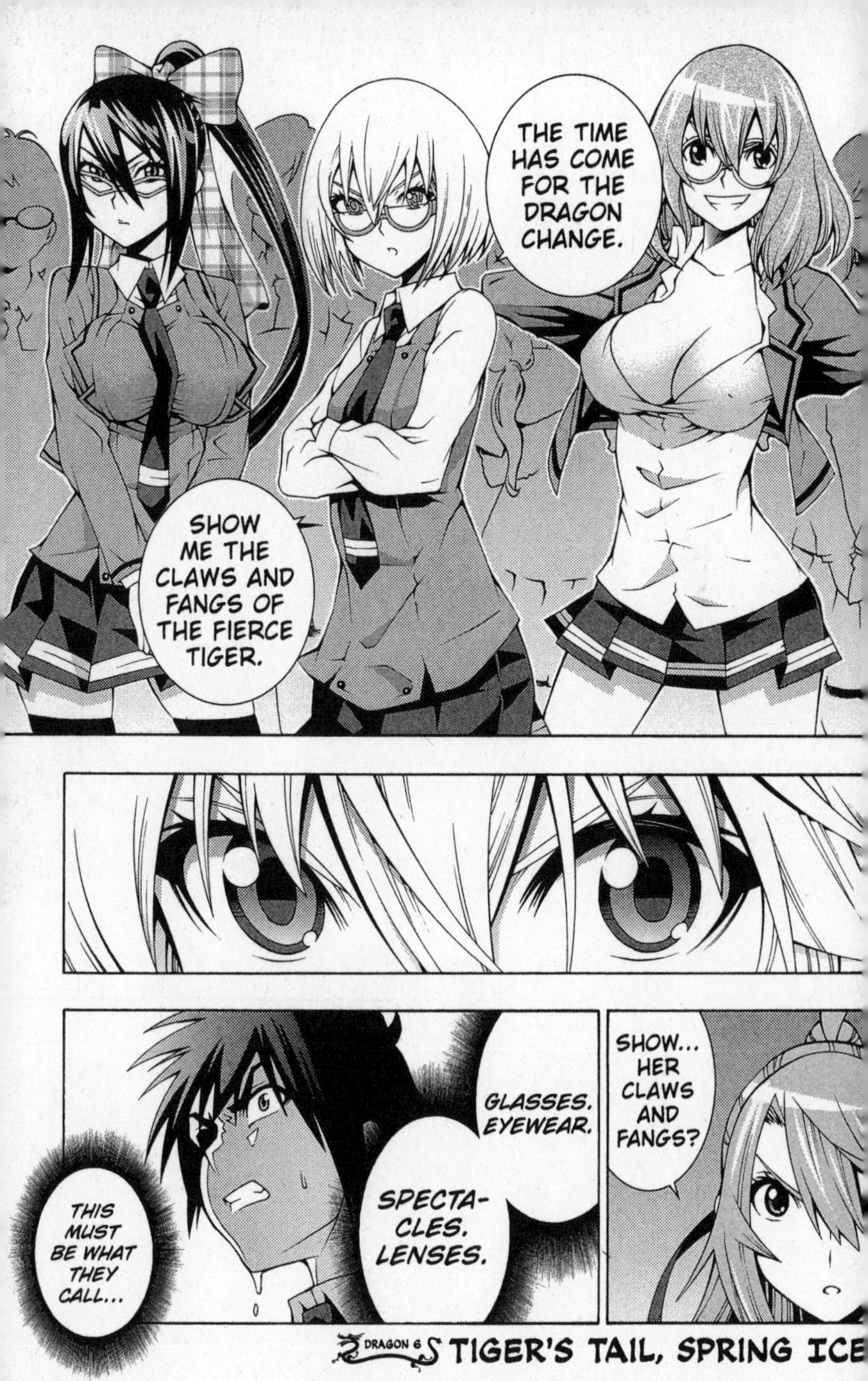
THE TIME HAS COME FOR THE DRAGON CHANGE.
SHOW ME THE CLAWS AND FANGS OF THE FIERCE TIGER.
SHOW... HER CLAWS AND FANGS?
GLASSES. EYEWEAR.
SPECTA- CLES. LENSES.
THIS MUST BE WHAT THEY CALL...

DRAGON 6 TIGER'S TAIL, SPRING ICE

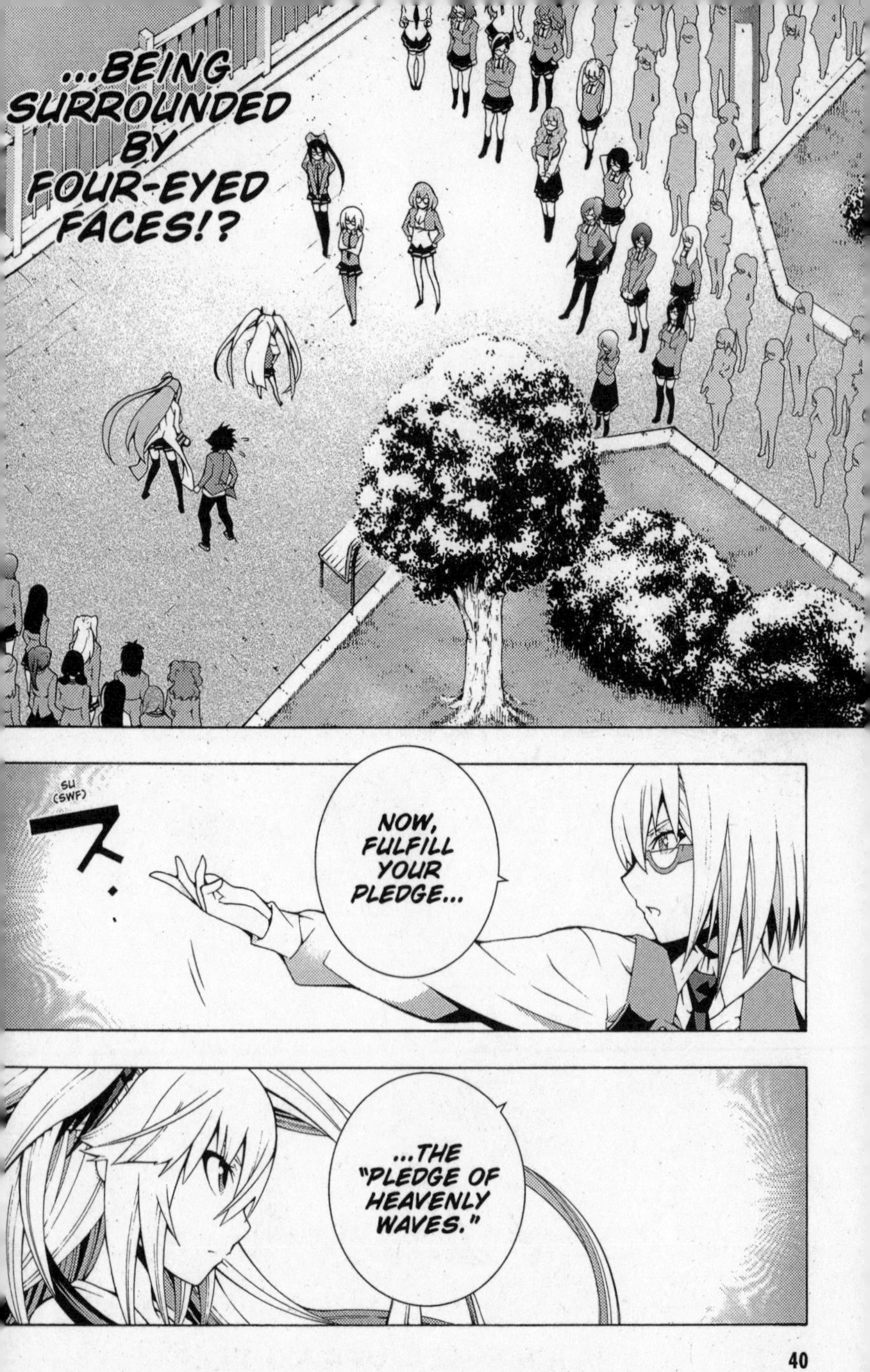
...BEING SURROUNDED BY FOUR-EYED FACES!?
NOW, FULFILL YOUR PLEDGE...
SU (SWF)
...THE "PLEDGE OF HEAVENLY WAVES."

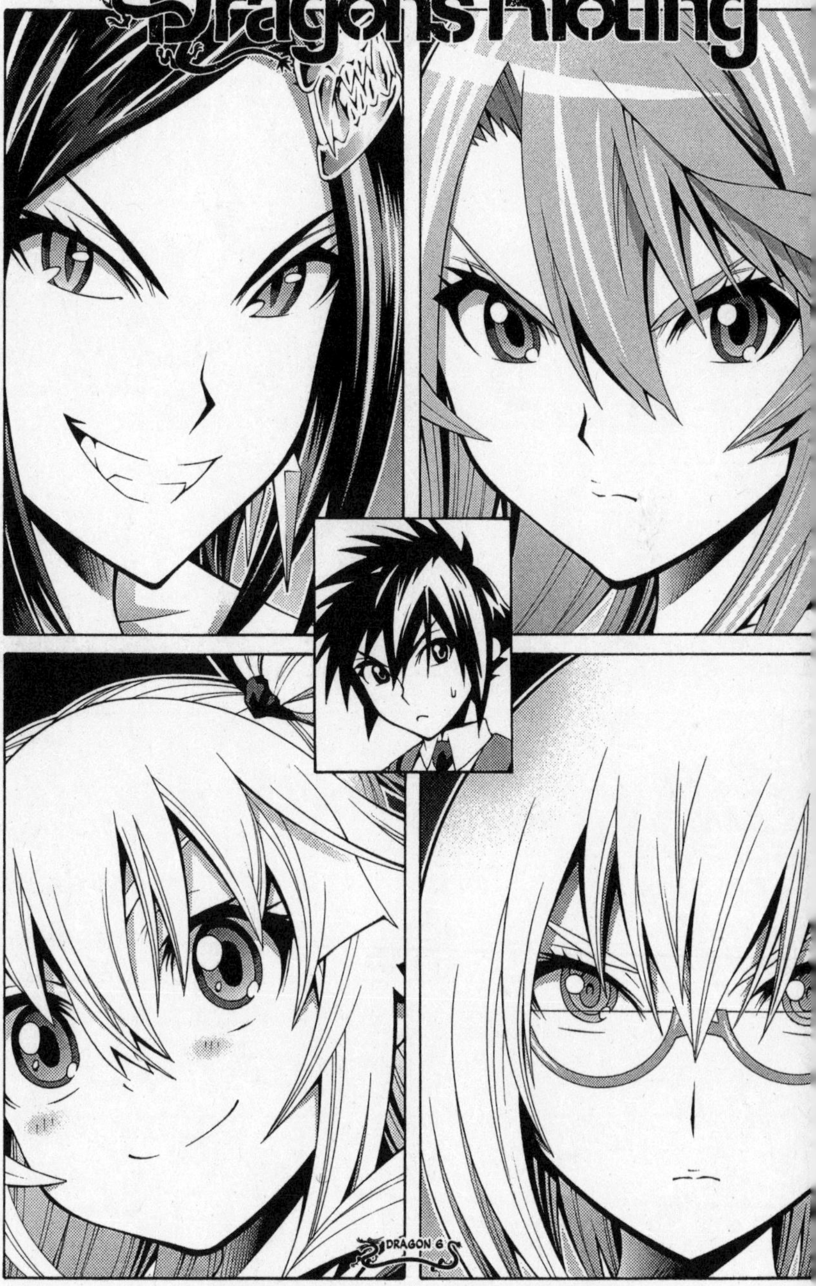
DRAGON 6

TIGER'S TAIL, SPRING ICE

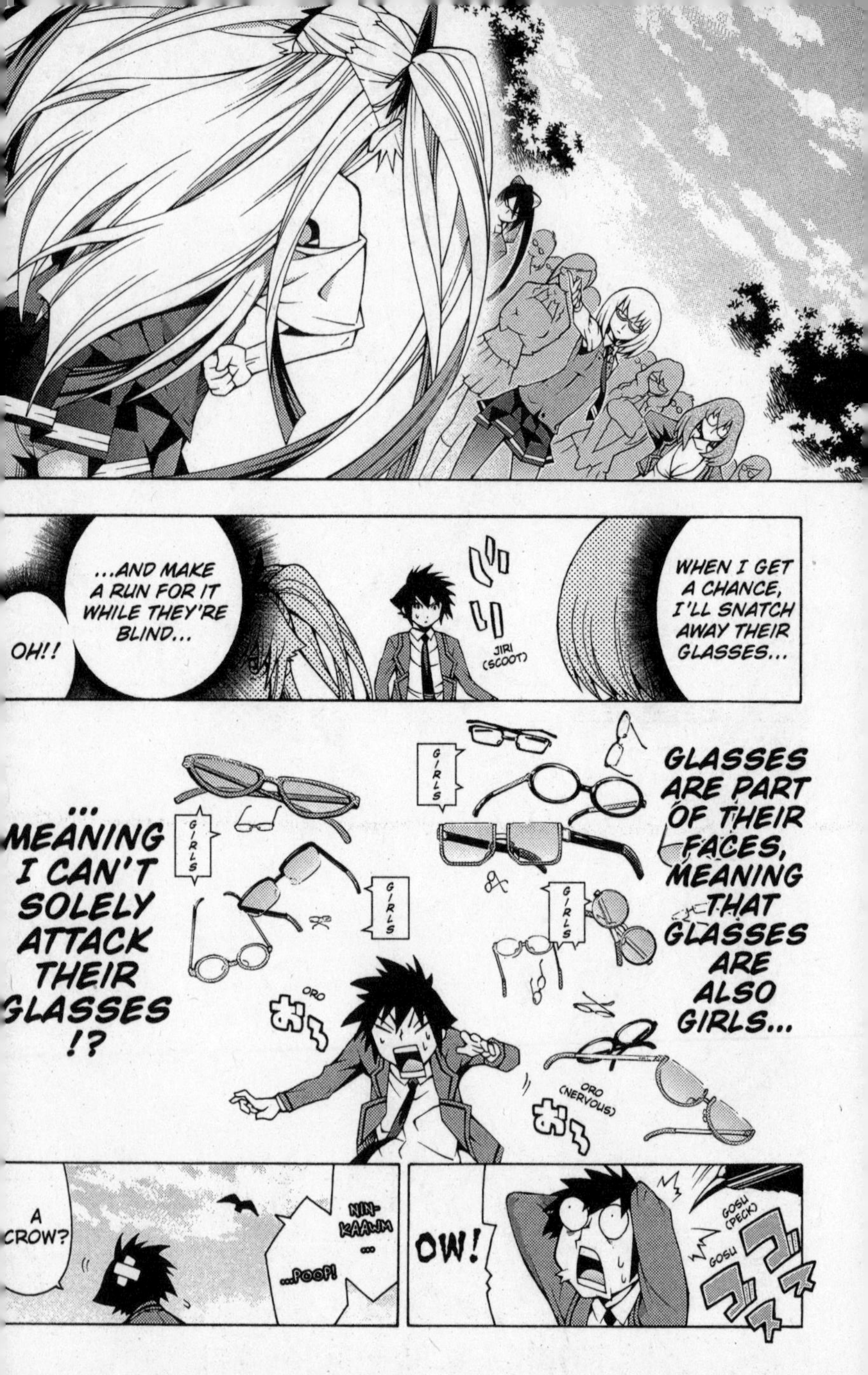

WHEN I GET A CHANCE, I'LL SNATCH AWAY THEIR GLASSES...
JIRI (SCOOT)
...AND MAKE A RUN FOR IT WHILE THEY'RE BLIND...
OH!!
GLASSES ARE PART OF THEIR FACES, MEANING THAT GLASSES ARE ALSO GIRLS...
GIRLS
GIRLS
GIRLS
GIRLS
...MEANING I CAN'T SOLELY ATTACK THEIR GLASSES!?
ORO
ORO (NERVOUS)
GOSU (PECK)
GOSU
OW!
NIN-KAAWM...
...POOP!
A CROW?

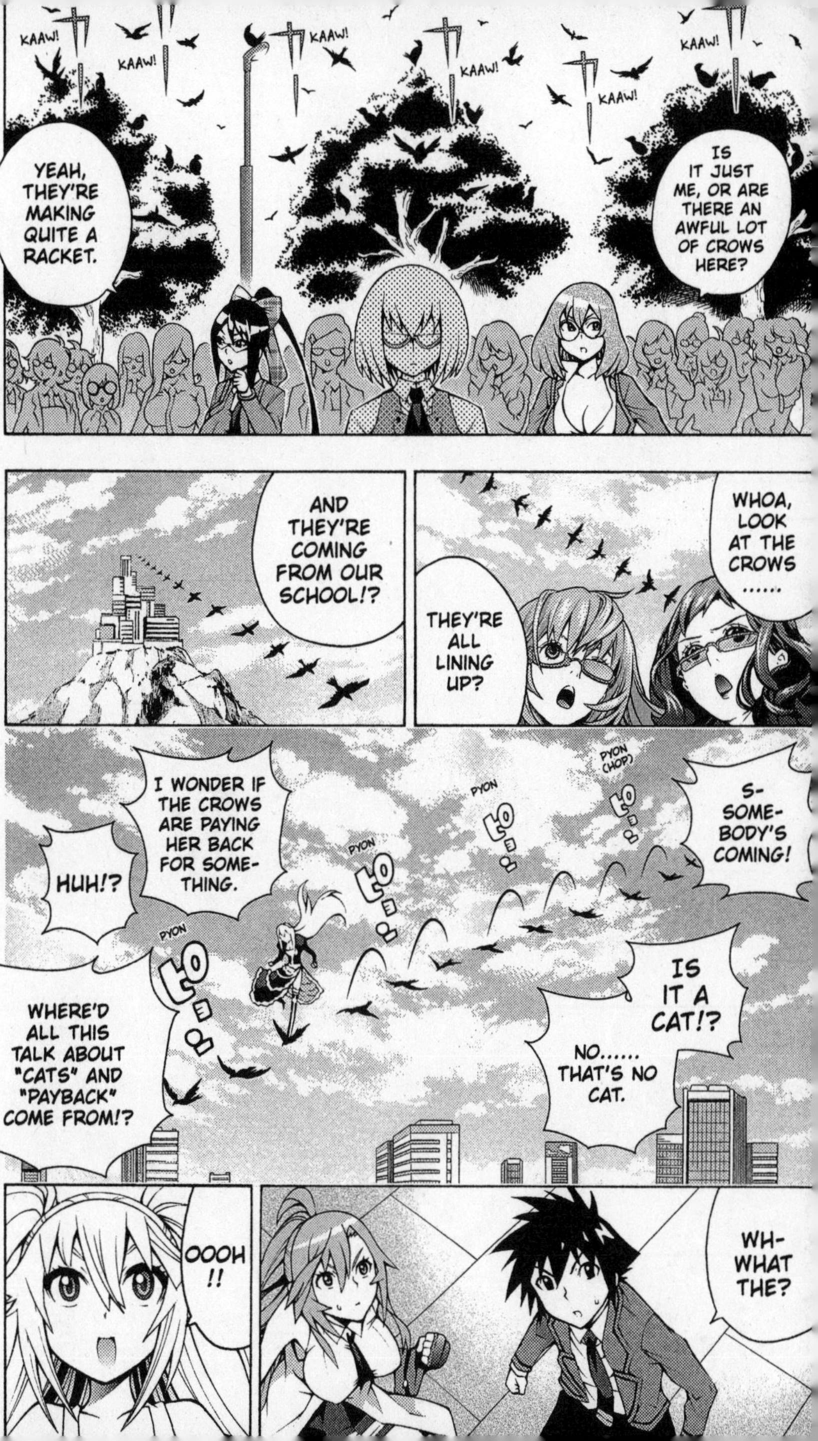
KAAW!
KAAW!
KAAW!
KAAW!
KAAW!
KAAW!
IS IT JUST ME, OR ARE THERE AN AWFUL LOT OF CROWS HERE?
YEAH, THEY'RE MAKING QUITE A RACKET.
WHOA, LOOK AT THE CROWS......
THEY'RE ALL LINING UP?
AND THEY'RE COMING FROM OUR SCHOOL!?
S-SOMEBODY'S COMING!
PYON (HOP)
PYON
PYON
PYON
I WONDER IF THE CROWS ARE PAYING HER BACK FOR SOME-THING.
HUH!?
IS IT A CAT!?
NO...... THAT'S NO CAT.
WHERE'D ALL THIS TALK ABOUT "CATS" AND "PAYBACK" COME FROM!?
WH-WHAT THE?
OOOH!!

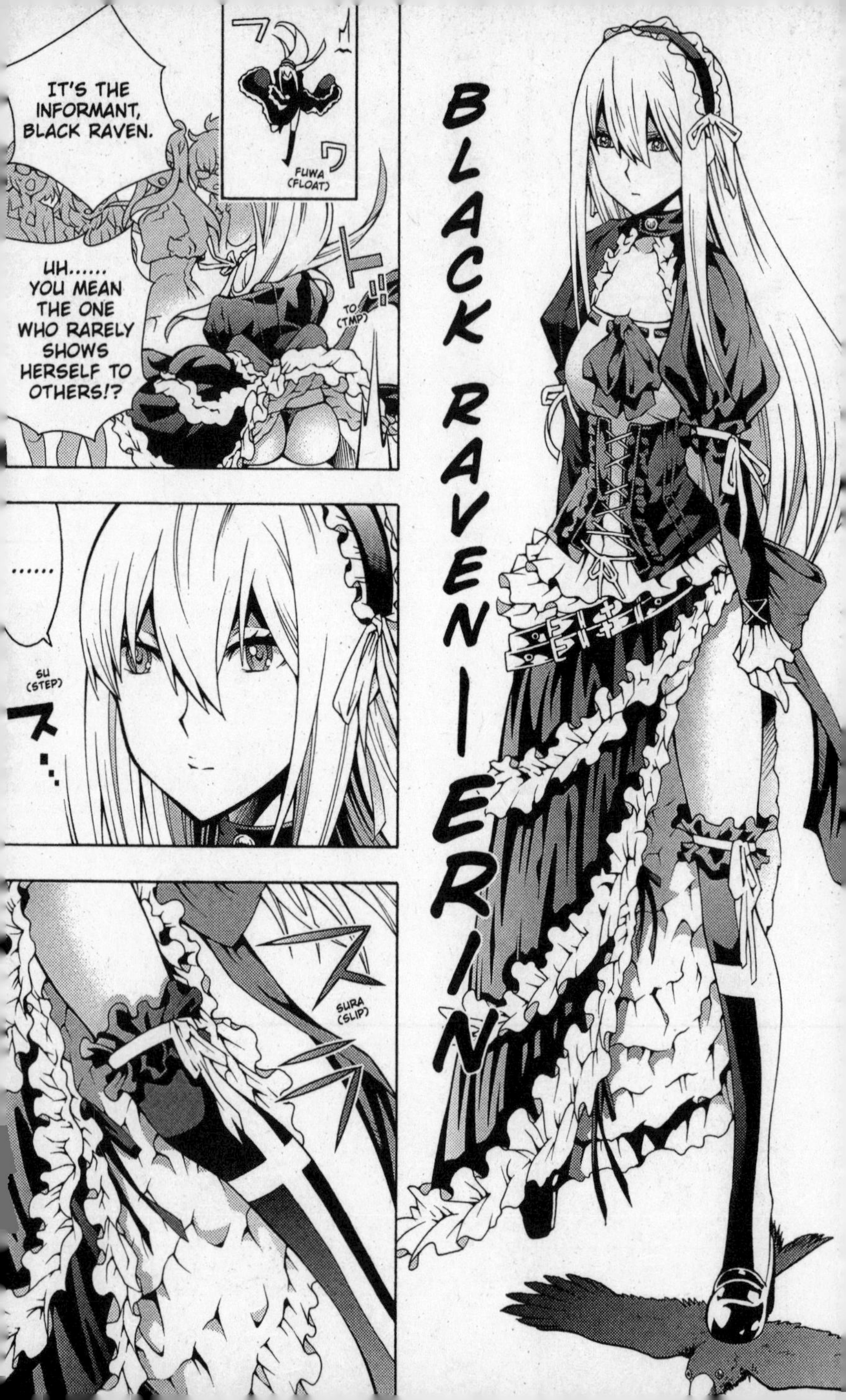
BLACK RAVEN ERIN
FUWA (FLOAT)
IT'S THE INFORMANT, BLACK RAVEN.
TO (TMP)
UH...... YOU MEAN THE ONE WHO RARELY SHOWS HERSELF TO OTHERS!?
......
SU (STEP)
SURA (SLIP)

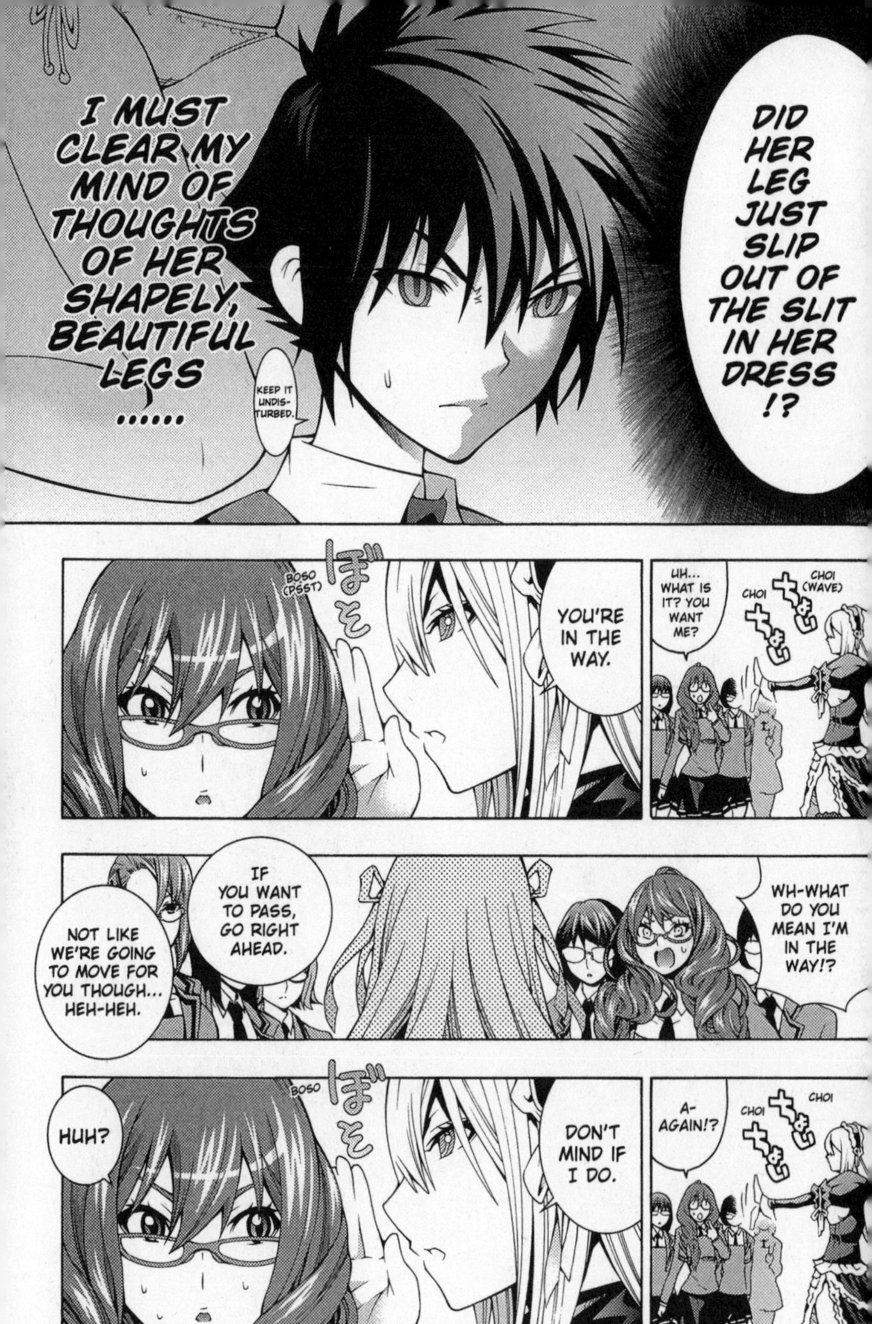

DID HER LEG JUST SLIP OUT OF THE SLIT IN HER DRESS !?
I MUST CLEAR MY MIND OF THOUGHTS OF HER SHAPELY, BEAUTIFUL LEGS ......
KEEP IT UNDIS-TURBED.
CHOI (WAVE)
CHOI
UH... WHAT IS IT? YOU WANT ME?
YOU'RE IN THE WAY.
ぼそ
BOSO (PSST)
WH-WHAT DO YOU MEAN I'M IN THE WAY!?
IF YOU WANT TO PASS, GO RIGHT AHEAD.
NOT LIKE WE'RE GOING TO MOVE FOR YOU THOUGH... HEH-HEH.
CHOI
CHOI
A-AGAIN!?
DON'T MIND IF I DO.
ぼそ
BOSO
HUH?

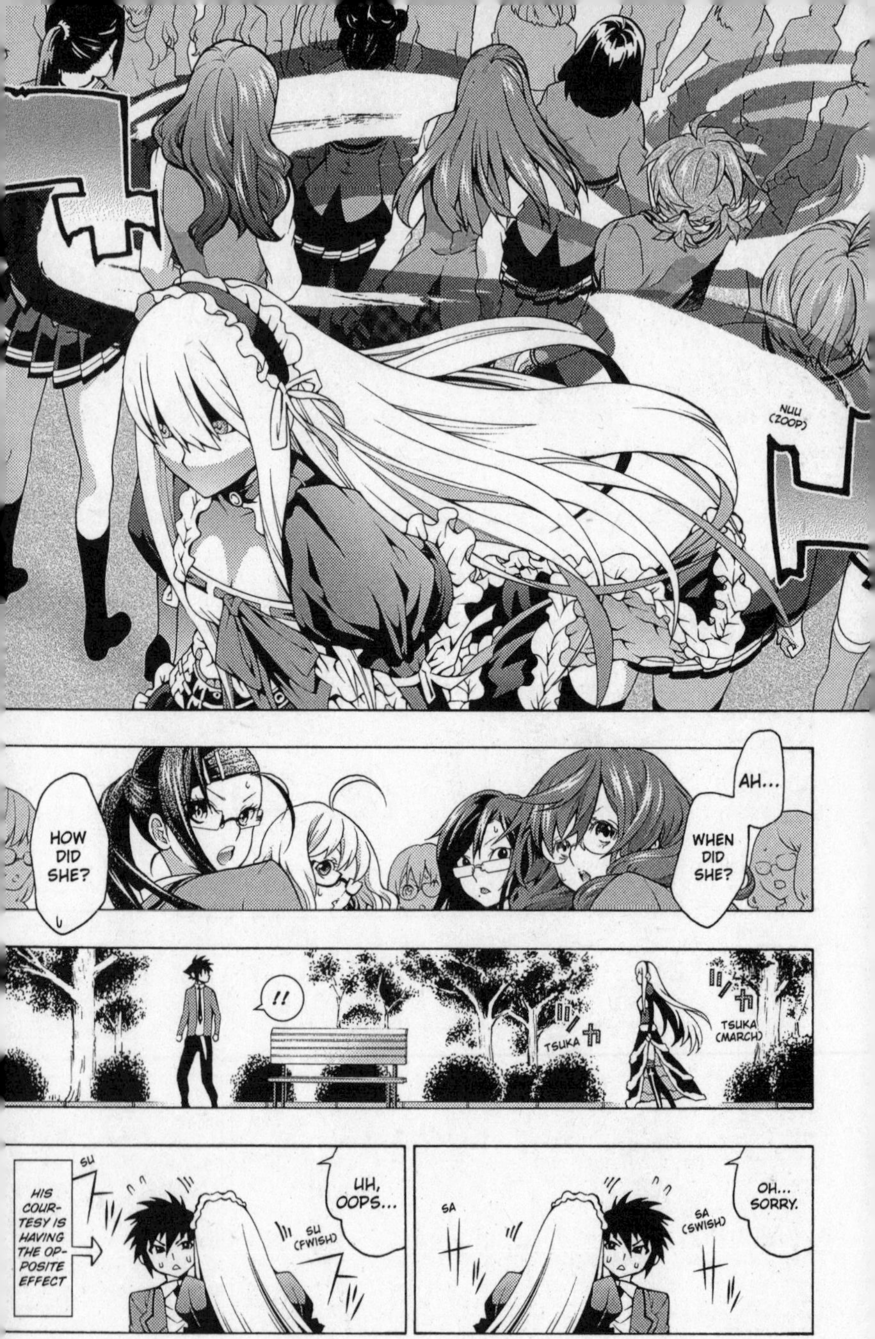
NUU (ZOOP)
AH...
WHEN DID SHE?
HOW DID SHE?
TSUKA (MARCH)
TSUKA
!!
OH... SORRY.
SA (SWISH)
SA
UH, OOPS...
SU (FWISH)
SU
HIS COURTESY IS HAVING THE OPPOSITE EFFECT

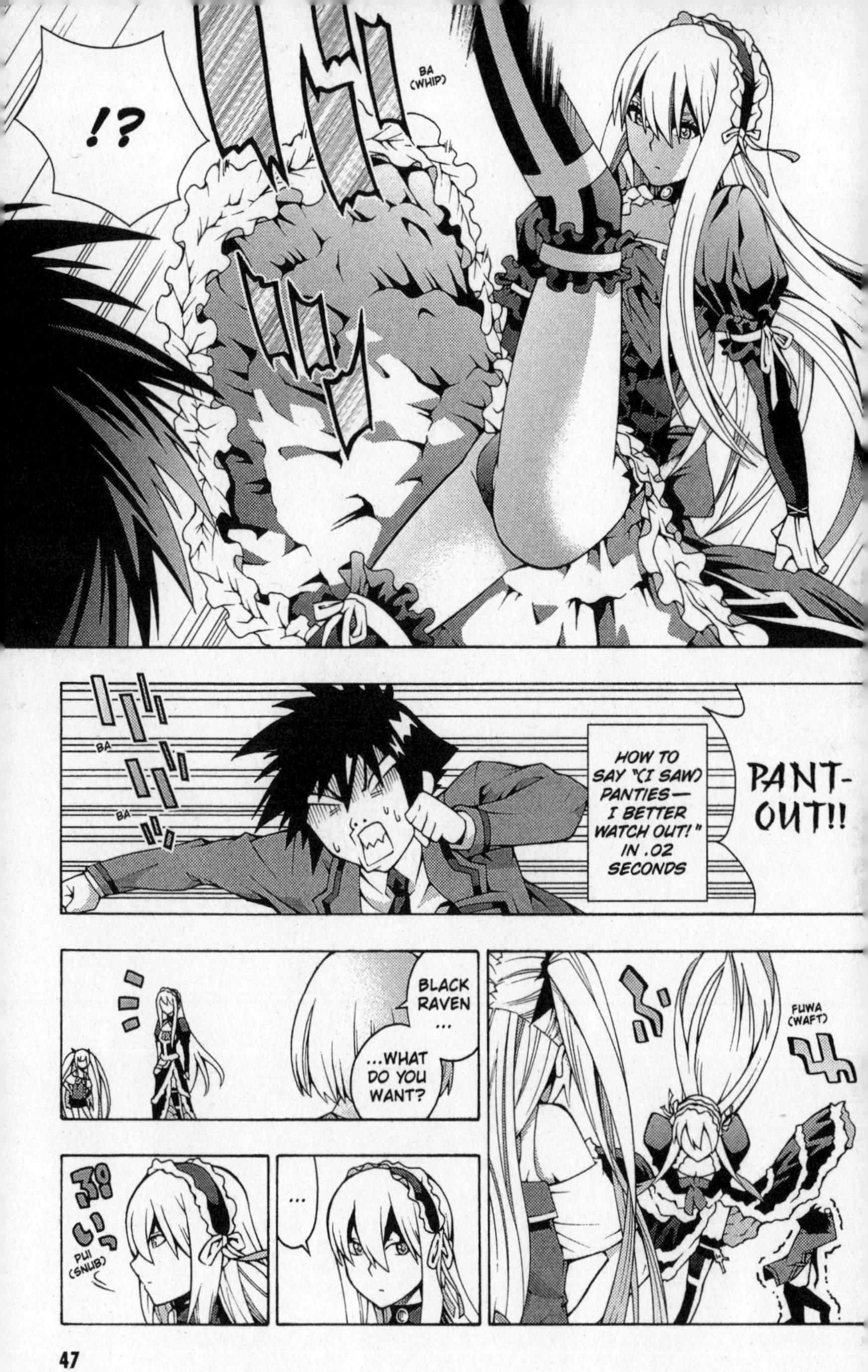
BA
(WHIP)
!?
PANT-
OUT!!
HOW TO SAY "(I SAW) PANTIES— I BETTER WATCH OUT!" IN .02 SECONDS
BA
BA
FUWA
(WAFT)
BLACK RAVEN ...
...WHAT DO YOU WANT?
...
PUI
(SNUB)

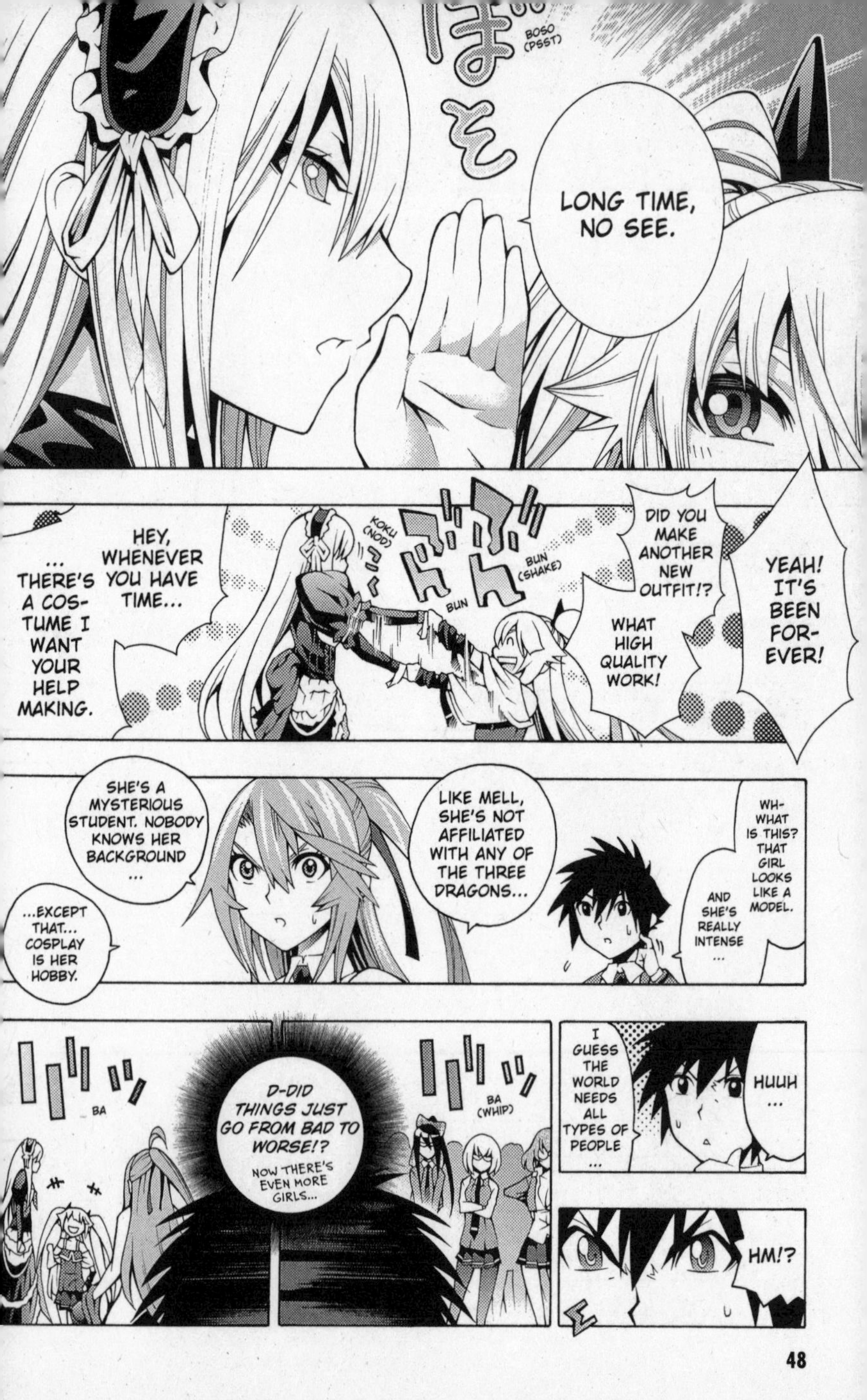
ぼそ
BOSO (PSST)
LONG TIME, NO SEE.
YEAH! IT'S BEEN FOR-EVER!
DID YOU MAKE ANOTHER NEW OUTFIT!?
WHAT HIGH QUALITY WORK!
BUN (SHAKE)
BUN
KOKU (NOD)
HEY, WHENEVER YOU HAVE TIME...
...THERE'S A COS-TUME I WANT YOUR HELP MAKING.
WH-WHAT IS THIS? THAT GIRL LOOKS LIKE A MODEL.
AND SHE'S REALLY INTENSE...
LIKE MELL, SHE'S NOT AFFILIATED WITH ANY OF THE THREE DRAGONS...
SHE'S A MYSTERIOUS STUDENT. NOBODY KNOWS HER BACKGROUND...
...EXCEPT THAT... COSPLAY IS HER HOBBY.
HUUH...
I GUESS THE WORLD NEEDS ALL TYPES OF PEOPLE...
HM!?
BA (WHIP)
D-DID THINGS JUST GO FROM BAD TO WORSE!?
NOW THERE'S EVEN MORE GIRLS...
BA

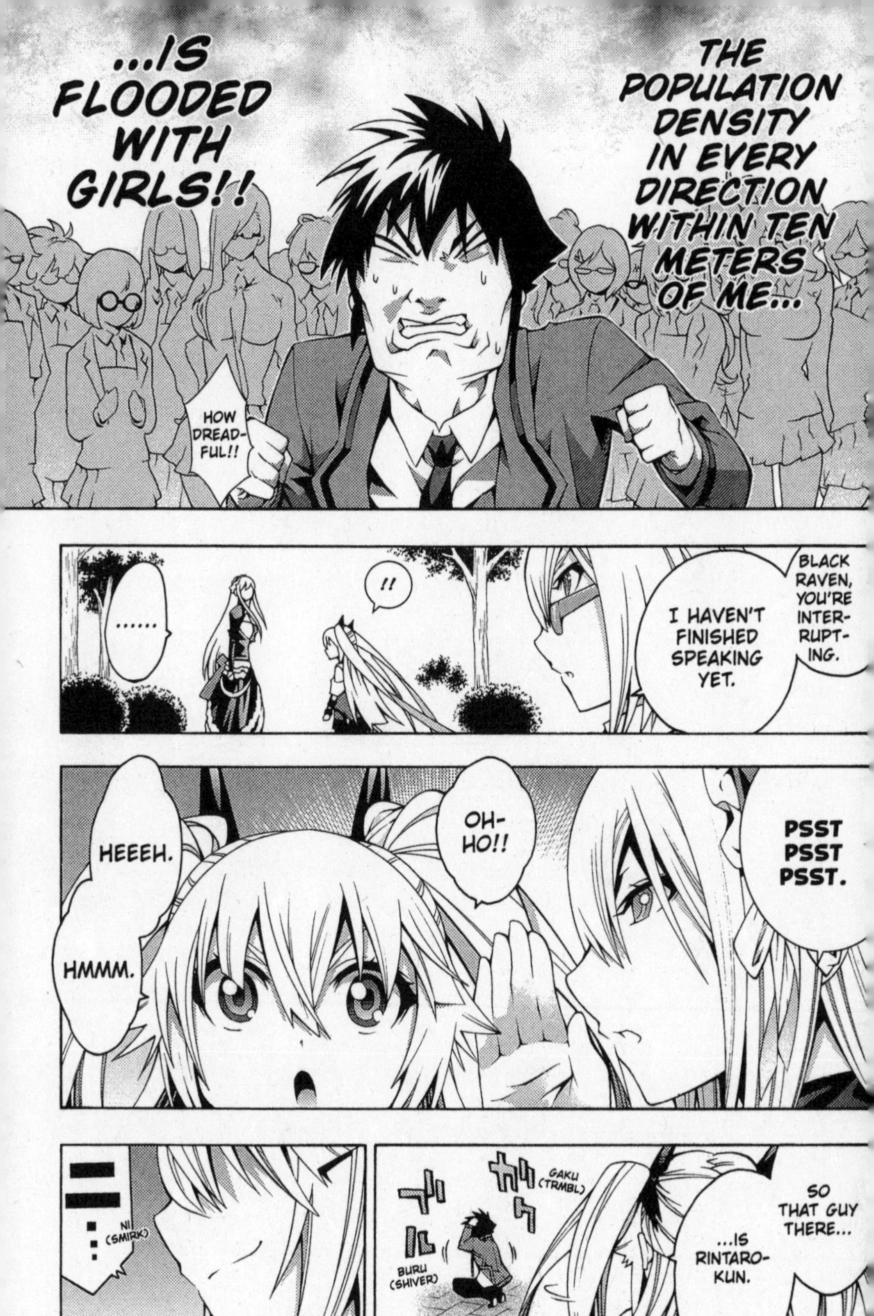
THE POPULATION DENSITY IN EVERY DIRECTION WITHIN TEN METERS OF ME...
...IS FLOODED WITH GIRLS!!
HOW DREAD-FUL!!
BLACK RAVEN, YOU'RE INTER-RUPT-ING.
I HAVEN'T FINISHED SPEAKING YET.
!!
......
PSST PSST PSST.
OH-HO!!
HEEEH.
HMMM.
SO THAT GUY THERE...
...IS RINTARO-KUN.
GAKU (TRMBL)
BURU (SHIVER)
NI (SMIRK)

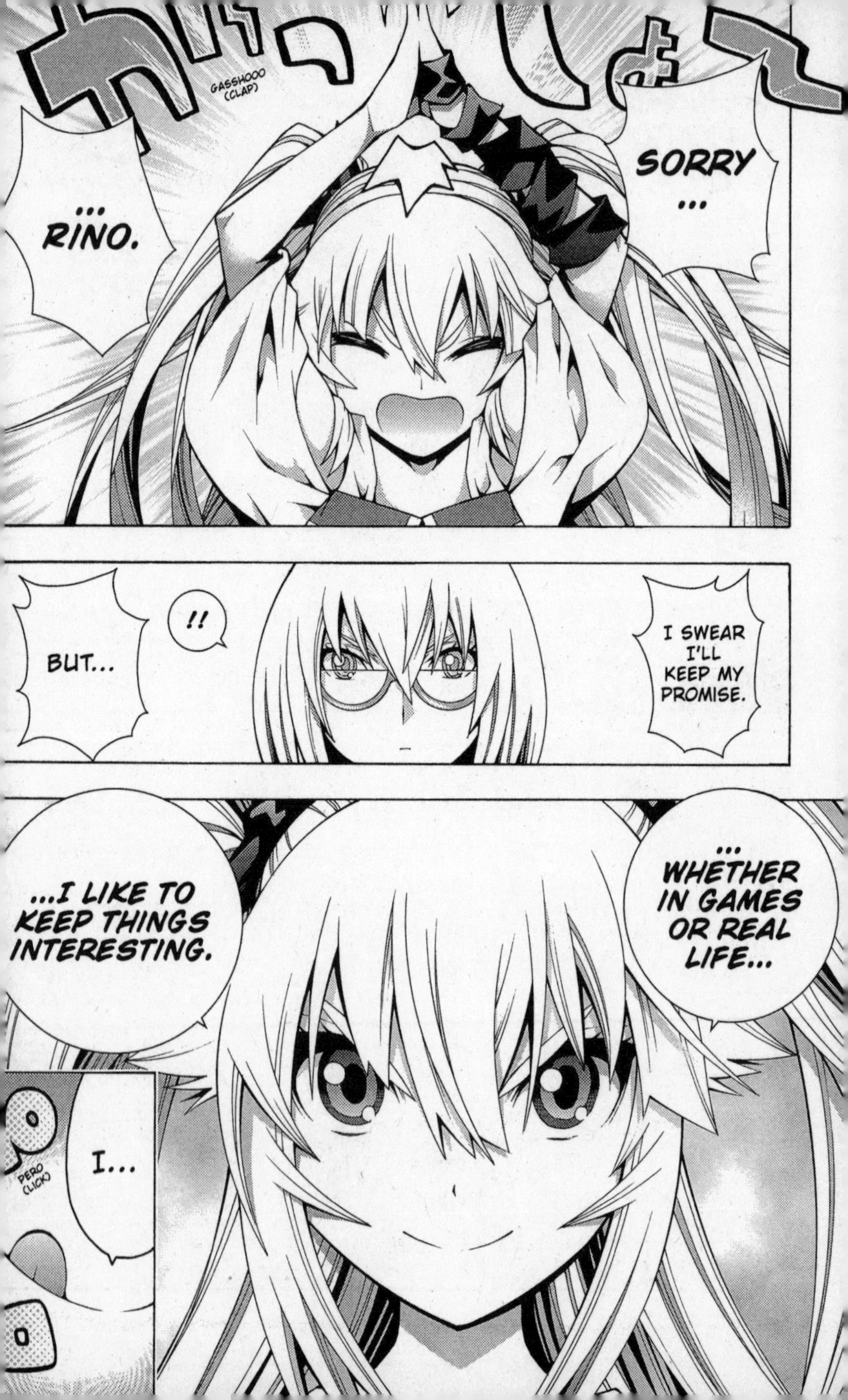
GASSHOOO (CLAP)
SORRY ...
... RINO.
I SWEAR I'LL KEEP MY PROMISE.
!!
BUT...
... WHETHER IN GAMES OR REAL LIFE...
...I LIKE TO KEEP THINGS INTERESTING.
I...
PERO (LICK)

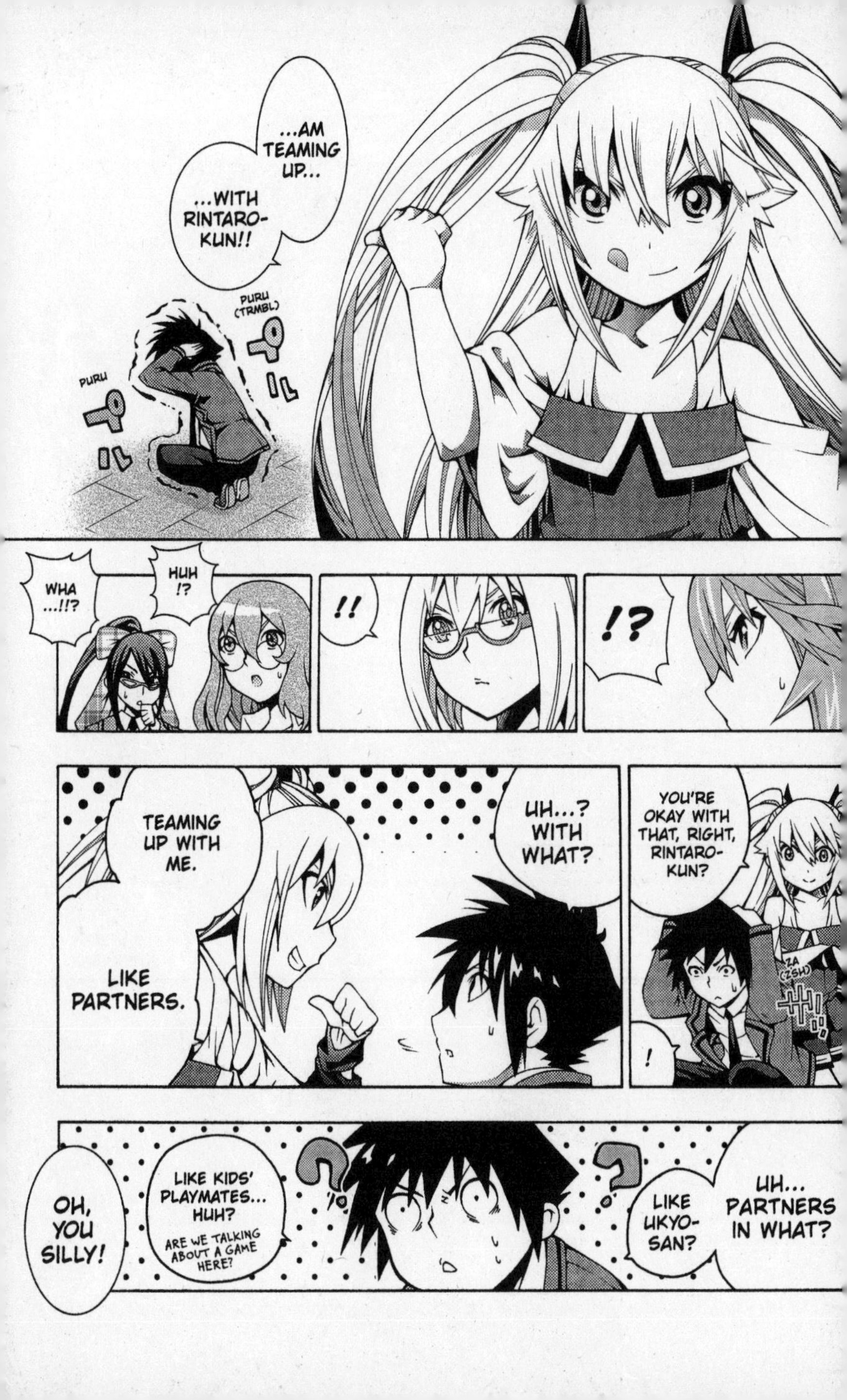
...AM TEAMING UP...
...WITH RINTARO-KUN!!
PURU (TRMBL)
PURU
!?
!!
HUH !?
WHA ...!!?
YOU'RE OKAY WITH THAT, RIGHT, RINTARO-KUN?
ZA (ZSH)
!
UH...? WITH WHAT?
TEAMING UP WITH ME.
LIKE PARTNERS.
UH... PARTNERS IN WHAT?
LIKE UKYO-SAN?
LIKE KIDS' PLAYMATES... HUH?
ARE WE TALKING ABOUT A GAME HERE?
OH, YOU SILLY!

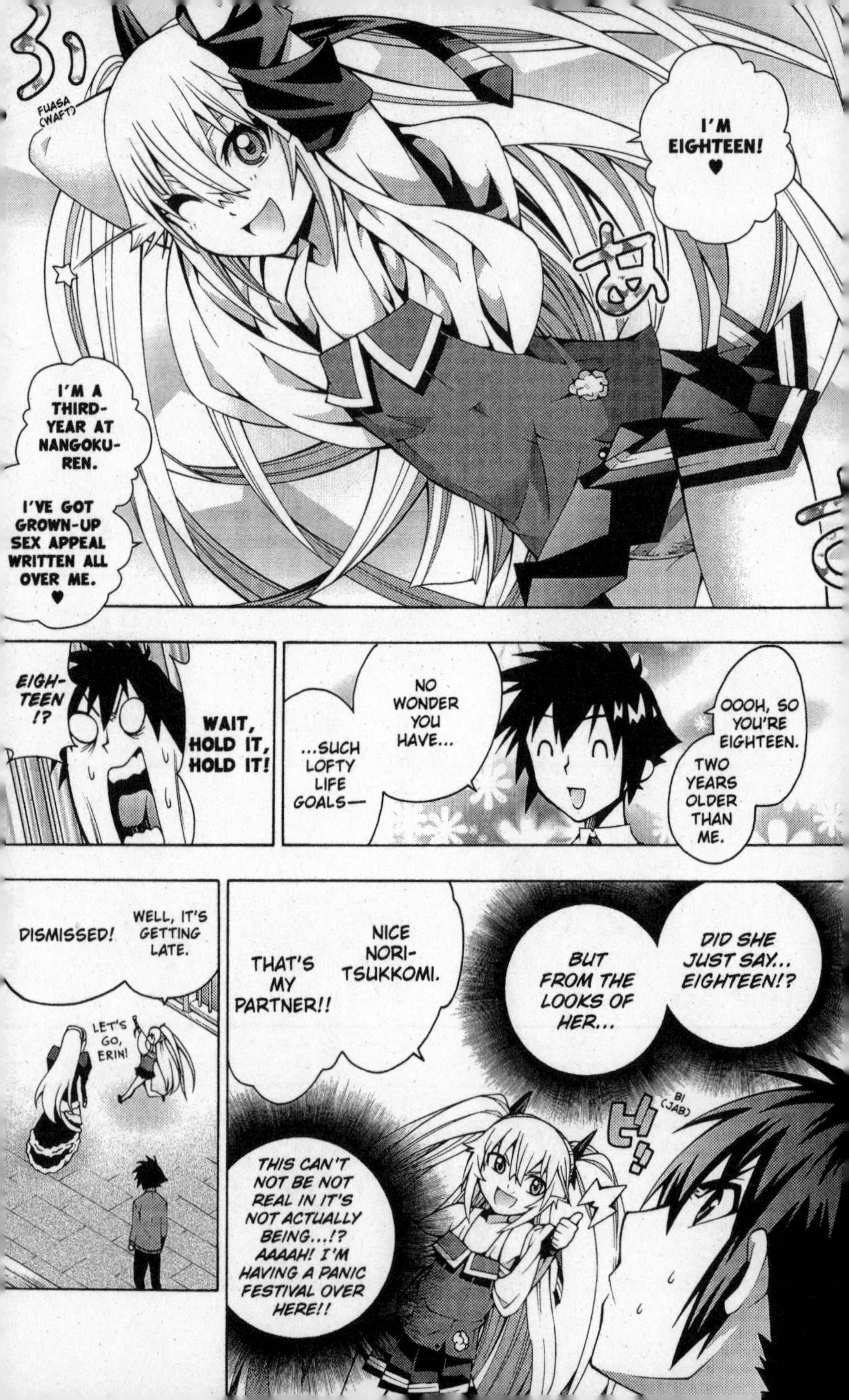
I'M EIGHTEEN! ♥
FUASA (WAFT)
I'M A THIRD-YEAR AT NANGOKU-REN.
I'VE GOT GROWN-UP SEX APPEAL WRITTEN ALL OVER ME. ♥
OOOH, SO YOU'RE EIGHTEEN.
TWO YEARS OLDER THAN ME.
NO WONDER YOU HAVE...
...SUCH LOFTY LIFE GOALS—
WAIT, HOLD IT, HOLD IT!
EIGHTEEN!?
DID SHE JUST SAY... EIGHTEEN!?
BUT FROM THE LOOKS OF HER...
NICE NORI-TSUKKOMI.
THAT'S MY PARTNER!!
BI (JAB)
THIS CAN'T NOT BE NOT REAL IN IT'S NOT ACTUALLY BEING...!? AAAAH! I'M HAVING A PANIC FESTIVAL OVER HERE!!
WELL, IT'S GETTING LATE.
DISMISSED!
LET'S GO, ERIN!

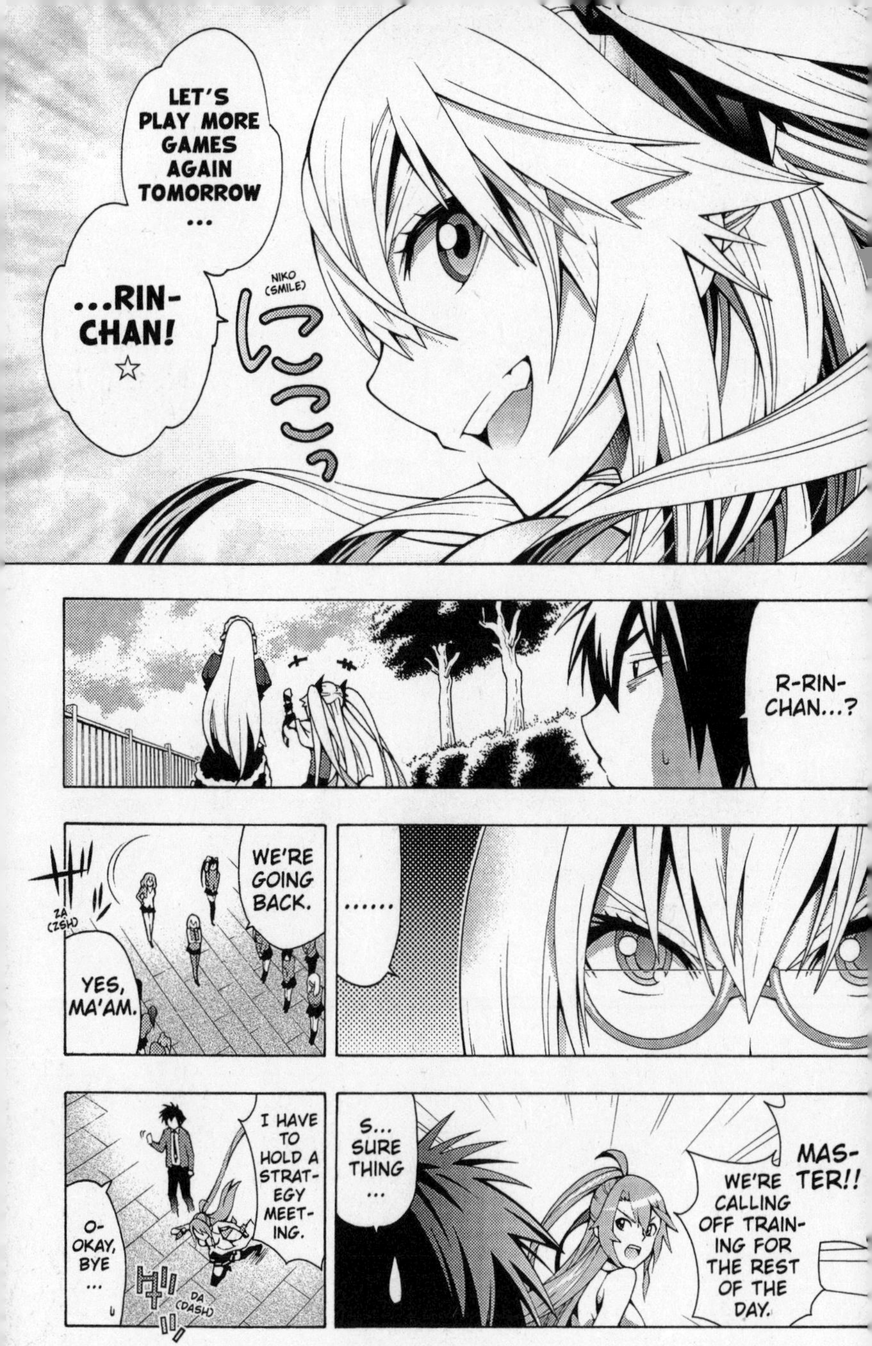
LET'S PLAY MORE GAMES AGAIN TOMORROW ...
...RIN-CHAN! ☆
NIKO (SMILE)
R-RIN-CHAN...?
......
WE'RE GOING BACK.
ZA (ZSH)
YES, MA'AM.
MAS-TER!!
WE'RE CALLING OFF TRAIN-ING FOR THE REST OF THE DAY.
S... SURE THING ...
I HAVE TO HOLD A STRAT-EGY MEET-ING.
O-OKAY, BYE ...
DA (DASH)

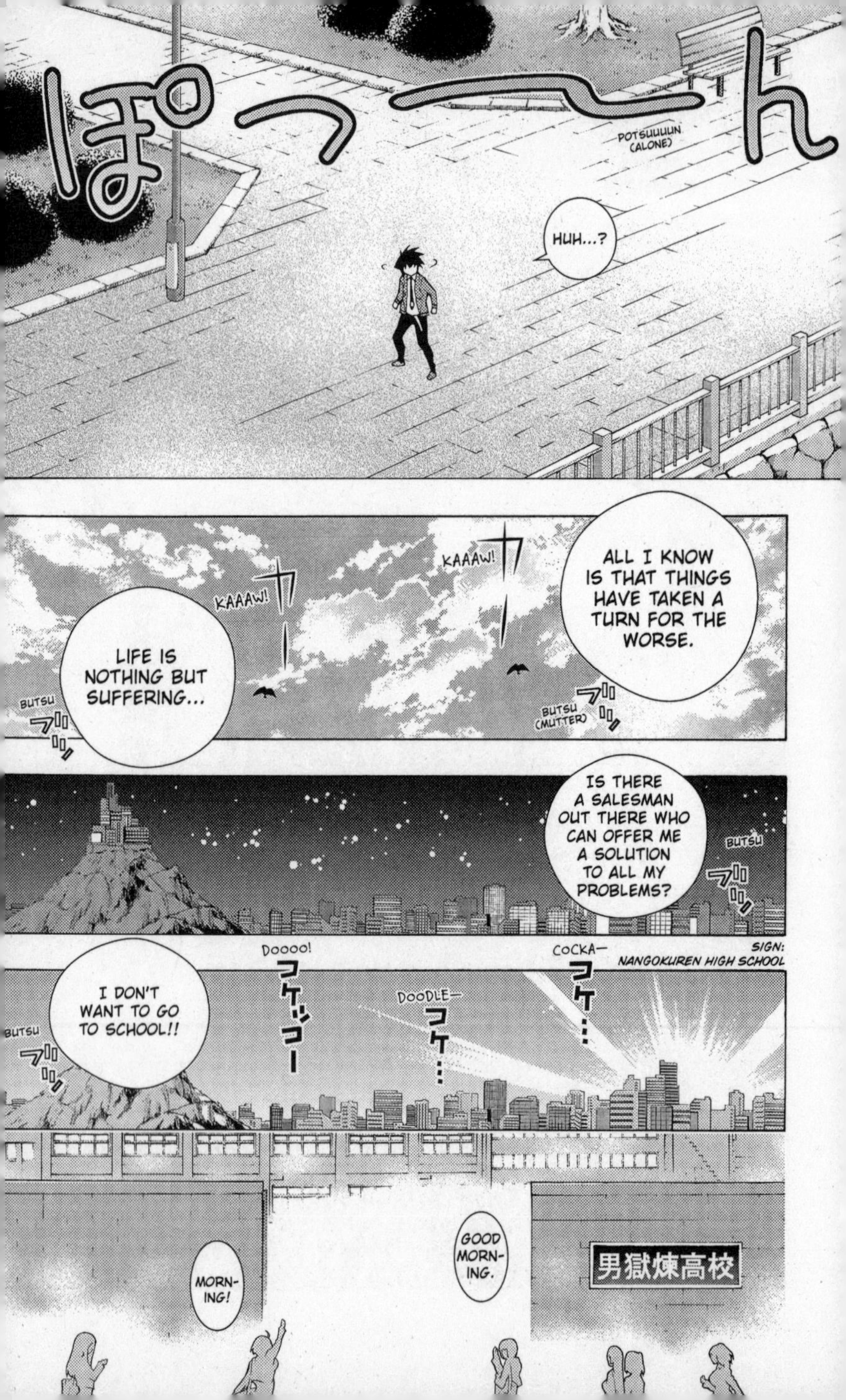
ぽつーーん
POTSUUUUN (ALONE)
HUH...?
ALL I KNOW IS THAT THINGS HAVE TAKEN A TURN FOR THE WORSE.
BUTSU (MUTTER)
ブツ
KAAAW!
カー
KAAAW!
カー
LIFE IS NOTHING BUT SUFFERING...
BUTSU
ブツ
BUTSU
ブツ
IS THERE A SALESMAN OUT THERE WHO CAN OFFER ME A SOLUTION TO ALL MY PROBLEMS?
SIGN: NANGOKUREN HIGH SCHOOL
COCKA—
コケ…
DOODLE—
コケ…
DOOOO!
コケッコー
I DON'T WANT TO GO TO SCHOOL!!
BUTSU
ブツ
男獄煉高校
GOOD MORNING.
MORNING!

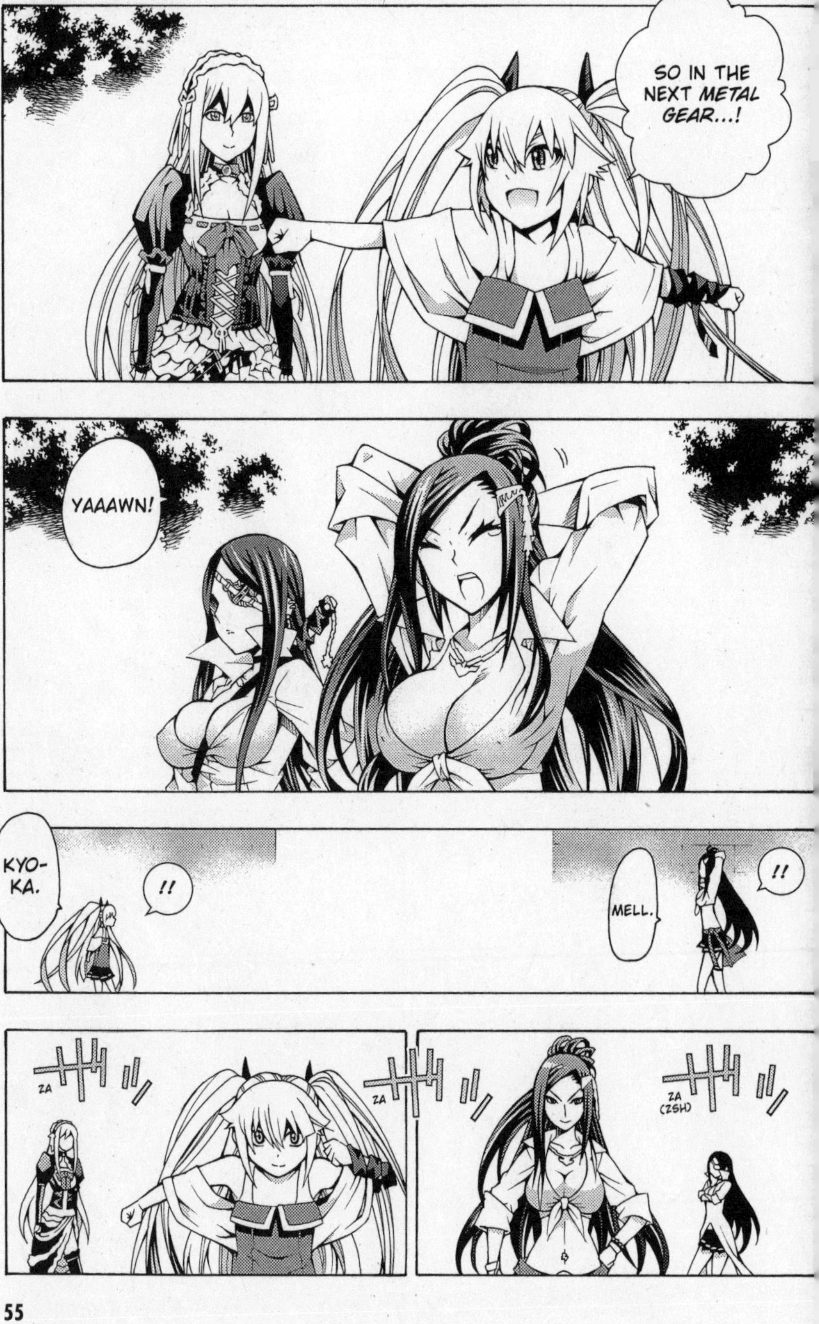
SO IN THE NEXT *METAL GEAR*...!
YAAAWN!
!!
MELL.
!!
KYO-KA.
ZA (ZSH)
ZA
ZA

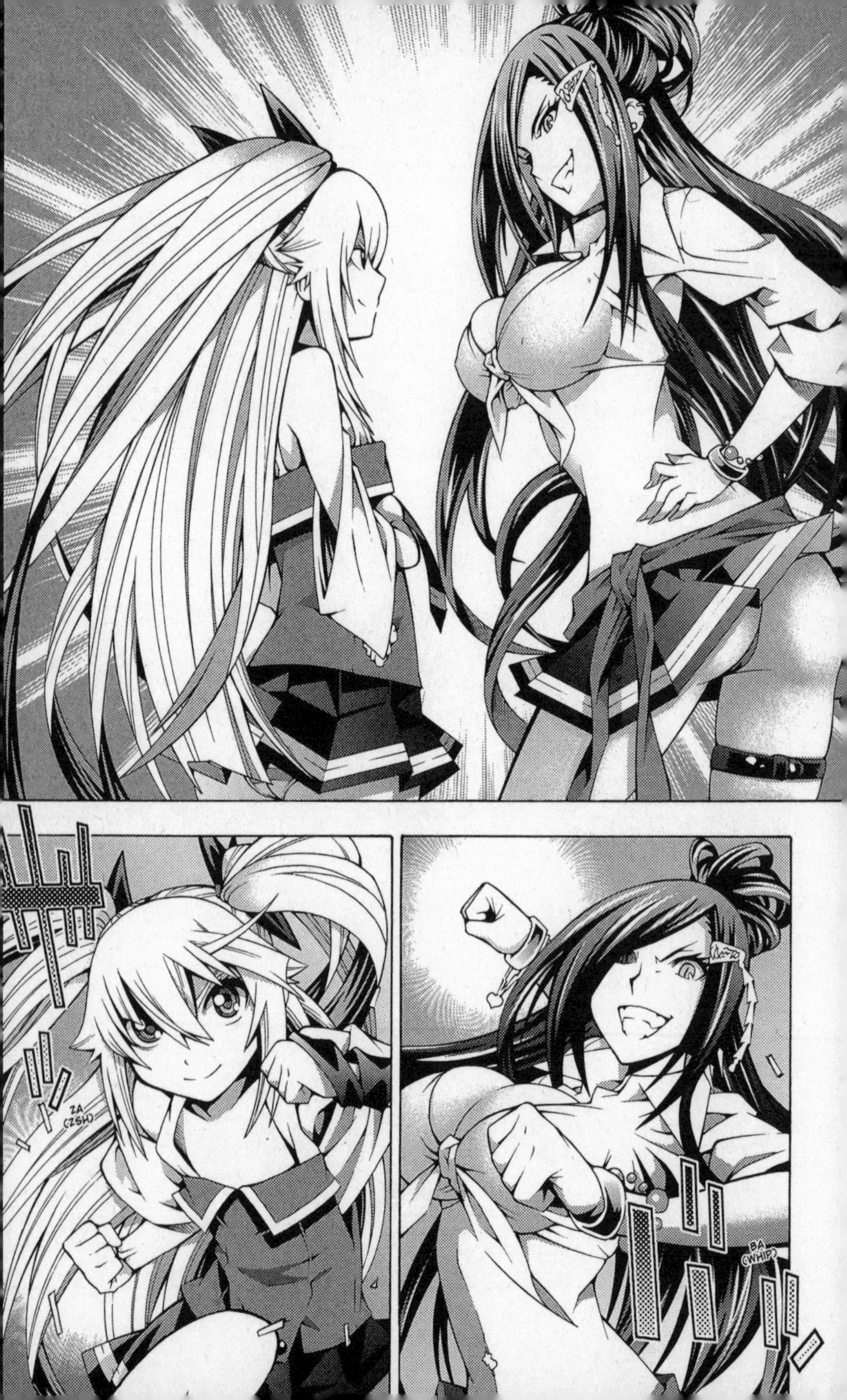
BA
(WHIP)
ZA
(ZSH)

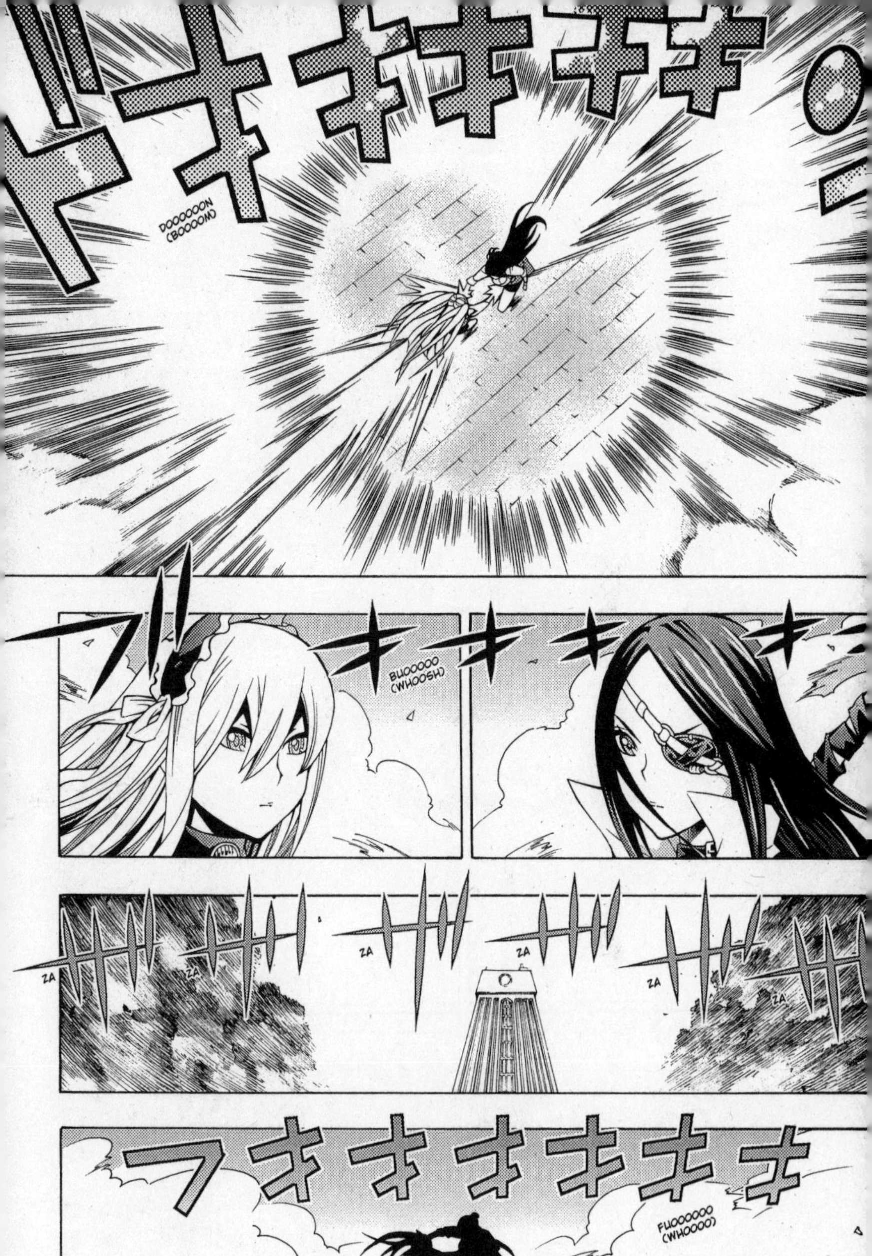
DOOOOOON
(BOOOOM)
BUOOOOO
(WHOOSH)
ZA
ZA
ZA
ZA
ZA
ZA
FUOOOOOO
(WHOOOO)

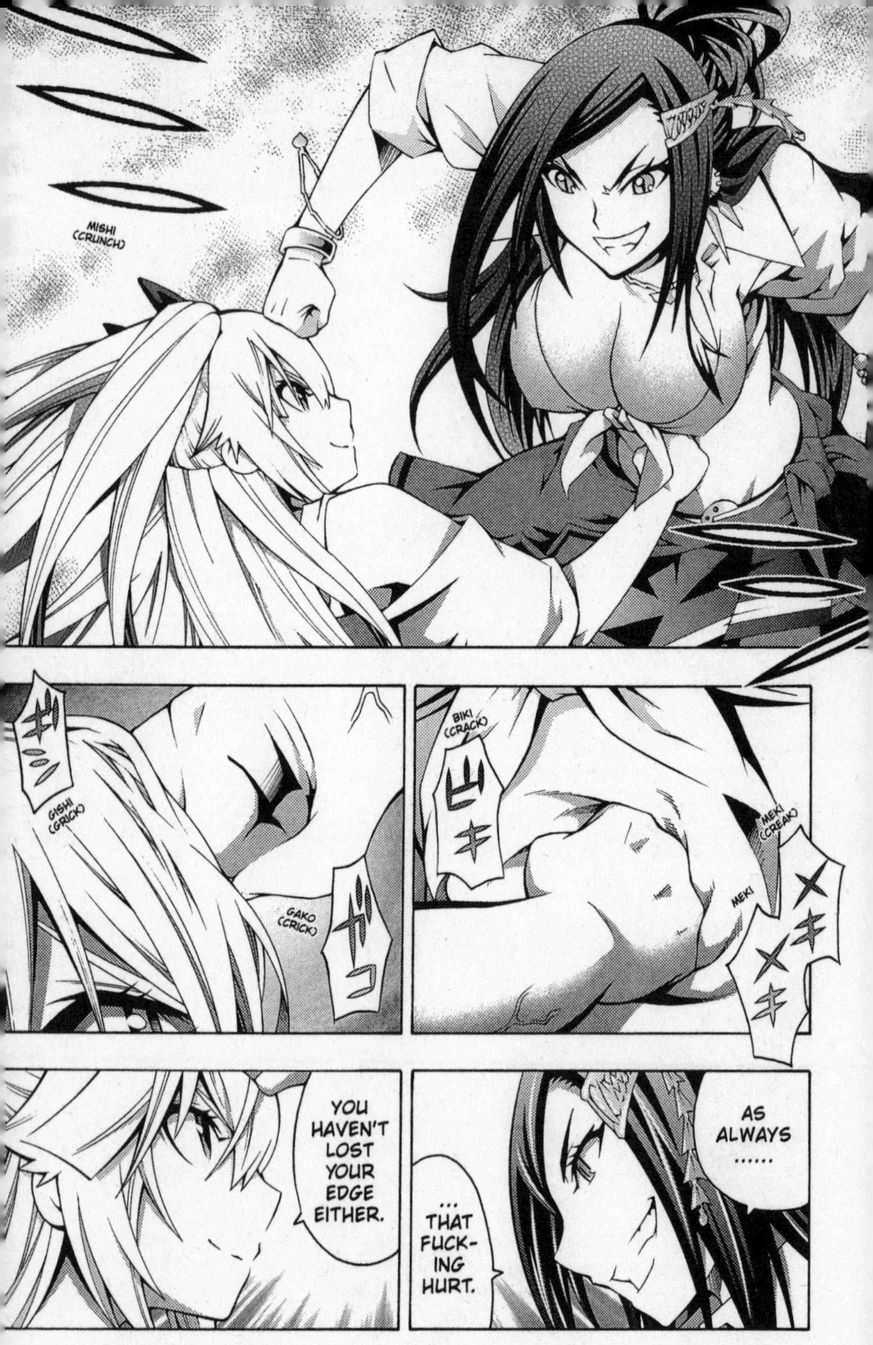
MISHI (CRUNCH)
BIKI (CRACK)
MEKI (CREAK)
MEKI
GISHI (GRICK)
GAKO (CRICK)
AS ALWAYS ......
... THAT FUCKING HURT.
YOU HAVEN'T LOST YOUR EDGE EITHER.

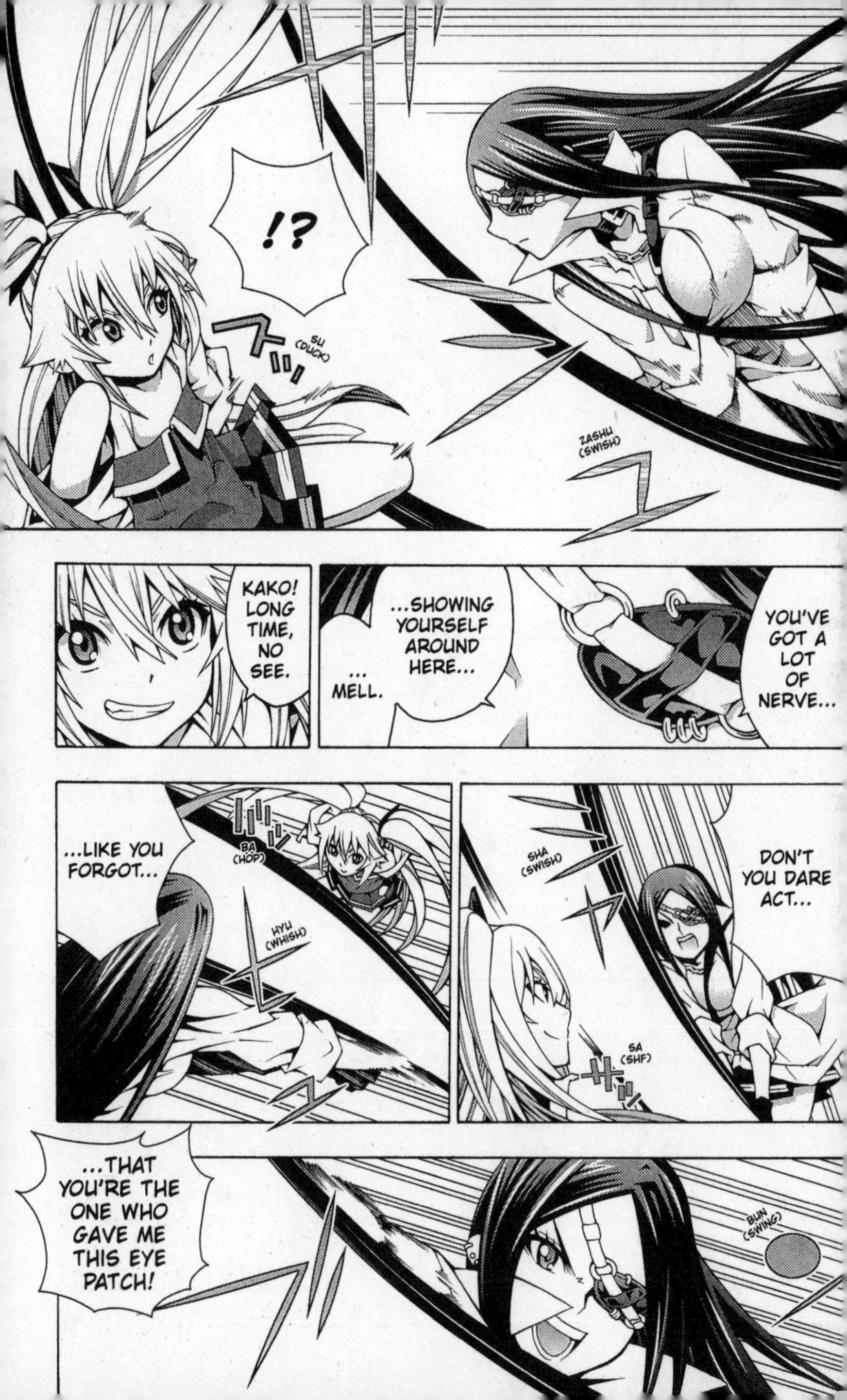
ZASHU (SWISH)
!?
SU (DUCK)
YOU'VE GOT A LOT OF NERVE...
...SHOWING YOURSELF AROUND HERE...
... MELL.
KAKO! LONG TIME, NO SEE.
DON'T YOU DARE ACT...
SHA (SWISH)
SA (SHF)
BA (HOP)
...LIKE YOU FORGOT...
HYU (WHISH)
BUN (SWING)
...THAT YOU'RE THE ONE WHO GAVE ME THIS EYE PATCH!

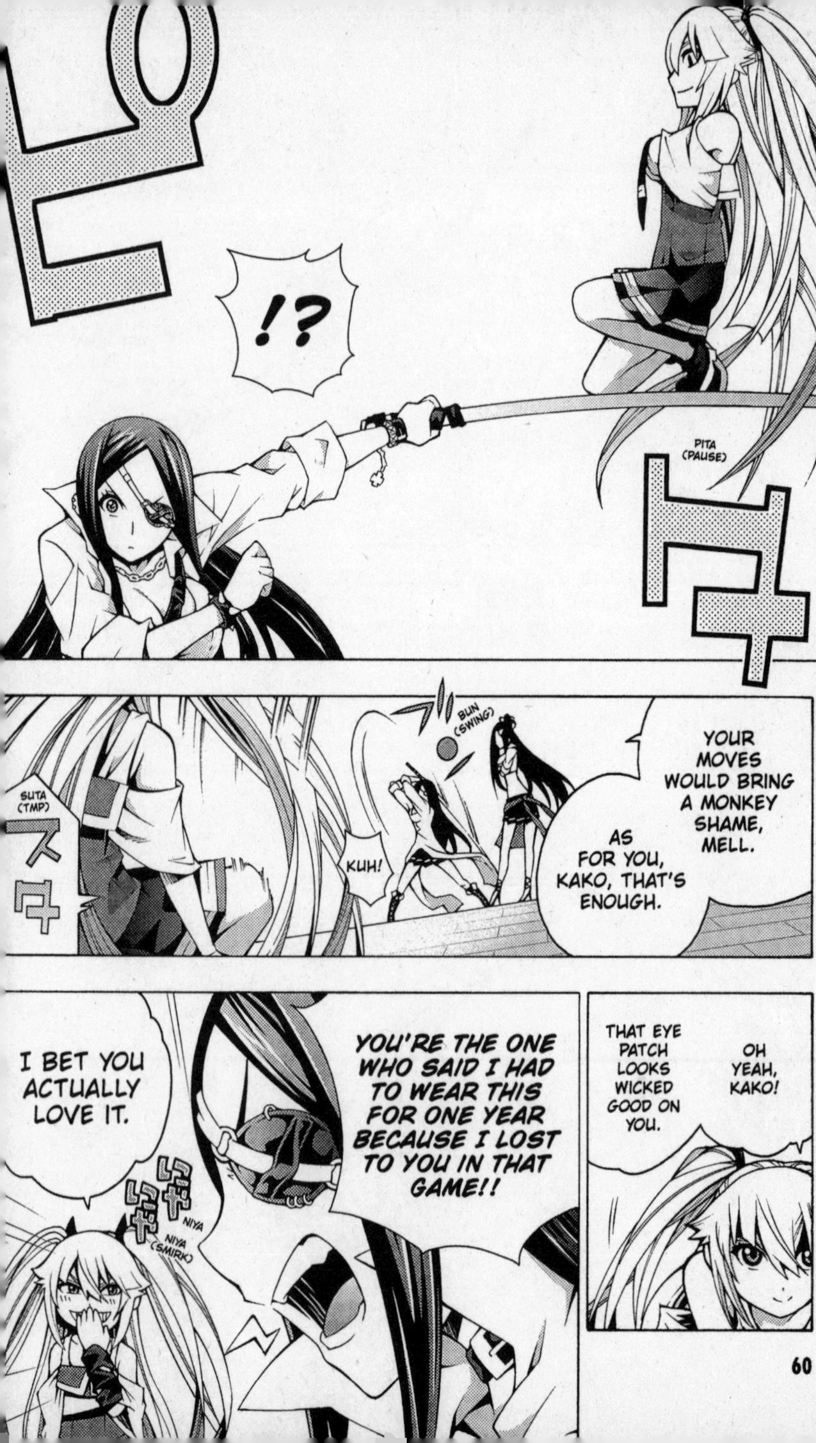
!?
PITA (PAUSE)
YOUR MOVES WOULD BRING A MONKEY SHAME, MELL.
AS FOR YOU, KAKO, THAT'S ENOUGH.
BUN (SWING)
KUH!
SUTA (TMP)
OH YEAH, KAKO!
THAT EYE PATCH LOOKS WICKED GOOD ON YOU.
YOU'RE THE ONE WHO SAID I HAD TO WEAR THIS FOR ONE YEAR BECAUSE I LOST TO YOU IN THAT GAME!!
I BET YOU ACTUALLY LOVE IT.
NIYA NIYA (SMIRK)

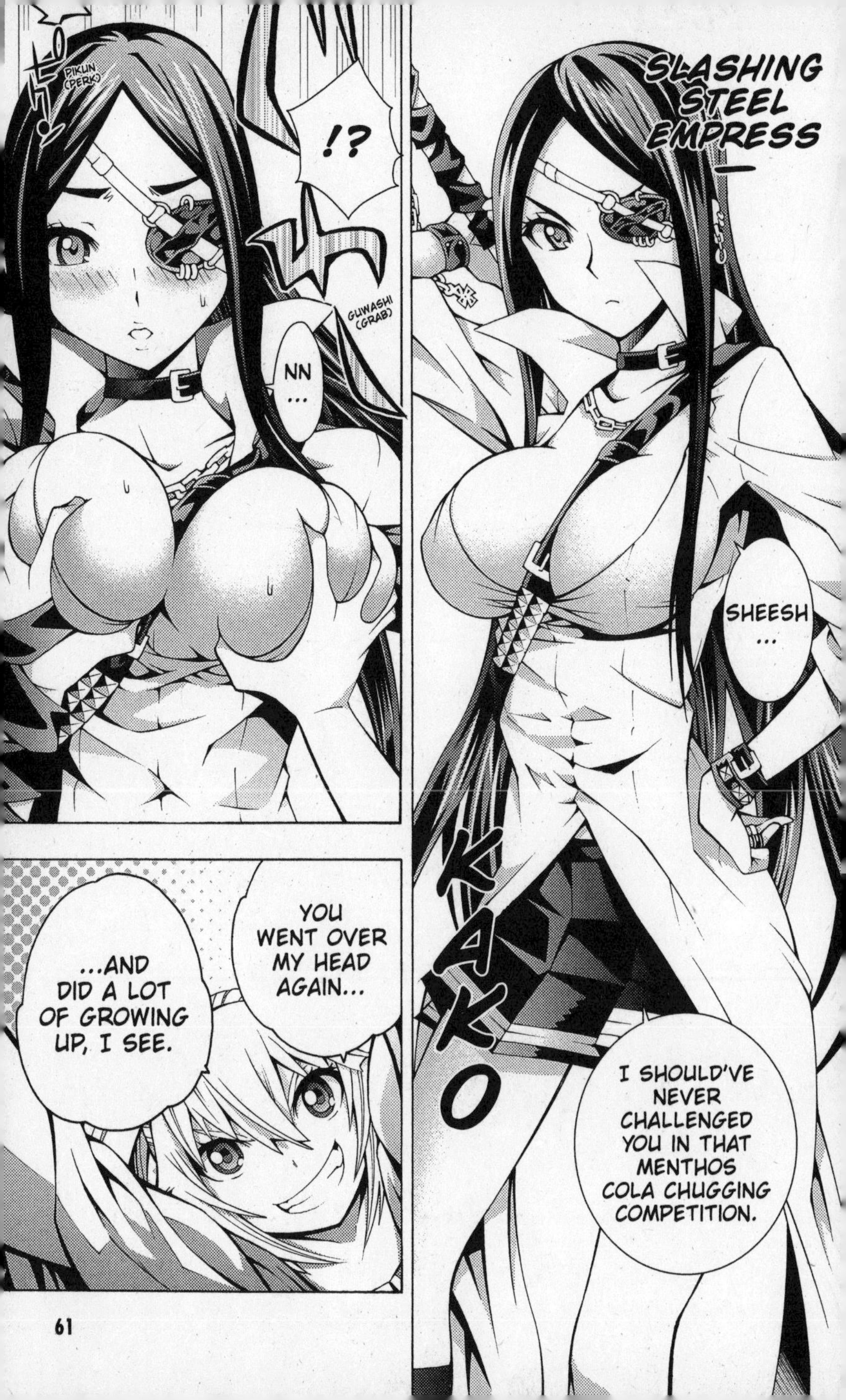
SLASHING STEEL EMPRESS—
SHEESH...
KAKO
I SHOULD'VE NEVER CHALLENGED YOU IN THAT MENTHOS COLA CHUGGING COMPETITION.
PIKUN (PERK)
!?
GUWASHI (GRAB)
NN...
YOU WENT OVER MY HEAD AGAIN...
...AND DID A LOT OF GROWING UP, I SEE.

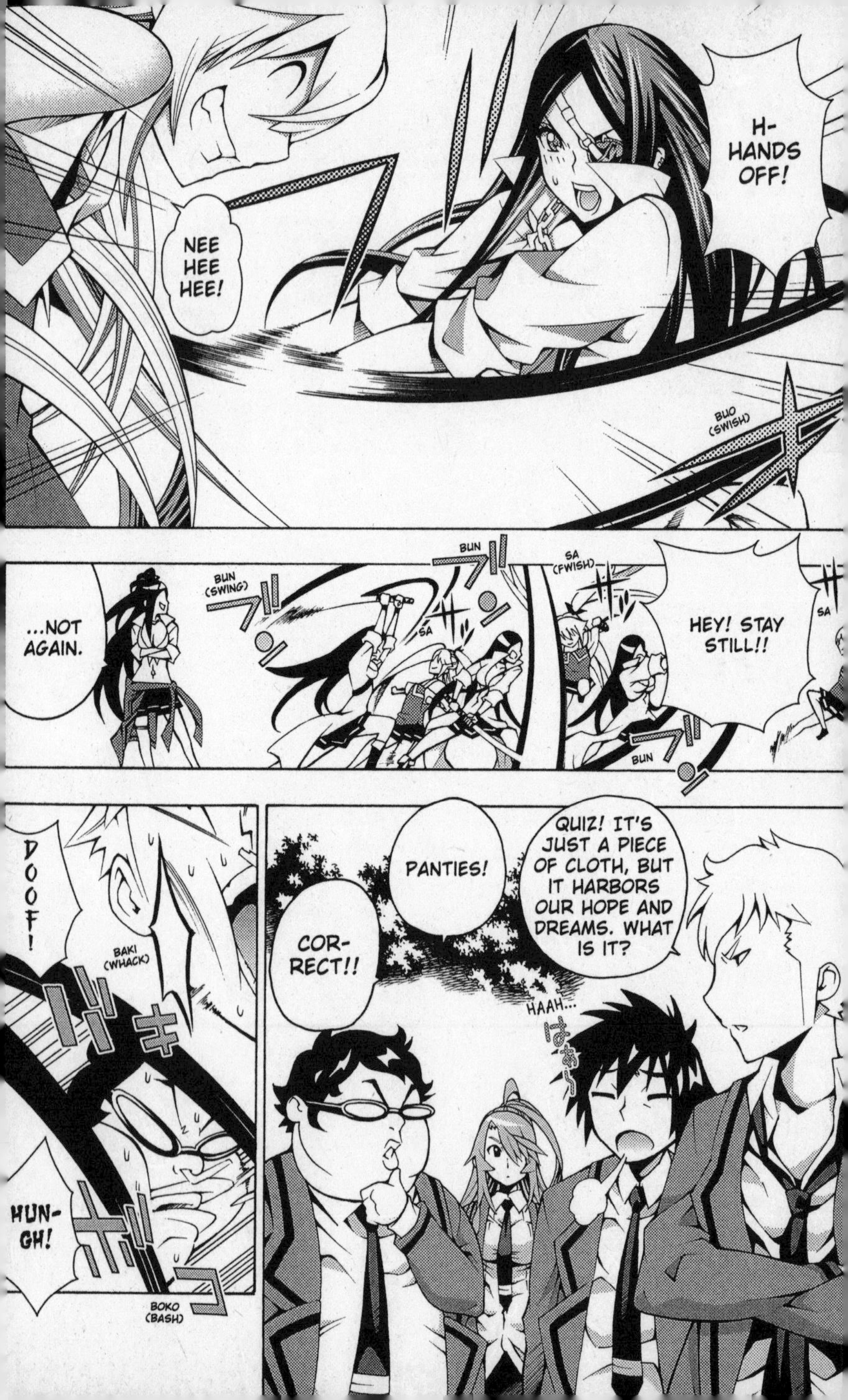
H- HANDS OFF!
NEE HEE HEE!
BUO (SWISH)
HEY! STAY STILL!!
SA
SA (FWISH)
BUN
BUN
SA
BUN (SWING)
...NOT AGAIN.
QUIZ! IT'S JUST A PIECE OF CLOTH, BUT IT HARBORS OUR HOPE AND DREAMS. WHAT IS IT?
PANTIES!
COR- RECT!!
HAAH...
DOOOF!
BAKI (WHACK)
HUN- GH!
BOKO (BASH)

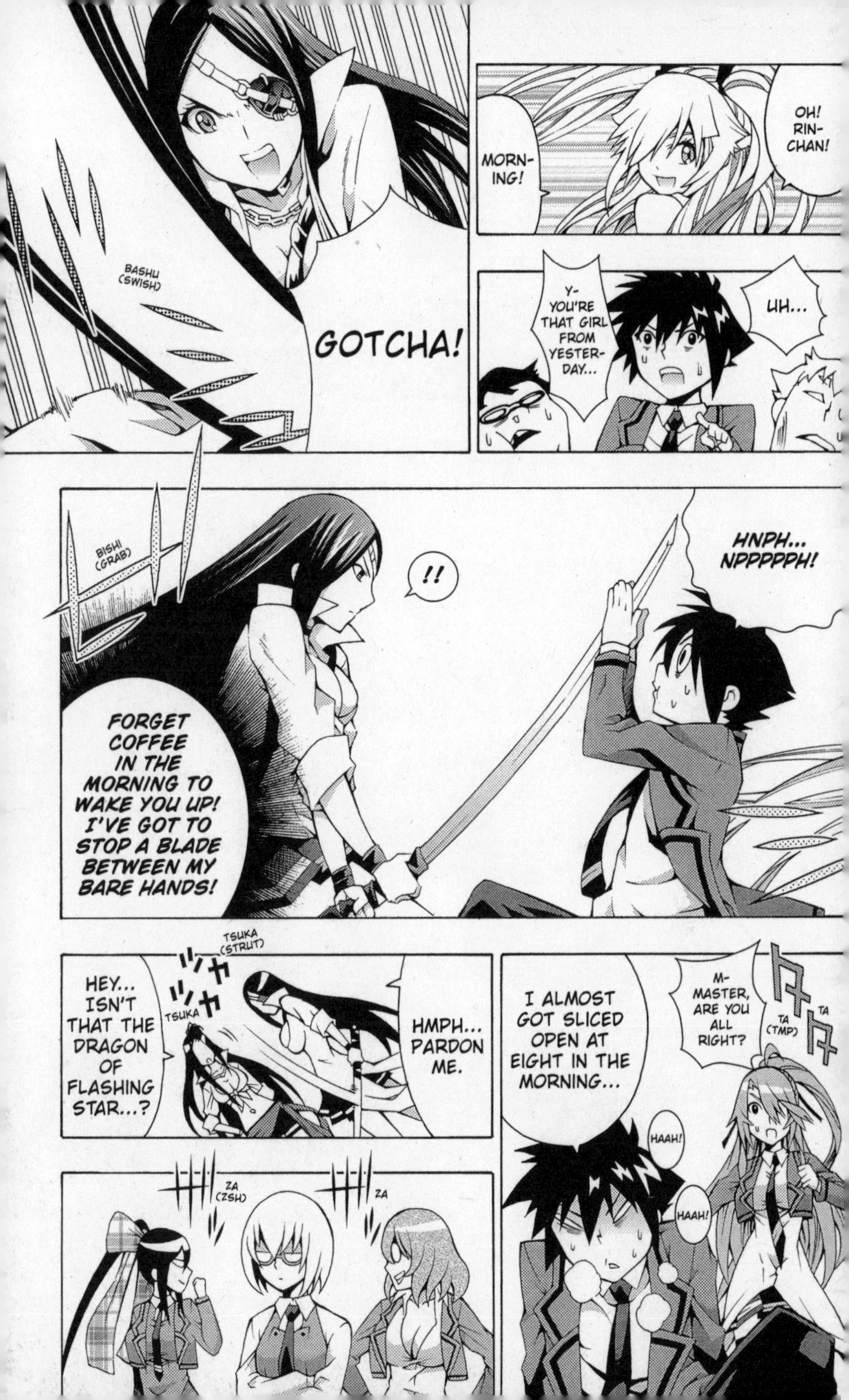
OH! RIN-CHAN!
MORNING!
UH...
Y-YOU'RE THAT GIRL FROM YESTER-DAY...
BASHU (SWISH)
GOTCHA!
HNPH... NPPPPPH!
!!
BISHI (GRAB)
FORGET COFFEE IN THE MORNING TO WAKE YOU UP! I'VE GOT TO STOP A BLADE BETWEEN MY BARE HANDS!
TA TA (TMP)
M-MASTER, ARE YOU ALL RIGHT?
I ALMOST GOT SLICED OPEN AT EIGHT IN THE MORNING...
HAAH!
HAAH!
HMPH... PARDON ME.
TSUKA (STRUT)
TSUKA
HEY... ISN'T THAT THE DRAGON OF FLASHING STAR...?
ZA
ZA (ZSH)

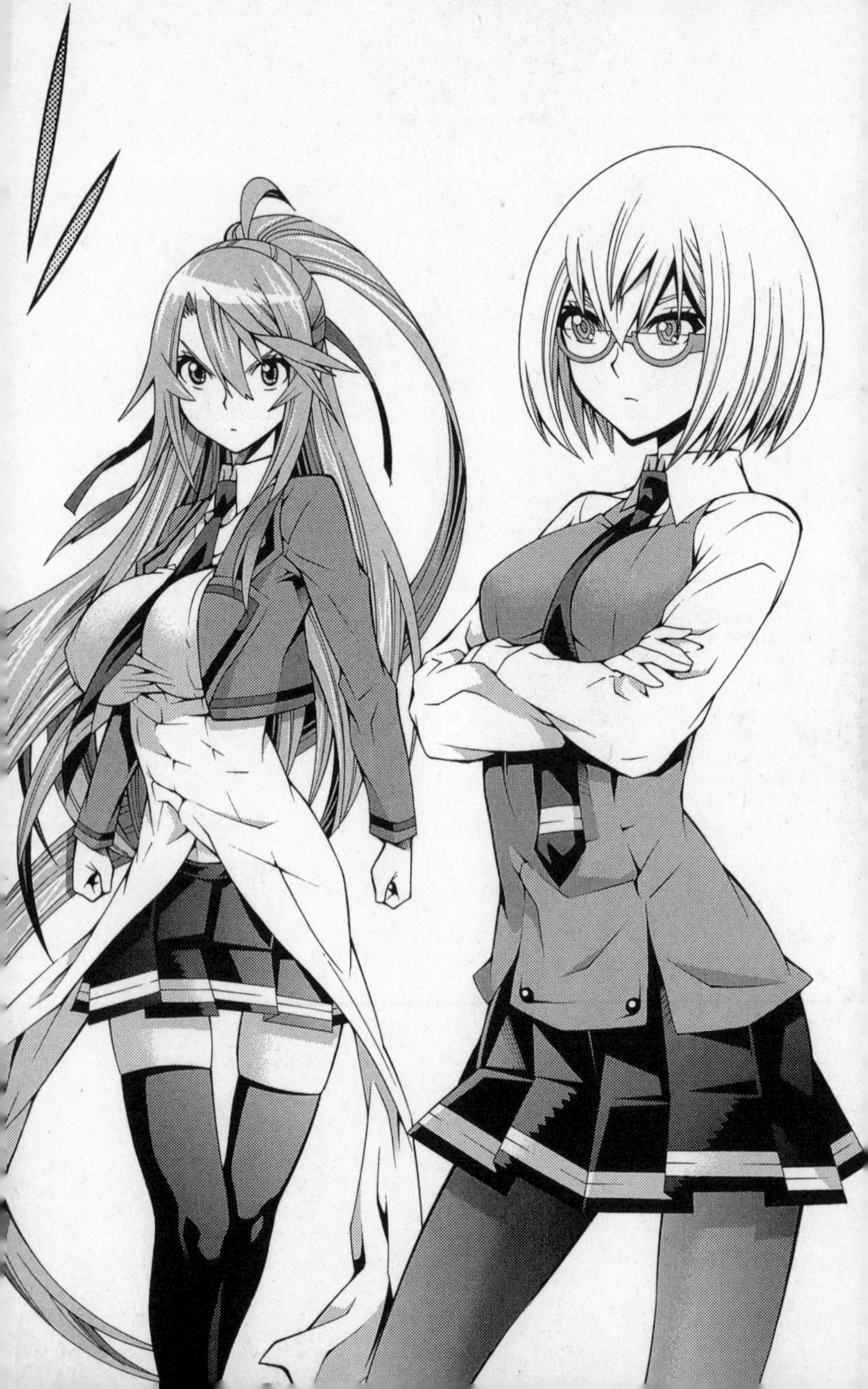

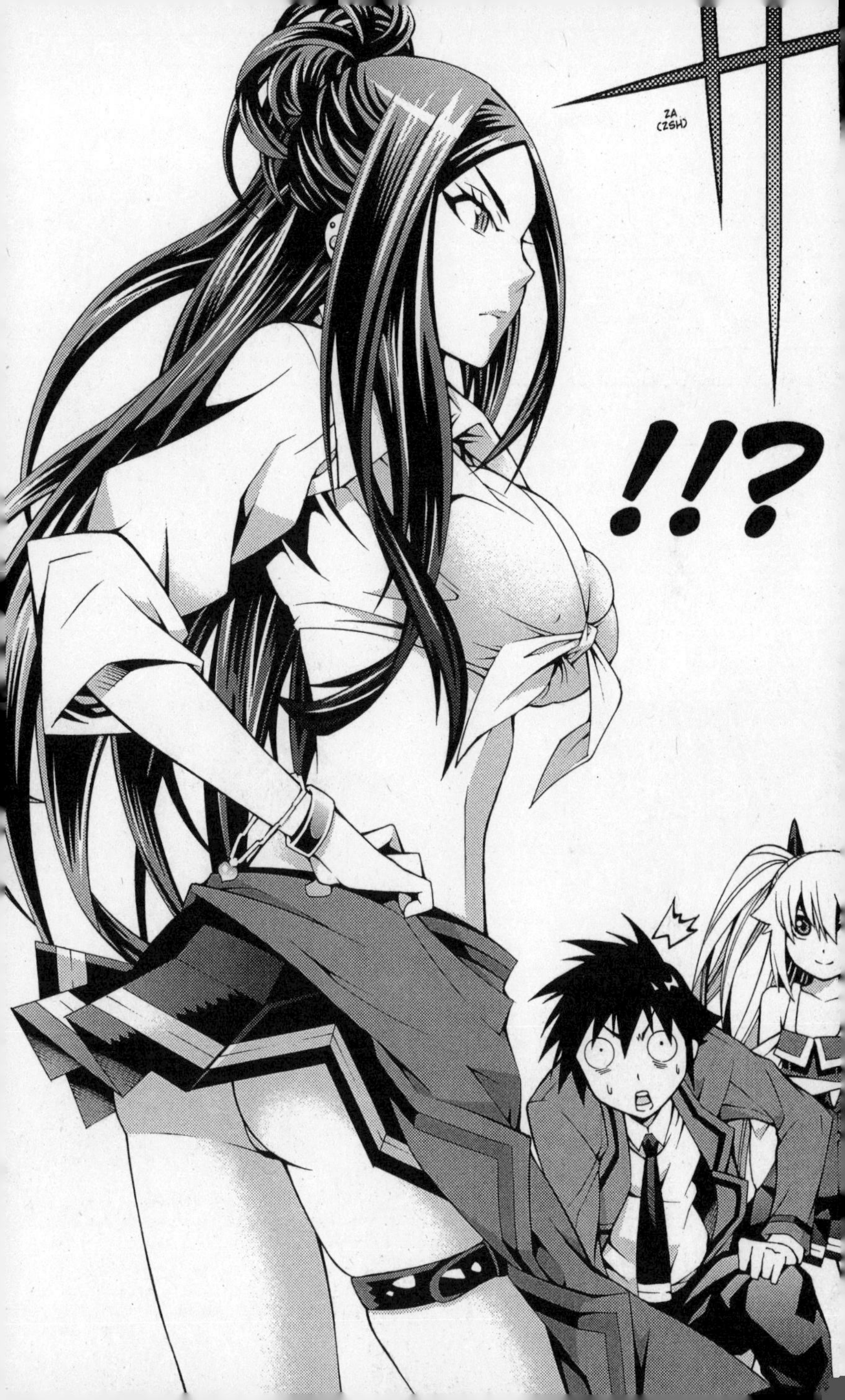
ZA
(ZSH)
!!?

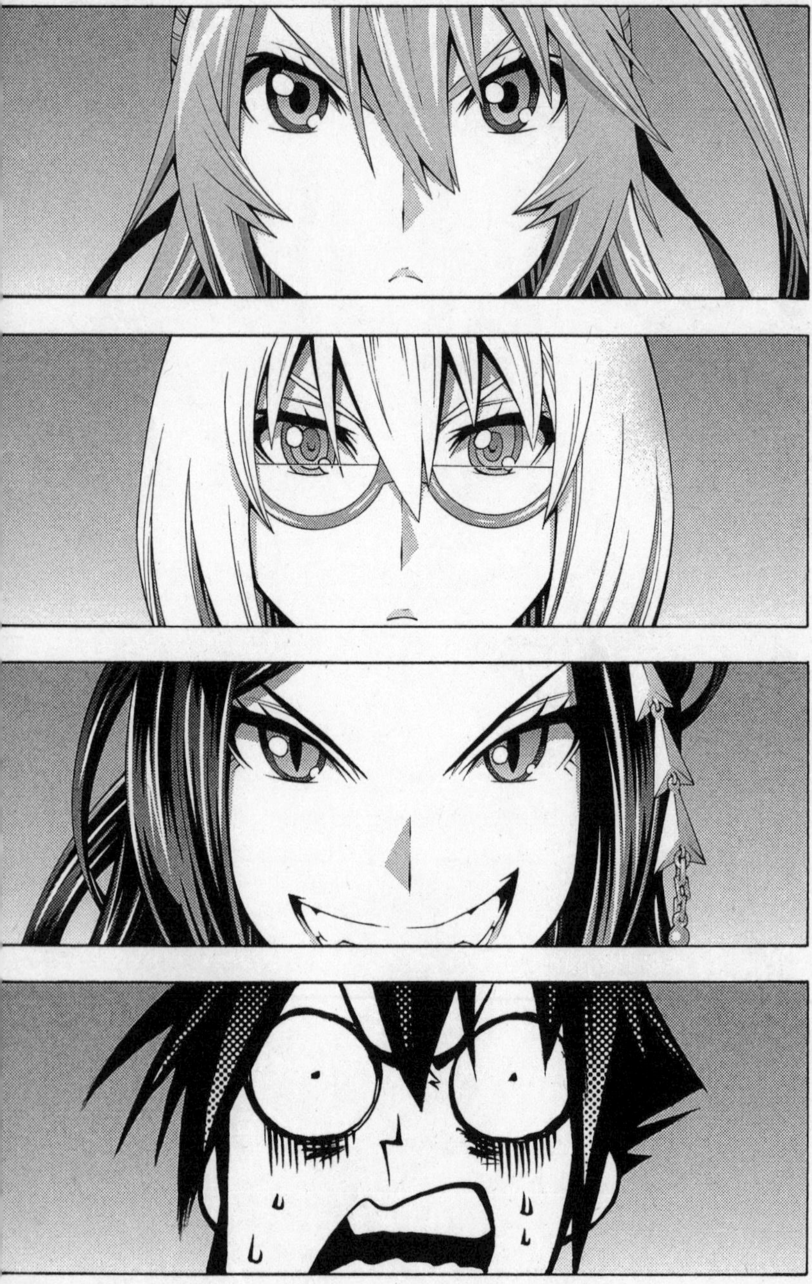

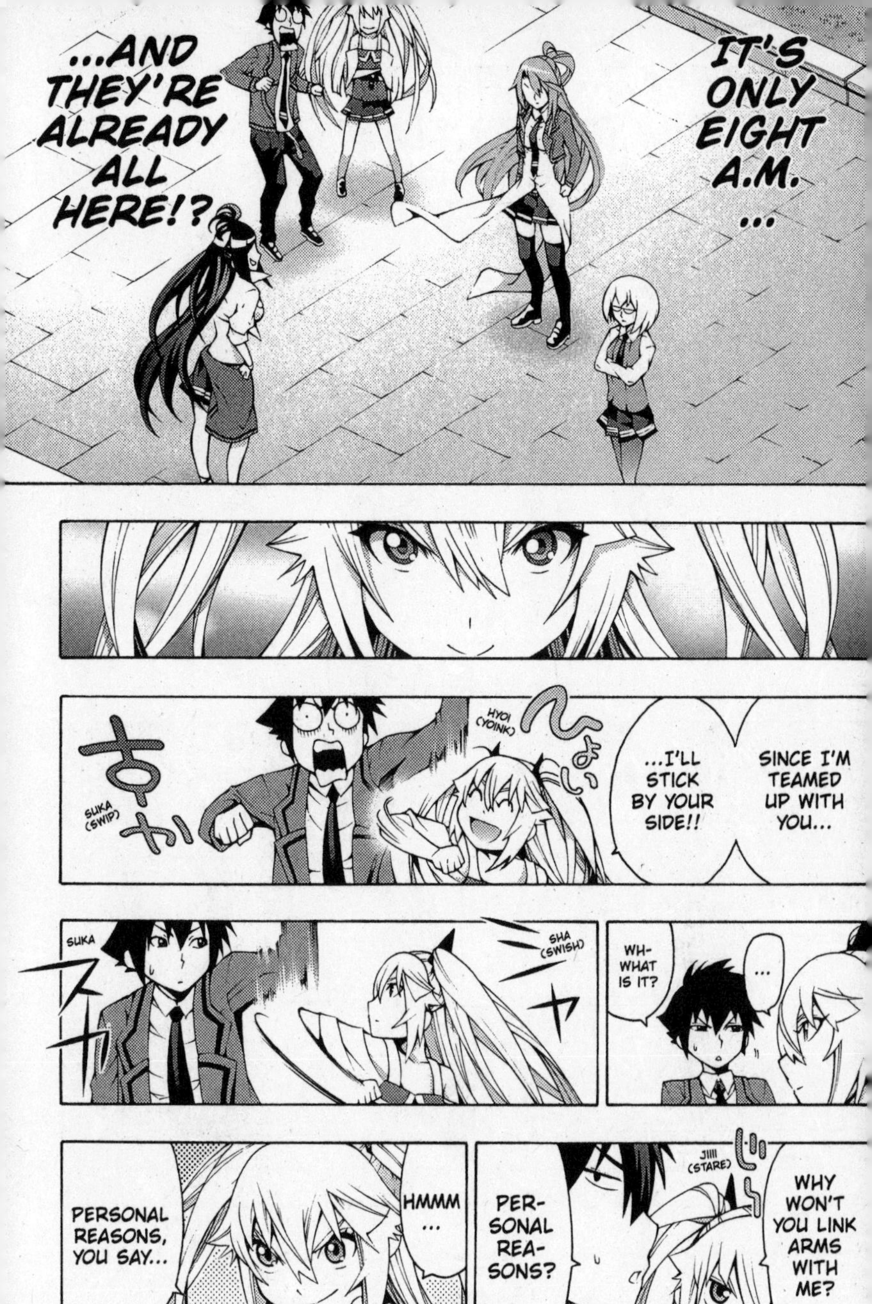
IT'S ONLY EIGHT A.M. ...
...AND THEY'RE ALREADY ALL HERE!?
SINCE I'M TEAMED UP WITH YOU...
...I'LL STICK BY YOUR SIDE!!
HYOI (YOINK)
SUKA (SWIP)
...
WH- WHAT IS IT?
SHA (SWISH)
SUKA
WHY WON'T YOU LINK ARMS WITH ME?
JIIII (STARE)
PER- SONAL REA- SONS?
HMMM ...
PERSONAL REASONS, YOU SAY...

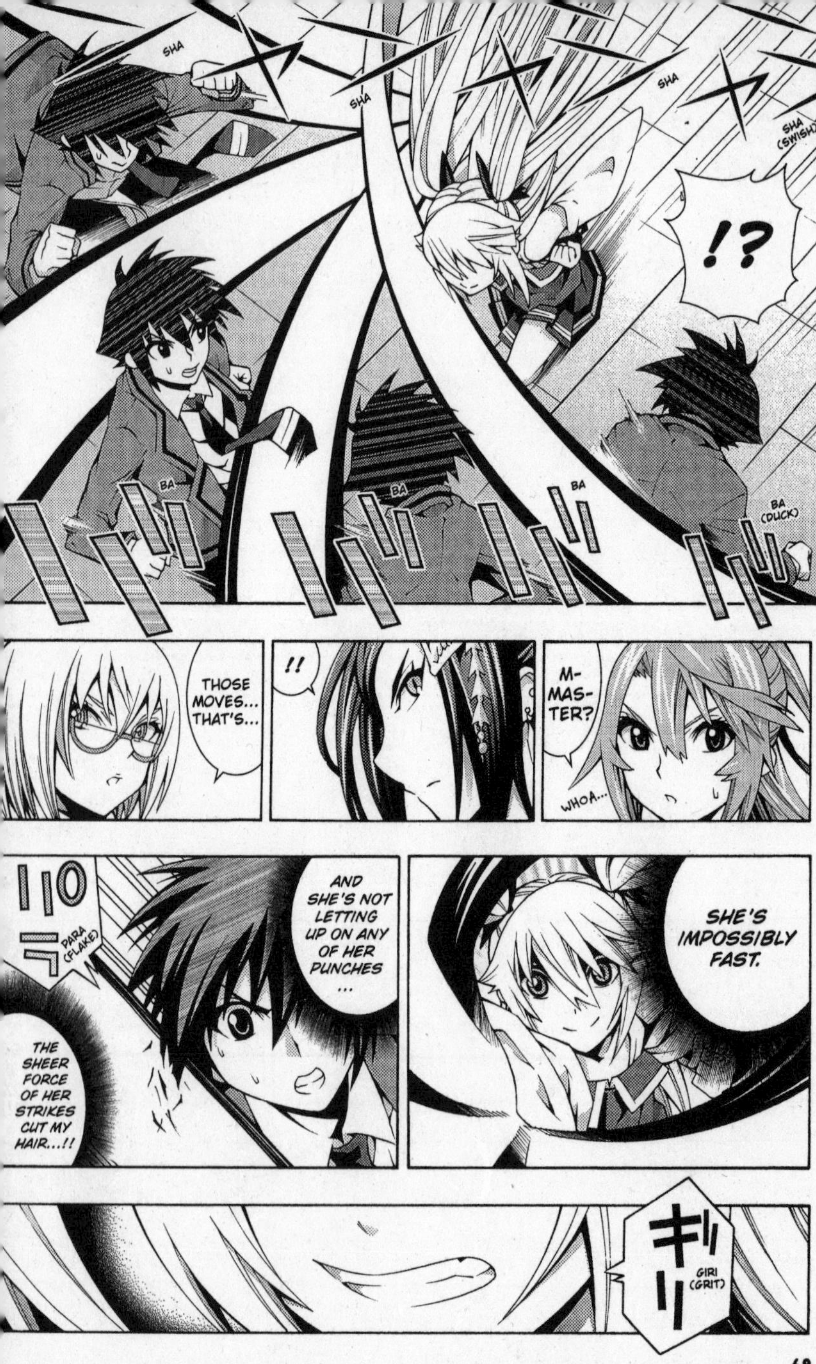
SHA (SWISH)
!?
SHA
SHA
SHA
BA (DUCK)
BA
BA
BA
M-MASTER?
WHOA...
!!
THOSE MOVES... THAT'S...
SHE'S IMPOSSIBLY FAST.
AND SHE'S NOT LETTING UP ON ANY OF HER PUNCHES ...
PARA (FLAKE)
THE SHEER FORCE OF HER STRIKES CUT MY HAIR...!!
GIRI (GRIT)

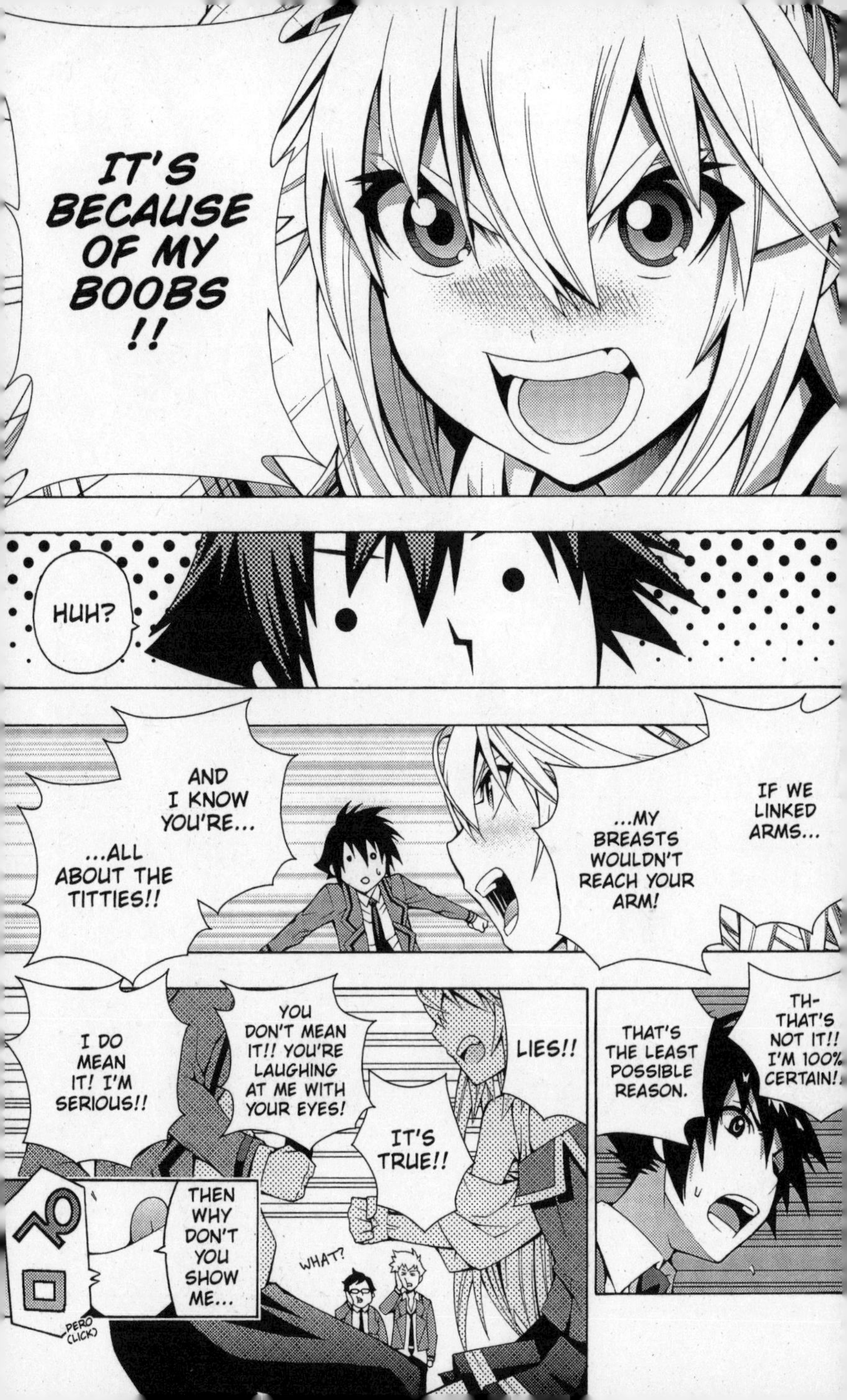
IT'S BECAUSE OF MY BOOBS!!
HUH?
IF WE LINKED ARMS...
...MY BREASTS WOULDN'T REACH YOUR ARM!
AND I KNOW YOU'RE...
...ALL ABOUT THE TITTIES!!
TH-THAT'S NOT IT!! I'M 100% CERTAIN!
THAT'S THE LEAST POSSIBLE REASON.
LIES!!
YOU DON'T MEAN IT!! YOU'RE LAUGHING AT ME WITH YOUR EYES!
I DO MEAN IT! I'M SERIOUS!!
IT'S TRUE!!
THEN WHY DON'T YOU SHOW ME...
WHAT?
PERO (LICK)

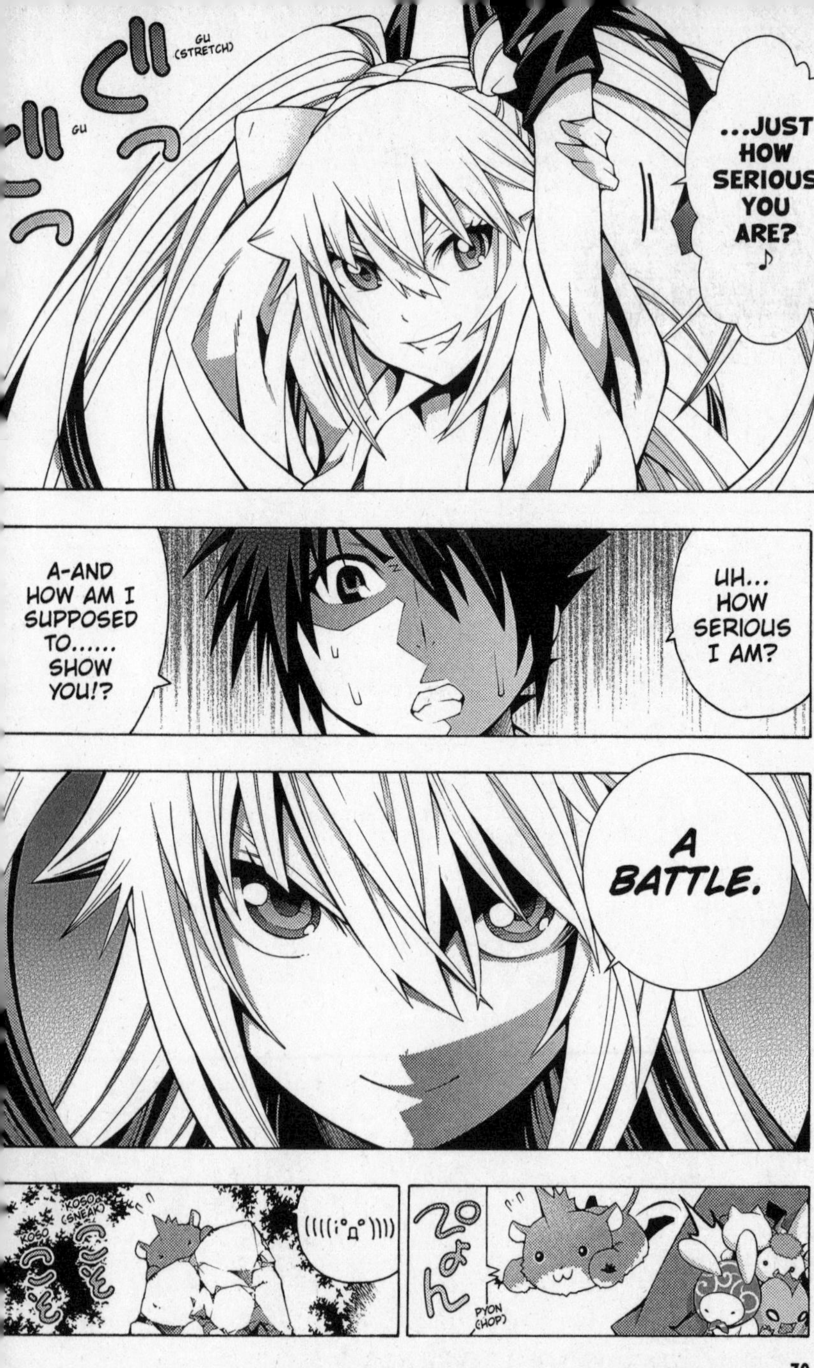
...JUST HOW SERIOUS YOU ARE? ♪
GU (STRETCH)
GU
UH... HOW SERIOUS I AM?
A-AND HOW AM I SUPPOSED TO...... SHOW YOU!?
A BATTLE.
PYON (HOP)
(((;°Д°)))
KOSO (SNEAK)
KOSO

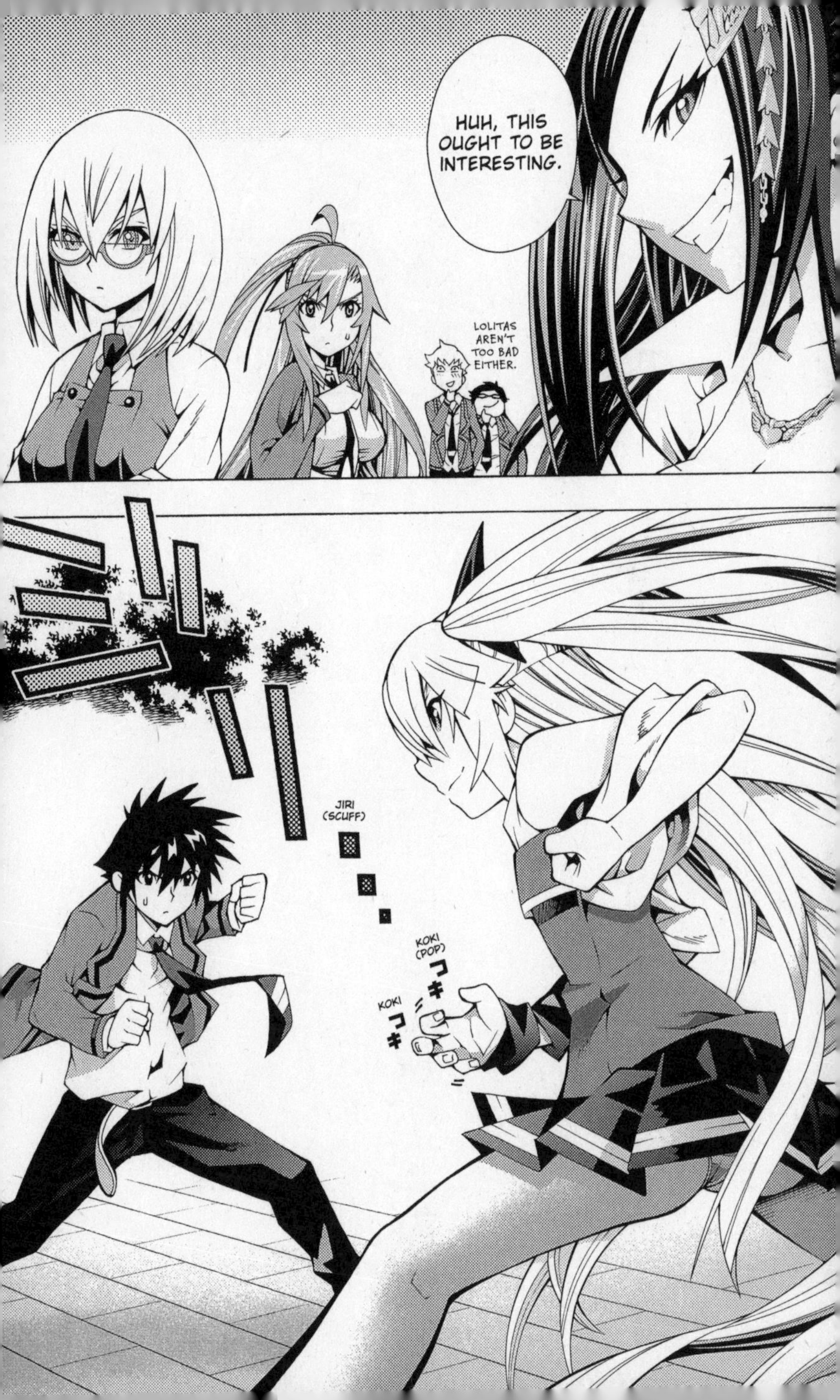
HUH, THIS OUGHT TO BE INTERESTING.
LOLITAS AREN'T TOO BAD EITHER.
JIRI (SCUFF)
KOKI (POP) コキ
KOKI コキ

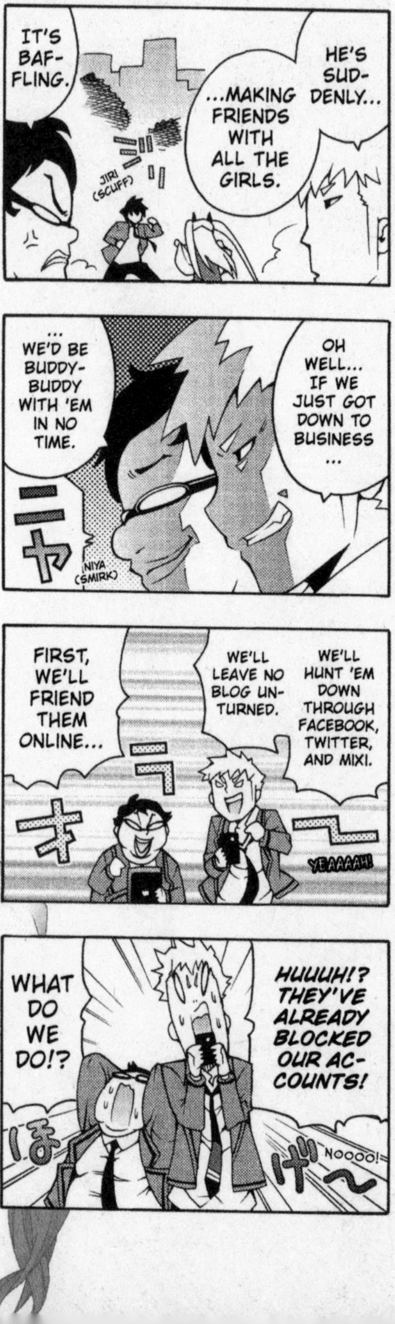
HE'S SUDDENLY...
...MAKING FRIENDS WITH ALL THE GIRLS.
JIRI (SCUFF)
IT'S BAFFLING.
OH WELL... IF WE JUST GOT DOWN TO BUSINESS ...
... WE'D BE BUDDY-BUDDY WITH 'EM IN NO TIME.
NIYA (SMIRK)
WE'LL HUNT 'EM DOWN THROUGH FACEBOOK, TWITTER, AND MIXI.
WE'LL LEAVE NO BLOG UNTURNED.
FIRST, WE'LL FRIEND THEM ONLINE...
YEAAAAH!
HUUUH!? THEY'VE ALREADY BLOCKED OUR ACCOUNTS!
WHAT DO WE DO!?
NOOOO!

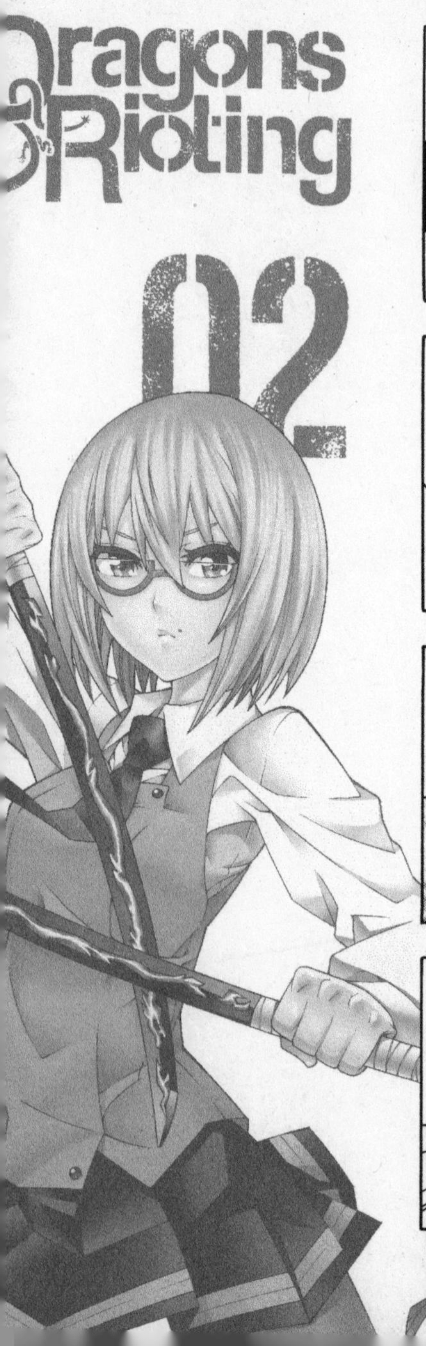
Dragons Rioting
02

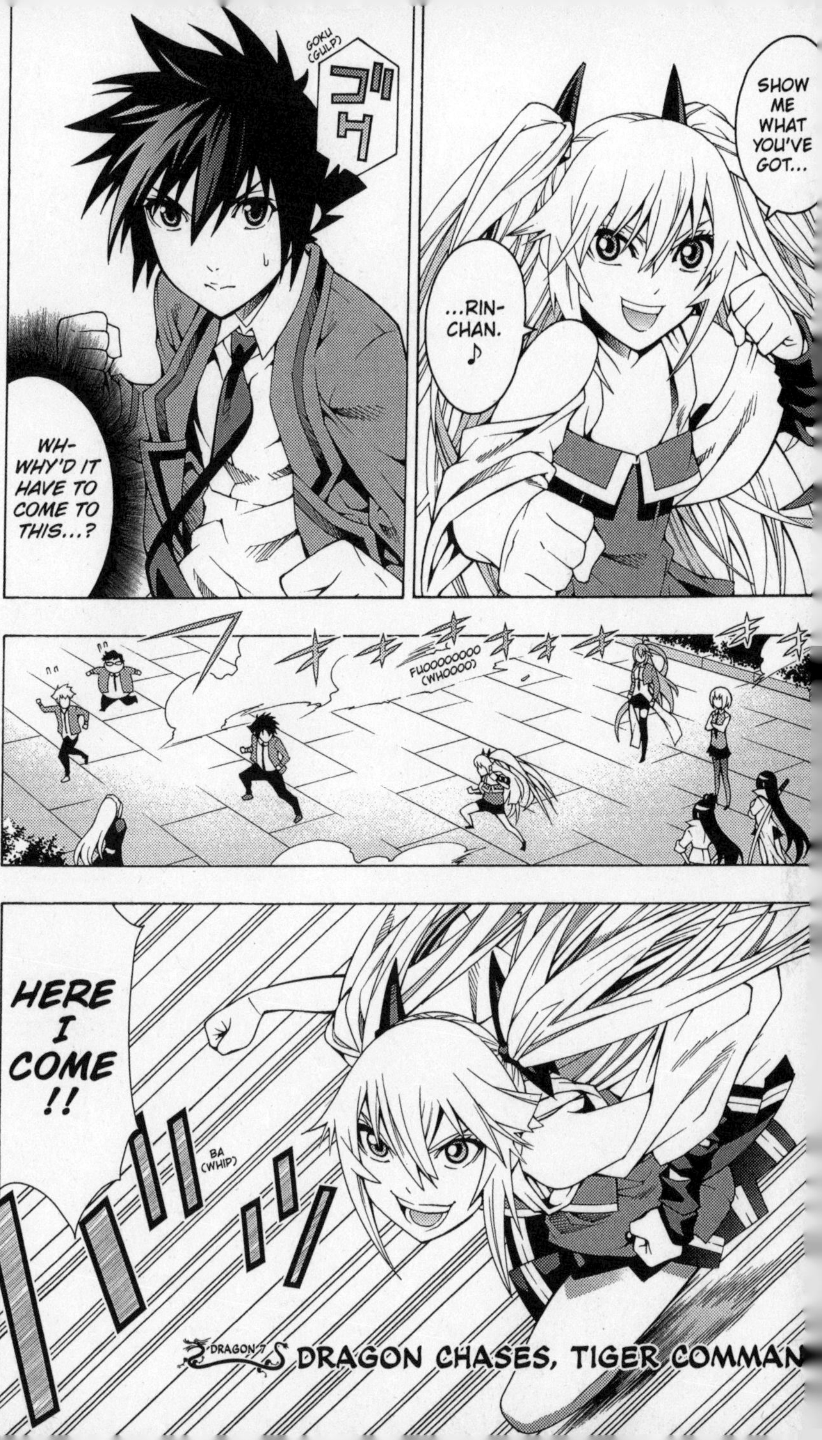
SHOW ME WHAT YOU'VE GOT...
...RIN-CHAN. ♪
ゴク
GOKU (GULP)
WH-WHY'D IT HAVE TO COME TO THIS...?
FUOOOOOOOO (WHOOOO)
HERE I COME!!
BA (WHIP)
DRAGON 7
DRAGON CHASES, TIGER COMMAN

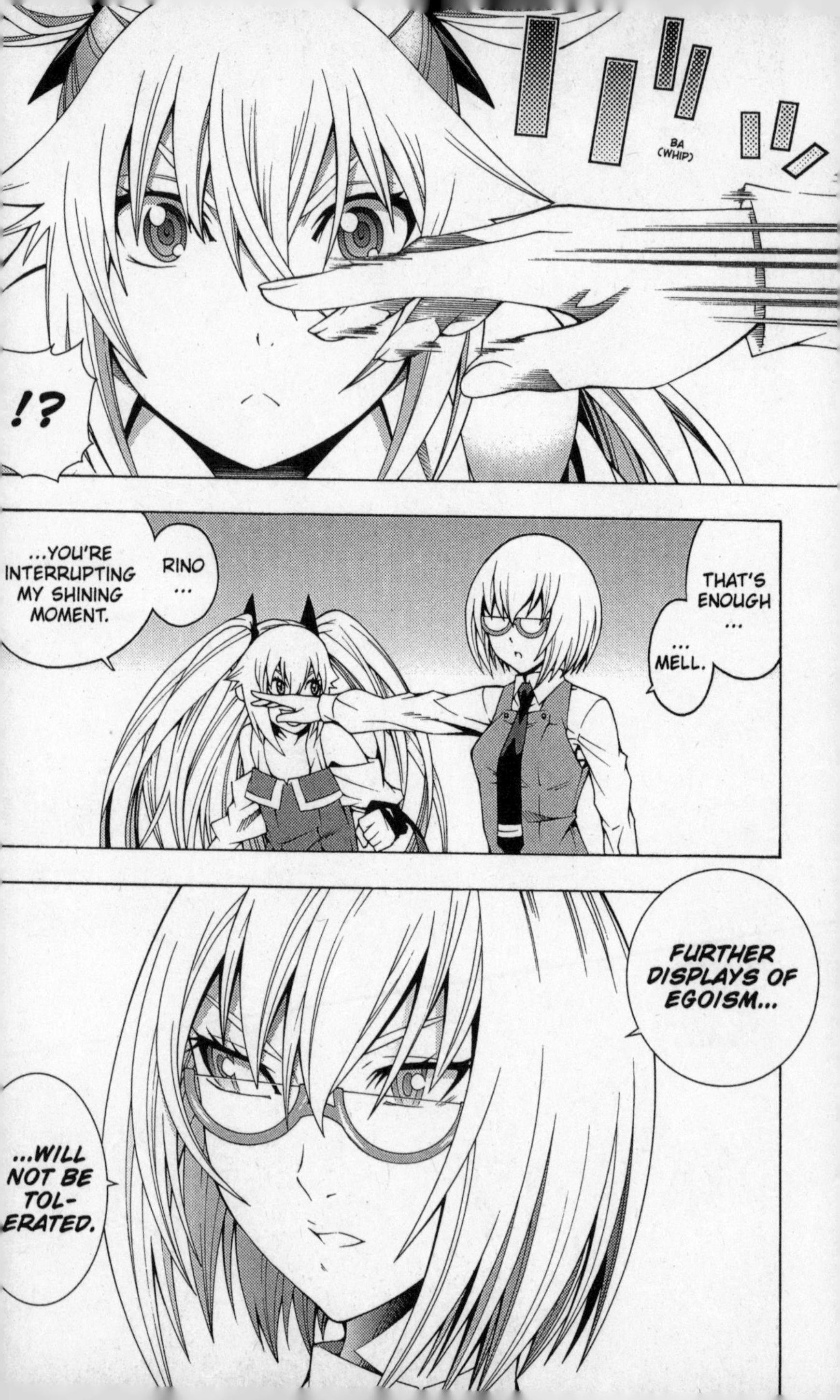
BA (WHIP)
!?
THAT'S ENOUGH... ...MELL.
RINO...
...YOU'RE INTERRUPTING MY SHINING MOMENT.
FURTHER DISPLAYS OF EGOISM...
...WILL NOT BE TOL-ERATED.

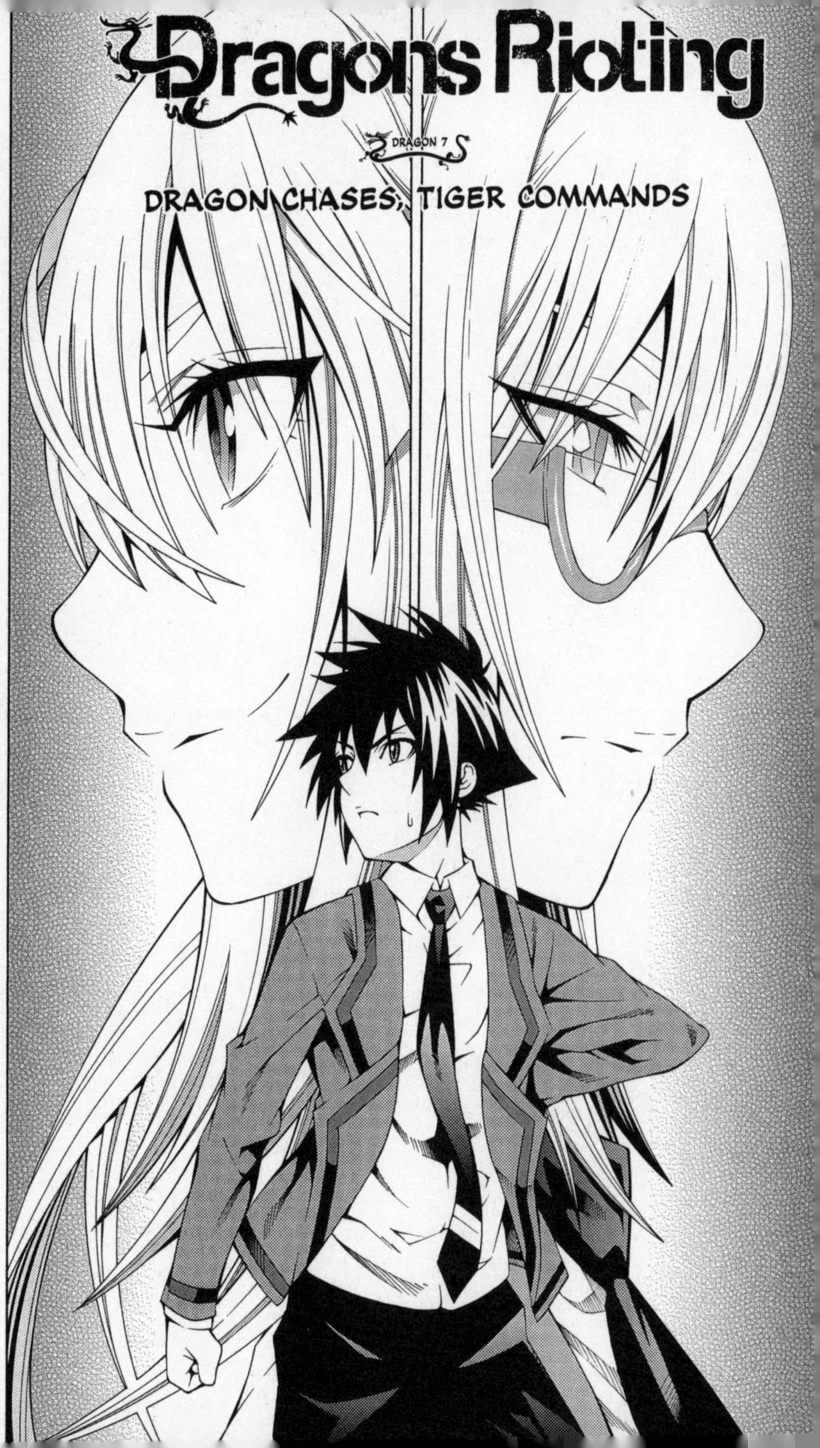
Dragons Rioting
DRAGON 7
DRAGON CHASES, TIGER COMMANDS

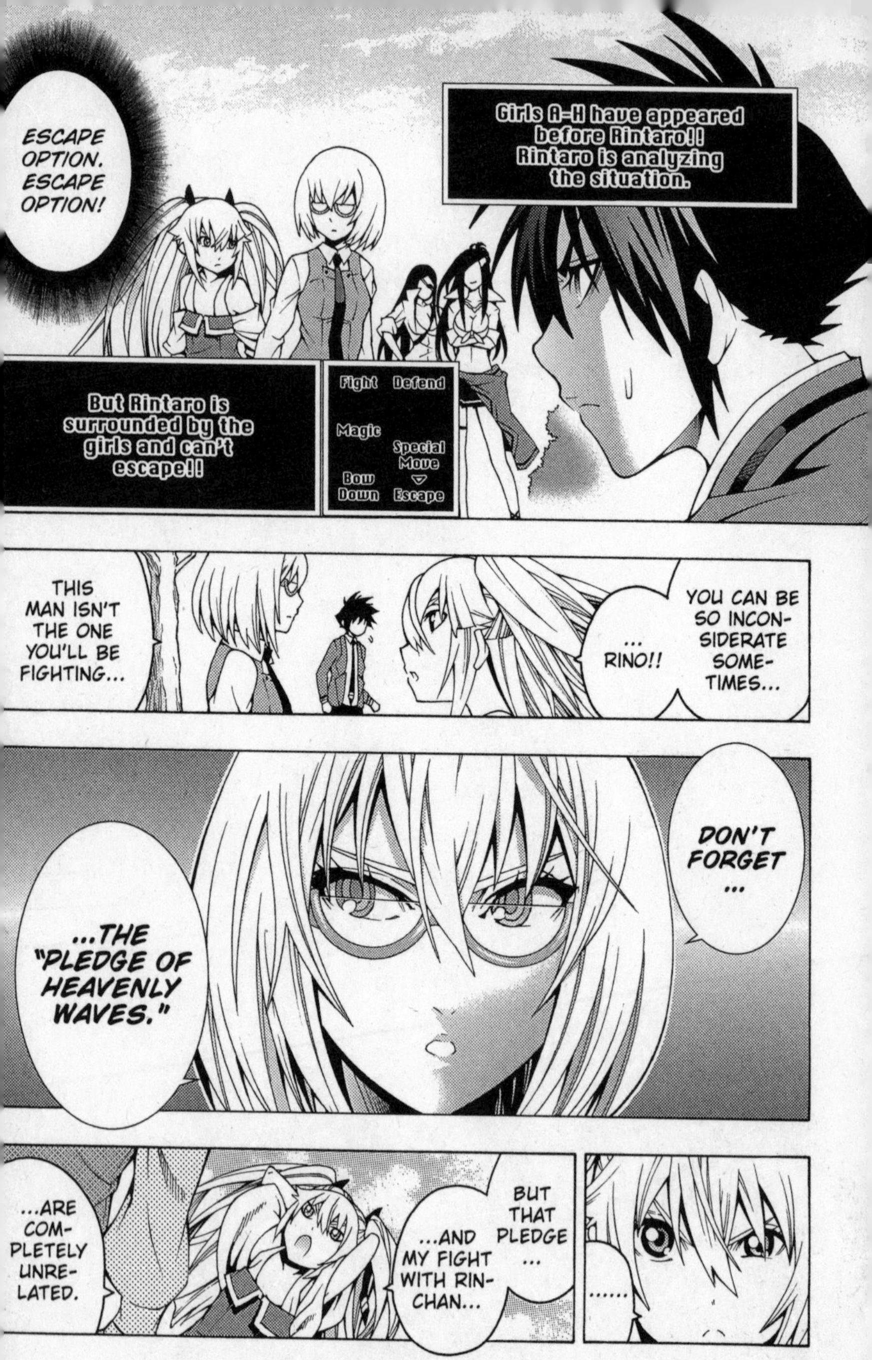
Girls A-H have appeared before Rintaro!! Rintaro is analyzing the situation.
ESCAPE OPTION. ESCAPE OPTION!
Fight Defend Magic Special Move Bow Down Escape
But Rintaro is surrounded by the girls and can't escape!!
YOU CAN BE SO INCONSIDERATE SOMETIMES...
...RINO!!
THIS MAN ISN'T THE ONE YOU'LL BE FIGHTING...
DON'T FORGET ...
...THE "PLEDGE OF HEAVENLY WAVES."
......
BUT THAT PLEDGE ...
...AND MY FIGHT WITH RIN-CHAN...
...ARE COMPLETELY UNRELATED.

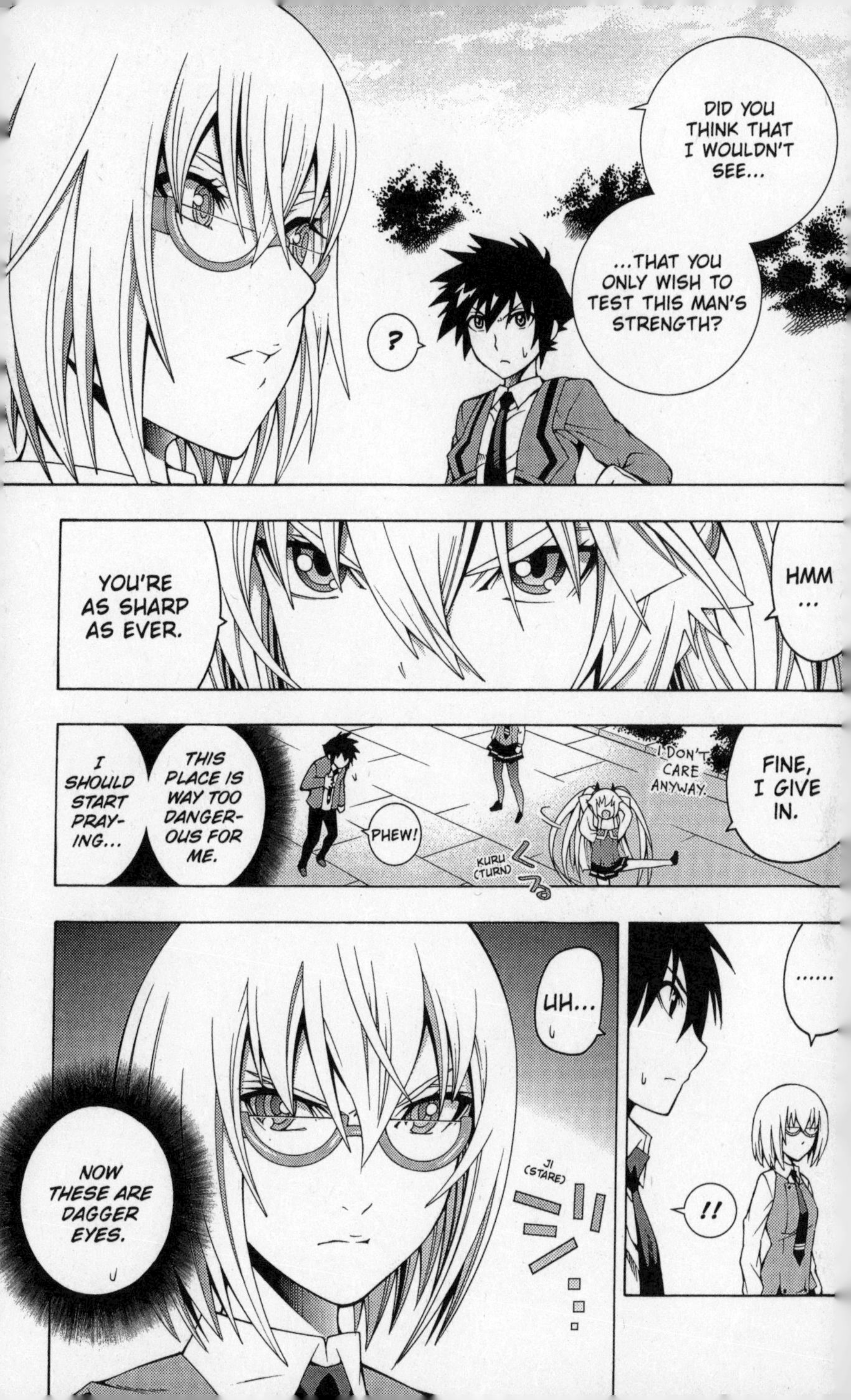

DID YOU THINK THAT I WOULDN'T SEE...
...THAT YOU ONLY WISH TO TEST THIS MAN'S STRENGTH?
?
HMM...
YOU'RE AS SHARP AS EVER.
FINE, I GIVE IN.
I DON'T CARE ANYWAY.
KURU (TURN)
PHEW!
THIS PLACE IS WAY TOO DANGER-OUS FOR ME.
I SHOULD START PRAY-ING...
......
!!
UH...
JI (STARE)
NOW THESE ARE DAGGER EYES.

ス
SU
(SWF)

YES,
MA'AM.

GOT
IT.

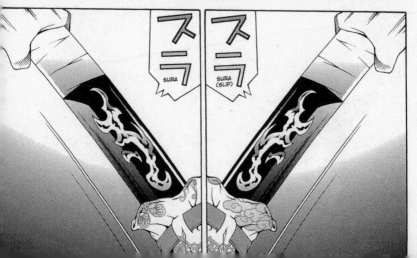

ス
ラ
SURA

ス
ラ
SURA
(SLIP)

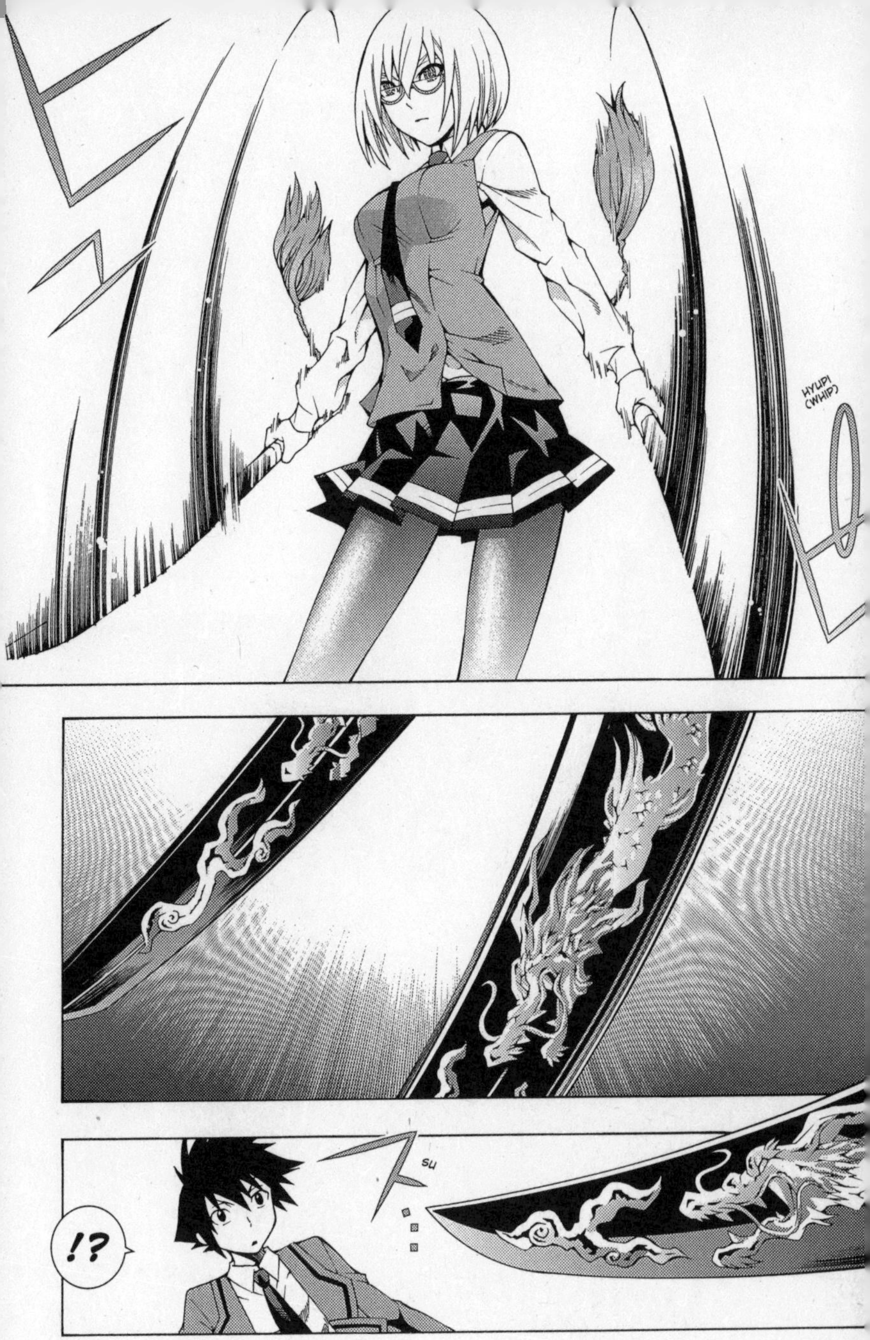
HYUP! (WHIP)
SU
!?

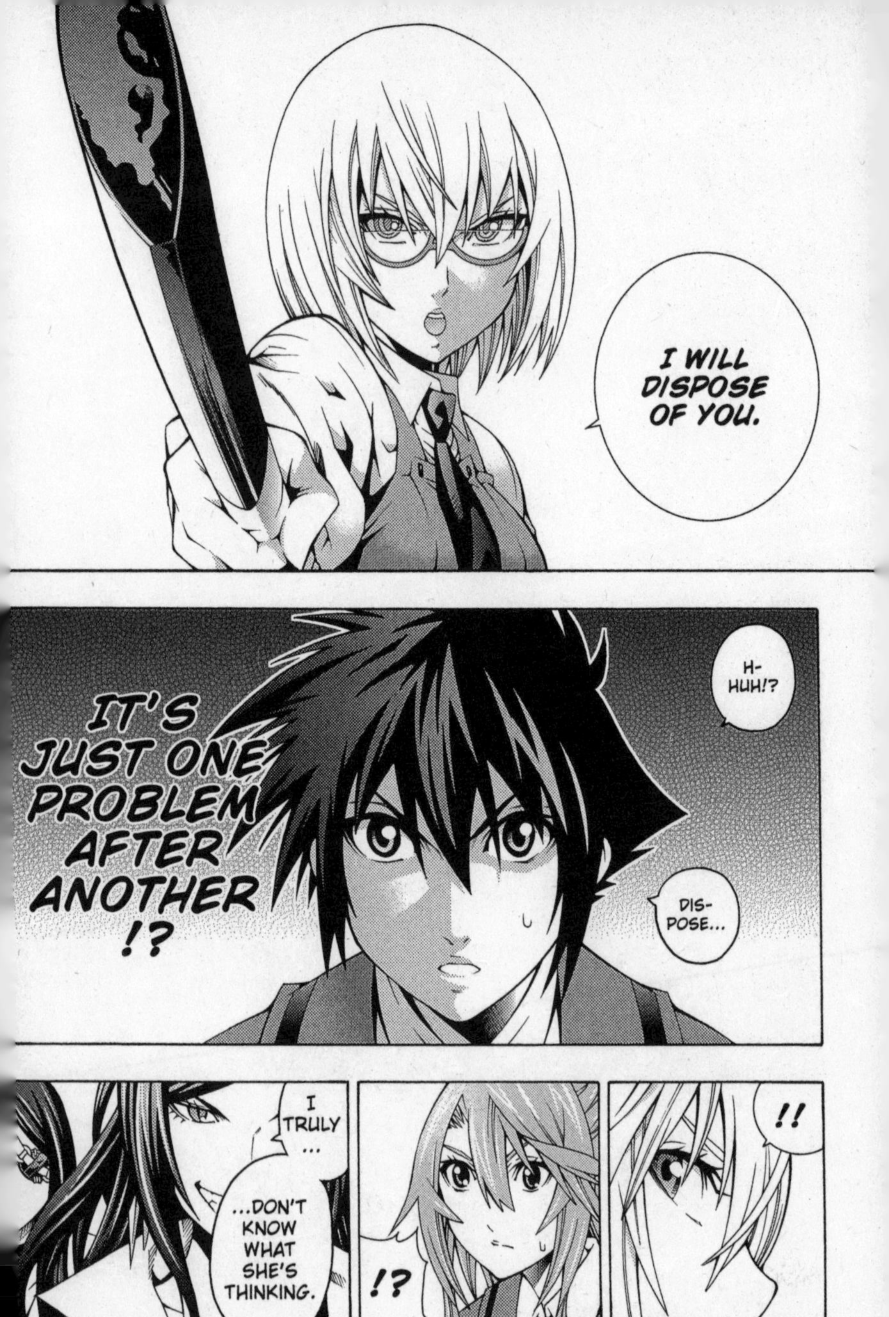
I WILL DISPOSE OF YOU.
H-HUH!?
DIS-POSE...
IT'S JUST ONE PROBLEM AFTER ANOTHER!?
!!
!?
I TRULY...
...DON'T KNOW WHAT SHE'S THINKING.

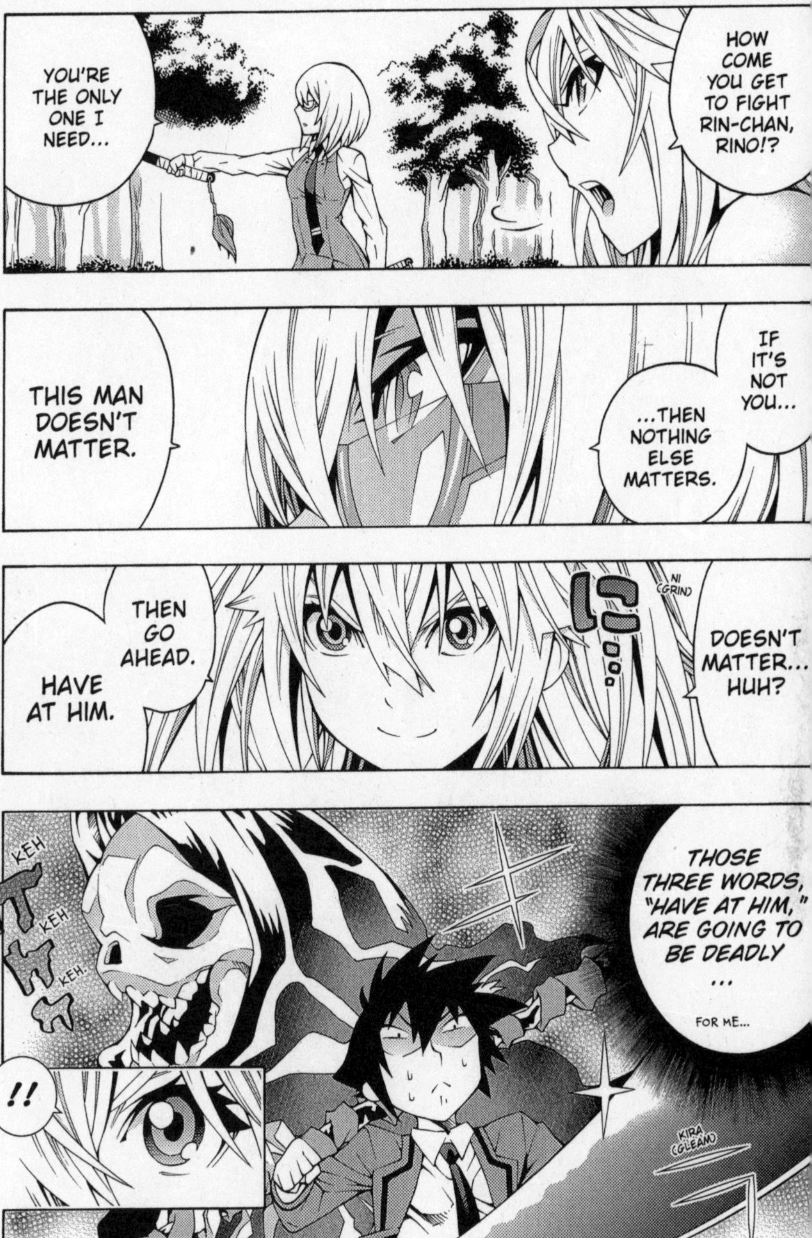
HOW COME YOU GET TO FIGHT RIN-CHAN, RINO!?
YOU'RE THE ONLY ONE I NEED...
IF IT'S NOT YOU...
...THEN NOTHING ELSE MATTERS.
THIS MAN DOESN'T MATTER.
NI (GRIN)
DOESN'T MATTER... HUH?
THEN GO AHEAD.
HAVE AT HIM.
THOSE THREE WORDS, "HAVE AT HIM," ARE GOING TO BE DEADLY ...
FOR ME...
KIRA (GLEAM)
KEH
KEH
KEH.
!!

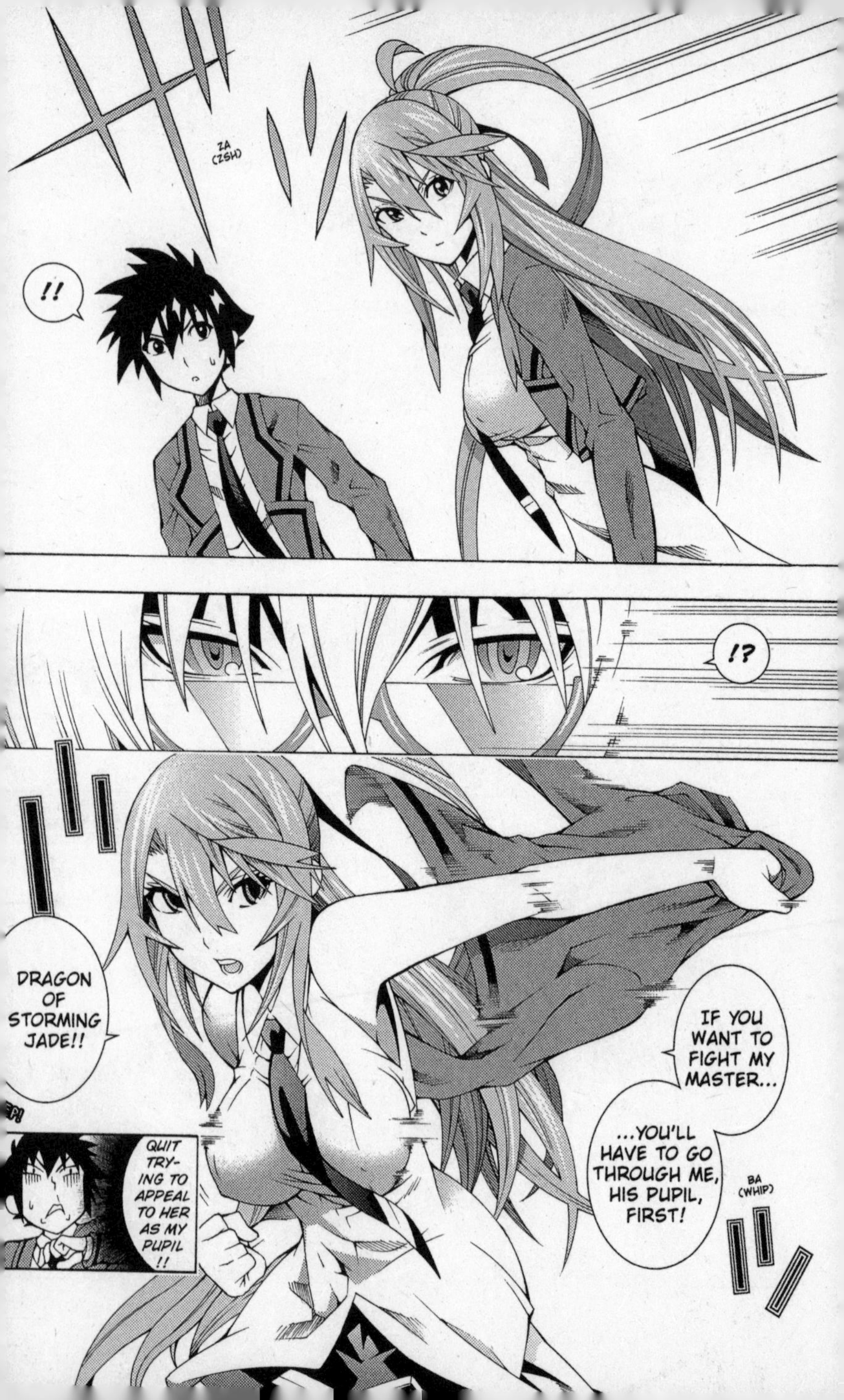
ZA (ZSH)
!!
!?
IF YOU WANT TO FIGHT MY MASTER...
...YOU'LL HAVE TO GO THROUGH ME, HIS PUPIL, FIRST!
BA (WHIP)
DRAGON OF STORMING JADE!!
QUIT TRY-ING TO APPEAL TO HER AS MY PUPIL!!

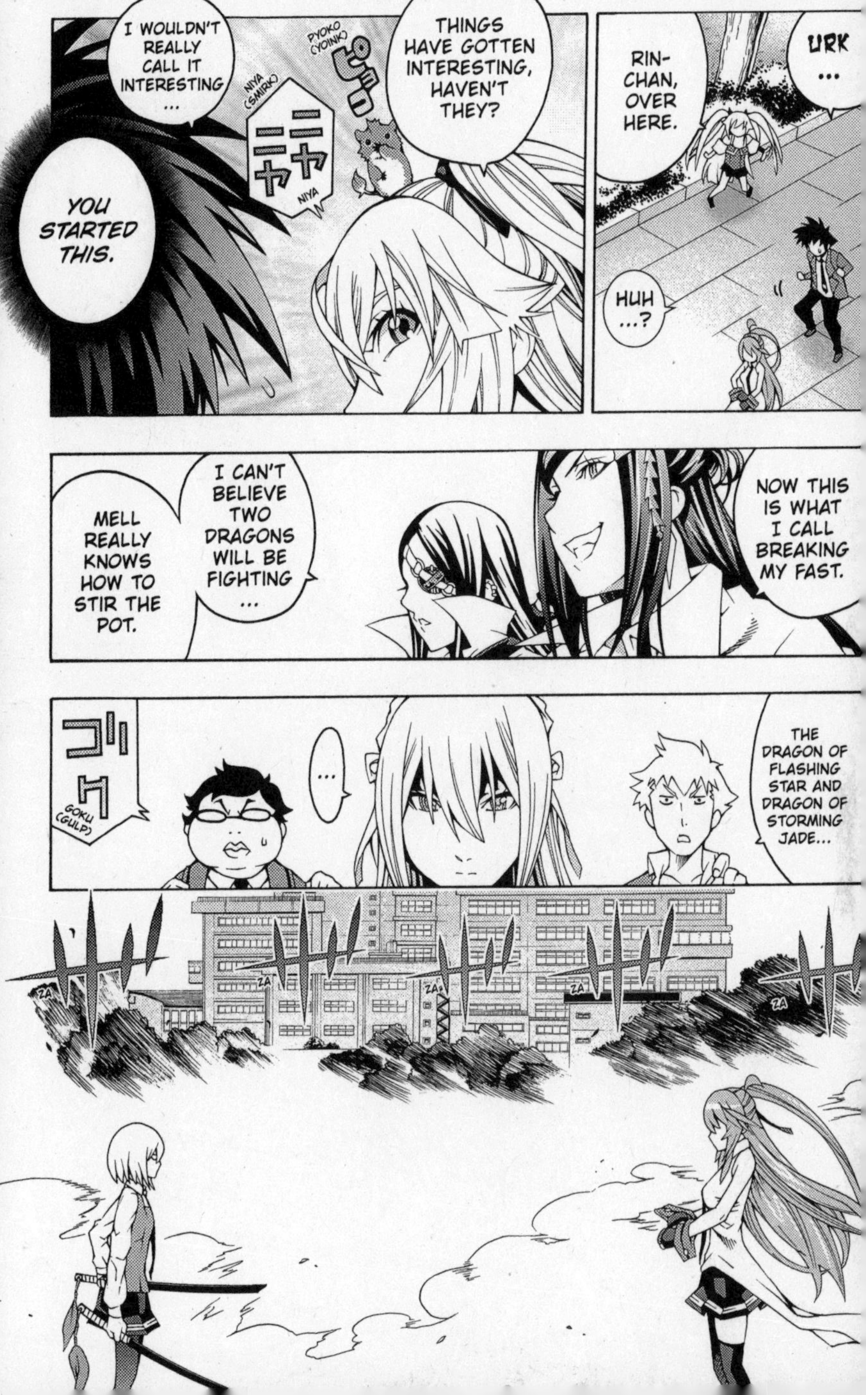
URK ...
RIN-CHAN, OVER HERE.
HUH ...?
THINGS HAVE GOTTEN INTERESTING, HAVEN'T THEY?
PYOKO (YOINK)
NIYA (SMIRK)
NIYA
I WOULDN'T REALLY CALL IT INTERESTING ...
YOU STARTED THIS.
NOW THIS IS WHAT I CALL BREAKING MY FAST.
I CAN'T BELIEVE TWO DRAGONS WILL BE FIGHTING ...
MELL REALLY KNOWS HOW TO STIR THE POT.
THE DRAGON OF FLASHING STAR AND DRAGON OF STORMING JADE...
...
GOKU (GULP)
ZA
ZA
ZA
ZA
ZA

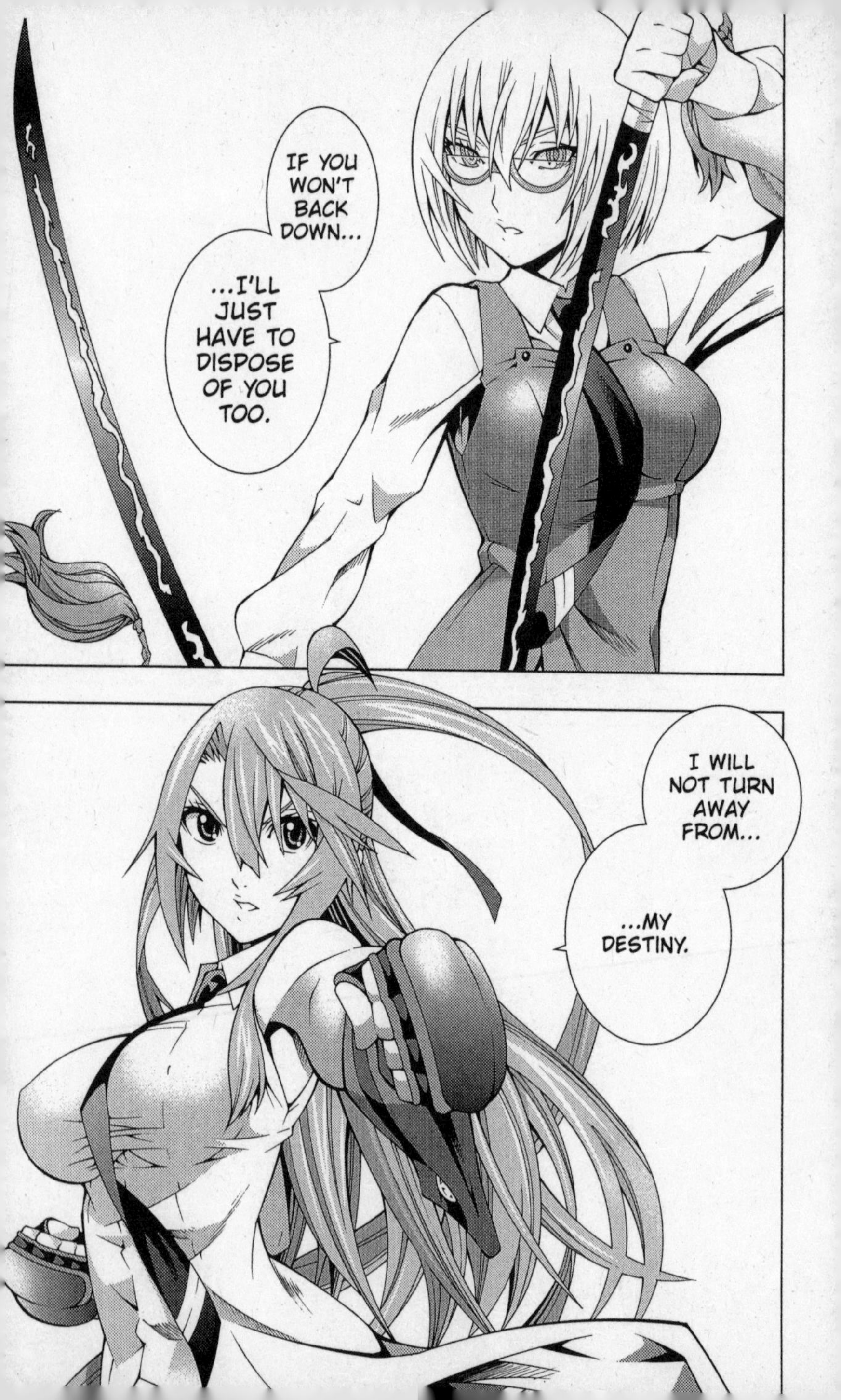
IF YOU WON'T BACK DOWN...
...I'LL JUST HAVE TO DISPOSE OF YOU TOO.
I WILL NOT TURN AWAY FROM...
...MY DESTINY.

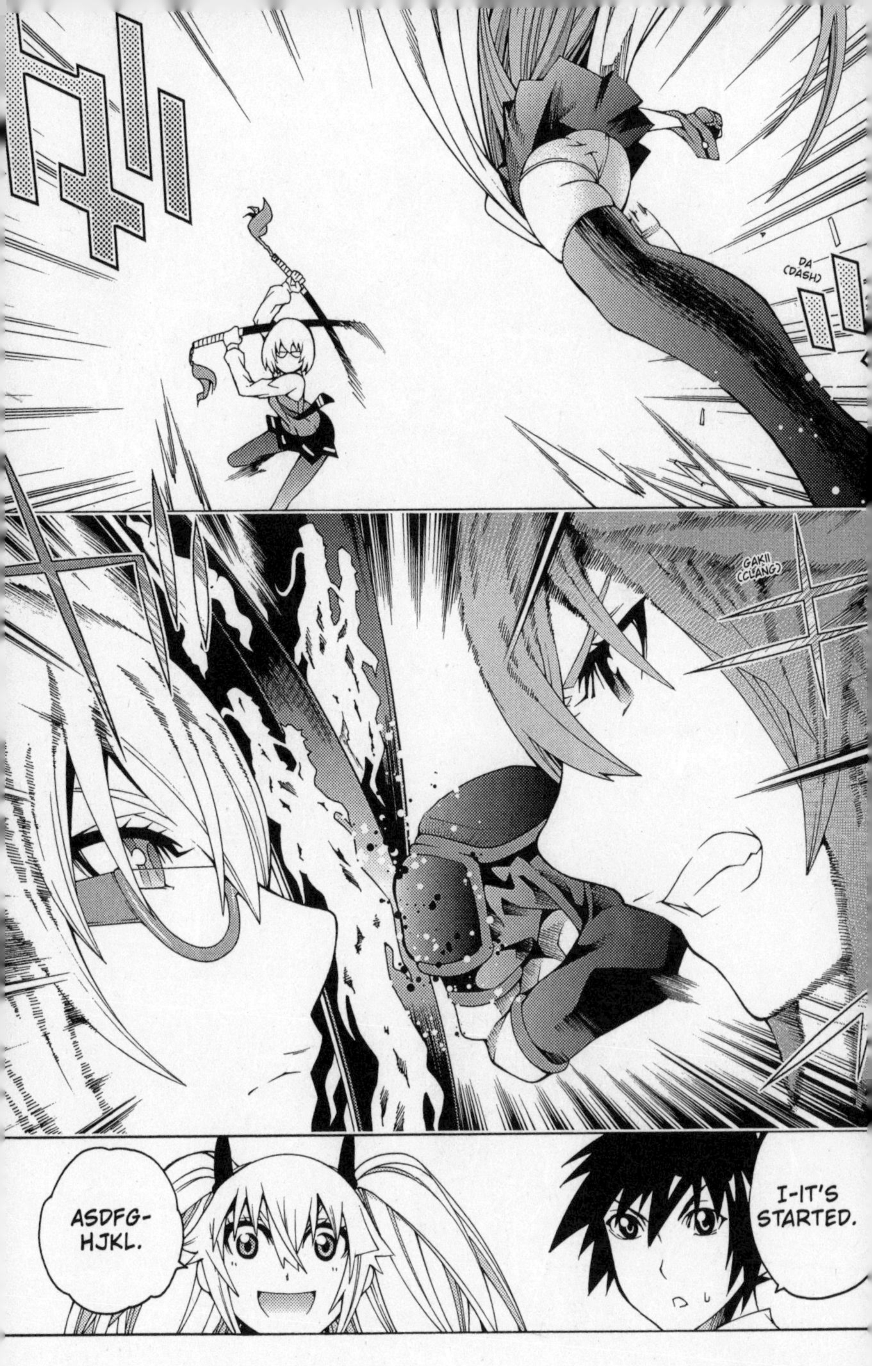
DA (DASH)
GAKII (CLANG)
I-IT'S STARTED.
ASDFG-HJKL.

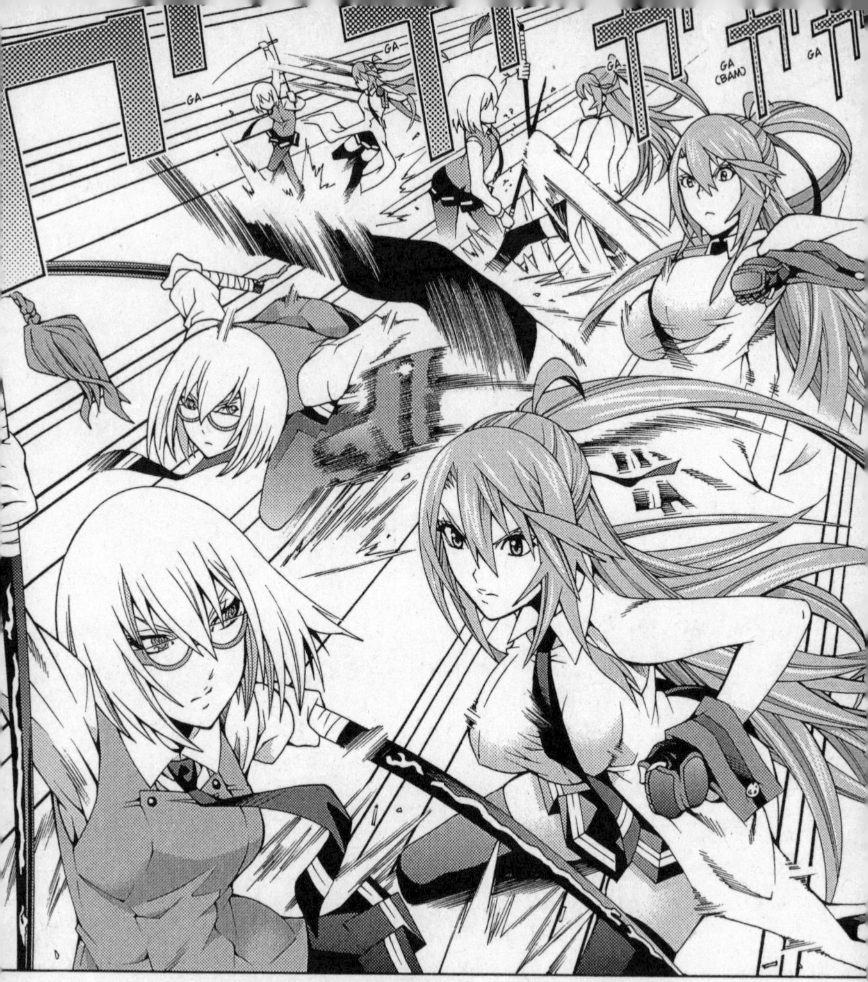
GA
GA (BAM)
GA
GA

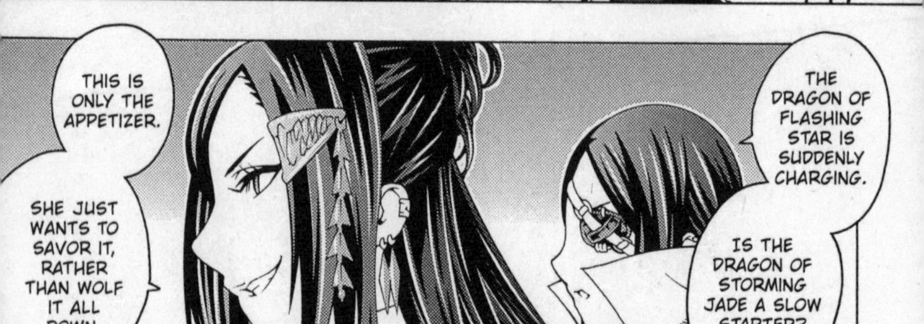
THE DRAGON OF FLASHING STAR IS SUDDENLY CHARGING.
IS THE DRAGON OF STORMING JADE A SLOW STARTER?
THIS IS ONLY THE APPETIZER.
SHE JUST WANTS TO SAVOR IT, RATHER THAN WOLF IT ALL DOWN.

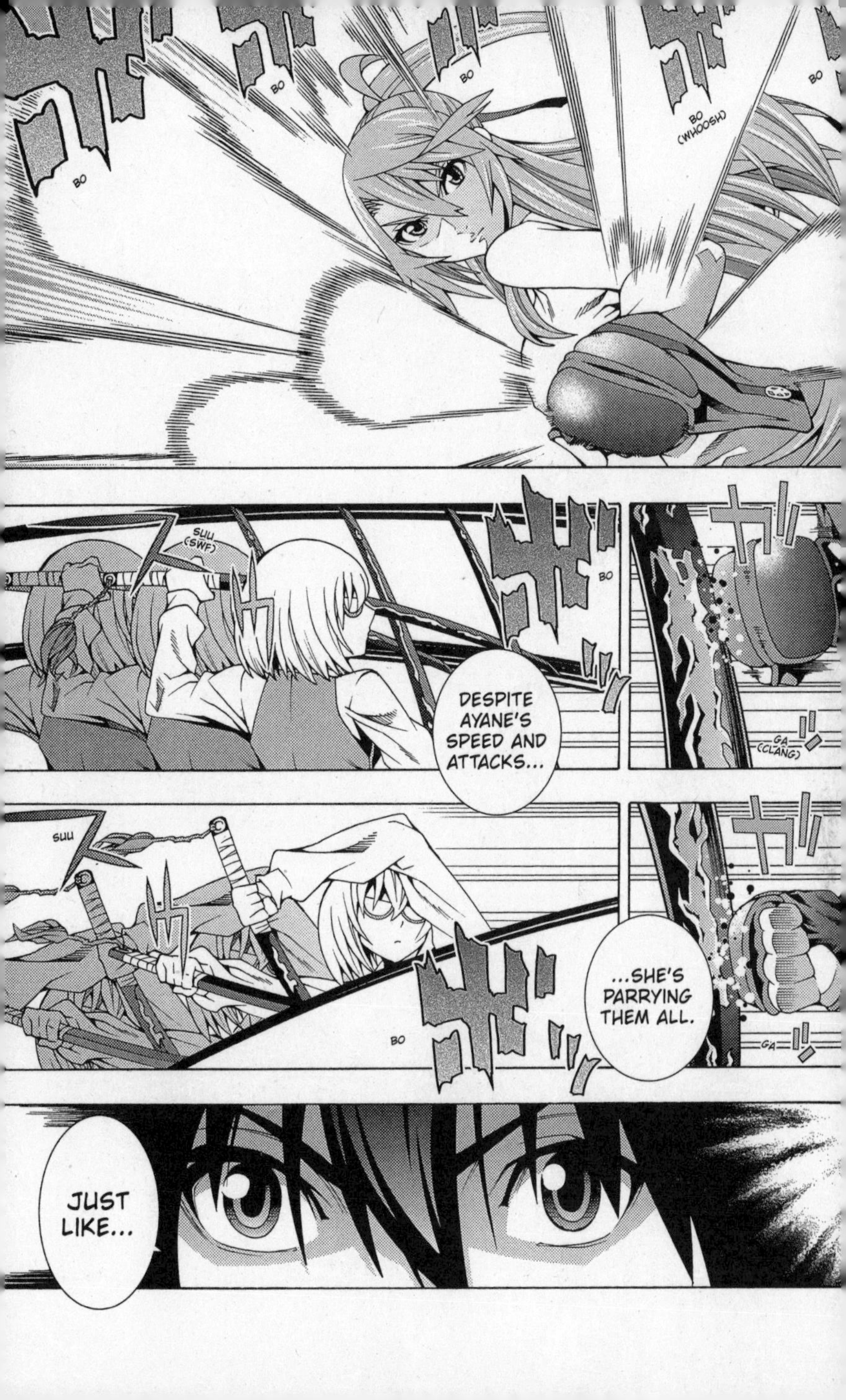
BO
BO (WHOOSH)
BO
BO
BO
GA (CLANG)
BO
SUU (SWF)
DESPITE AYANE'S SPEED AND ATTACKS...
GA
...SHE'S PARRYING THEM ALL.
BO
SUU
JUST LIKE...

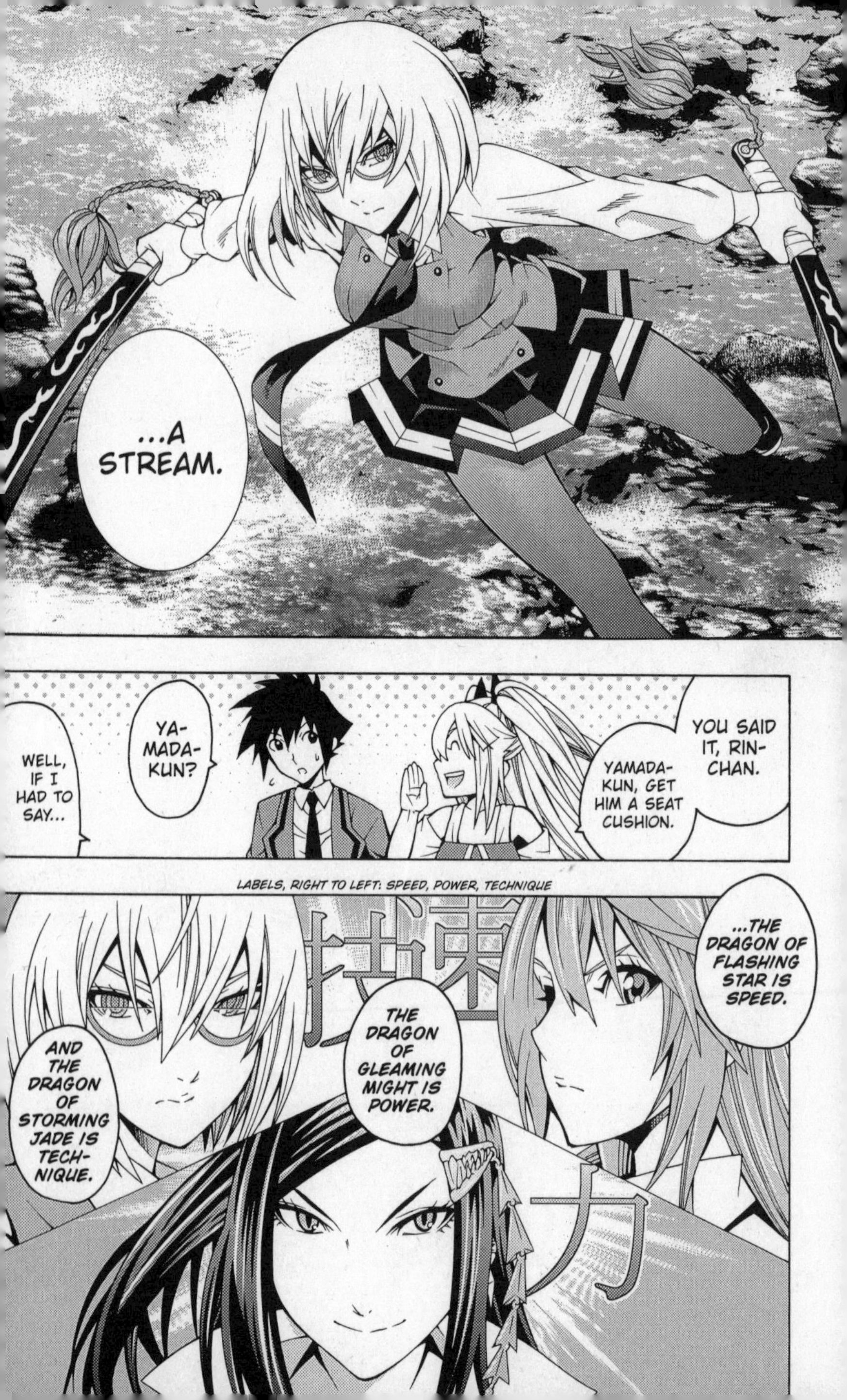
...A STREAM.
YOU SAID IT, RIN-CHAN.
YAMADA-KUN, GET HIM A SEAT CUSHION.
YA-MADA-KUN?
WELL, IF I HAD TO SAY...
LABELS, RIGHT TO LEFT: SPEED, POWER, TECHNIQUE
...THE DRAGON OF FLASHING STAR IS SPEED.
THE DRAGON OF GLEAMING MIGHT IS POWER.
AND THE DRAGON OF STORMING JADE IS TECH-NIQUE.

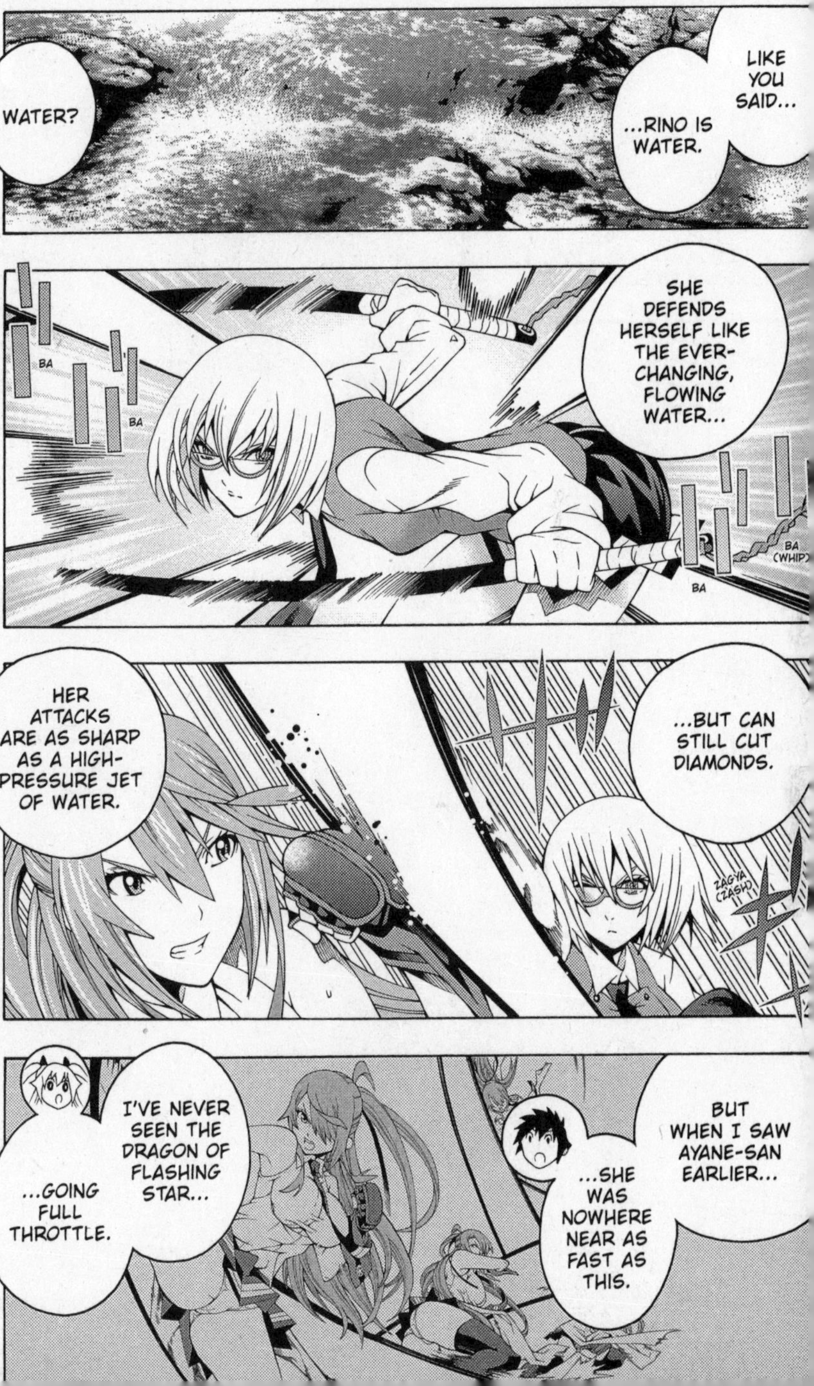
LIKE YOU SAID...
...RINO IS WATER.
WATER?
SHE DEFENDS HERSELF LIKE THE EVER-CHANGING, FLOWING WATER...
BA (WHIP)
BA
BA
BA
...BUT CAN STILL CUT DIAMONDS.
ZAGYA (ZASH)
HER ATTACKS ARE AS SHARP AS A HIGH-PRESSURE JET OF WATER.
BUT WHEN I SAW AYANE-SAN EARLIER...
...SHE WAS NOWHERE NEAR AS FAST AS THIS.
I'VE NEVER SEEN THE DRAGON OF FLASHING STAR...
...GOING FULL THROTTLE.

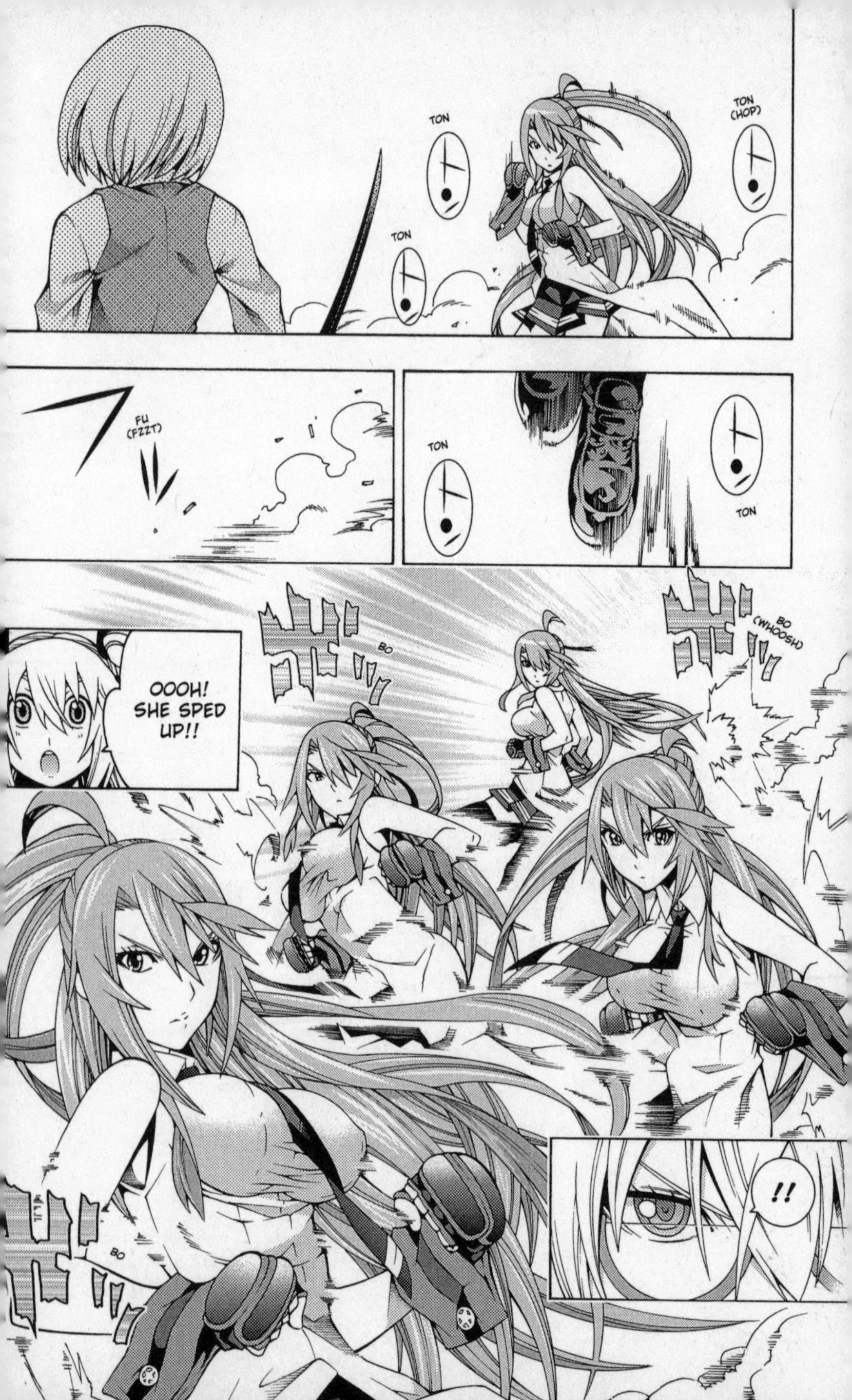
TON (HOP)
TON
TON
TON
TON
FU (FZZT)
BO (WHOOSH)
BO
OOOH! SHE SPED UP!!
!!
BO

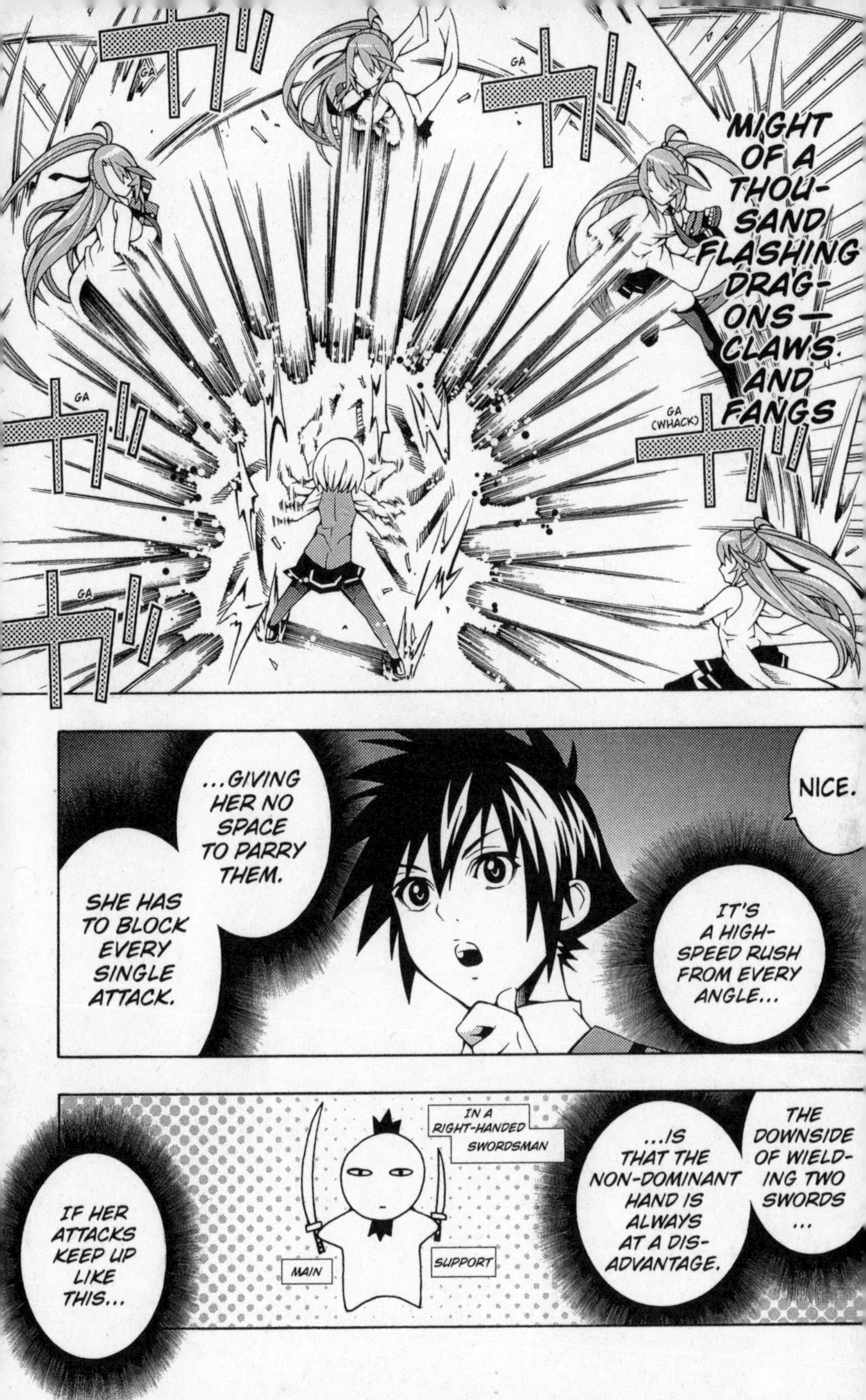
GA
MIGHT OF A THOUSAND FLASHING DRAGONS—CLAWS AND FANGS
GA (WHACK)
GA
GA
GA
NICE.
IT'S A HIGH-SPEED RUSH FROM EVERY ANGLE...
...GIVING HER NO SPACE TO PARRY THEM.
SHE HAS TO BLOCK EVERY SINGLE ATTACK.
THE DOWNSIDE OF WIELDING TWO SWORDS...
...IS THAT THE NON-DOMINANT HAND IS ALWAYS AT A DISADVANTAGE.
IN A RIGHT-HANDED SWORDSMAN
SUPPORT
MAIN
IF HER ATTACKS KEEP UP LIKE THIS...

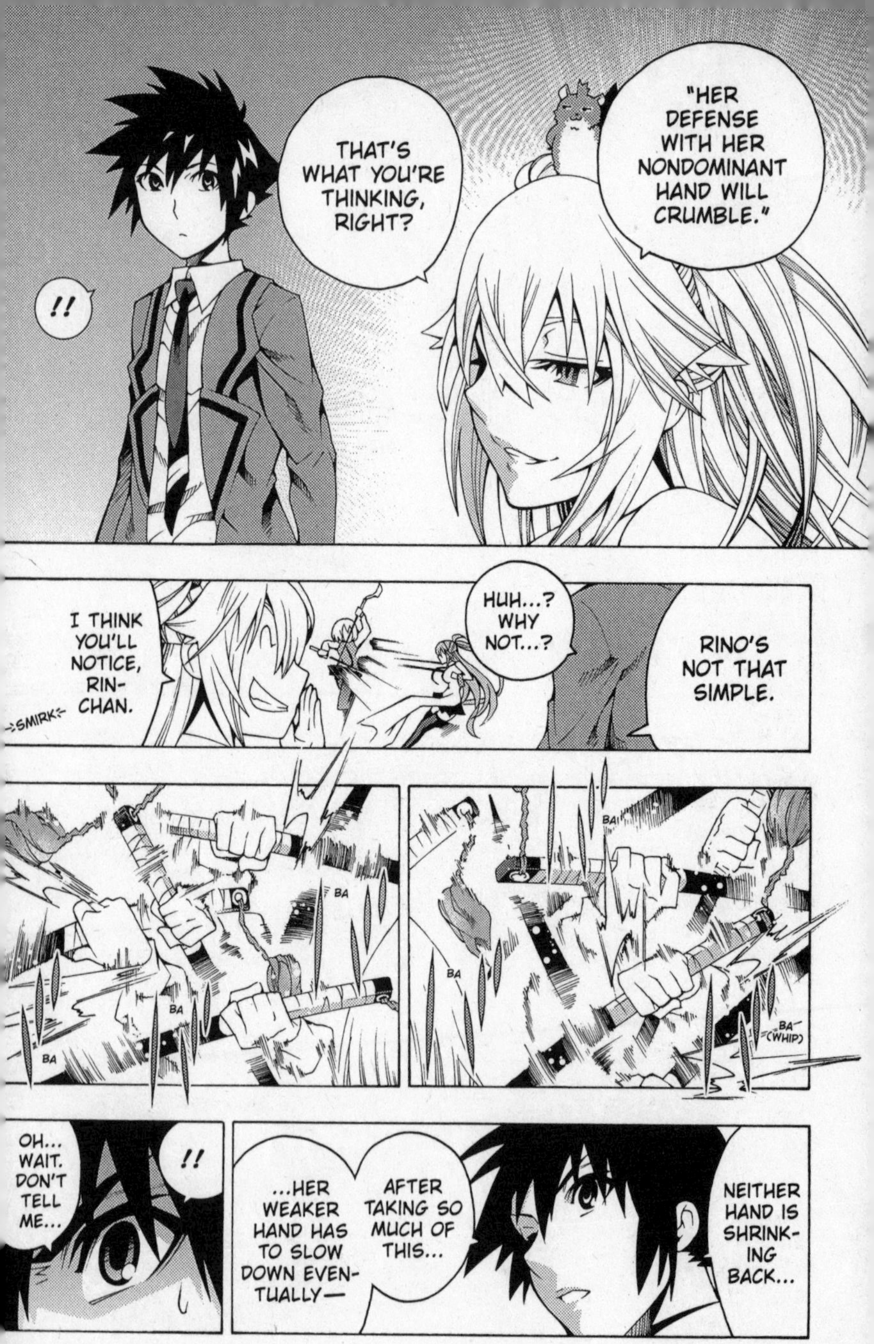
"HER DEFENSE WITH HER NONDOMINANT HAND WILL CRUMBLE."
THAT'S WHAT YOU'RE THINKING, RIGHT?
!!
RINO'S NOT THAT SIMPLE.
HUH...? WHY NOT...?
I THINK YOU'LL NOTICE, RIN-CHAN.
SMIRK
BA
BA
BA (WHIP)
BA
BA
BA
NEITHER HAND IS SHRINKING BACK...
AFTER TAKING SO MUCH OF THIS...
...HER WEAKER HAND HAS TO SLOW DOWN EVENTUALLY—
!!
OH... WAIT. DON'T TELL ME...

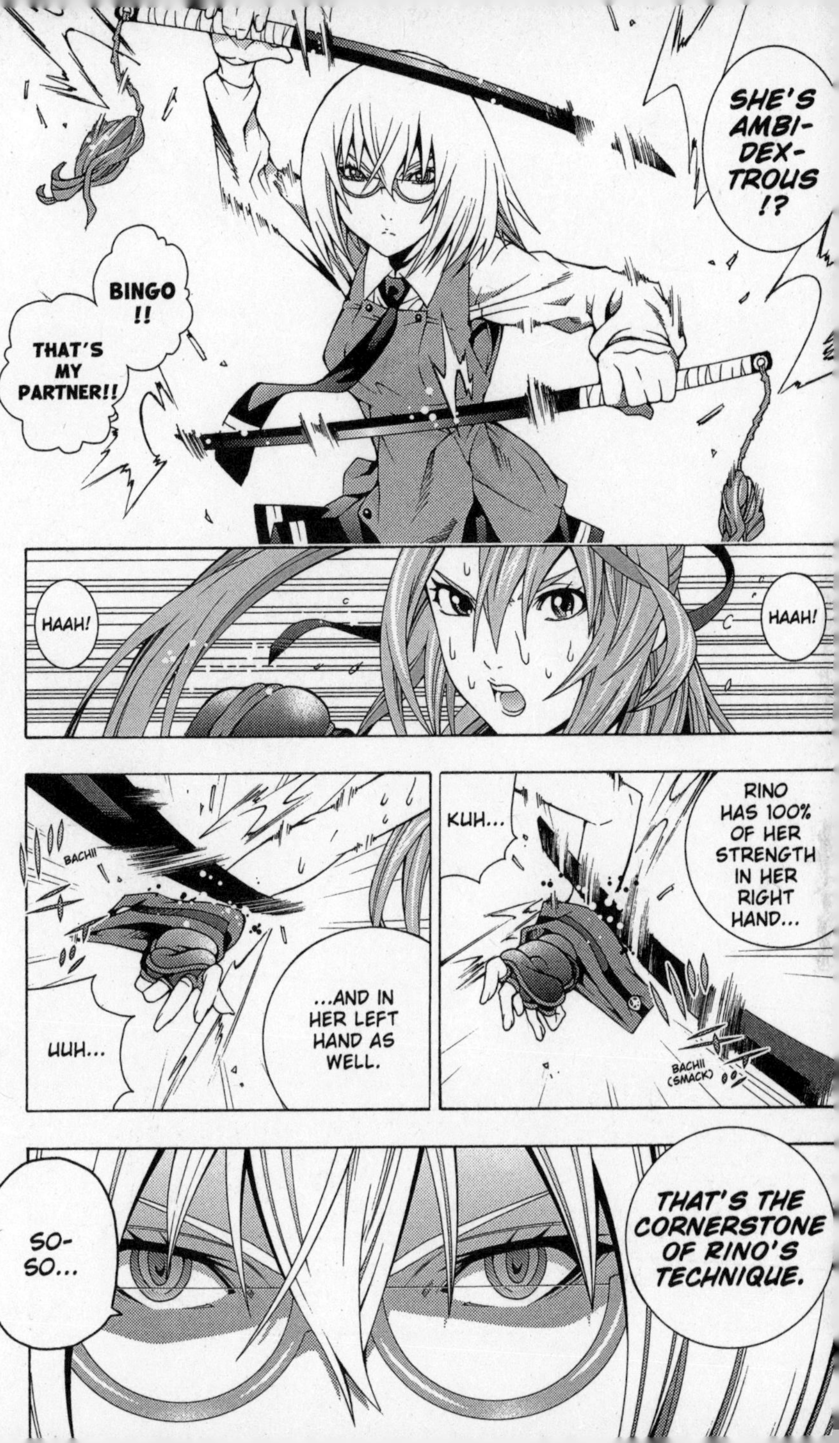
SHE'S AMBI-DEX-TROUS!?
BINGO!!
THAT'S MY PARTNER!!
HAAH!
HAAH!
RINO HAS 100% OF HER STRENGTH IN HER RIGHT HAND...
KUH...
BACHII (SMACK)
...AND IN HER LEFT HAND AS WELL.
BACHII
UUH...
THAT'S THE CORNERSTONE OF RINO'S TECHNIQUE.
SO-SO...

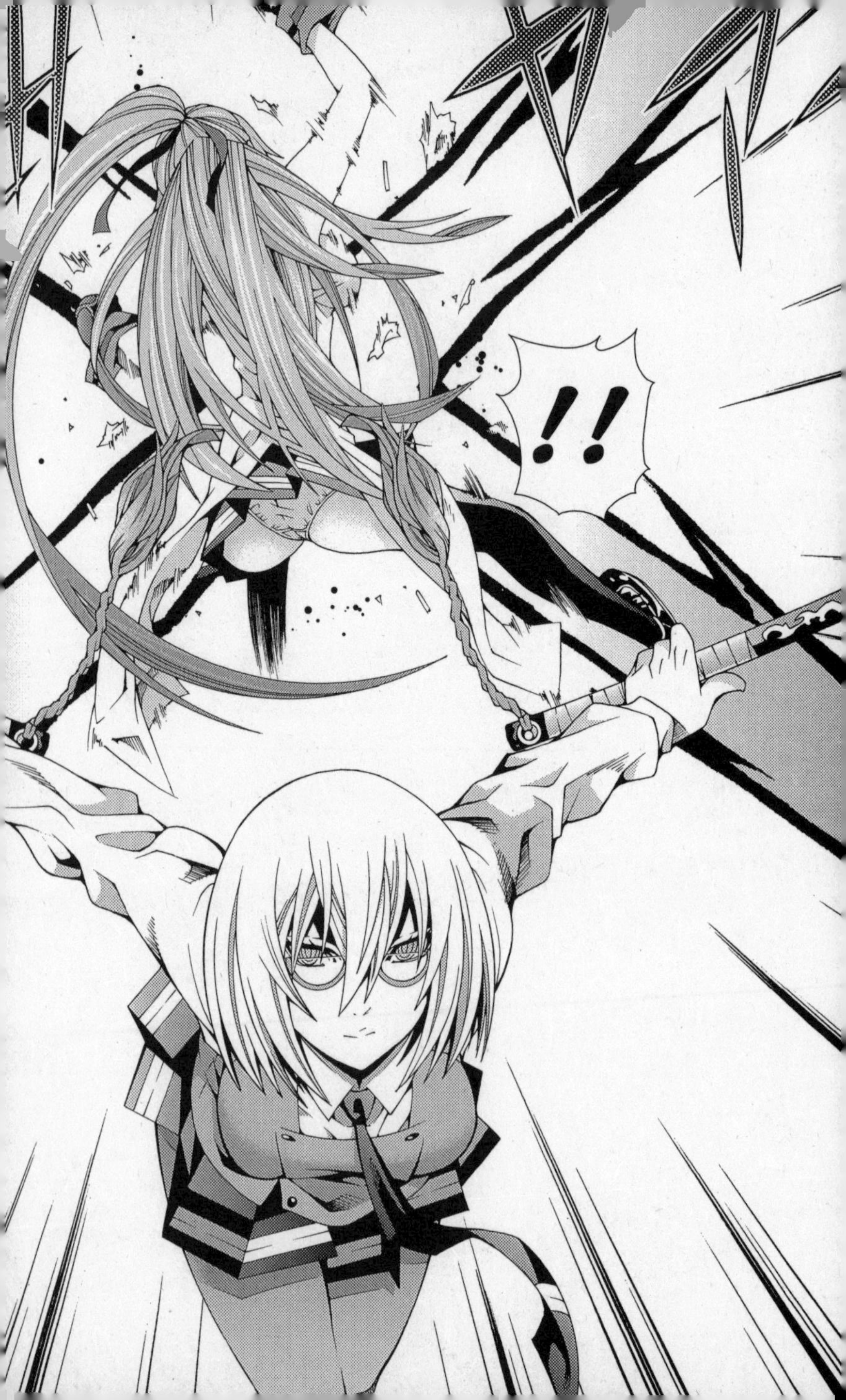
!!

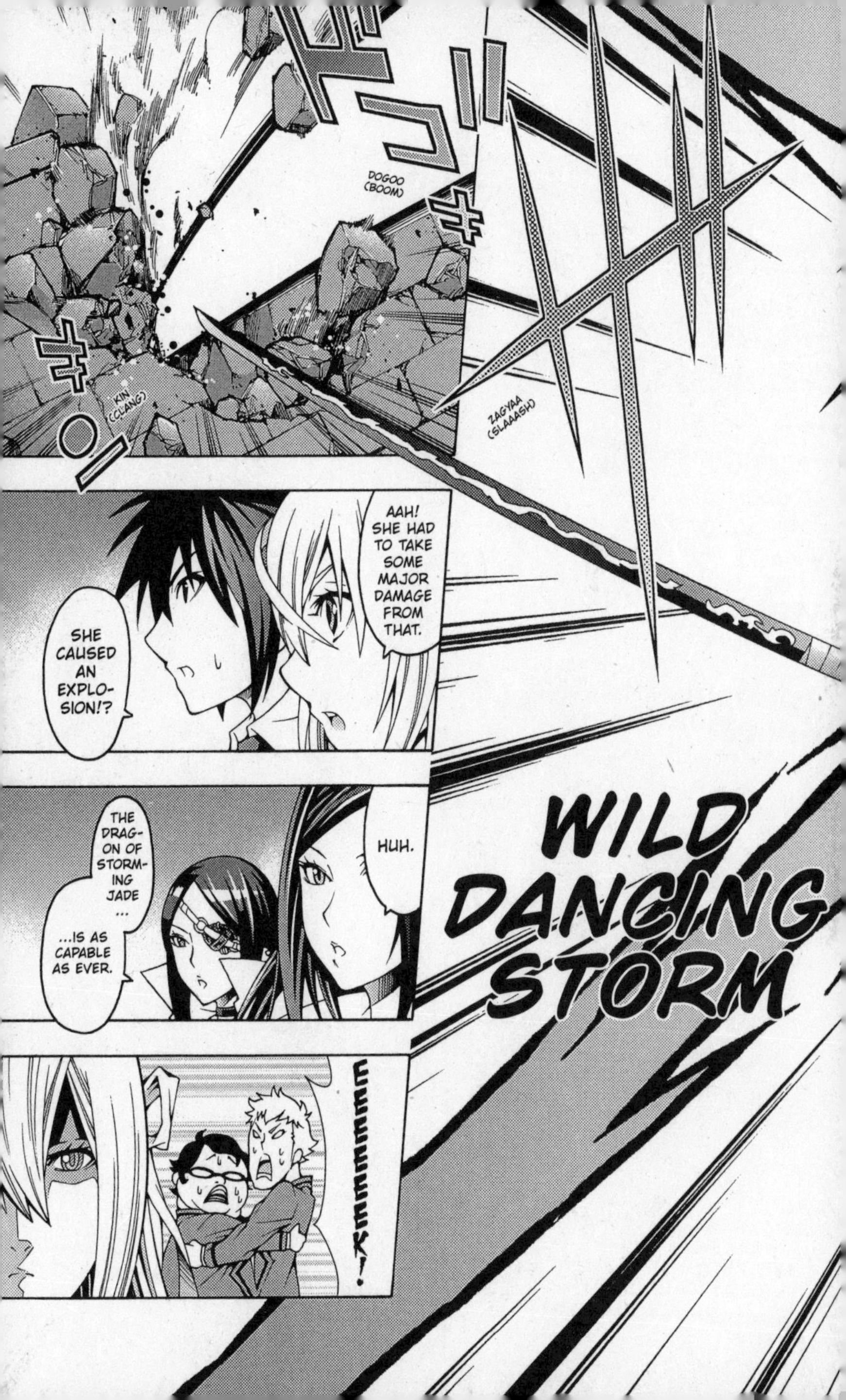
ZAGYAA (SLAAASH)
WILD DANCING STORM
DOGOO (BOOM)
KIN (CLANG)
AAH! SHE HAD TO TAKE SOME MAJOR DAMAGE FROM THAT.
SHE CAUSED AN EXPLOSION!?
HUH.
THE DRAGON OF STORMING JADE ...
...IS AS CAPABLE AS EVER.
EEEEEEEK!

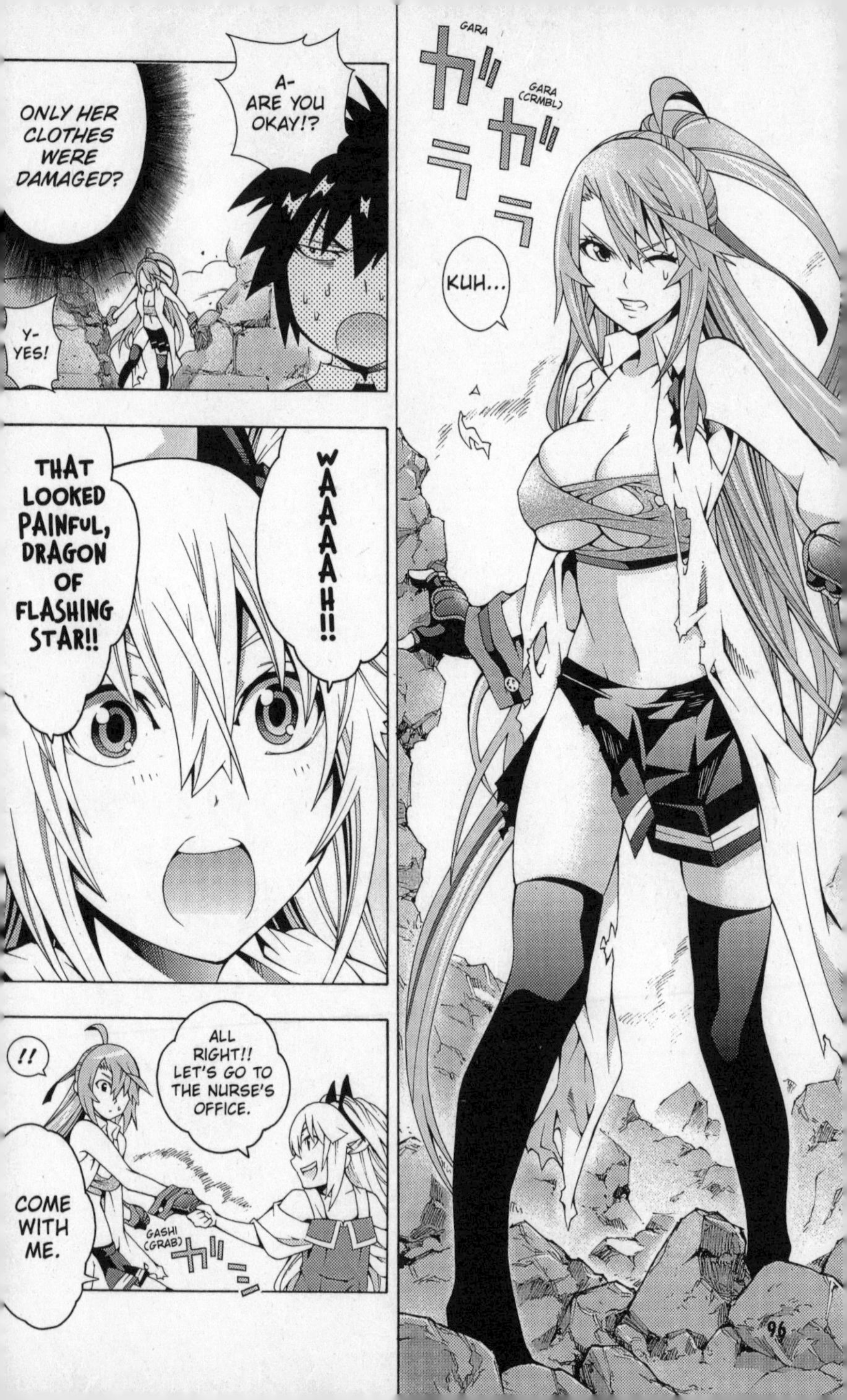
GARA
GARA (CRMBL)
KUH...
A- ARE YOU OKAY!?
ONLY HER CLOTHES WERE DAMAGED?
Y- YES!
WAAAAAH!!
THAT LOOKED PAINFUL, DRAGON OF FLASHING STAR!!
ALL RIGHT!! LET'S GO TO THE NURSE'S OFFICE.
!!
COME WITH ME.
GASHI (GRAB)

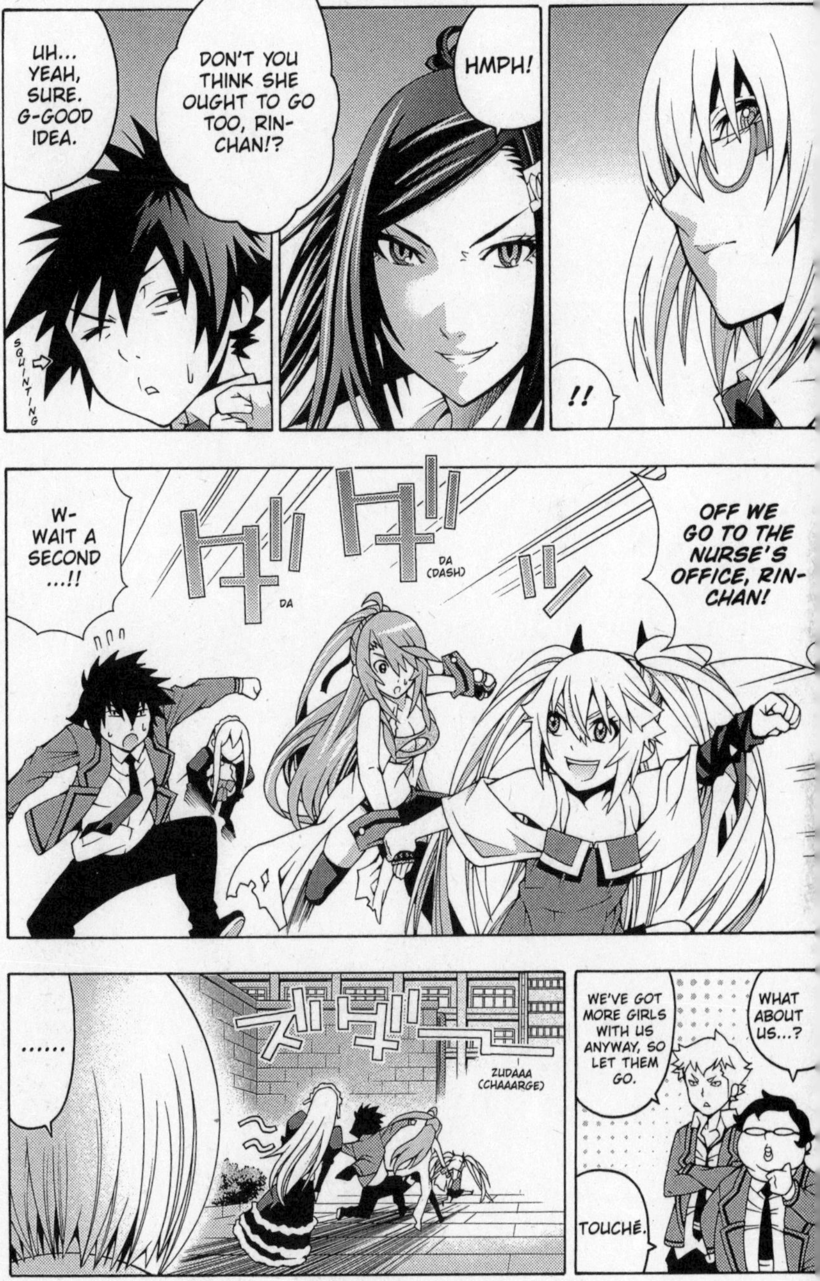
!!
HMPH!
DON'T YOU THINK SHE OUGHT TO GO TOO, RIN-CHAN!?
UH... YEAH, SURE. G-GOOD IDEA.
SQUINTING
OFF WE GO TO THE NURSE'S OFFICE, RIN-CHAN!
DA (DASH)
DA
W-WAIT A SECOND ...!!
WHAT ABOUT US...?
WE'VE GOT MORE GIRLS WITH US ANYWAY, SO LET THEM GO.
TOUCHÉ.
ZUDAAA (CHAAARGE)
......

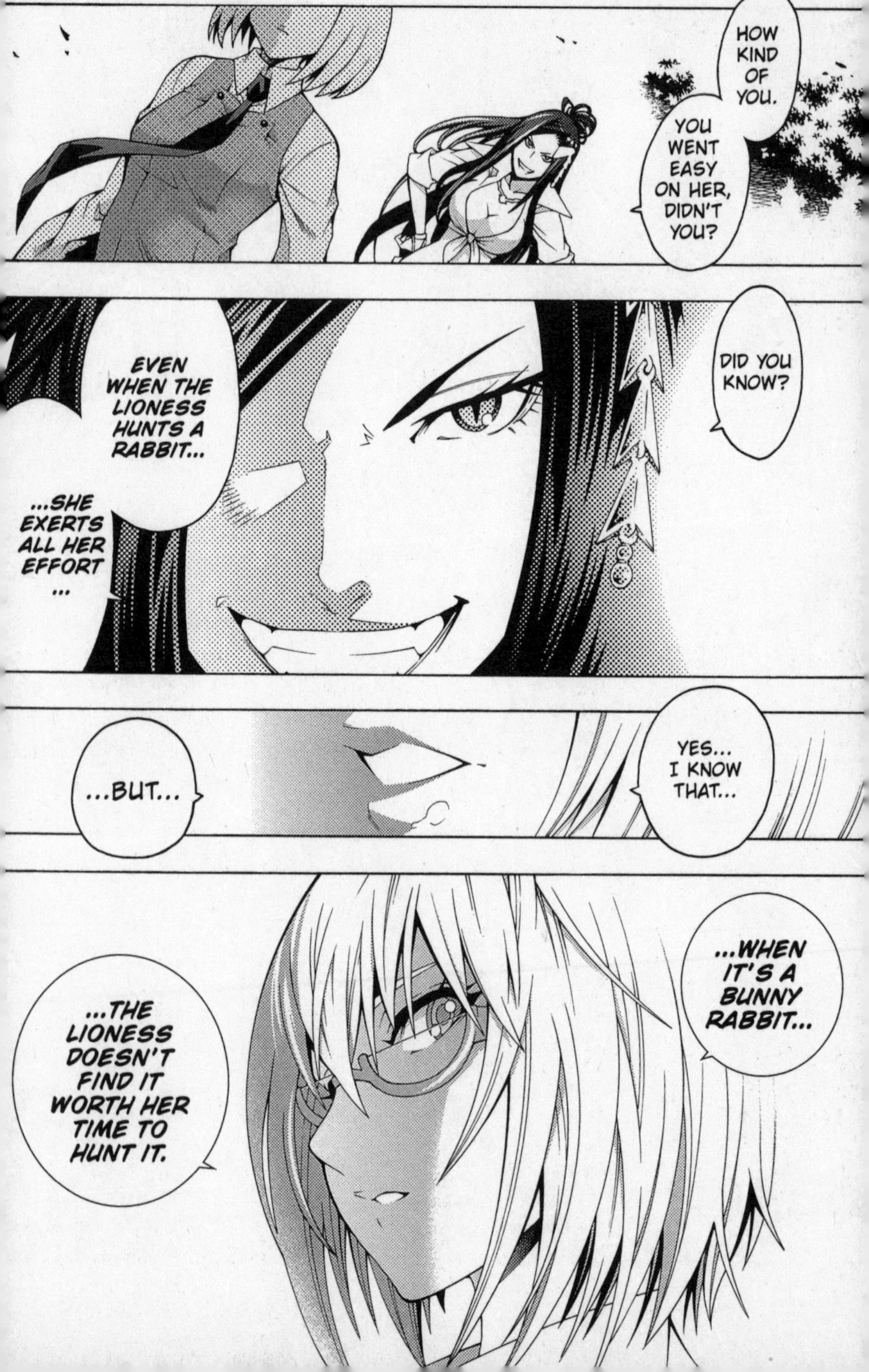
HOW KIND OF YOU.
YOU WENT EASY ON HER, DIDN'T YOU?
DID YOU KNOW?
EVEN WHEN THE LIONESS HUNTS A RABBIT...
...SHE EXERTS ALL HER EFFORT...
YES... I KNOW THAT...
...BUT...
...WHEN IT'S A BUNNY RABBIT...
...THE LIONESS DOESN'T FIND IT WORTH HER TIME TO HUNT IT.

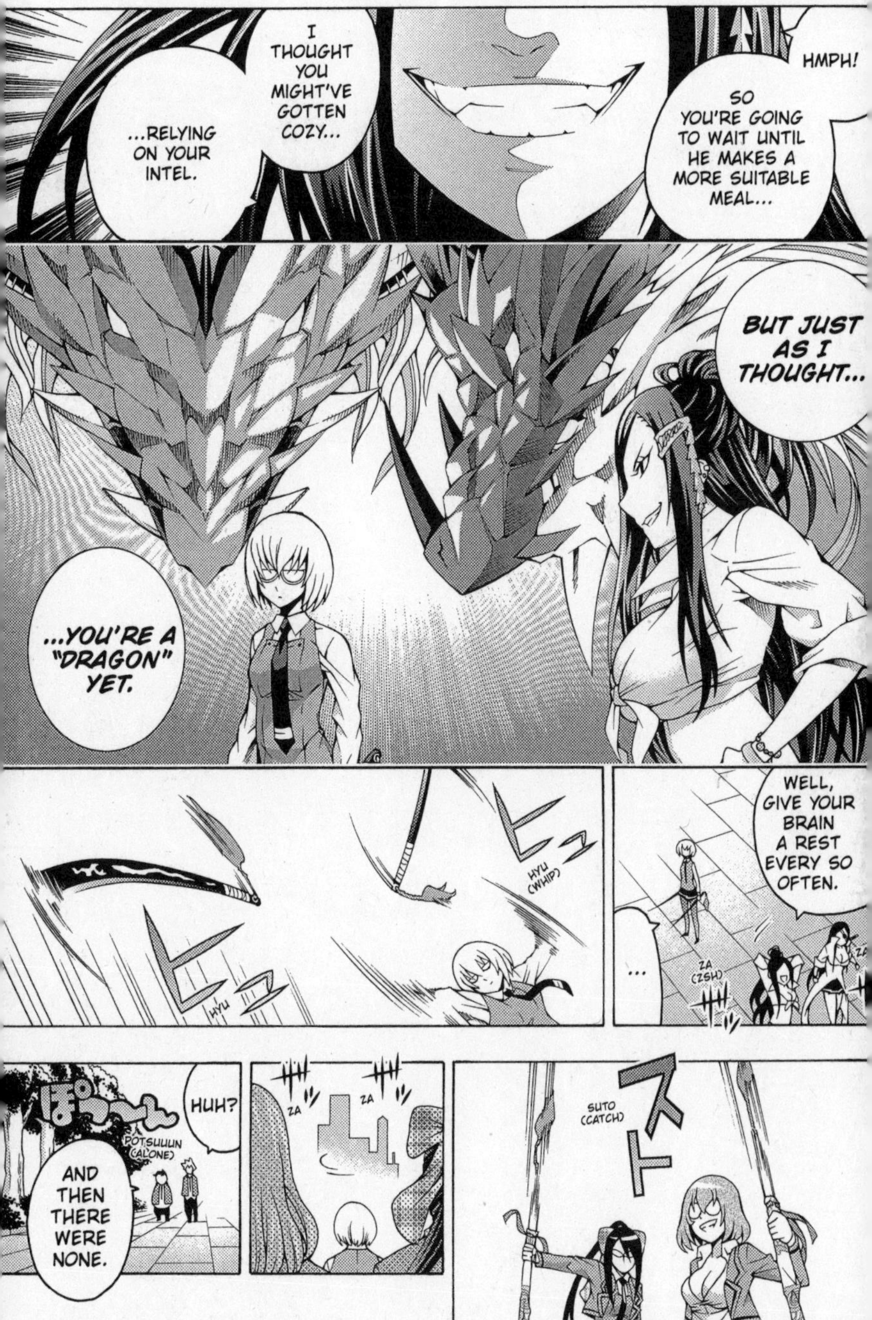
HMPH!
SO YOU'RE GOING TO WAIT UNTIL HE MAKES A MORE SUITABLE MEAL...
I THOUGHT YOU MIGHT'VE GOTTEN COZY...
...RELYING ON YOUR INTEL.
BUT JUST AS I THOUGHT...
...YOU'RE A "DRAGON" YET.
WELL, GIVE YOUR BRAIN A REST EVERY SO OFTEN.
...
ZA (ZSH)
HYU (WHIP)
HYU
SUTO (CATCH)
ZA
ZA
HUH?
POTSUUUN (ALONE)
AND THEN THERE WERE NONE.

LABEL: INFIRMARY

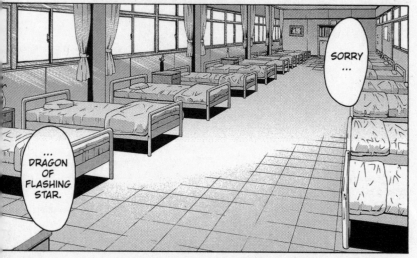

SORRY ...

... DRAGON OF FLASHING STAR.

YOU HAD TO GO THROUGH ALL THAT...

...BECAUSE I WANTED TO TAKE ON RIN-CHAN...

IT'S FINE...

I HAVE TO BATTLE HER EVENTUALLY ANYWAY...

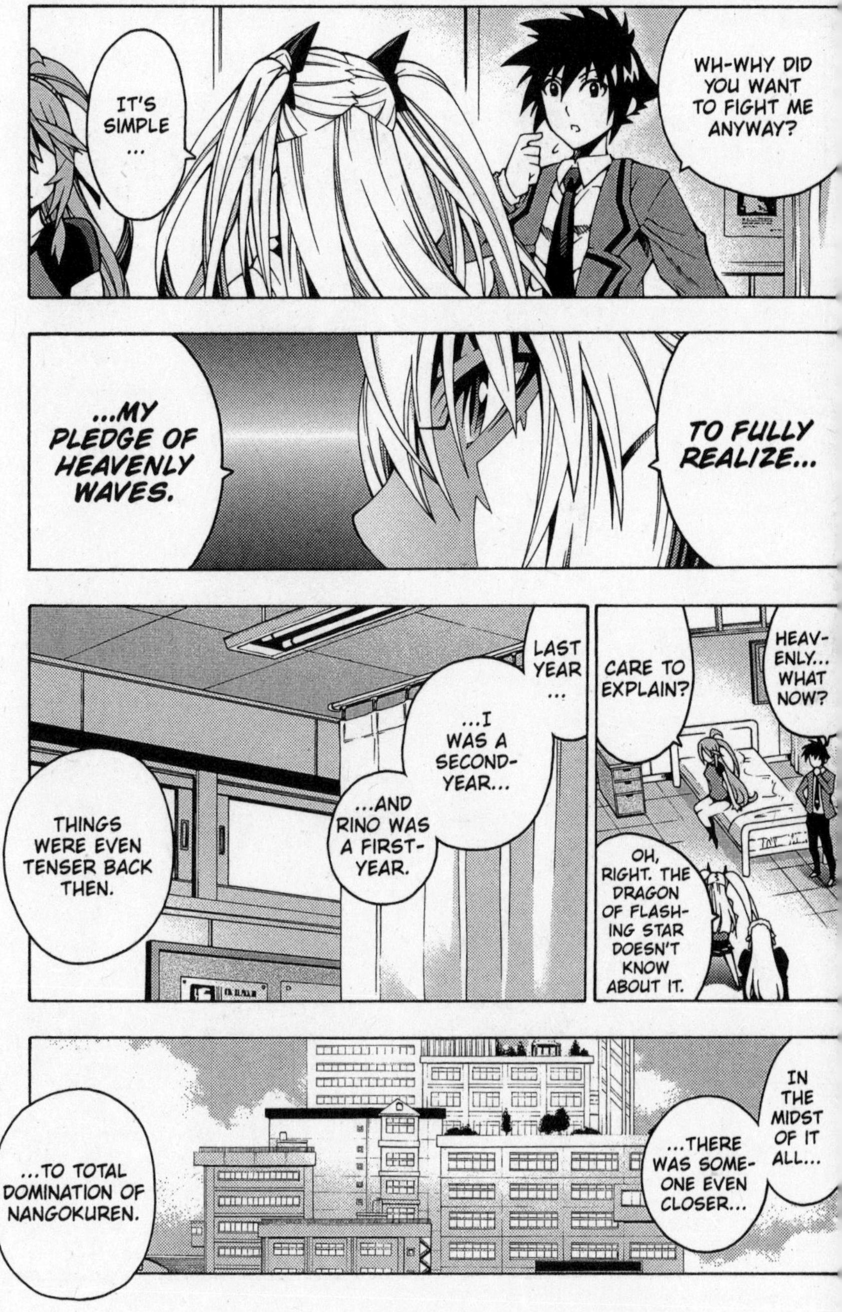
WH-WHY DID YOU WANT TO FIGHT ME ANYWAY?
IT'S SIMPLE ...
TO FULLY REALIZE...
...MY PLEDGE OF HEAVENLY WAVES.
HEAV-ENLY... WHAT NOW?
CARE TO EXPLAIN?
OH, RIGHT. THE DRAGON OF FLASH-ING STAR DOESN'T KNOW ABOUT IT.
LAST YEAR ...
...I WAS A SECOND-YEAR...
...AND RINO WAS A FIRST-YEAR.
THINGS WERE EVEN TENSER BACK THEN.
IN THE MIDST OF IT ALL...
...THERE WAS SOME-ONE EVEN CLOSER...
...TO TOTAL DOMINATION OF NANGOKUREN.

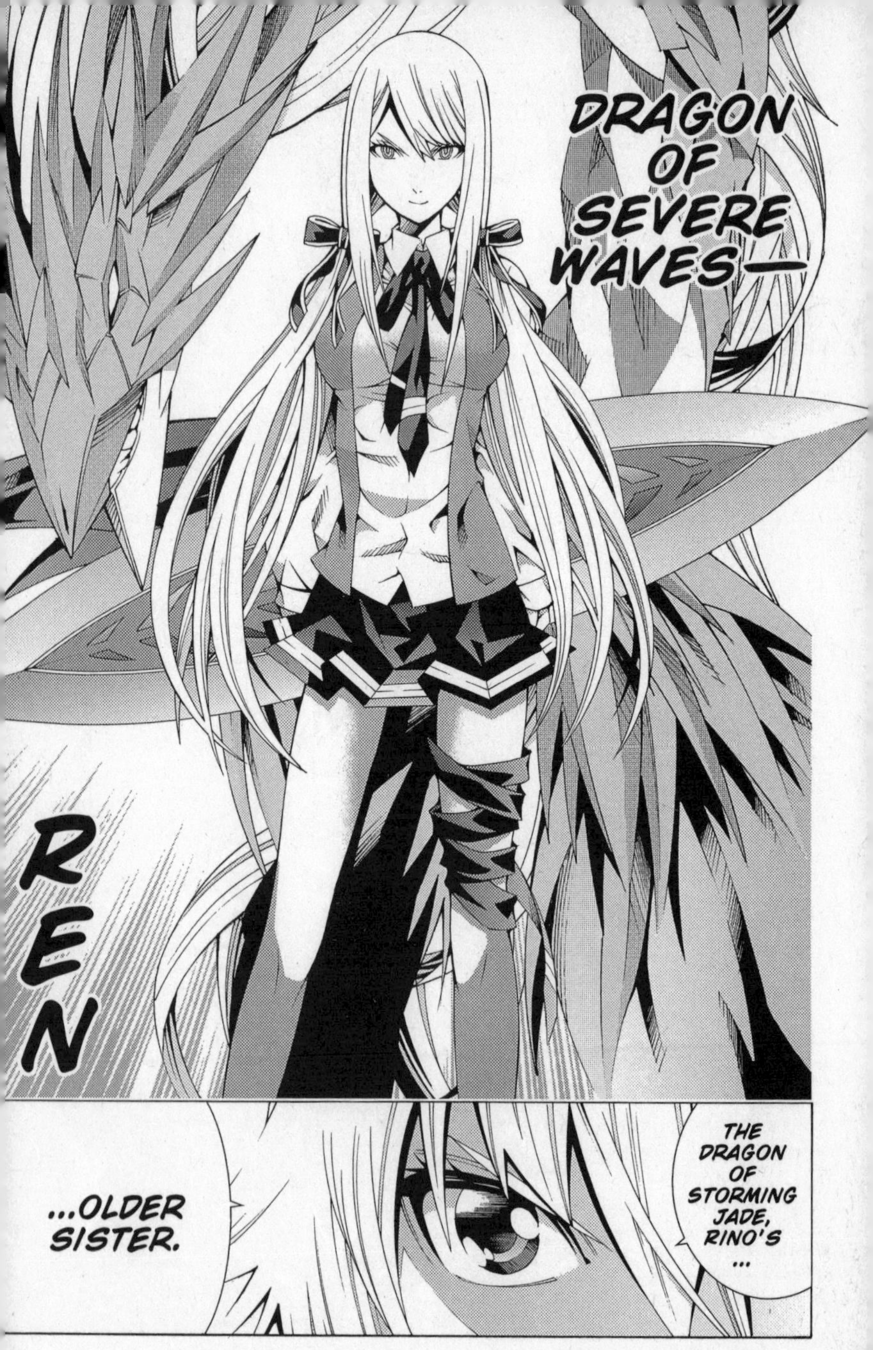
DRAGON OF SEVERE WAVES—
REN
THE DRAGON OF STORMING JADE, RINO'S ...
...OLDER SISTER.

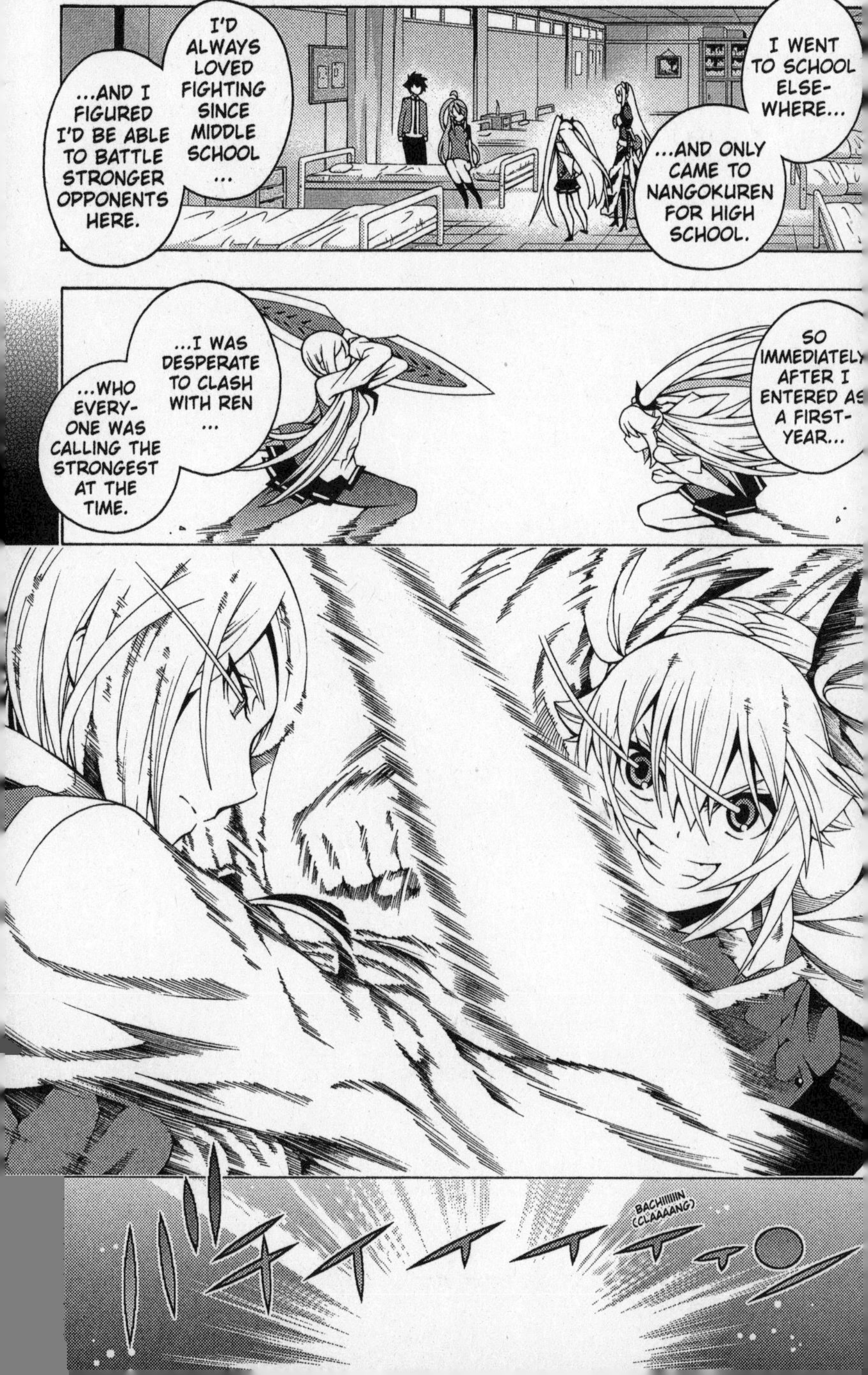
I WENT TO SCHOOL ELSE-WHERE...
...AND ONLY CAME TO NANGOKUREN FOR HIGH SCHOOL.
I'D ALWAYS LOVED FIGHTING SINCE MIDDLE SCHOOL...
...AND I FIGURED I'D BE ABLE TO BATTLE STRONGER OPPONENTS HERE.
SO IMMEDIATELY AFTER I ENTERED AS A FIRST-YEAR...
...I WAS DESPERATE TO CLASH WITH REN...
...WHO EVERY-ONE WAS CALLING THE STRONGEST AT THE TIME.
BACHIIIIIIN (CLAAAANG)

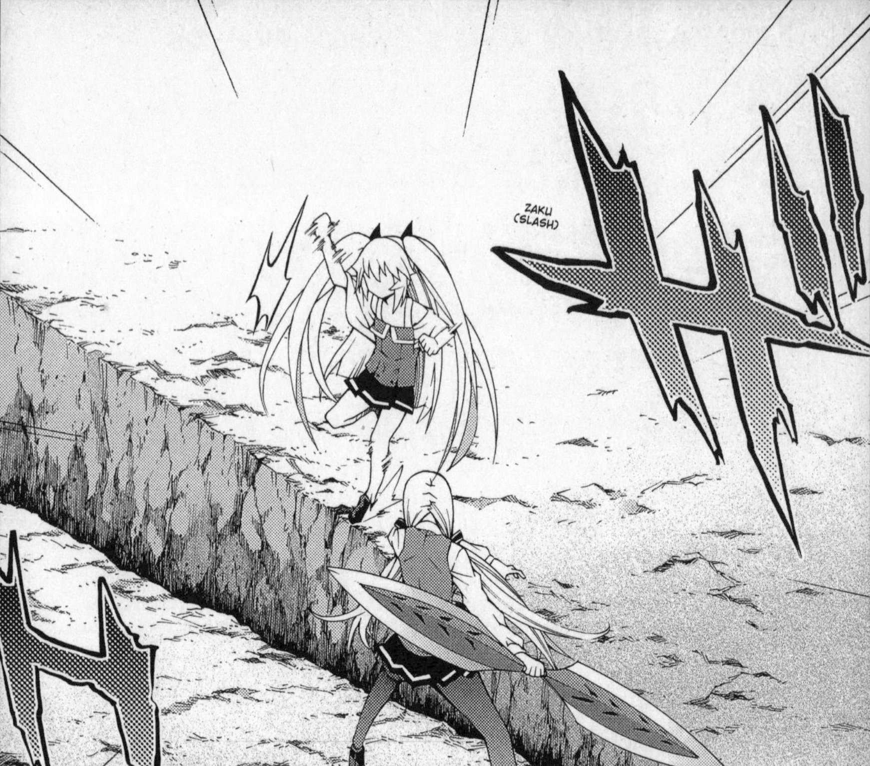
ZAKU
(SLASH)
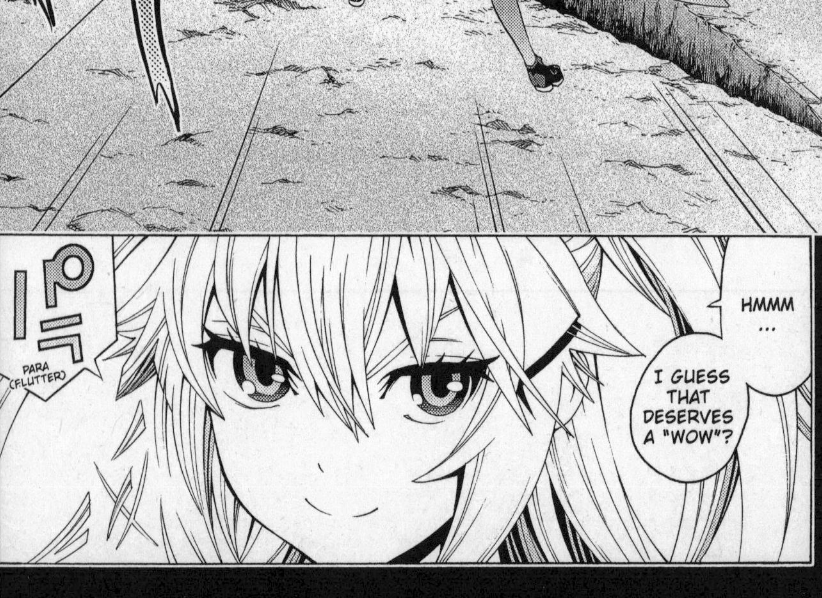
HMMM ...
I GUESS THAT DESERVES A "WOW"?
PARA
(FLUTTER)

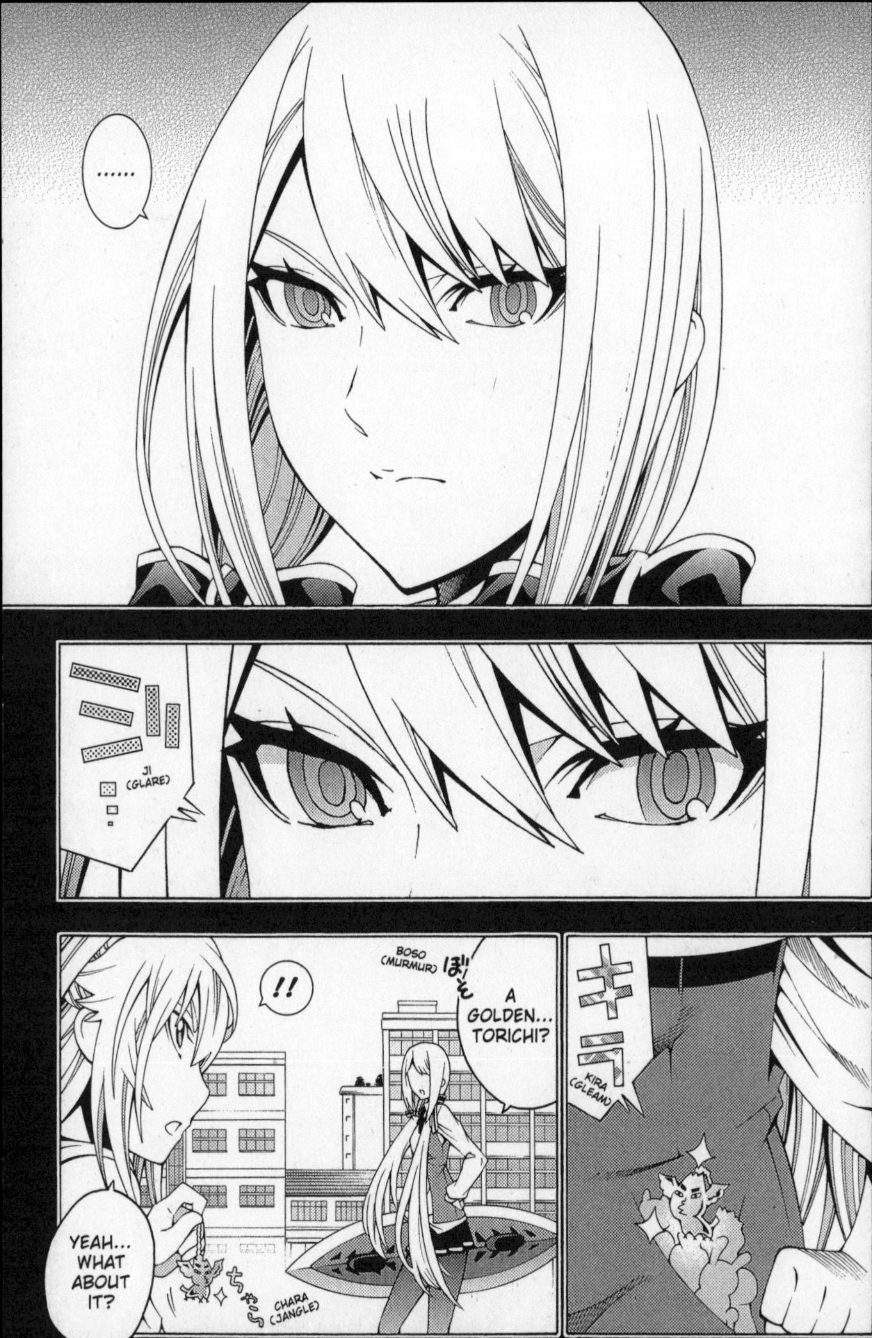
......
JI (GLARE)
キラ
KIRA (GLEAM)
ぼそ
BOSO (MURMUR)
A GOLDEN... TORICHI?
!!
YEAH... WHAT ABOUT IT?
ちゃら
CHARA (JANGLE)

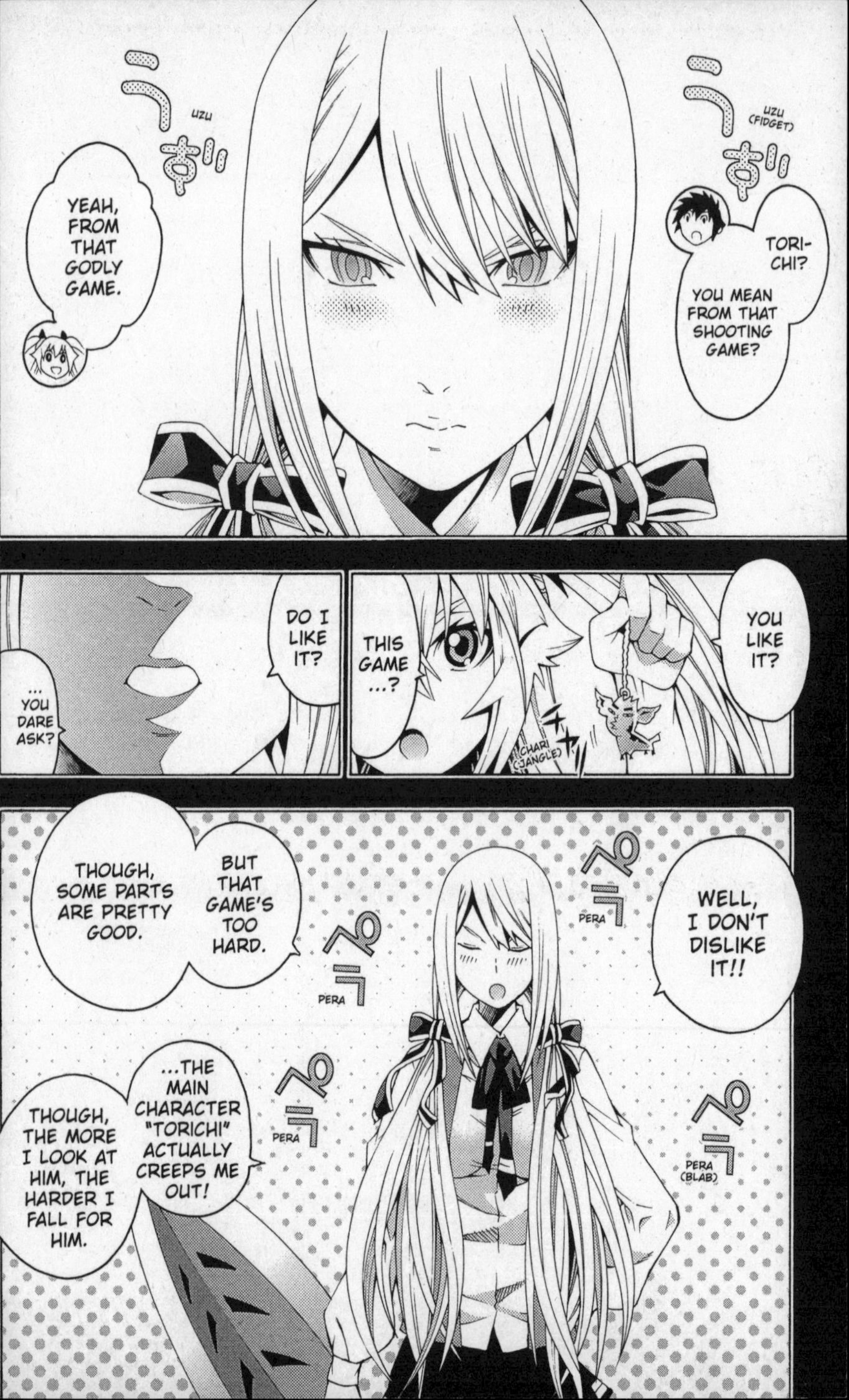
UZU (FIDGET)
TORI-CHI? YOU MEAN FROM THAT SHOOTING GAME?
UZU
YEAH, FROM THAT GODLY GAME.
YOU LIKE IT?
CHARI (JANGLE)
THIS GAME ...?
DO I LIKE IT?
... YOU DARE ASK?
WELL, I DON'T DISLIKE IT!!
PERA
BUT THAT GAME'S TOO HARD.
THOUGH, SOME PARTS ARE PRETTY GOOD.
PERA
PERA (BLAB)
...THE MAIN CHARACTER "TORICHI" ACTUALLY CREEPS ME OUT!
PERA
THOUGH, THE MORE I LOOK AT HIM, THE HARDER I FALL FOR HIM.

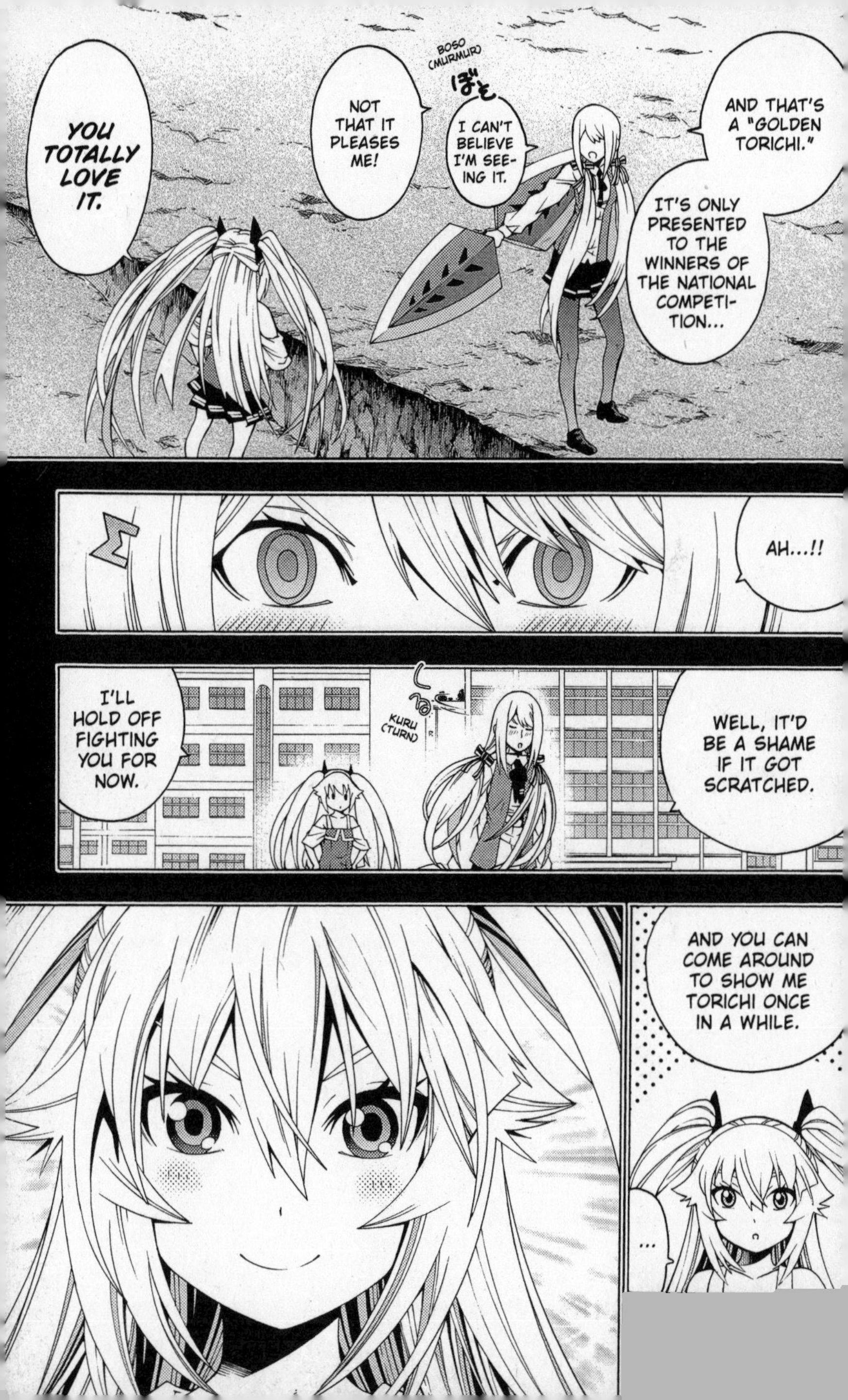
AND THAT'S A "GOLDEN TORICHI."
IT'S ONLY PRESENTED TO THE WINNERS OF THE NATIONAL COMPETITION...
BOSO (MURMUR)
ぼそ
I CAN'T BELIEVE I'M SEEING IT.
NOT THAT IT PLEASES ME!
YOU TOTALLY LOVE IT.
AH...!!
WELL, IT'D BE A SHAME IF IT GOT SCRATCHED.
KURU (TURN)
くる
I'LL HOLD OFF FIGHTING YOU FOR NOW.
AND YOU CAN COME AROUND TO SHOW ME TORICHI ONCE IN A WHILE.
...

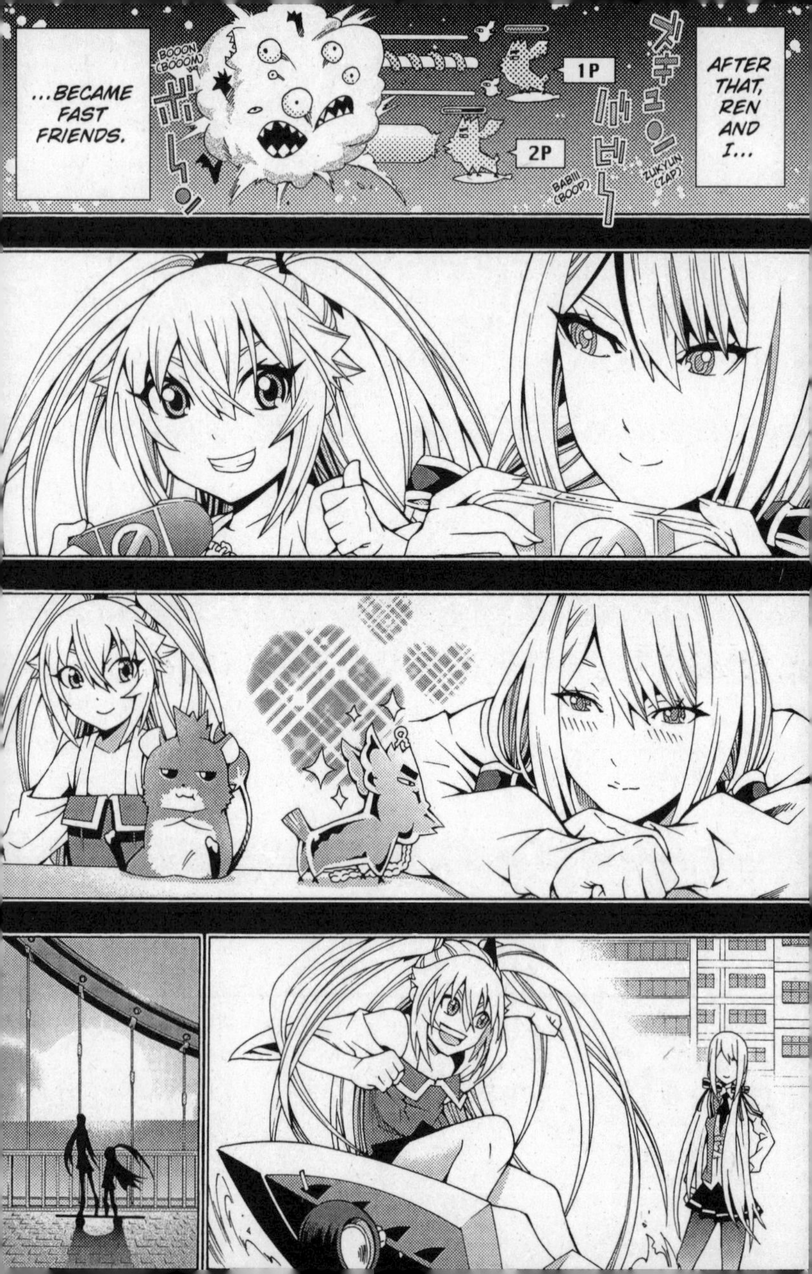
AFTER THAT, REN AND I...
ZUKYUN (ZAP)
BABIII (BOOP)
1P
2P
BOOON (BOOOM)
...BECAME FAST FRIENDS.

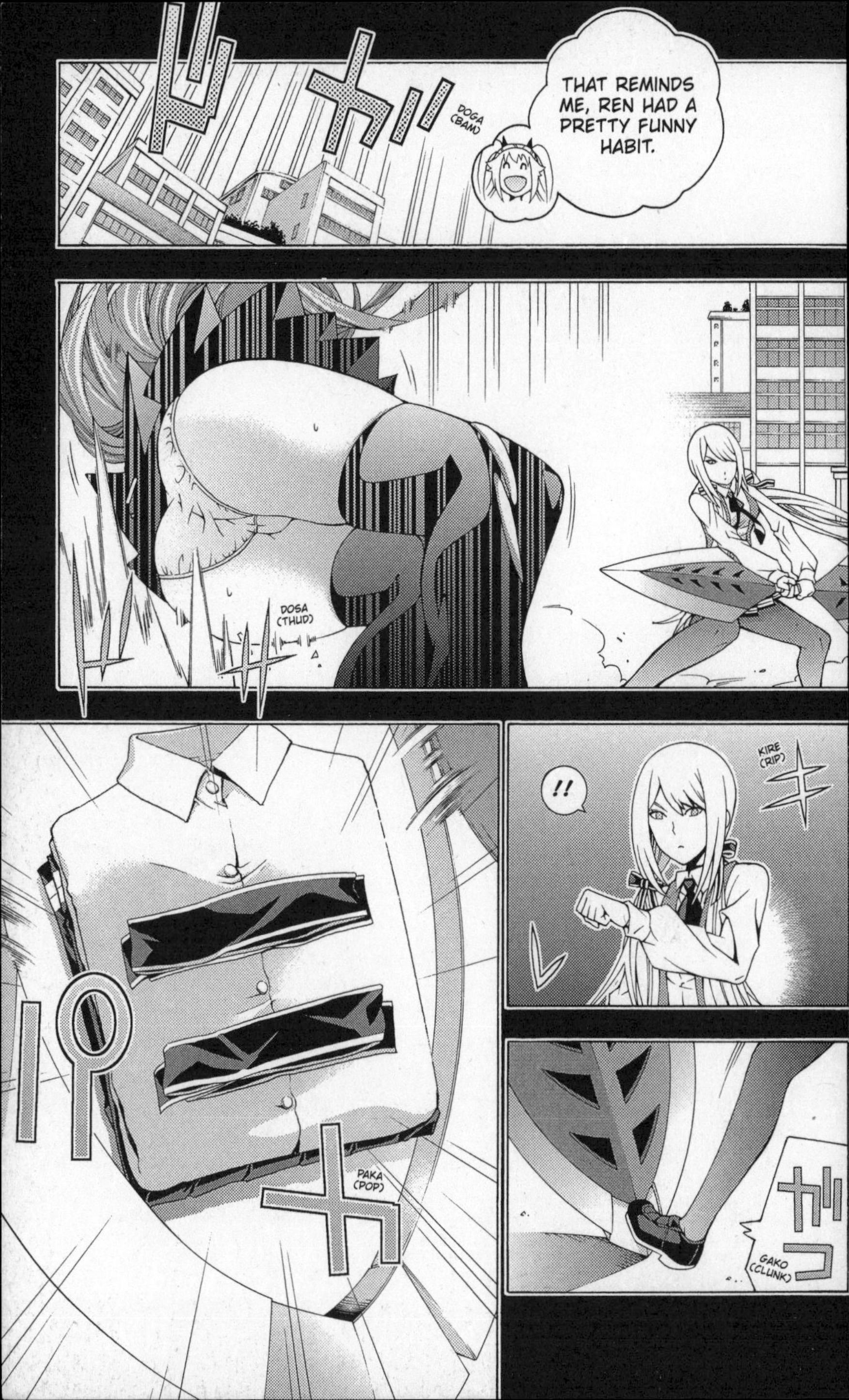
THAT REMINDS ME, REN HAD A PRETTY FUNNY HABIT.
DOGA (BAM)
DOSA (THUD)
KIRE (RIP)
!!
GAKO (CLUNK)
PAKA (POP)

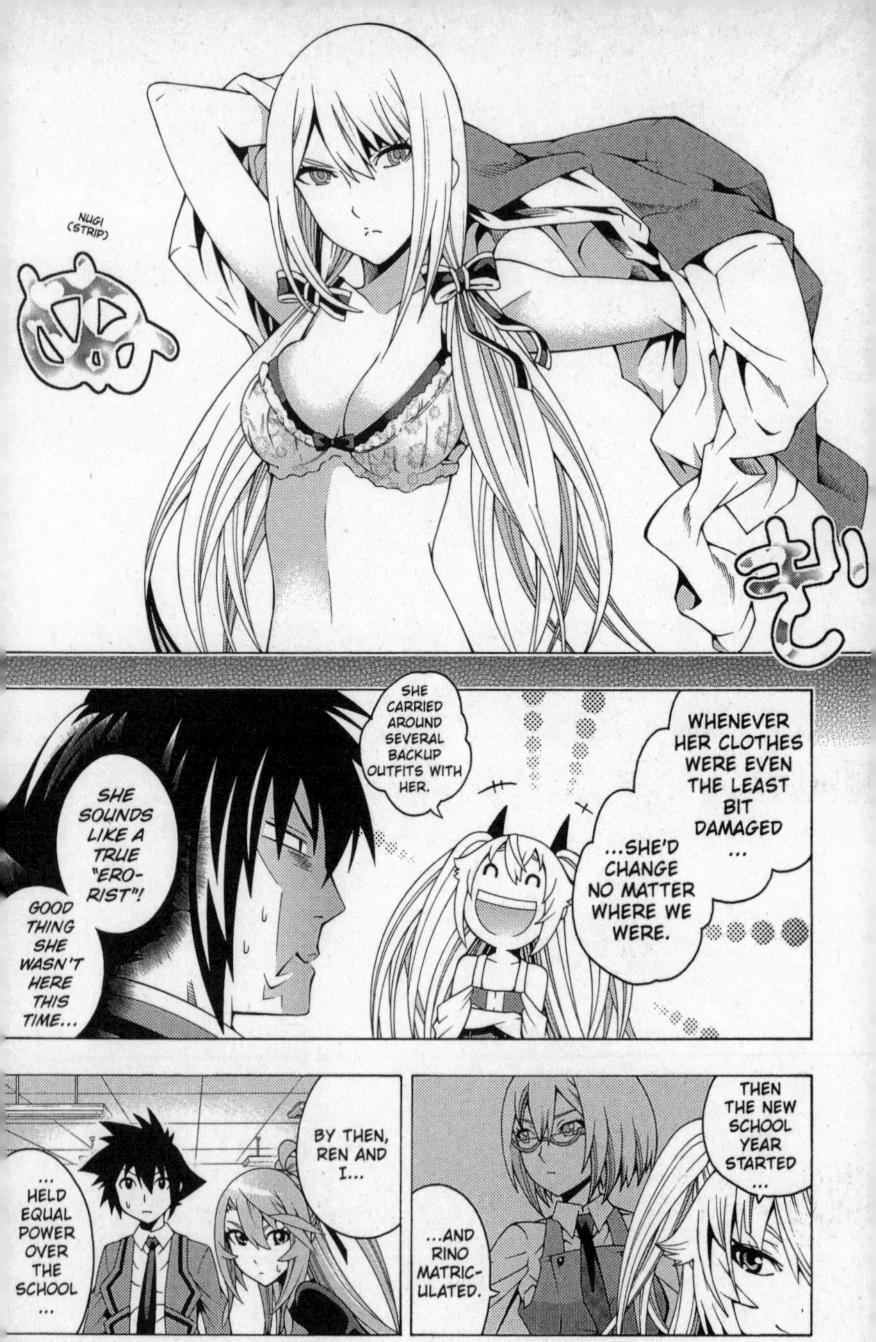
NUGI (STRIP)
WHENEVER HER CLOTHES WERE EVEN THE LEAST BIT DAMAGED ...
...SHE'D CHANGE NO MATTER WHERE WE WERE.
SHE CARRIED AROUND SEVERAL BACKUP OUTFITS WITH HER.
SHE SOUNDS LIKE A TRUE "ERO-RIST"!
GOOD THING SHE WASN'T HERE THIS TIME...
THEN THE NEW SCHOOL YEAR STARTED ...
...AND RINO MATRIC-ULATED.
BY THEN, REN AND I...
... HELD EQUAL POWER OVER THE SCHOOL ...

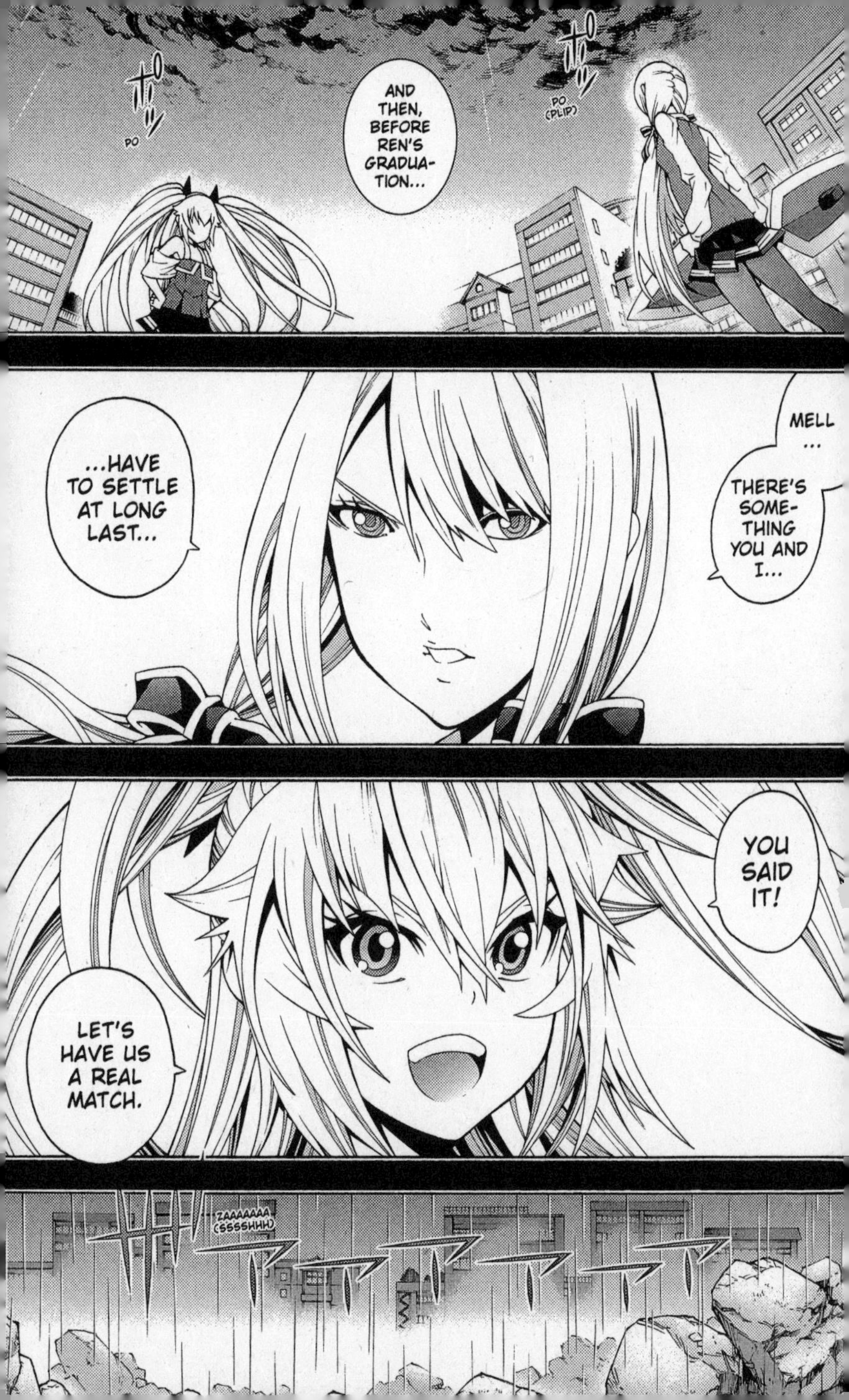
PO (PLIP)
AND THEN, BEFORE REN'S GRADUATION...
PO
MELL... THERE'S SOMETHING YOU AND I...
...HAVE TO SETTLE AT LONG LAST...
YOU SAID IT!
LET'S HAVE US A REAL MATCH.
ZAAAAAAA (SSSSHHH)

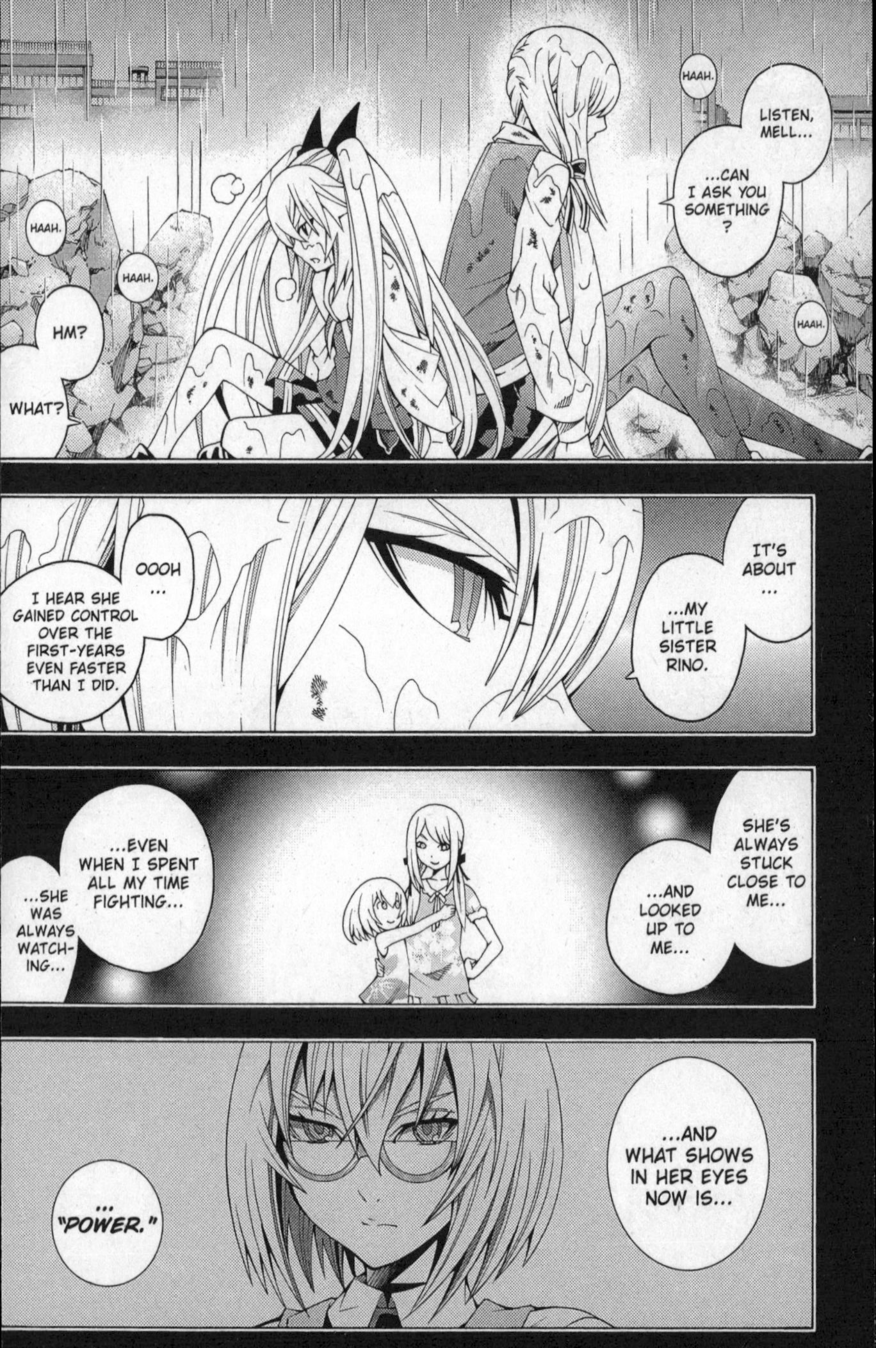
HAAH.
LISTEN, MELL...
...CAN I ASK YOU SOMETHING ?
HAAH.
HAAH.
HAAH.
HM?
WHAT?
IT'S ABOUT ...
...MY LITTLE SISTER RINO.
OOOH ...
I HEAR SHE GAINED CONTROL OVER THE FIRST-YEARS EVEN FASTER THAN I DID.
SHE'S ALWAYS STUCK CLOSE TO ME...
...AND LOOKED UP TO ME...
...EVEN WHEN I SPENT ALL MY TIME FIGHTING...
...SHE WAS ALWAYS WATCHING...
...AND WHAT SHOWS IN HER EYES NOW IS...
... "POWER."

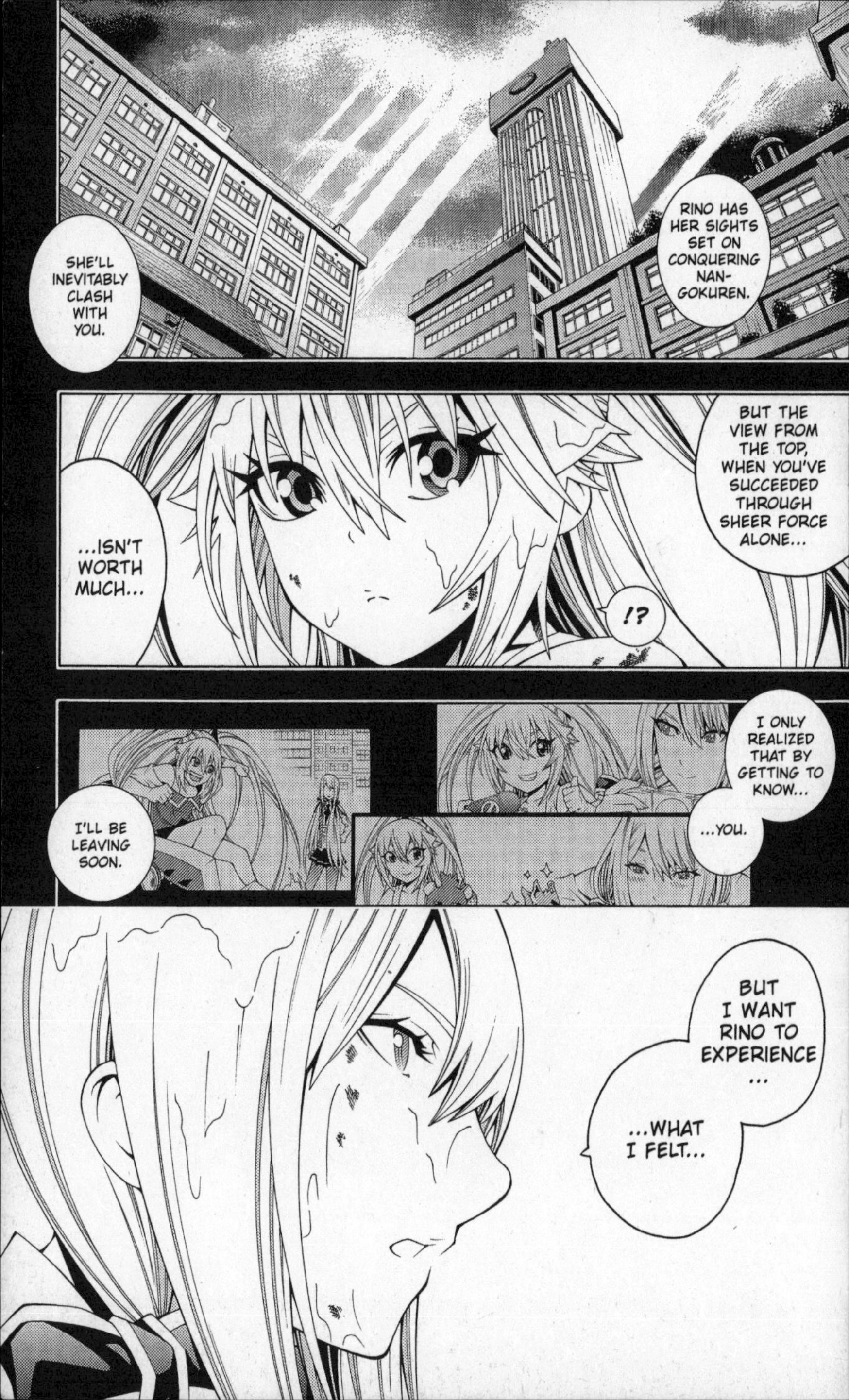
RINO HAS HER SIGHTS SET ON CONQUERING NAN-GOKUREN.
SHE'LL INEVITABLY CLASH WITH YOU.
BUT THE VIEW FROM THE TOP, WHEN YOU'VE SUCCEEDED THROUGH SHEER FORCE ALONE...
...ISN'T WORTH MUCH...
!?
I ONLY REALIZED THAT BY GETTING TO KNOW...
...YOU.
I'LL BE LEAVING SOON.
BUT I WANT RINO TO EXPERIENCE...
...WHAT I FELT...

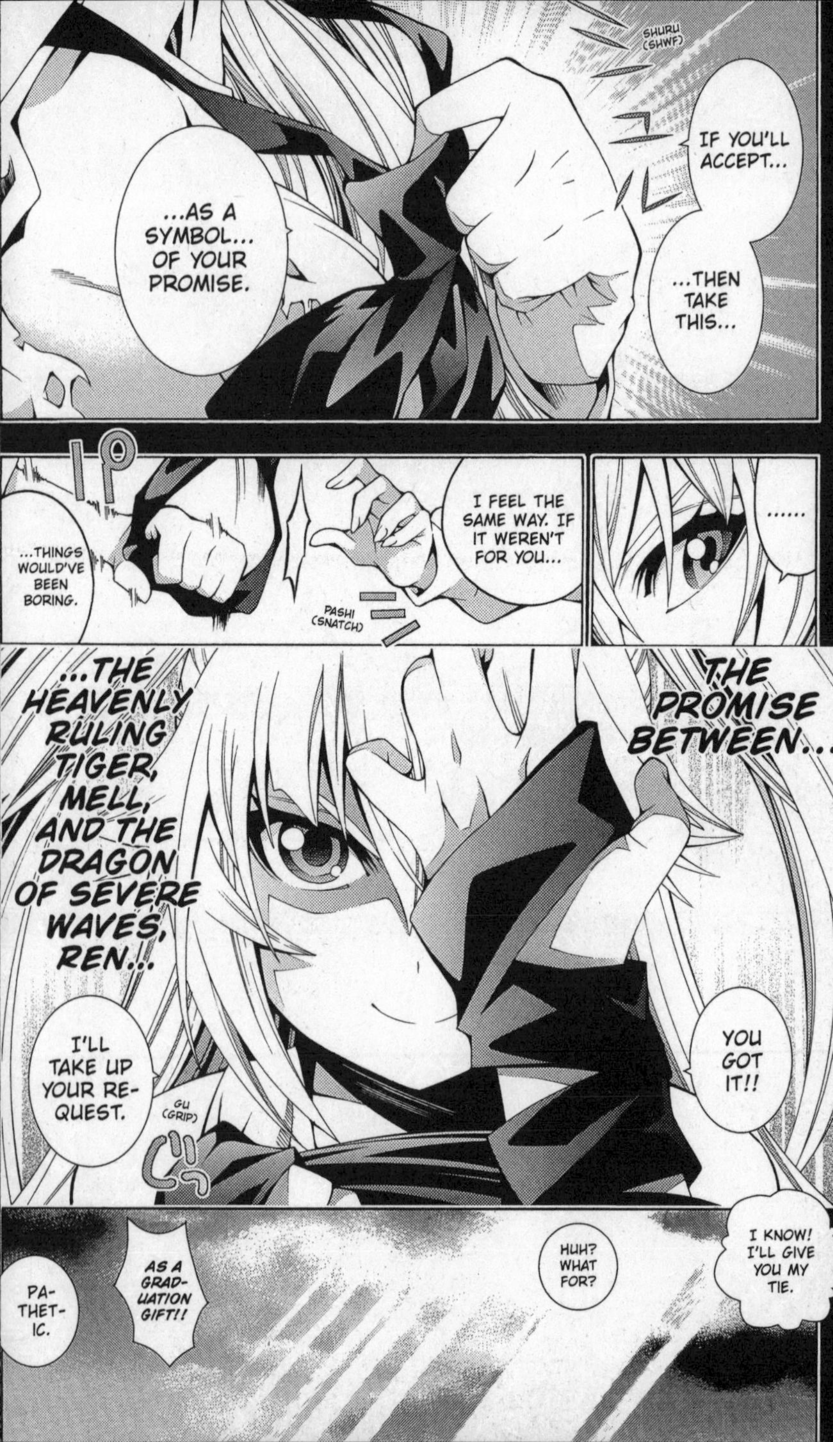

SHURU (SHWF)
IF YOU'LL ACCEPT...
...THEN TAKE THIS...
...AS A SYMBOL... OF YOUR PROMISE.
......
I FEEL THE SAME WAY. IF IT WEREN'T FOR YOU...
PASHI (SNATCH)
...THINGS WOULD'VE BEEN BORING.
THE PROMISE BETWEEN...
...THE HEAVENLY RULING TIGER, MELL, AND THE DRAGON OF SEVERE WAVES, REN...
YOU GOT IT!!
I'LL TAKE UP YOUR RE-QUEST.
GU (GRIP)
I KNOW! I'LL GIVE YOU MY TIE.
HUH? WHAT FOR?
AS A GRAD-UATION GIFT!!
PA-THET-IC.

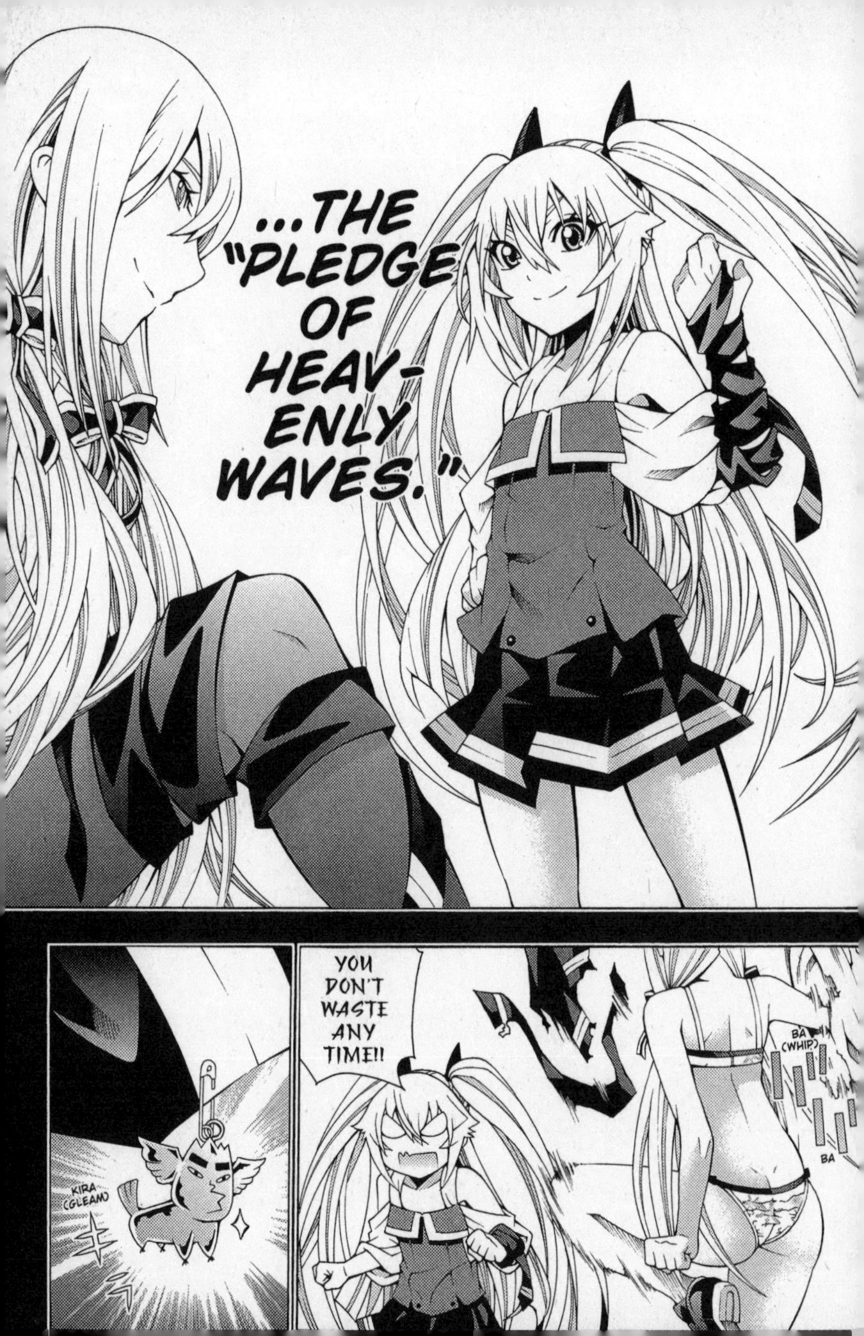
...THE "PLEDGE OF HEAV-ENLY WAVES."
YOU DON'T WASTE ANY TIME!!
BA (WHIP)
BA
KIRA (GLEAM)

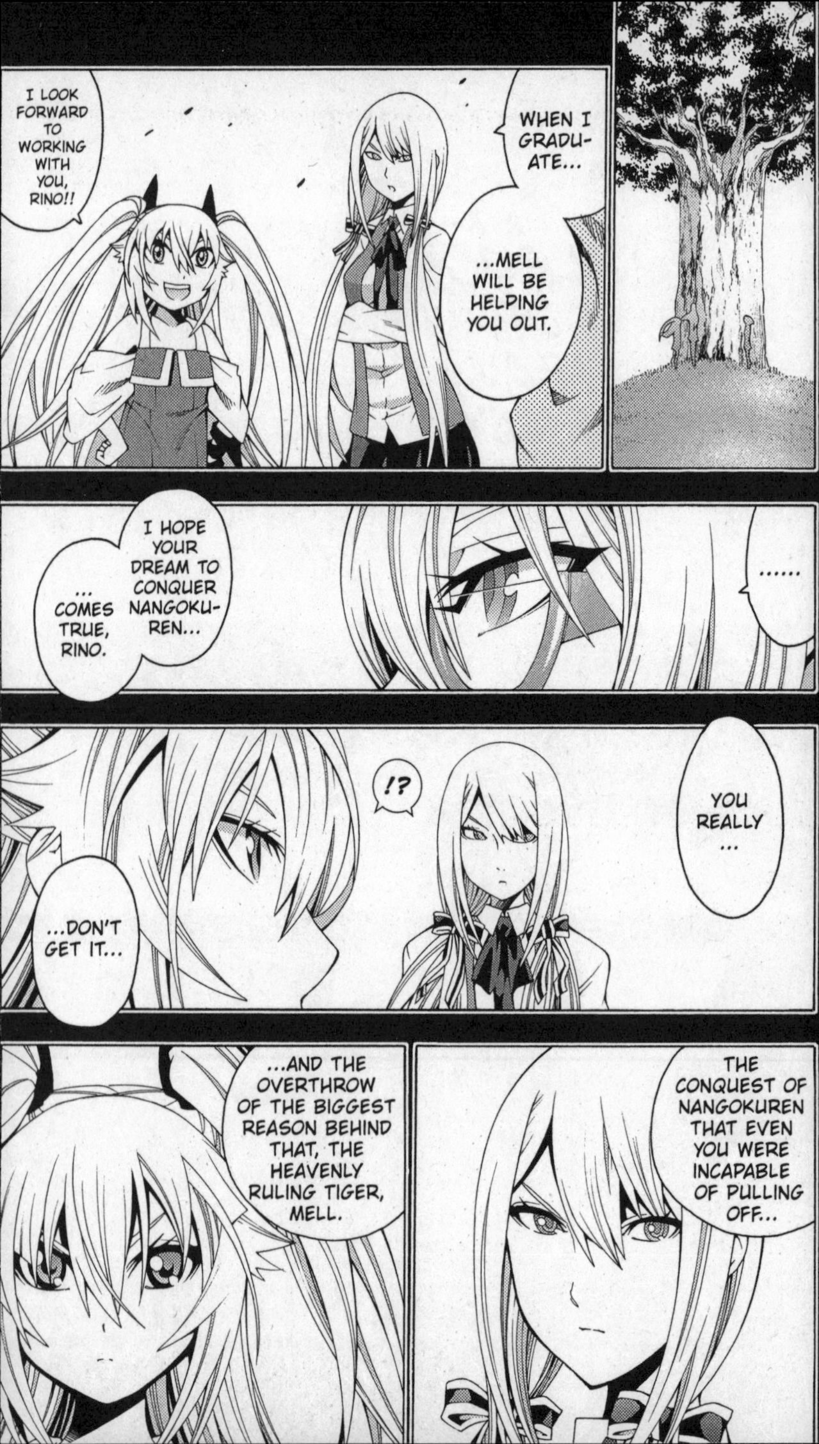
WHEN I GRADUATE...
...MELL WILL BE HELPING YOU OUT.
I LOOK FORWARD TO WORKING WITH YOU, RINO!!
......
I HOPE YOUR DREAM TO CONQUER NANGOKUREN...
...COMES TRUE, RINO.
YOU REALLY ...
!?
...DON'T GET IT...
THE CONQUEST OF NANGOKUREN THAT EVEN YOU WERE INCAPABLE OF PULLING OFF...
...AND THE OVERTHROW OF THE BIGGEST REASON BEHIND THAT, THE HEAVENLY RULING TIGER, MELL.

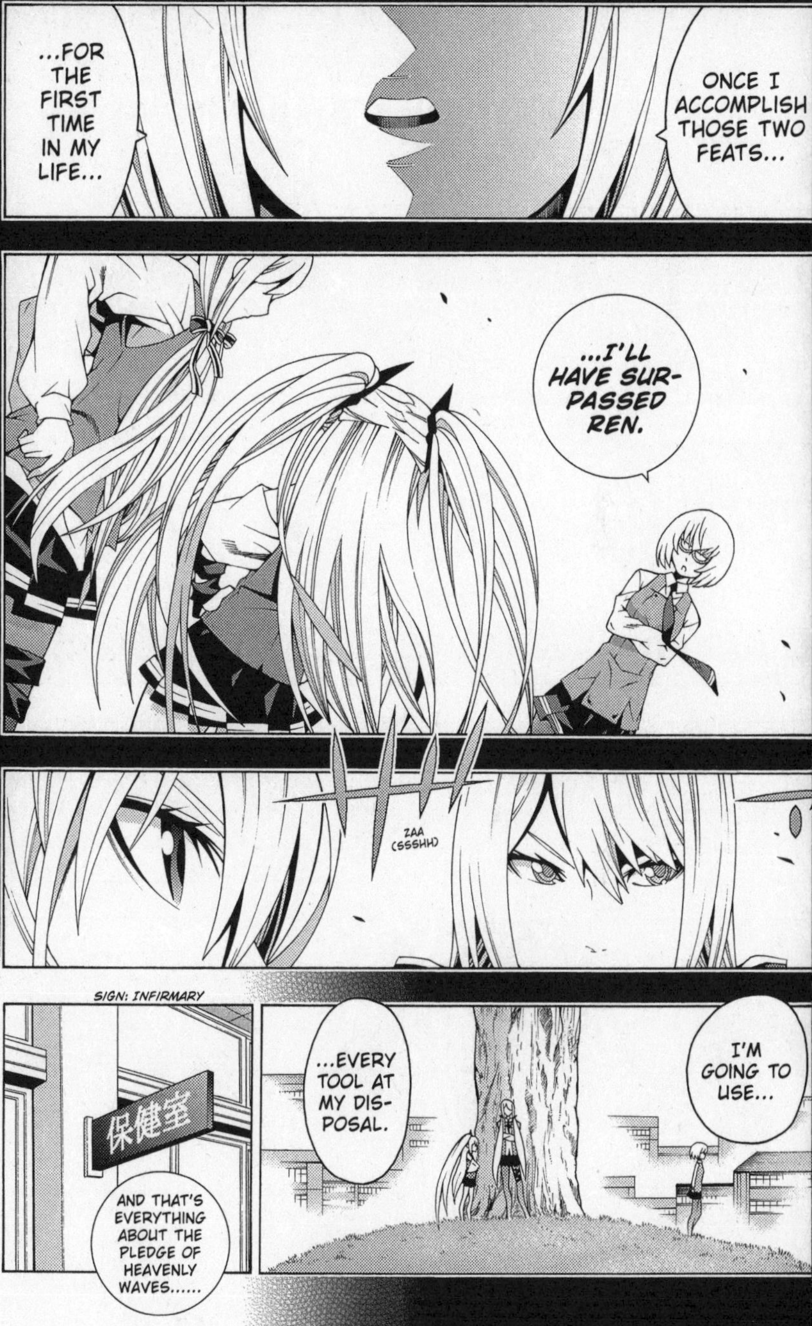

ONCE I ACCOMPLISH THOSE TWO FEATS...
...FOR THE FIRST TIME IN MY LIFE...
...I'LL HAVE SURPASSED REN.
ZAA (SSSHH)
I'M GOING TO USE...
...EVERY TOOL AT MY DISPOSAL.
SIGN: INFIRMARY
保健室
AND THAT'S EVERYTHING ABOUT THE PLEDGE OF HEAVENLY WAVES......

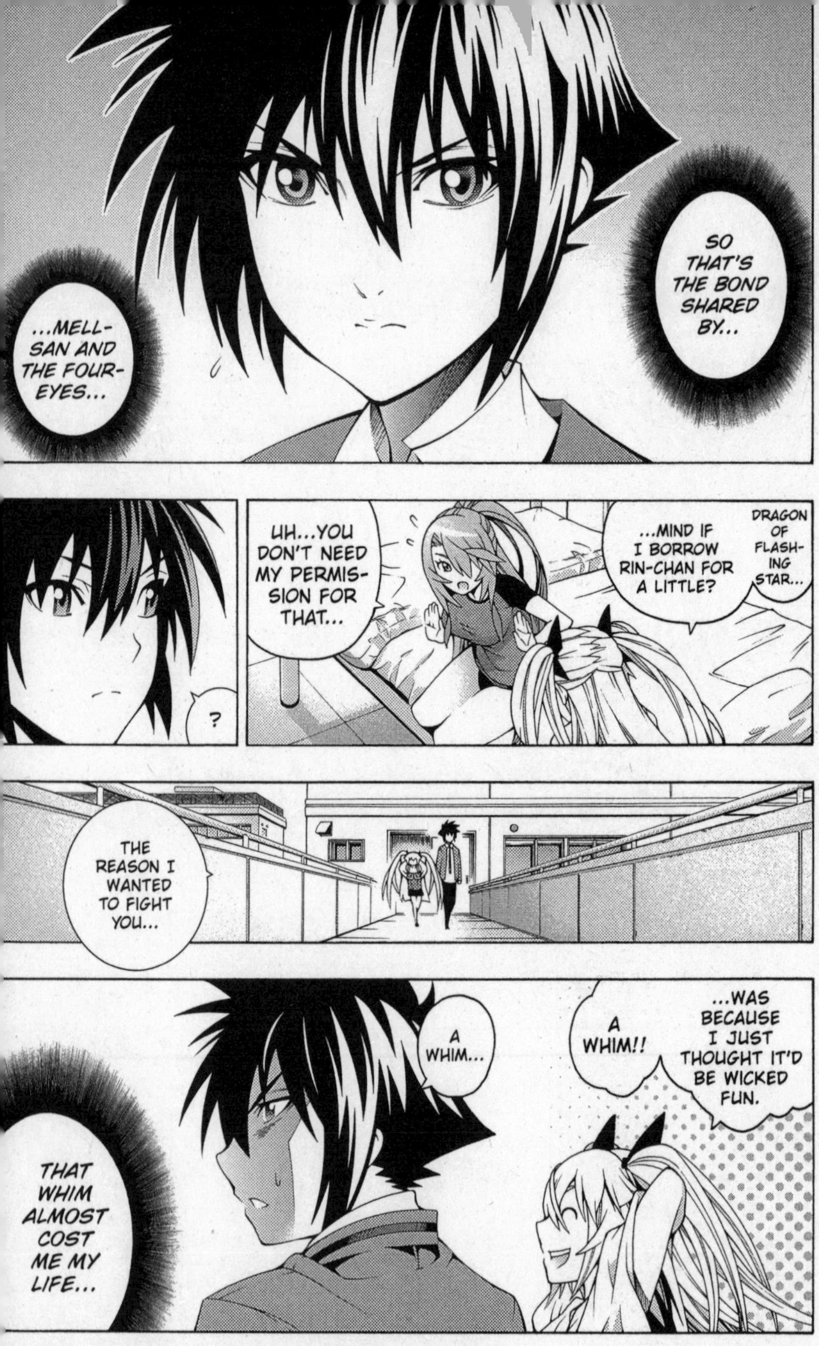
SO THAT'S THE BOND SHARED BY...
...MELL-SAN AND THE FOUR-EYES...
DRAGON OF FLASHING STAR...
...MIND IF I BORROW RIN-CHAN FOR A LITTLE?
UH...YOU DON'T NEED MY PERMISSION FOR THAT...
?
THE REASON I WANTED TO FIGHT YOU...
...WAS BECAUSE I JUST THOUGHT IT'D BE WICKED FUN.
A WHIM!!
A WHIM...
THAT WHIM ALMOST COST ME MY LIFE...

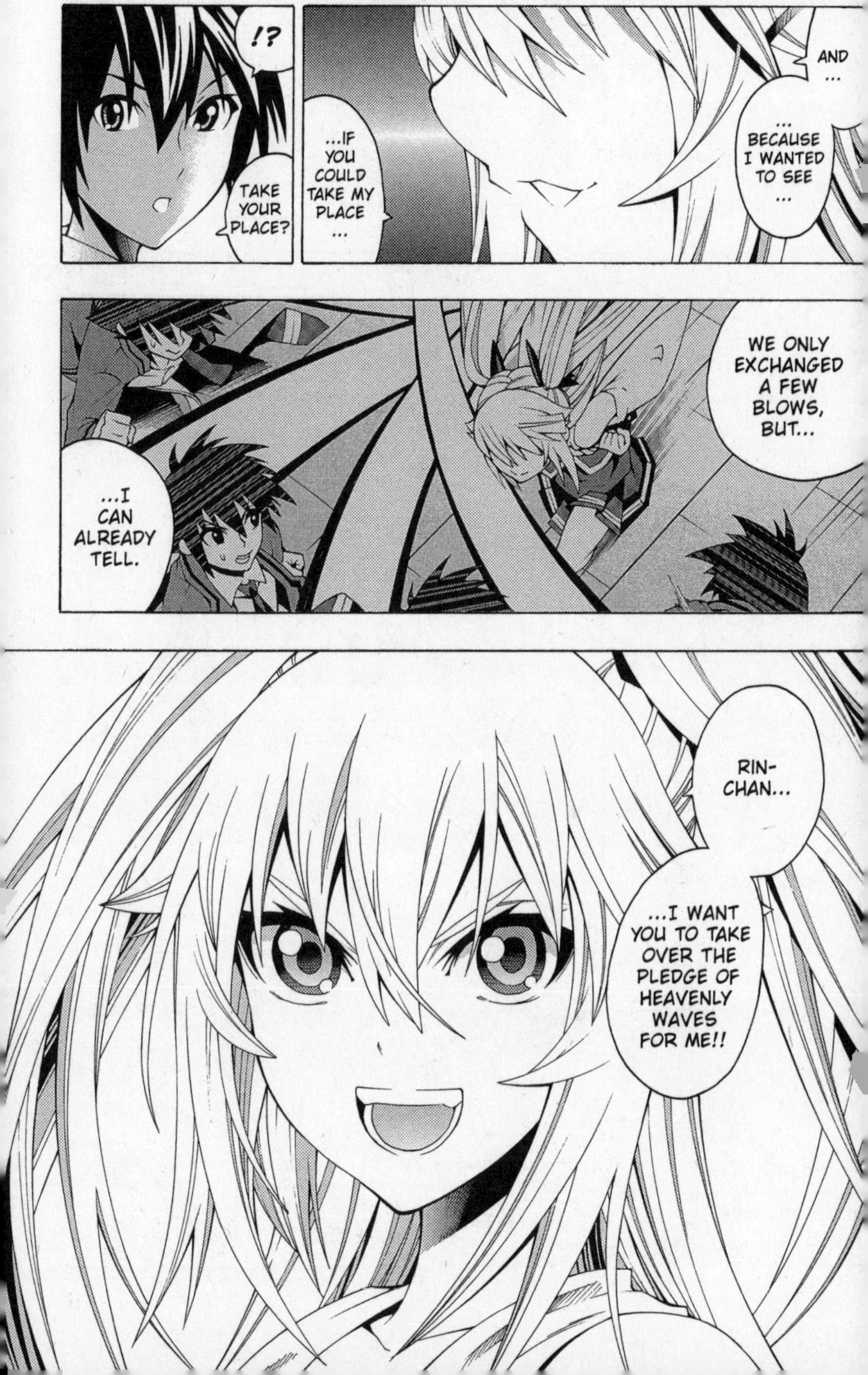
AND ...
... BECAUSE I WANTED TO SEE ...
...IF YOU COULD TAKE MY PLACE ...
!?
TAKE YOUR PLACE?
WE ONLY EXCHANGED A FEW BLOWS, BUT...
...I CAN ALREADY TELL.
RIN-CHAN...
...I WANT YOU TO TAKE OVER THE PLEDGE OF HEAVENLY WAVES FOR ME!!

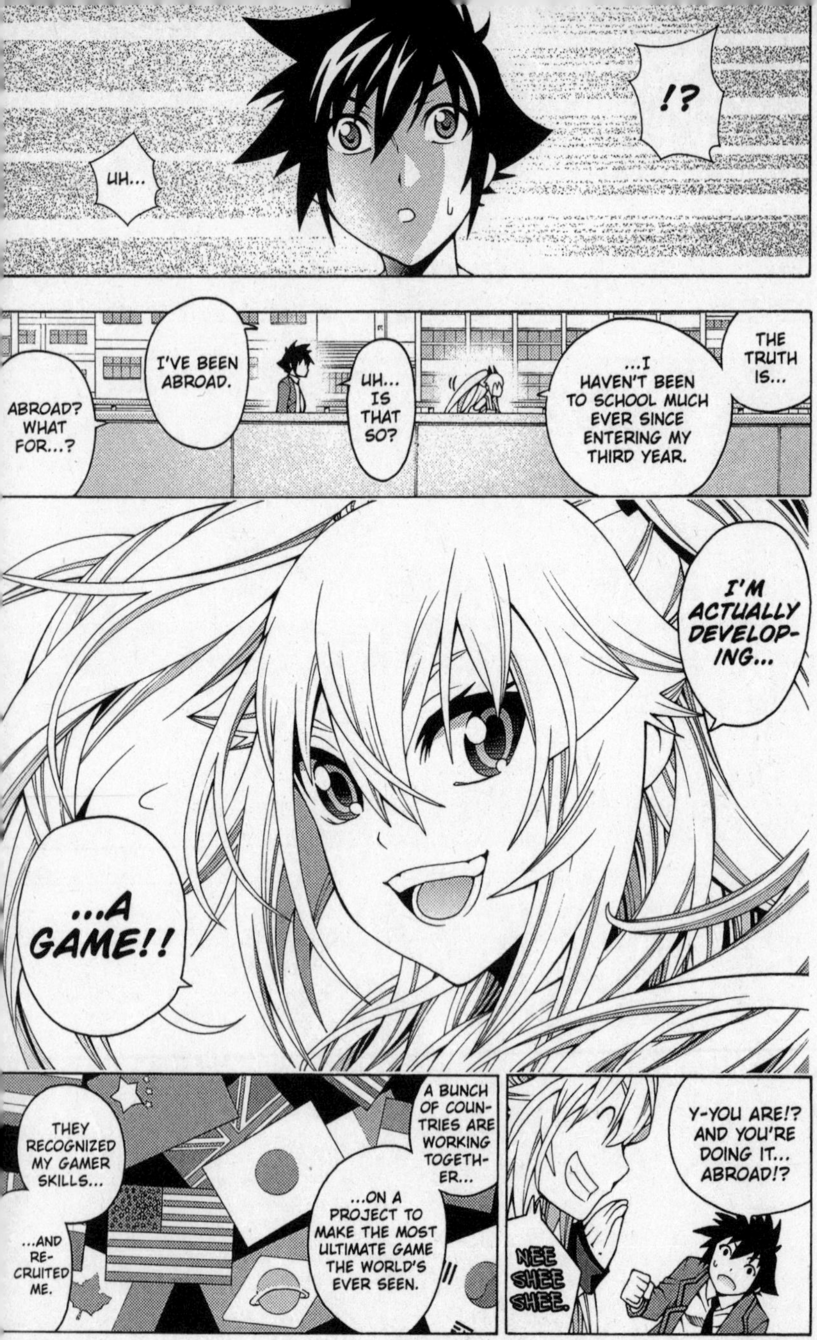
!?
UH...
THE TRUTH IS...
...I HAVEN'T BEEN TO SCHOOL MUCH EVER SINCE ENTERING MY THIRD YEAR.
UH... IS THAT SO?
I'VE BEEN ABROAD.
ABROAD? WHAT FOR...?
I'M ACTUALLY DEVELOPING...
...A GAME!!
Y-YOU ARE!? AND YOU'RE DOING IT... ABROAD!?
NEE SHEE SHEE.
A BUNCH OF COUNTRIES ARE WORKING TOGETHER...
...ON A PROJECT TO MAKE THE MOST ULTIMATE GAME THE WORLD'S EVER SEEN.
THEY RECOGNIZED MY GAMER SKILLS...
...AND RECRUITED ME.

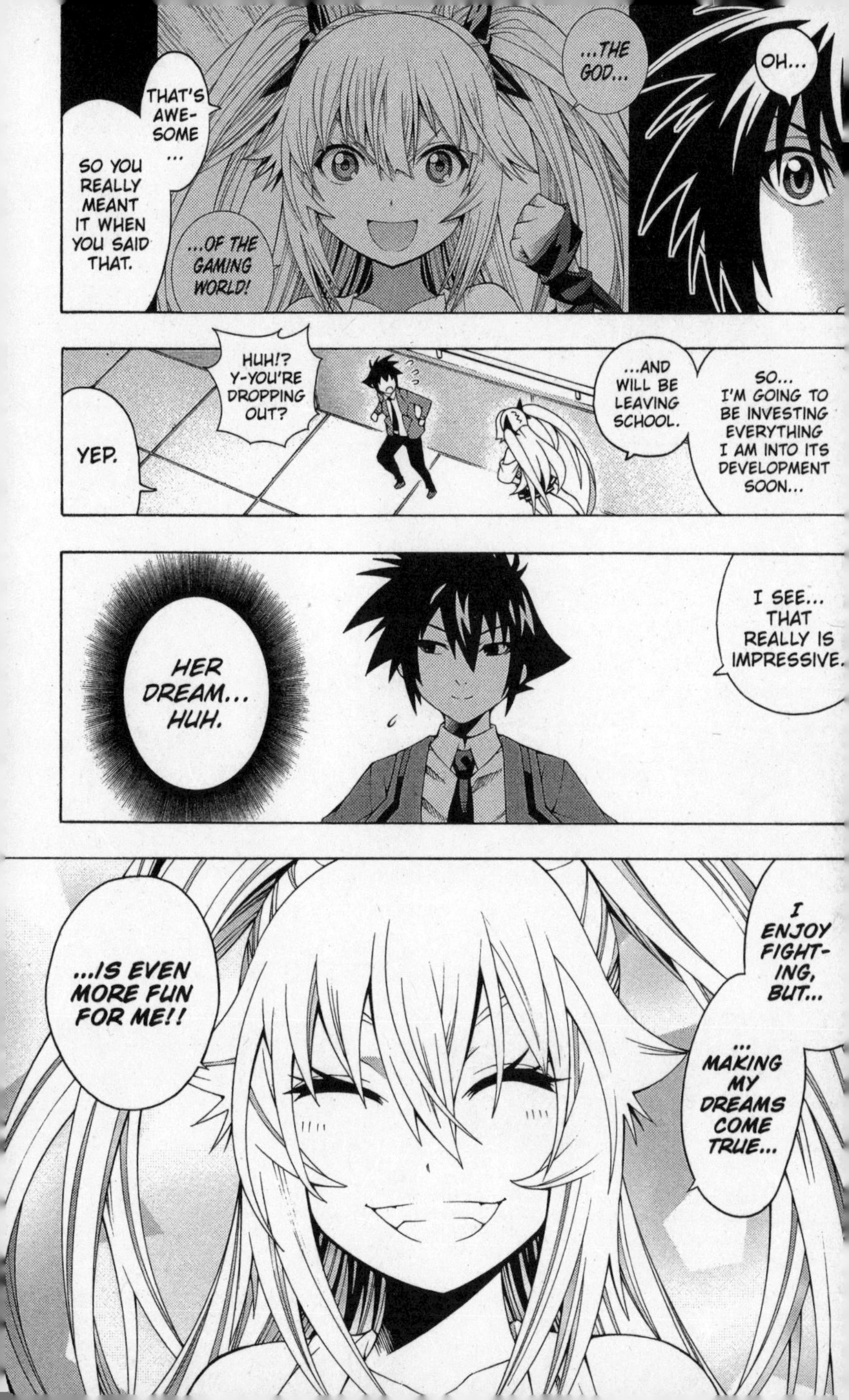
OH...
...THE GOD...
...OF THE GAMING WORLD!
THAT'S AWE-SOME...
SO YOU REALLY MEANT IT WHEN YOU SAID THAT.
SO... I'M GOING TO BE INVESTING EVERYTHING I AM INTO ITS DEVELOPMENT SOON...
...AND WILL BE LEAVING SCHOOL.
HUH!? Y-YOU'RE DROPPING OUT?
YEP.
I SEE... THAT REALLY IS IMPRESSIVE.
HER DREAM... HUH.
I ENJOY FIGHT-ING, BUT...
...MAKING MY DREAMS COME TRUE...
...IS EVEN MORE FUN FOR ME!!

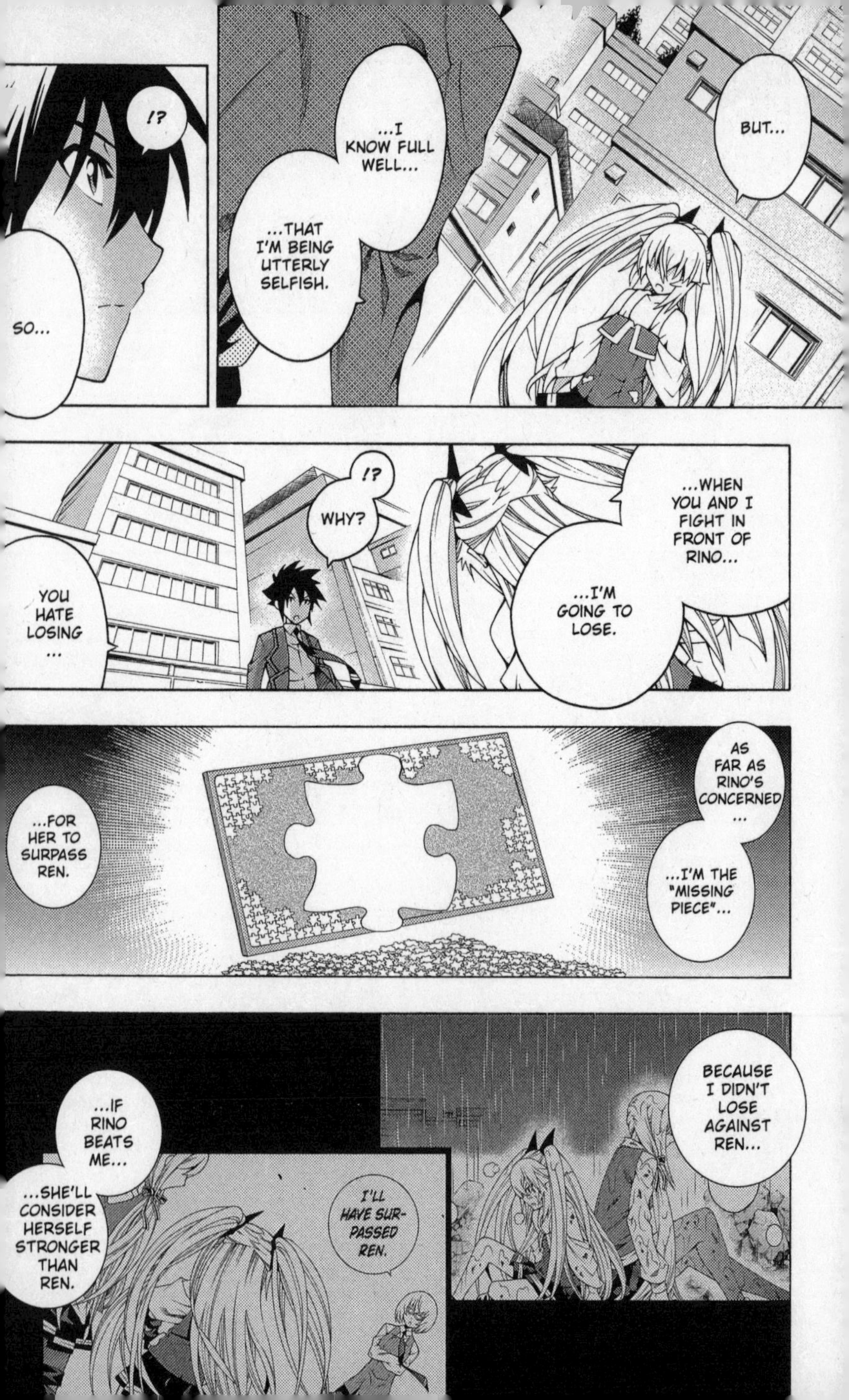
BUT...
...I KNOW FULL WELL...
...THAT I'M BEING UTTERLY SELFISH.
!?
SO...
...WHEN YOU AND I FIGHT IN FRONT OF RINO...
...I'M GOING TO LOSE.
!?
WHY?
YOU HATE LOSING ...
AS FAR AS RINO'S CONCERNED ...
...I'M THE "MISSING PIECE"...
...FOR HER TO SURPASS REN.
BECAUSE I DIDN'T LOSE AGAINST REN...
...IF RINO BEATS ME...
...SHE'LL CONSIDER HERSELF STRONGER THAN REN.
I'LL HAVE SUR-PASSED REN.

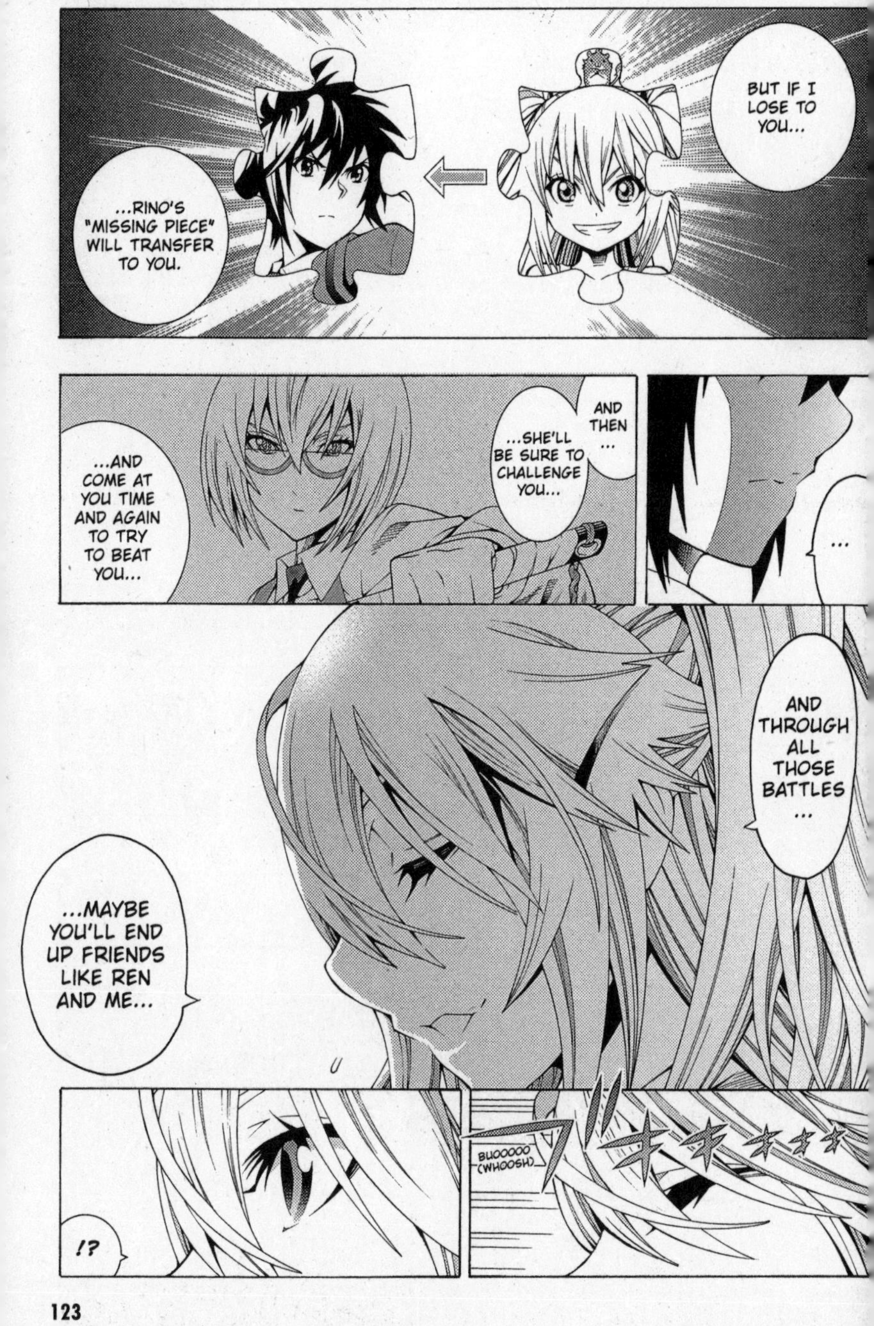
BUT IF I LOSE TO YOU...
...RINO'S "MISSING PIECE" WILL TRANSFER TO YOU.
...
AND THEN ...
...SHE'LL BE SURE TO CHALLENGE YOU...
...AND COME AT YOU TIME AND AGAIN TO TRY TO BEAT YOU...
AND THROUGH ALL THOSE BATTLES ...
...MAYBE YOU'LL END UP FRIENDS LIKE REN AND ME...
BUOOOOO (WHOOSH)
!?

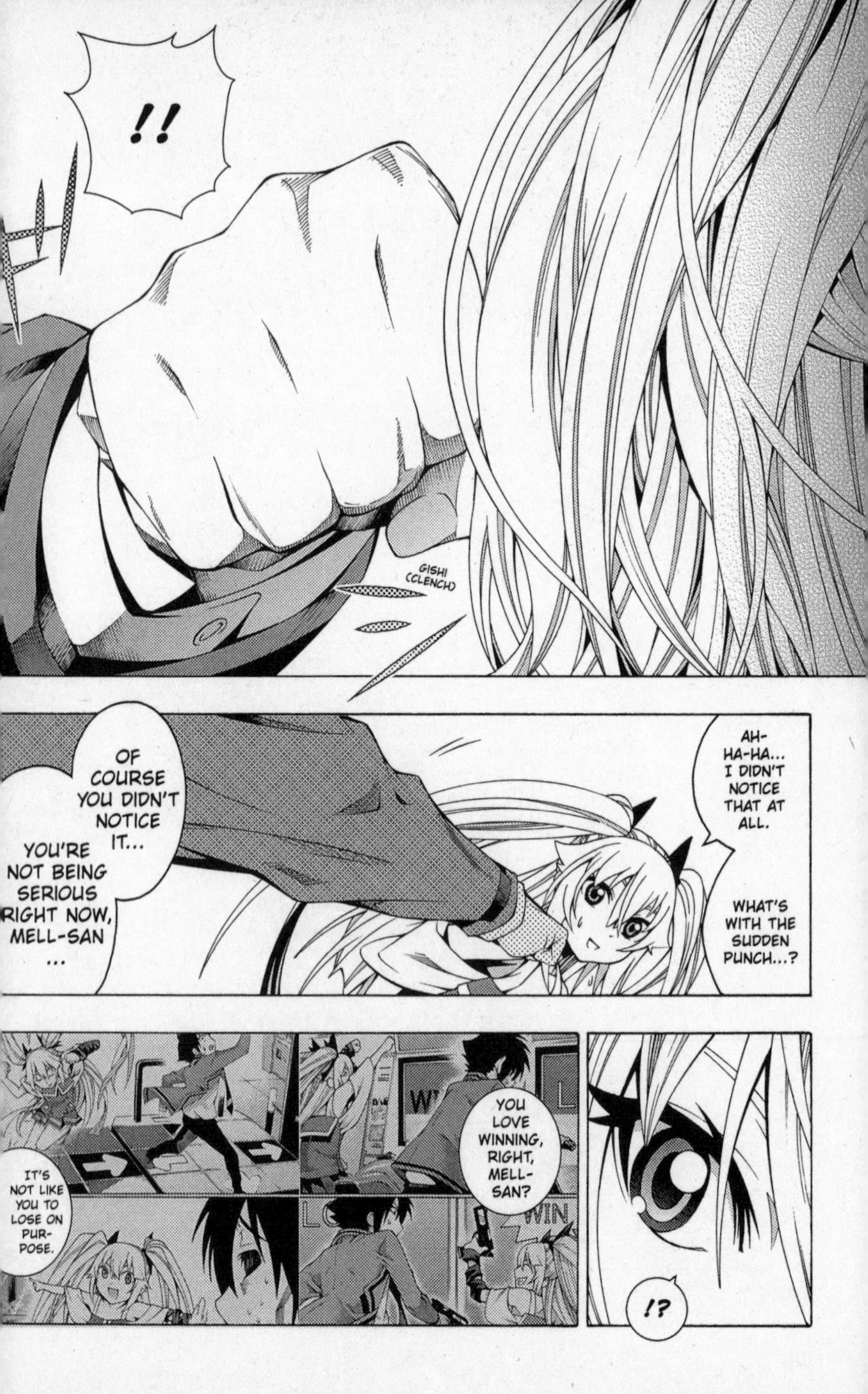
!!
GISHI (CLENCH)
AH-HA-HA... I DIDN'T NOTICE THAT AT ALL.
WHAT'S WITH THE SUDDEN PUNCH...?
OF COURSE YOU DIDN'T NOTICE IT...
YOU'RE NOT BEING SERIOUS RIGHT NOW, MELL-SAN ...
!?
YOU LOVE WINNING, RIGHT, MELL-SAN?
IT'S NOT LIKE YOU TO LOSE ON PUR-POSE.

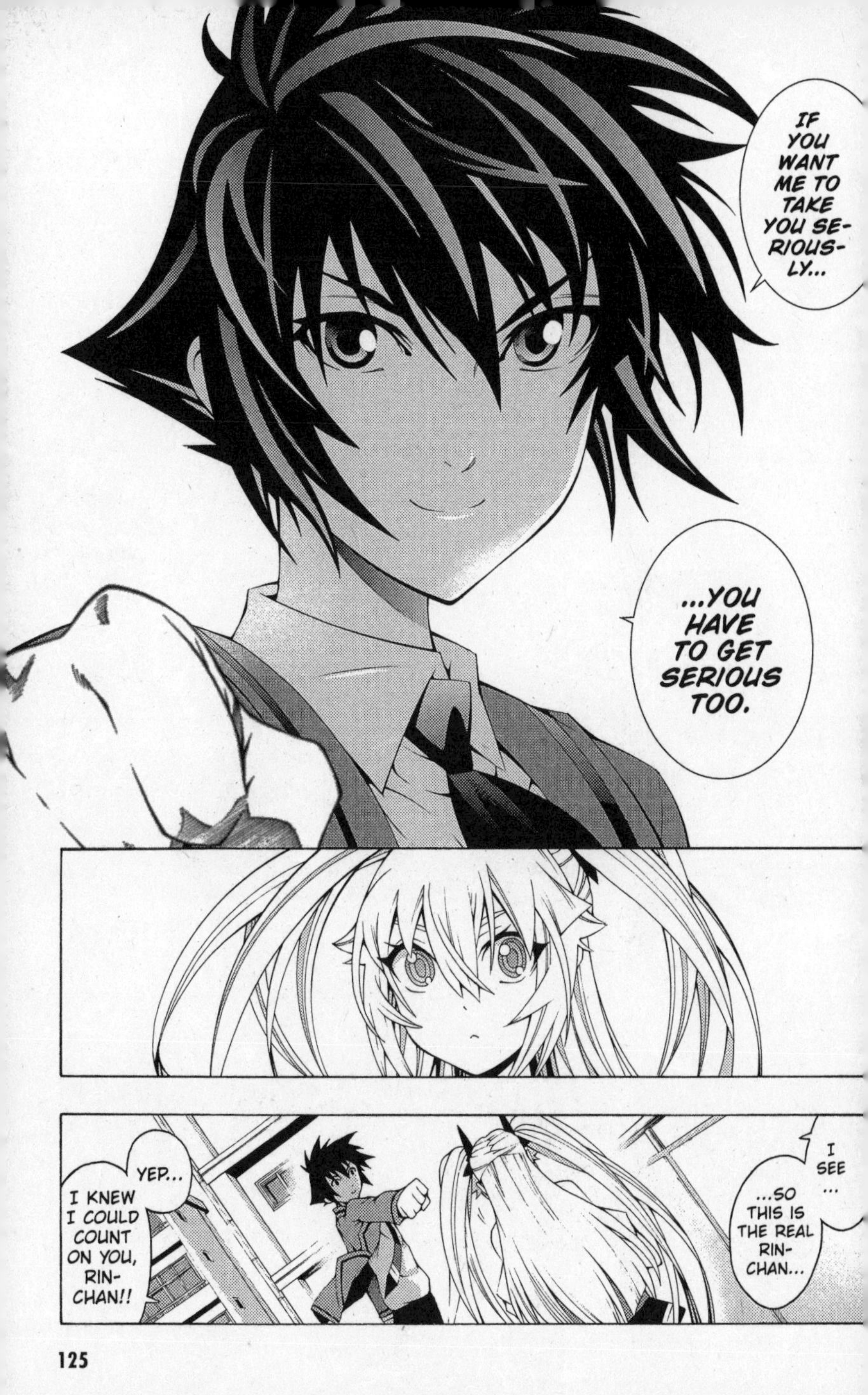
IF YOU WANT ME TO TAKE YOU SE-RIOUS-LY...
...YOU HAVE TO GET SERIOUS TOO.
I SEE...
...SO THIS IS THE REAL RIN-CHAN...
YEP...
I KNEW I COULD COUNT ON YOU, RIN-CHAN!!

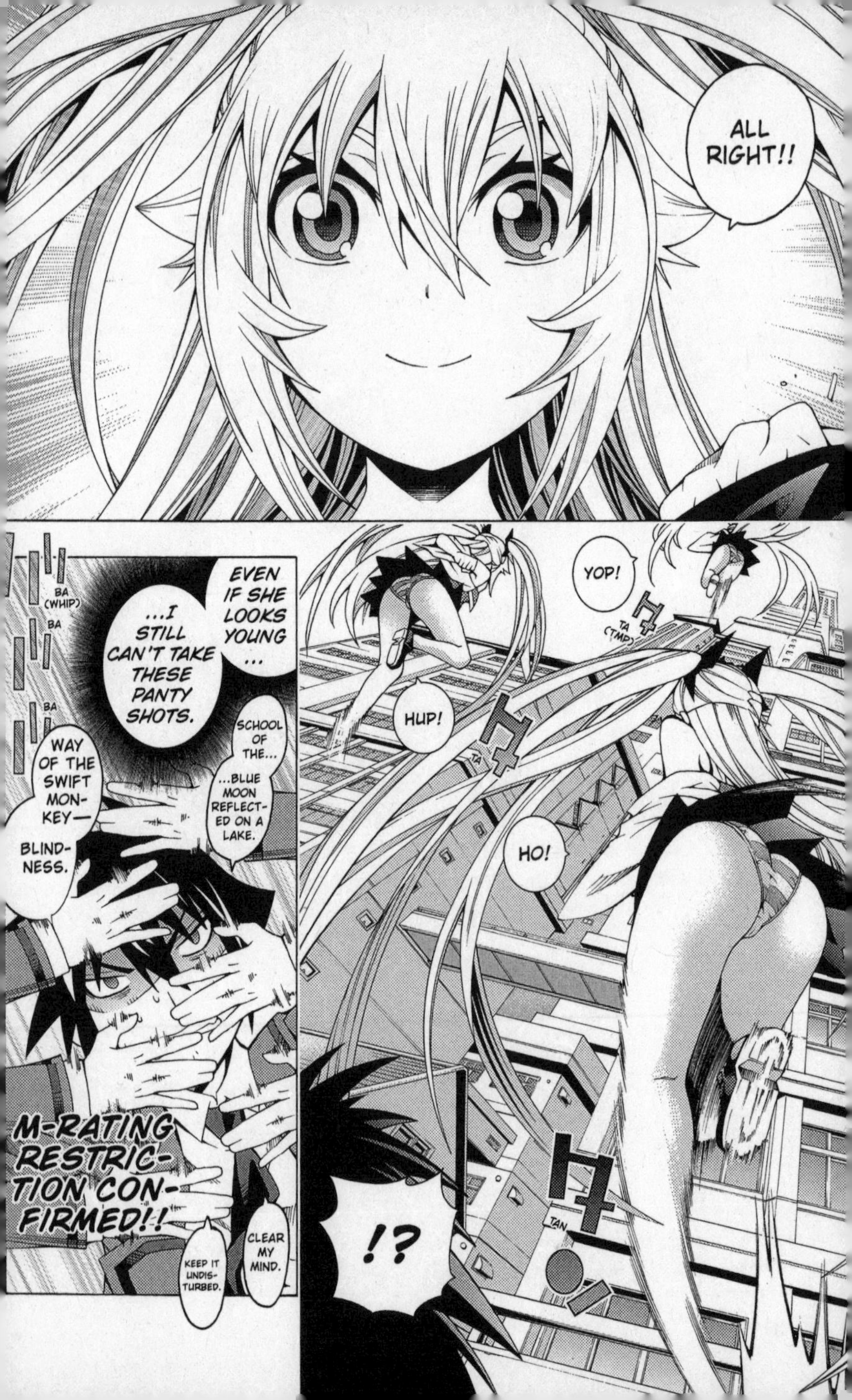
ALL RIGHT!!
YOP!
TA (TMP)
HUP!
TA
HO!
TAN
!?
EVEN IF SHE LOOKS YOUNG...
...I STILL CAN'T TAKE THESE PANTY SHOTS.
BA (WHIP)
BA
BA
SCHOOL OF THE...
...BLUE MOON REFLECTED ON A LAKE.
WAY OF THE SWIFT MONKEY—
BLINDNESS.
M-RATING RESTRICTION CONFIRMED!!
CLEAR MY MIND.
KEEP IT UNDISTURBED.

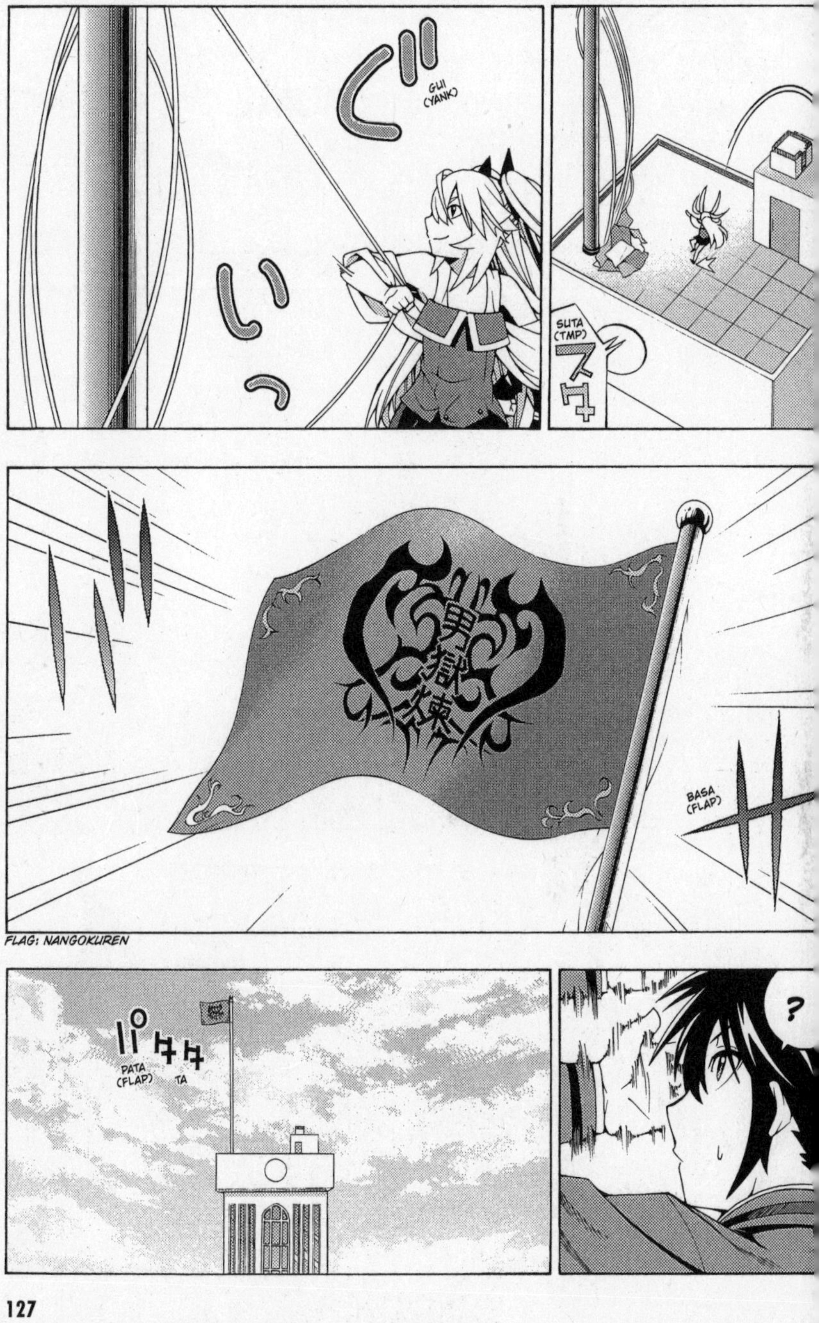
SUTA (TMP)
GUI (YANK)
BASA (FLAP)
FLAG: NANGOKUREN
?
PATA (FLAP) TA

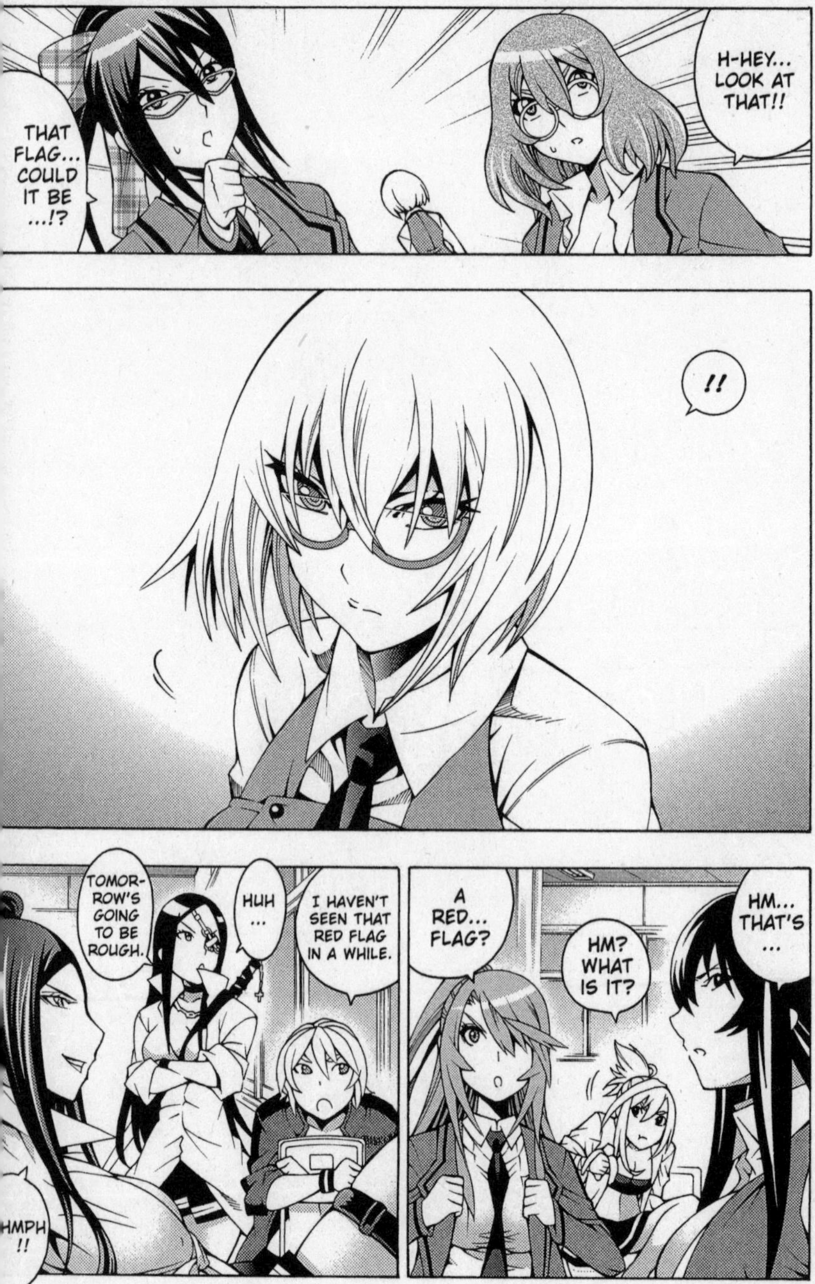
H-HEY... LOOK AT THAT!!
THAT FLAG... COULD IT BE ...!?
!!
HM... THAT'S ...
HM? WHAT IS IT?
A RED... FLAG?
I HAVEN'T SEEN THAT RED FLAG IN A WHILE.
HUH ...
TOMOR-ROW'S GOING TO BE ROUGH.
HMPH !!

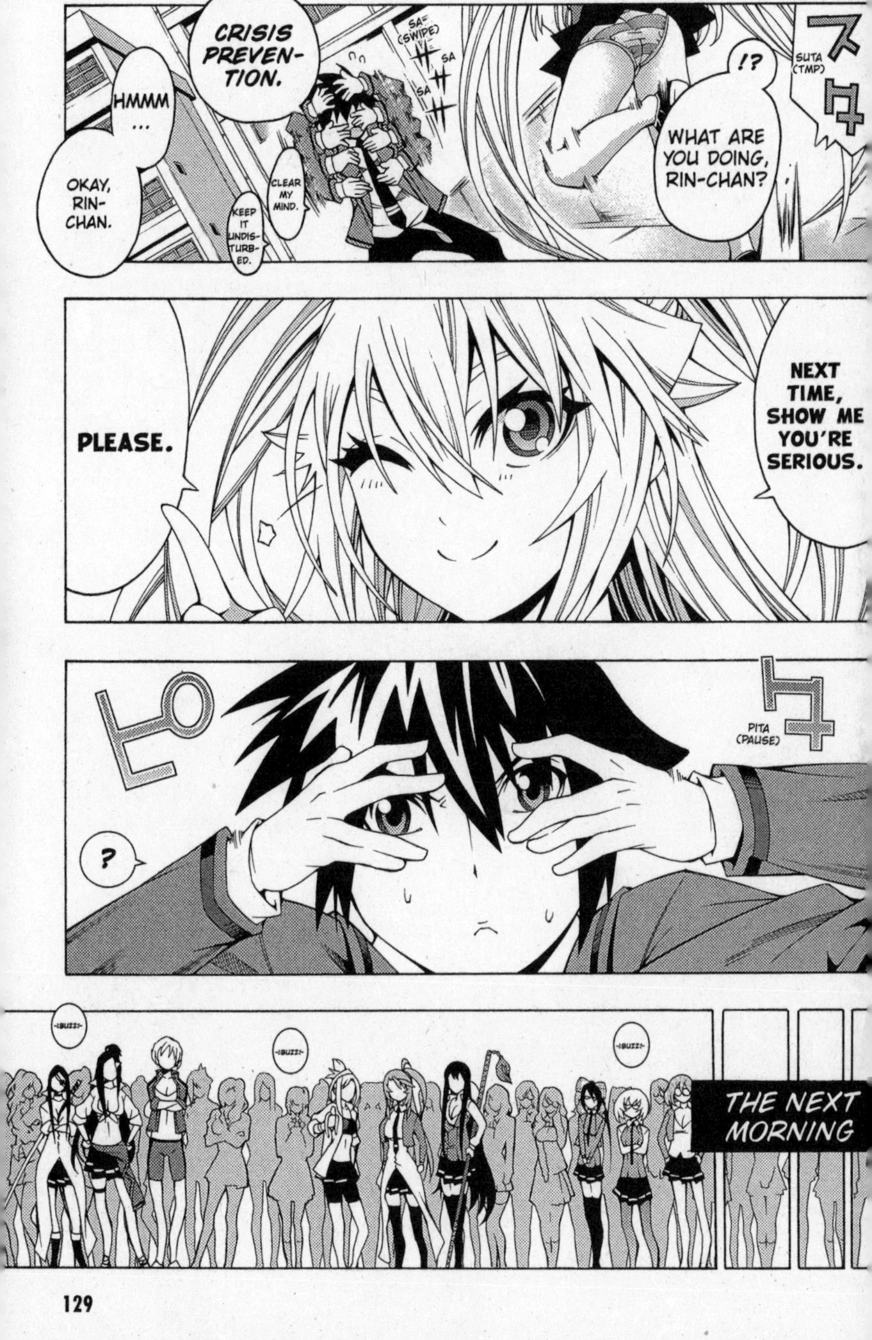

SUTA (TMP)
!?
WHAT ARE YOU DOING, RIN-CHAN?
SA (SWIPE)
SA
SA
CRISIS PREVEN-TION.
CLEAR MY MIND.
KEEP IT UNDIS-TURB-ED.
HMMM ...
OKAY, RIN-CHAN.
NEXT TIME, SHOW ME YOU'RE SERIOUS.
PLEASE.
PITA (PAUSE)
?
THE NEXT MORNING
-BUZZ-
-BUZZ-
-BUZZ-

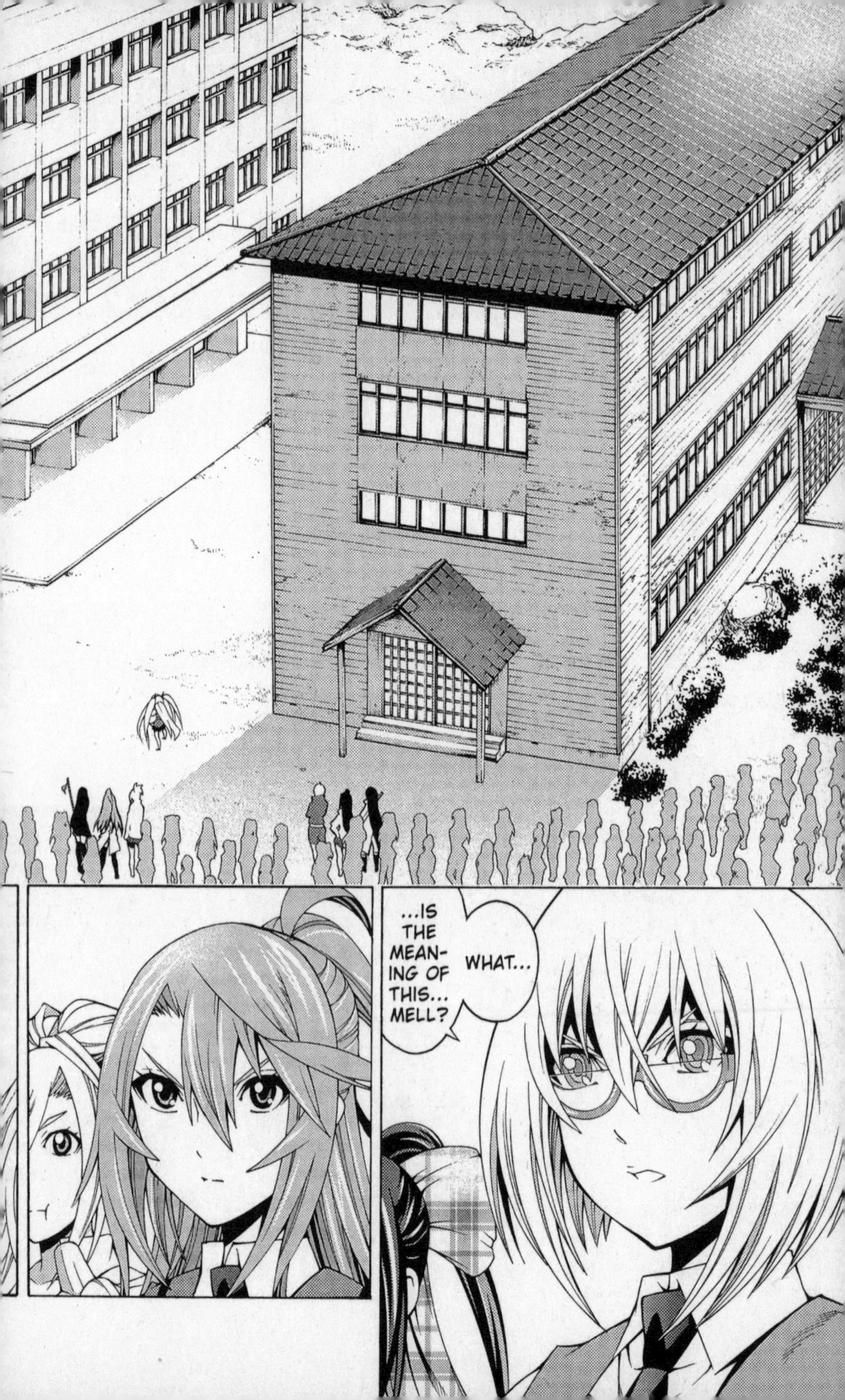
WHAT...
...IS THE MEANING OF THIS... MELL?

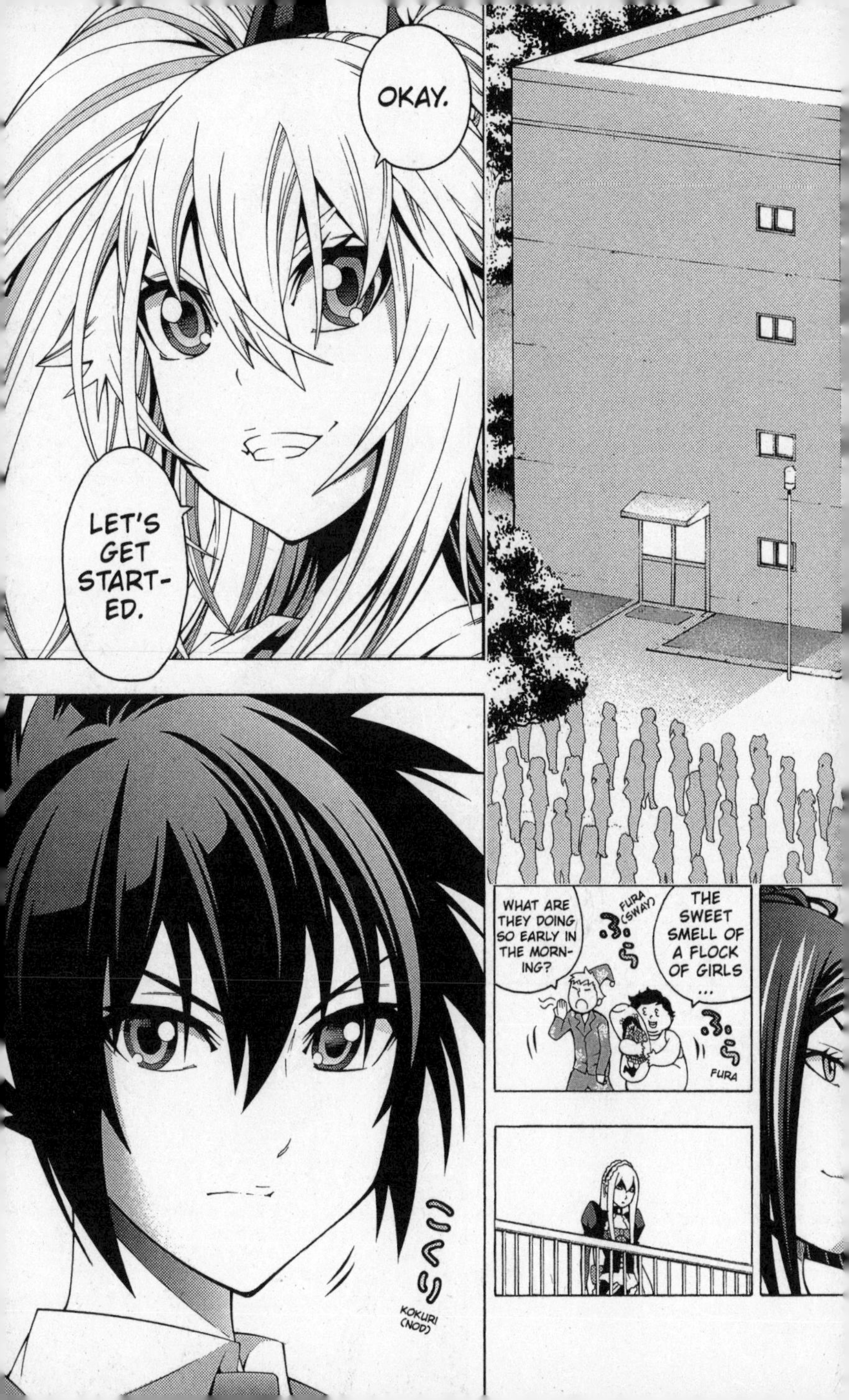

THE SWEET SMELL OF A FLOCK OF GIRLS ...
FURA (SWAY)
FURA
WHAT ARE THEY DOING SO EARLY IN THE MORNING?
OKAY.
LET'S GET START-ED.
KOKURI (NOD)

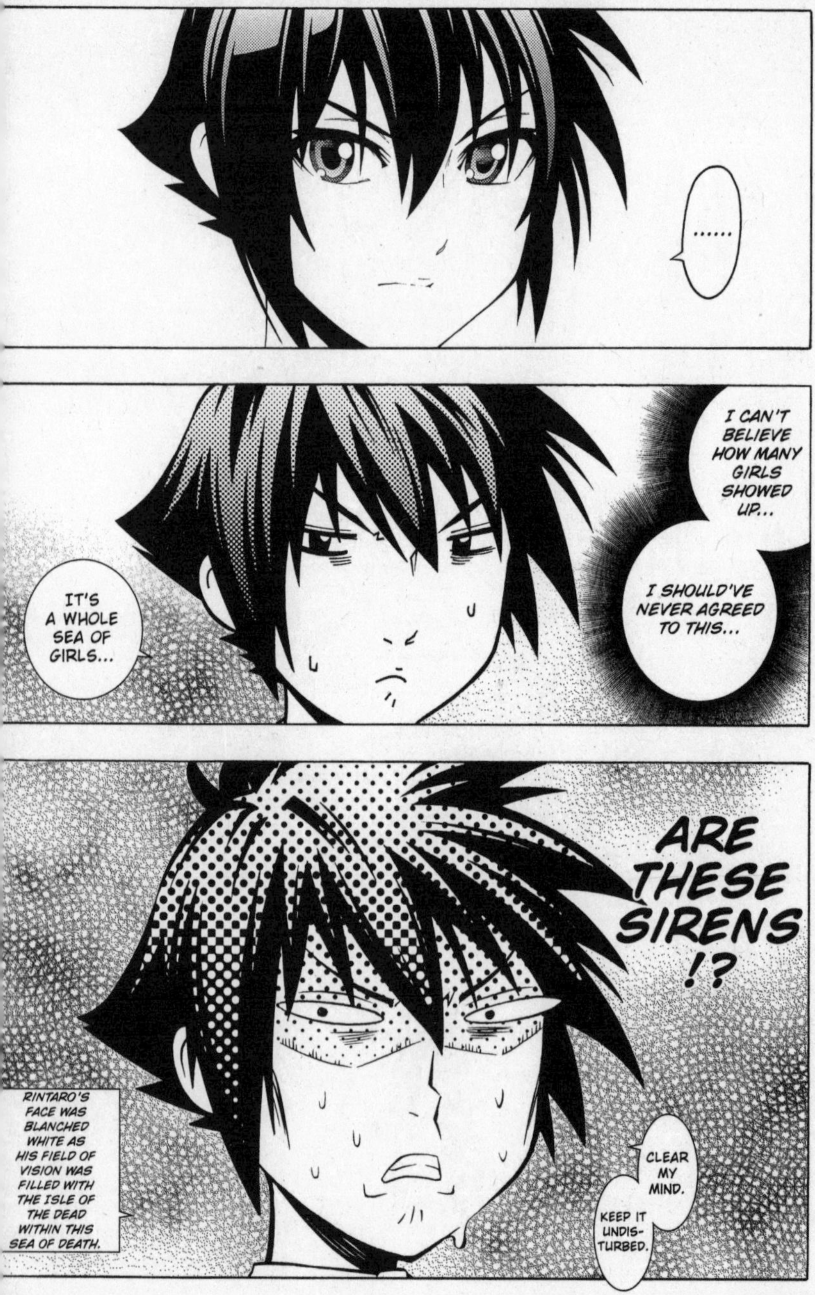
......
I CAN'T BELIEVE HOW MANY GIRLS SHOWED UP...
I SHOULD'VE NEVER AGREED TO THIS...
IT'S A WHOLE SEA OF GIRLS...
ARE THESE SIRENS !?
CLEAR MY MIND.
KEEP IT UNDIS-TURBED.
RINTARO'S FACE WAS BLANCHED WHITE AS HIS FIELD OF VISION WAS FILLED WITH THE ISLE OF THE DEAD WITHIN THIS SEA OF DEATH.

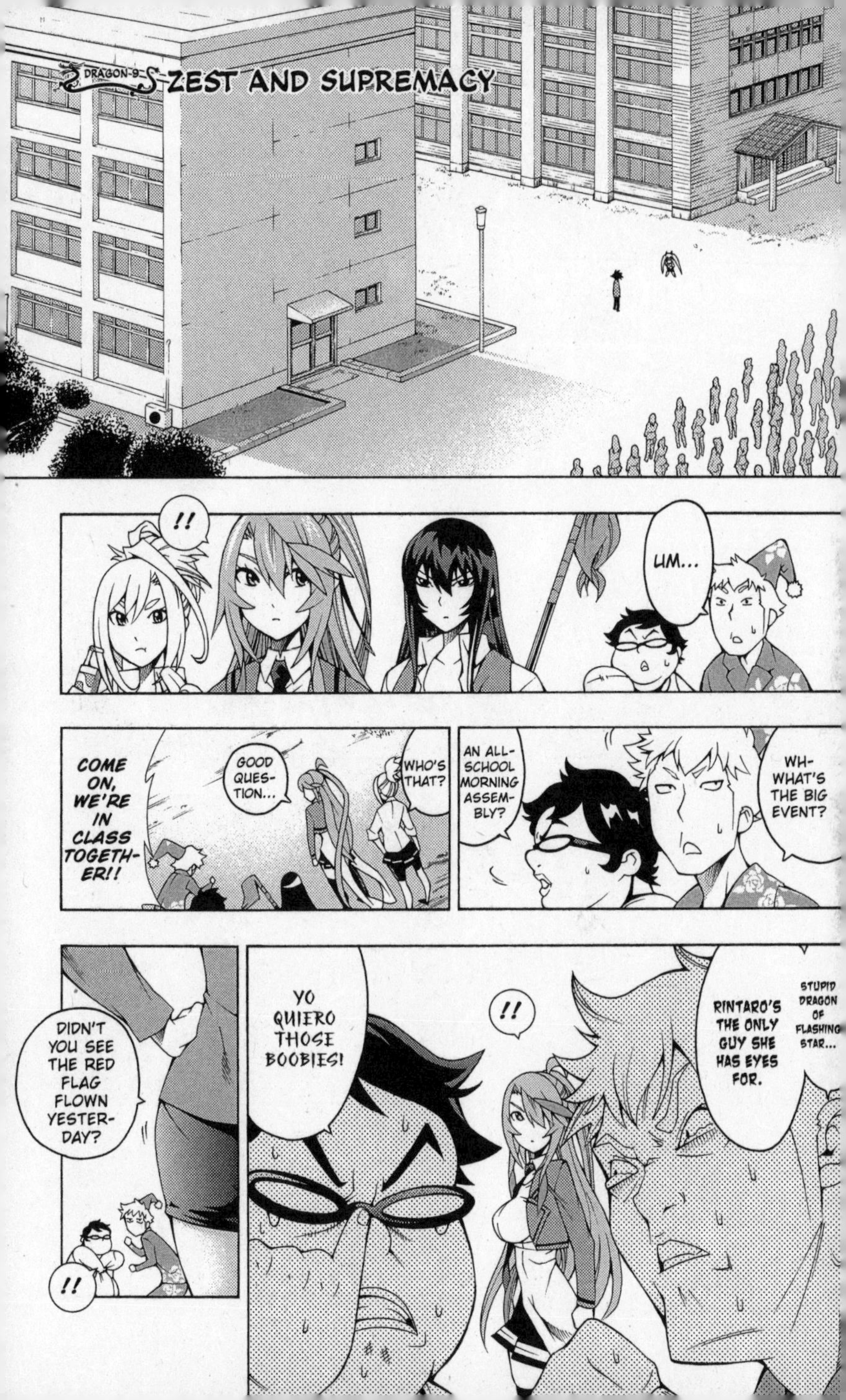
DRAGON-9 ZEST AND SUPREMACY
UM...
!!
WH-WHAT'S THE BIG EVENT?
AN ALL-SCHOOL MORNING ASSEMBLY?
WHO'S THAT?
GOOD QUESTION...
COME ON, WE'RE IN CLASS TOGETHER!!
STUPID DRAGON OF FLASHING STAR...
RINTARO'S THE ONLY GUY SHE HAS EYES FOR.
!!
YO QUIERO THOSE BOOBIES!
DIDN'T YOU SEE THE RED FLAG FLOWN YESTERDAY?
!!

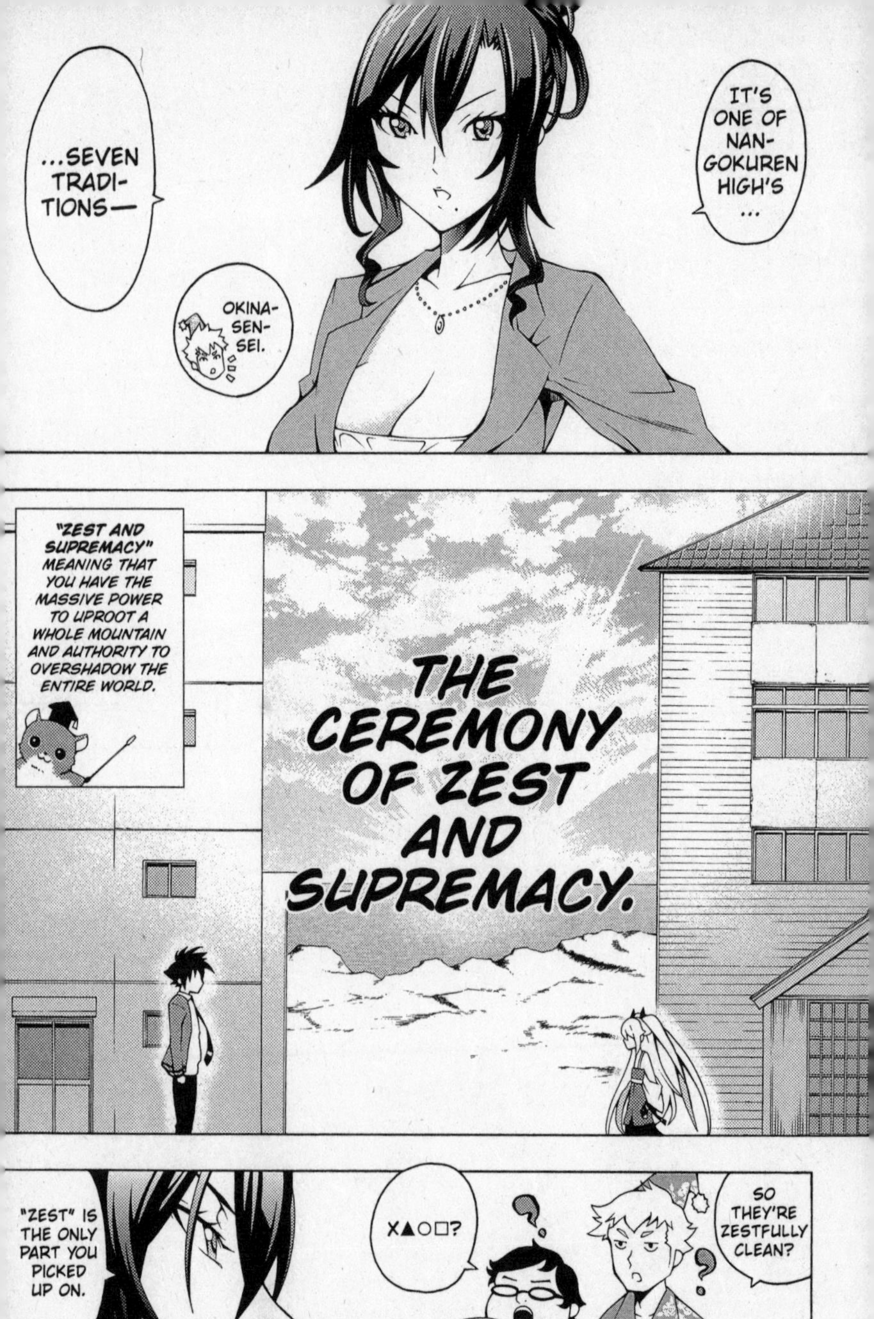
IT'S ONE OF NANGOKUREN HIGH'S ...
...SEVEN TRADITIONS—
OKINA-SENSEI.
THE CEREMONY OF ZEST AND SUPREMACY.
"ZEST AND SUPREMACY" MEANING THAT YOU HAVE THE MASSIVE POWER TO UPROOT A WHOLE MOUNTAIN AND AUTHORITY TO OVERSHADOW THE ENTIRE WORLD.
SO THEY'RE ZESTFULLY CLEAN?
X▲O□?
"ZEST" IS THE ONLY PART YOU PICKED UP ON.

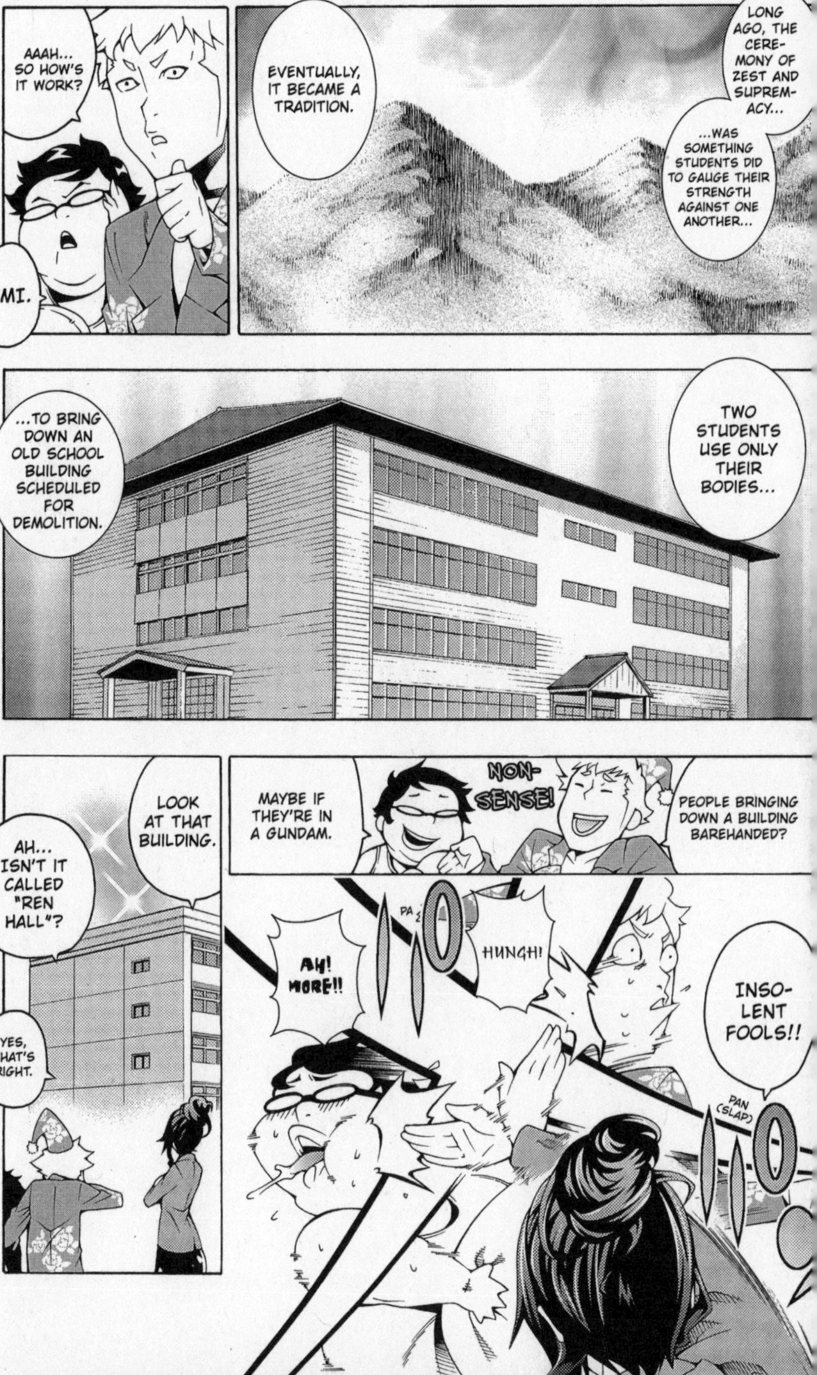
LONG AGO, THE CEREMONY OF ZEST AND SUPREMACY...
...WAS SOMETHING STUDENTS DID TO GAUGE THEIR STRENGTH AGAINST ONE ANOTHER...
EVENTUALLY, IT BECAME A TRADITION.
AAAH... SO HOW'S IT WORK?
NMI.
TWO STUDENTS USE ONLY THEIR BODIES...
...TO BRING DOWN AN OLD SCHOOL BUILDING SCHEDULED FOR DEMOLITION.
PEOPLE BRINGING DOWN A BUILDING BAREHANDED?
NON-SENSE!
MAYBE IF THEY'RE IN A GUNDAM.
INSOLENT FOOLS!!
PAN (SLAP)
HUNGH!
PA
AH! MORE!!
LOOK AT THAT BUILDING.
AH... ISN'T IT CALLED "REN HALL"?
YES, THAT'S RIGHT.

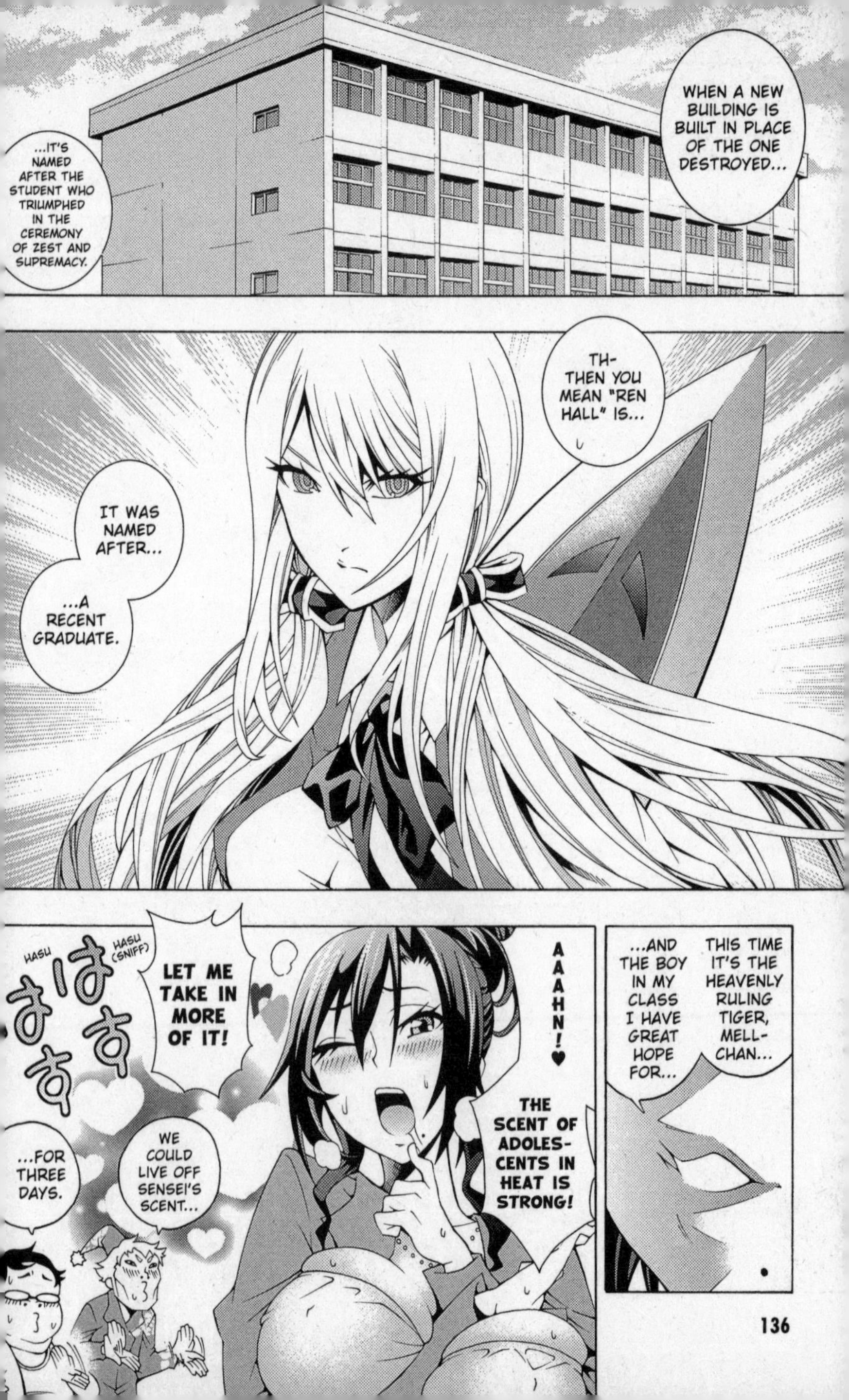
WHEN A NEW BUILDING IS BUILT IN PLACE OF THE ONE DESTROYED...
...IT'S NAMED AFTER THE STUDENT WHO TRIUMPHED IN THE CEREMONY OF ZEST AND SUPREMACY.
TH- THEN YOU MEAN "REN HALL" IS...
IT WAS NAMED AFTER...
...A RECENT GRADUATE.
THIS TIME IT'S THE HEAVENLY RULING TIGER, MELL-CHAN...
...AND THE BOY IN MY CLASS I HAVE GREAT HOPE FOR...
AAAAHN!♥
THE SCENT OF ADOLES-CENTS IN HEAT IS STRONG!
LET ME TAKE IN MORE OF IT!
HASU
HASU (SNIFF)
はすはす
WE COULD LIVE OFF SENSEI'S SCENT...
...FOR THREE DAYS.

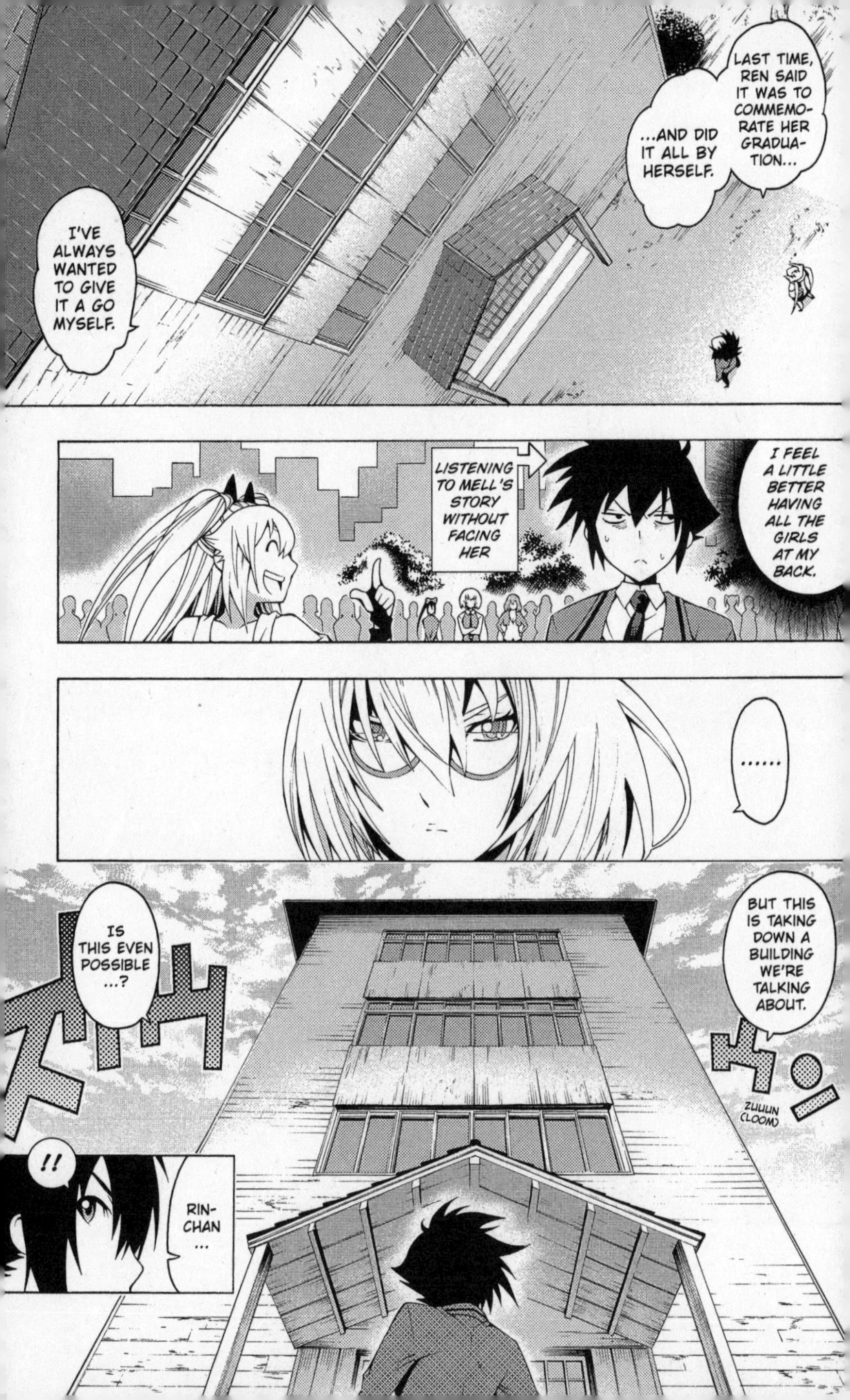
LAST TIME, REN SAID IT WAS TO COMMEMORATE HER GRADUATION...
...AND DID IT ALL BY HERSELF.
I'VE ALWAYS WANTED TO GIVE IT A GO MYSELF.
I FEEL A LITTLE BETTER HAVING ALL THE GIRLS AT MY BACK.
LISTENING TO MELL'S STORY WITHOUT FACING HER
......
BUT THIS IS TAKING DOWN A BUILDING WE'RE TALKING ABOUT.
ZUUUN (LOOM)
IS THIS EVEN POSSIBLE ...?
RIN-CHAN ...
!!

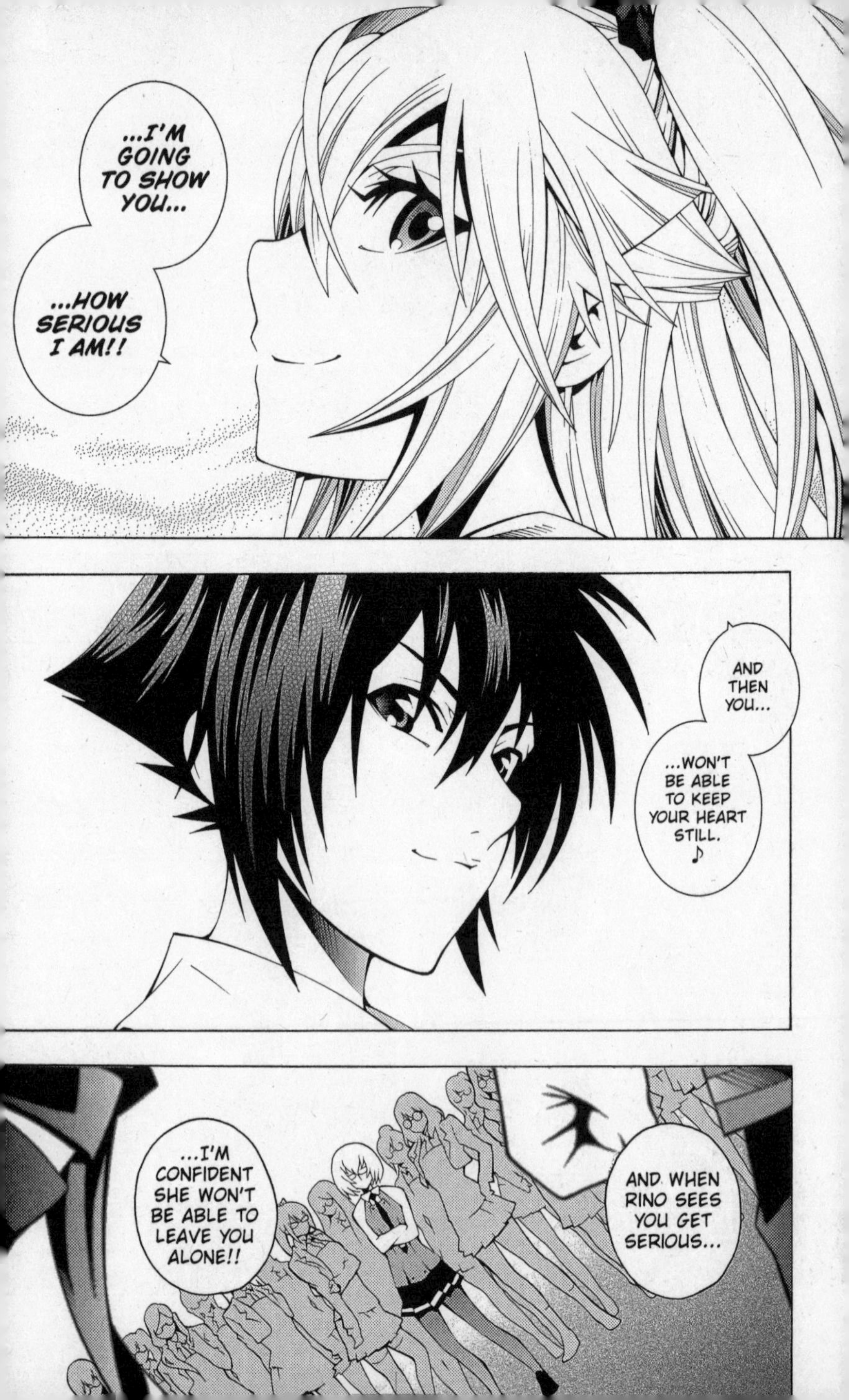
...I'M GOING TO SHOW YOU...
...HOW SERIOUS I AM!!
AND THEN YOU...
...WON'T BE ABLE TO KEEP YOUR HEART STILL. ♪
AND WHEN RINO SEES YOU GET SERIOUS...
...I'M CONFIDENT SHE WON'T BE ABLE TO LEAVE YOU ALONE!!

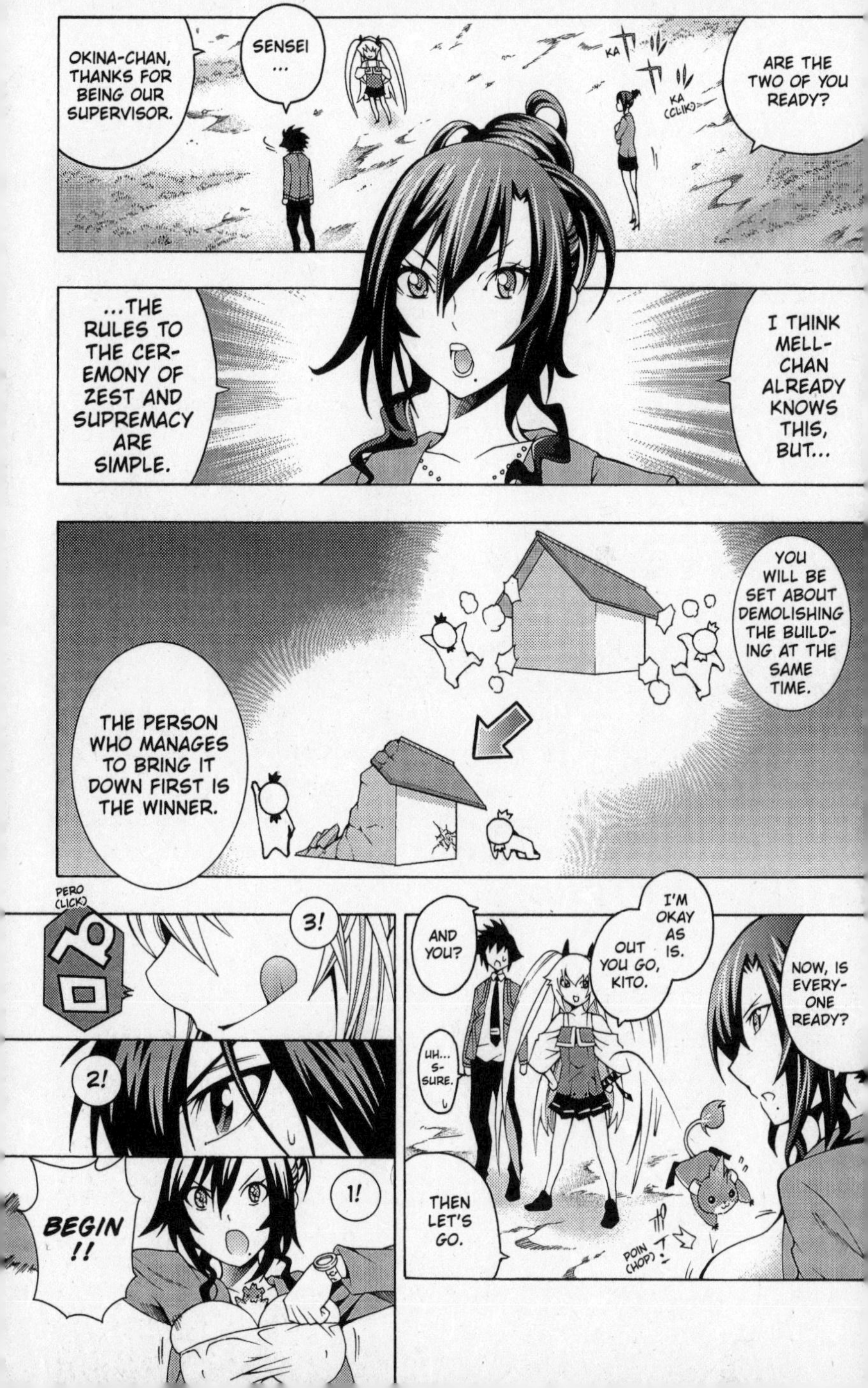
ARE THE TWO OF YOU READY?
KA KA (CLIK)
SENSEI ...
OKINA-CHAN, THANKS FOR BEING OUR SUPERVISOR.
I THINK MELL-CHAN ALREADY KNOWS THIS, BUT...
...THE RULES TO THE CER-EMONY OF ZEST AND SUPREMACY ARE SIMPLE.
YOU WILL BE SET ABOUT DEMOLISHING THE BUILD-ING AT THE SAME TIME.
THE PERSON WHO MANAGES TO BRING IT DOWN FIRST IS THE WINNER.
NOW, IS EVERY-ONE READY?
I'M OKAY AS IS.
OUT YOU GO, KITO.
AND YOU?
UH... S-SURE.
POIN (HOP)
THEN LET'S GO.
PERO (LICK)
3!
2!
1!
BEGIN !!

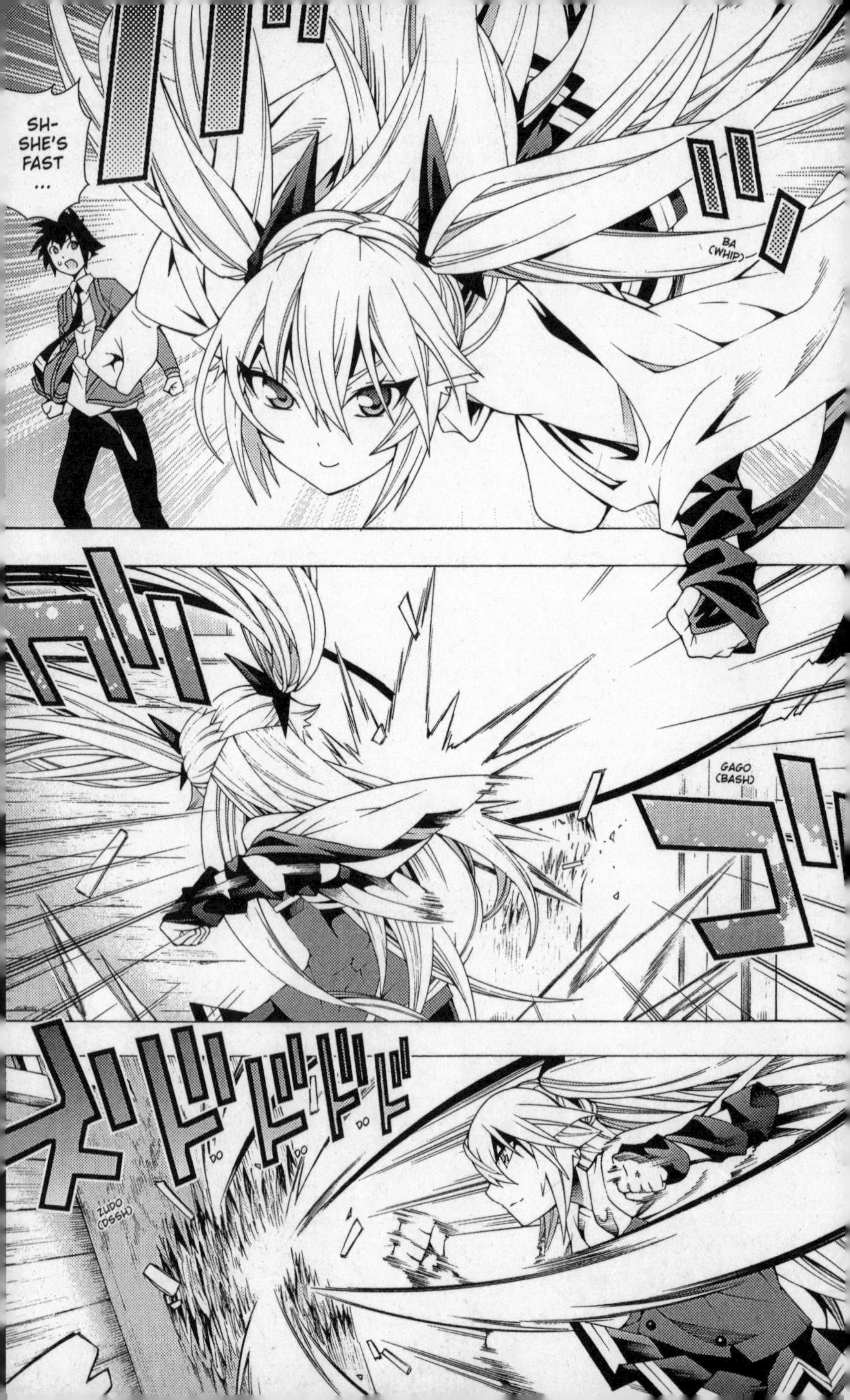
BA (WHIP)
SH-SHE'S FAST ...
GAGO (BASH)
DO
DO
DO
ZUDO (DSSH)

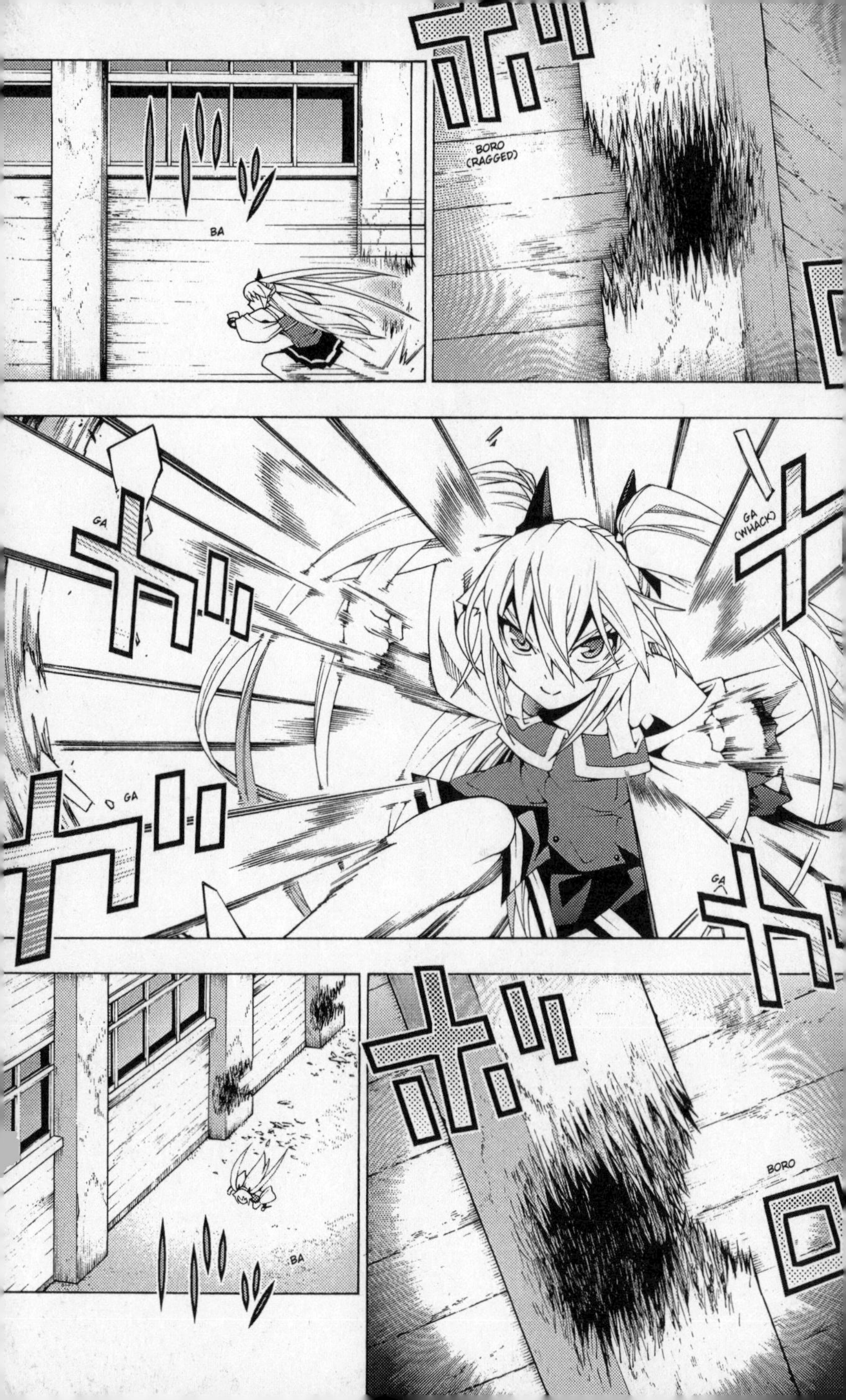
BORO
(RAGGED)
BA
GA
(WHACK)
GA
GA
GA
BORO
BA

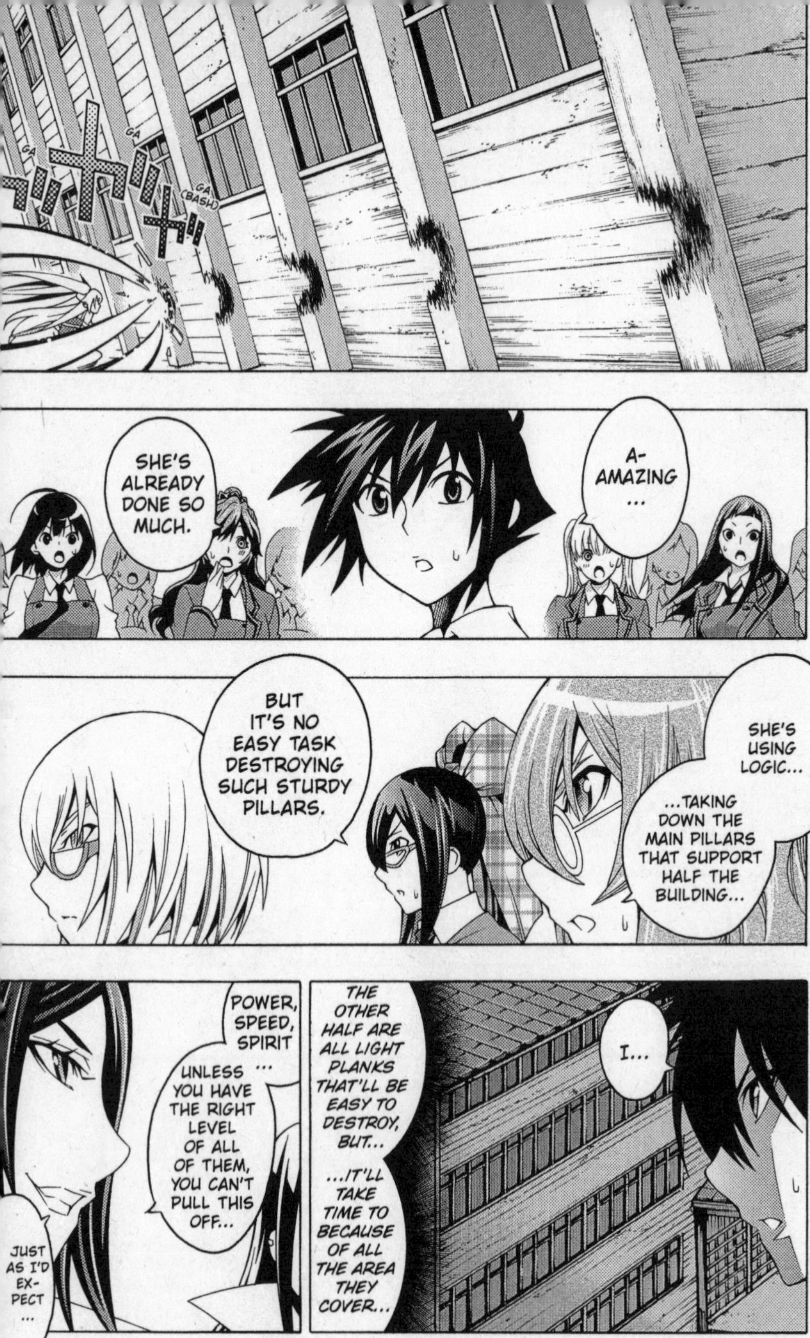
GA
GA
GA
(BASH)
A-AMAZING...
SHE'S ALREADY DONE SO MUCH.
SHE'S USING LOGIC...
...TAKING DOWN THE MAIN PILLARS THAT SUPPORT HALF THE BUILDING...
BUT IT'S NO EASY TASK DESTROYING SUCH STURDY PILLARS.
I...
THE OTHER HALF ARE ALL LIGHT PLANKS THAT'LL BE EASY TO DESTROY, BUT...
...IT'LL TAKE TIME TO BECAUSE OF ALL THE AREA THEY COVER...
POWER, SPEED, SPIRIT...
UNLESS YOU HAVE THE RIGHT LEVEL OF ALL OF THEM, YOU CAN'T PULL THIS OFF...
JUST AS I'D EX-PECT...

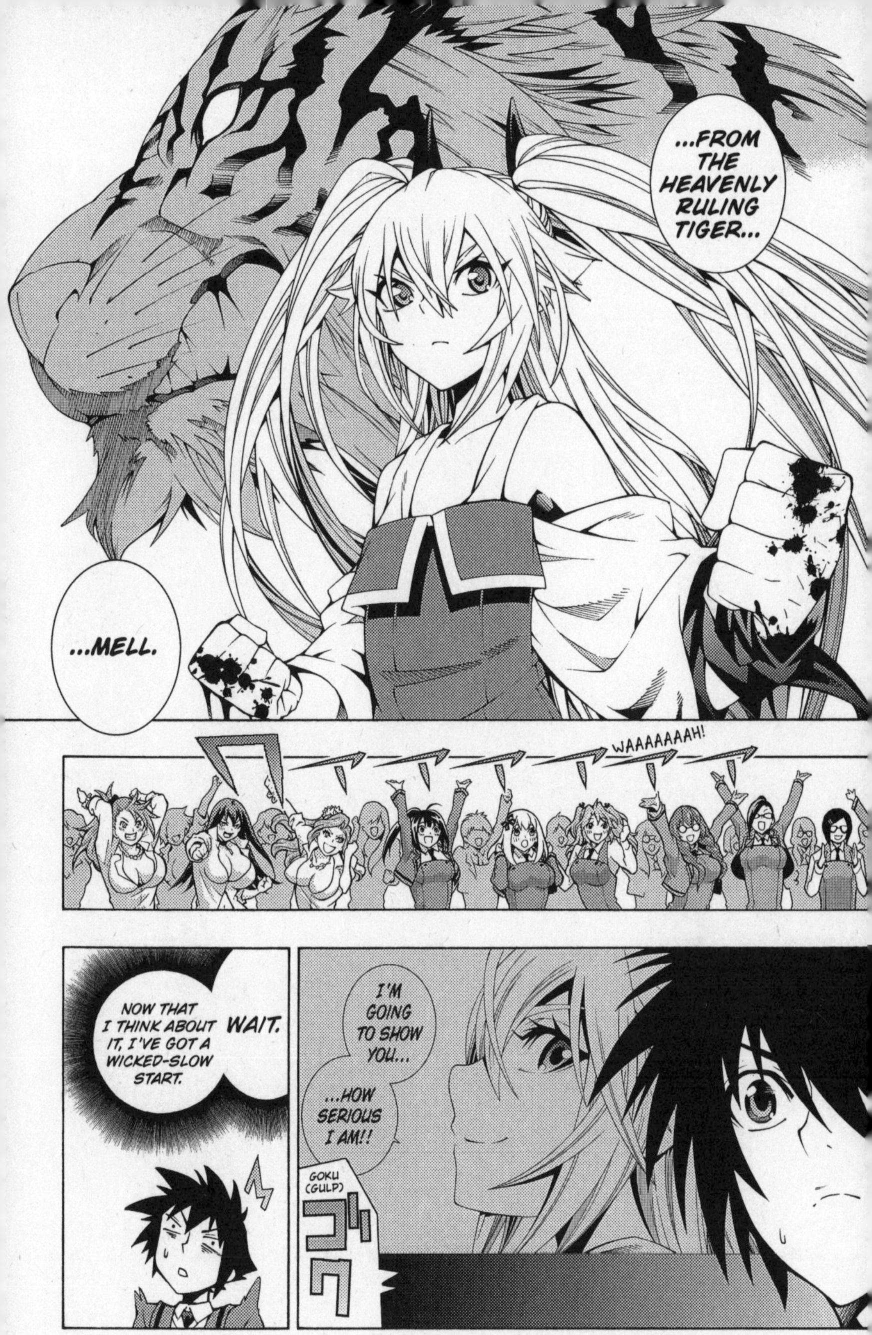
...FROM THE HEAVENLY RULING TIGER...
...MELL.
WAAAAAAAH!
I'M GOING TO SHOW YOU...
...HOW SERIOUS I AM!!
GOKU (GULP)
WAIT.
NOW THAT I THINK ABOUT IT, I'VE GOT A WICKED-SLOW START.

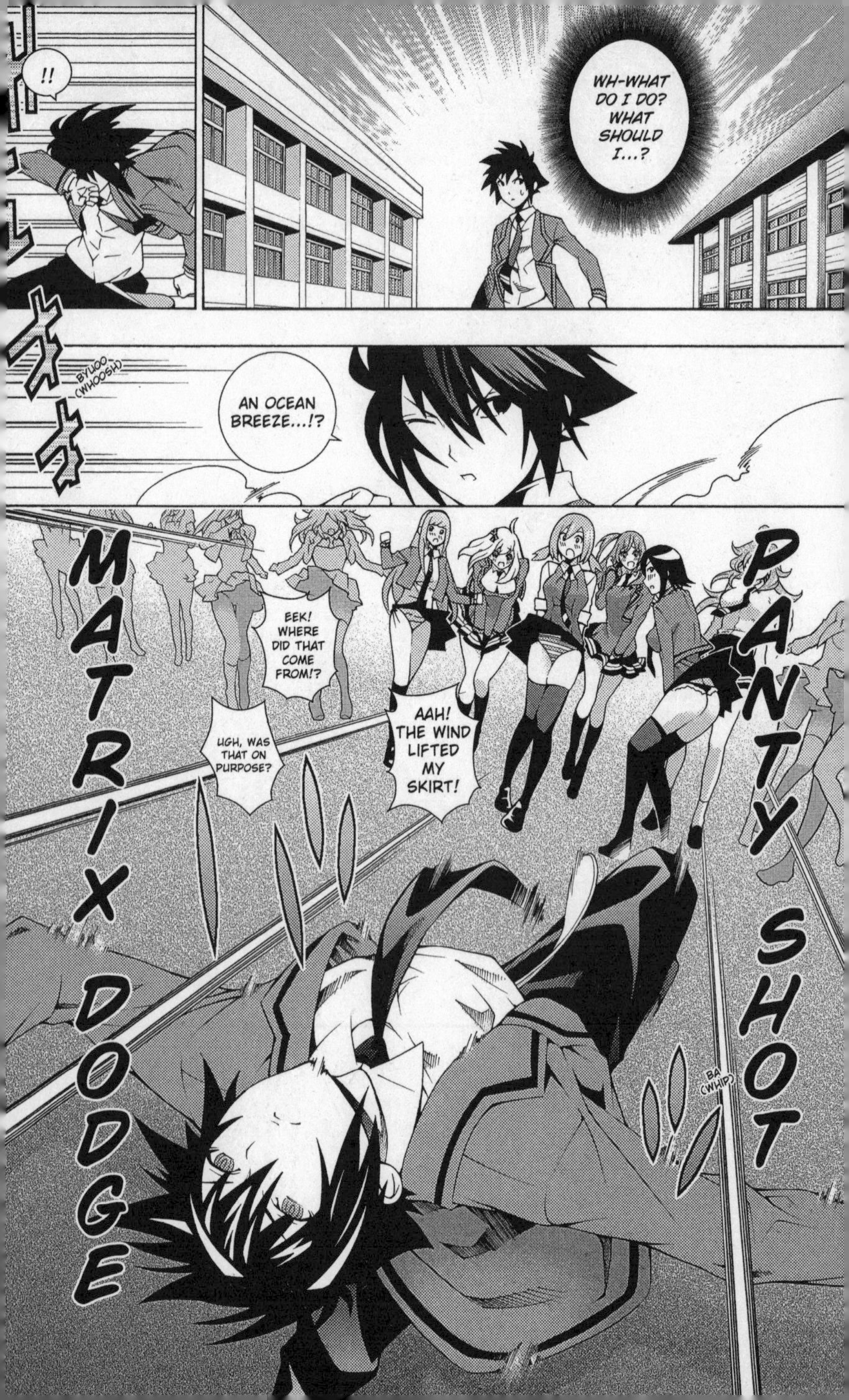
WH-WHAT DO I DO? WHAT SHOULD I...?
!!
BYUOO (WHOOSH)
AN OCEAN BREEZE...!?
PANTY SHOT
AAH! THE WIND LIFTED MY SKIRT!
EEK! WHERE DID THAT COME FROM!?
UGH, WAS THAT ON PURPOSE?
BA (WHIP)
MATRIX DODGE

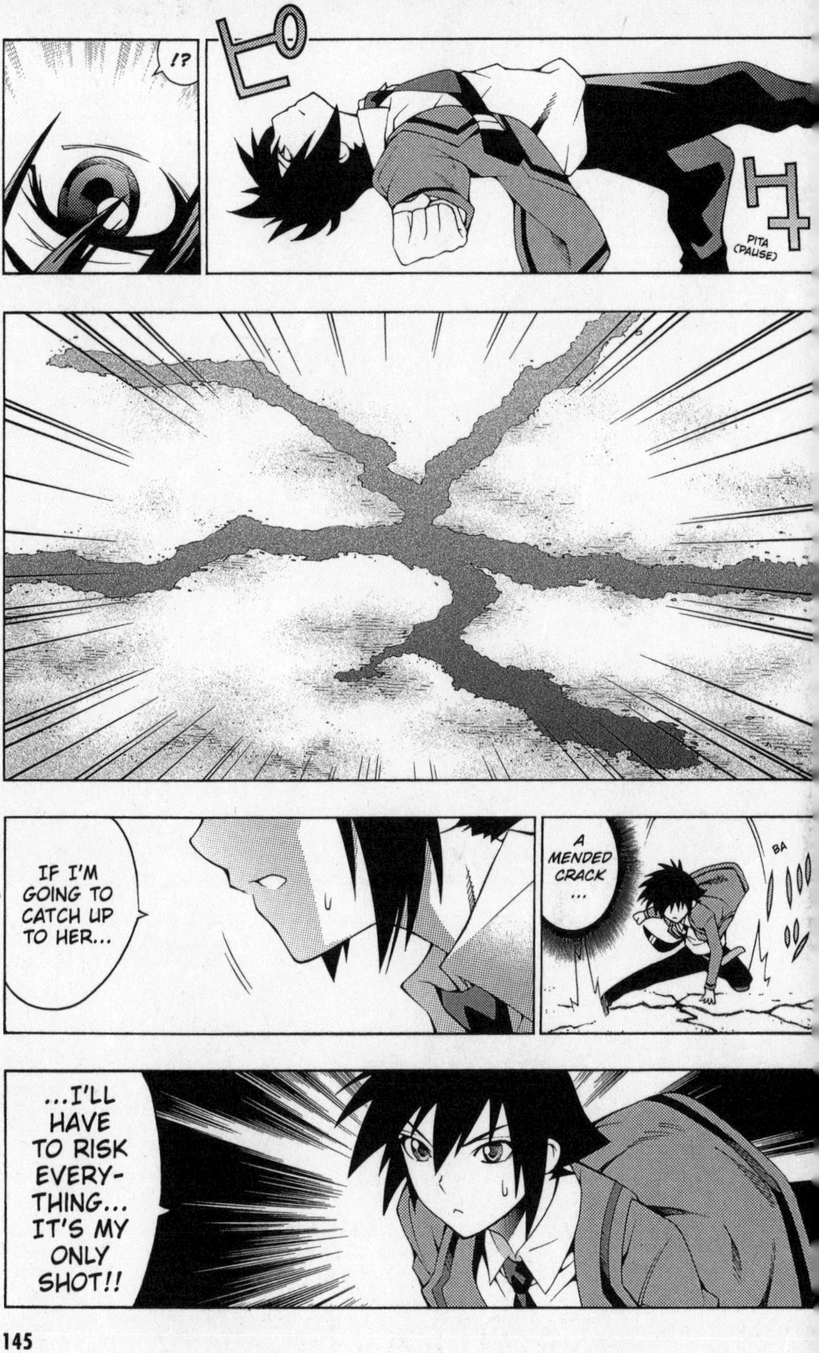
PITA (PAUSE)
!?
A MENDED CRACK ...
BA
IF I'M GOING TO CATCH UP TO HER...
...I'LL HAVE TO RISK EVERY-THING... IT'S MY ONLY SHOT!!

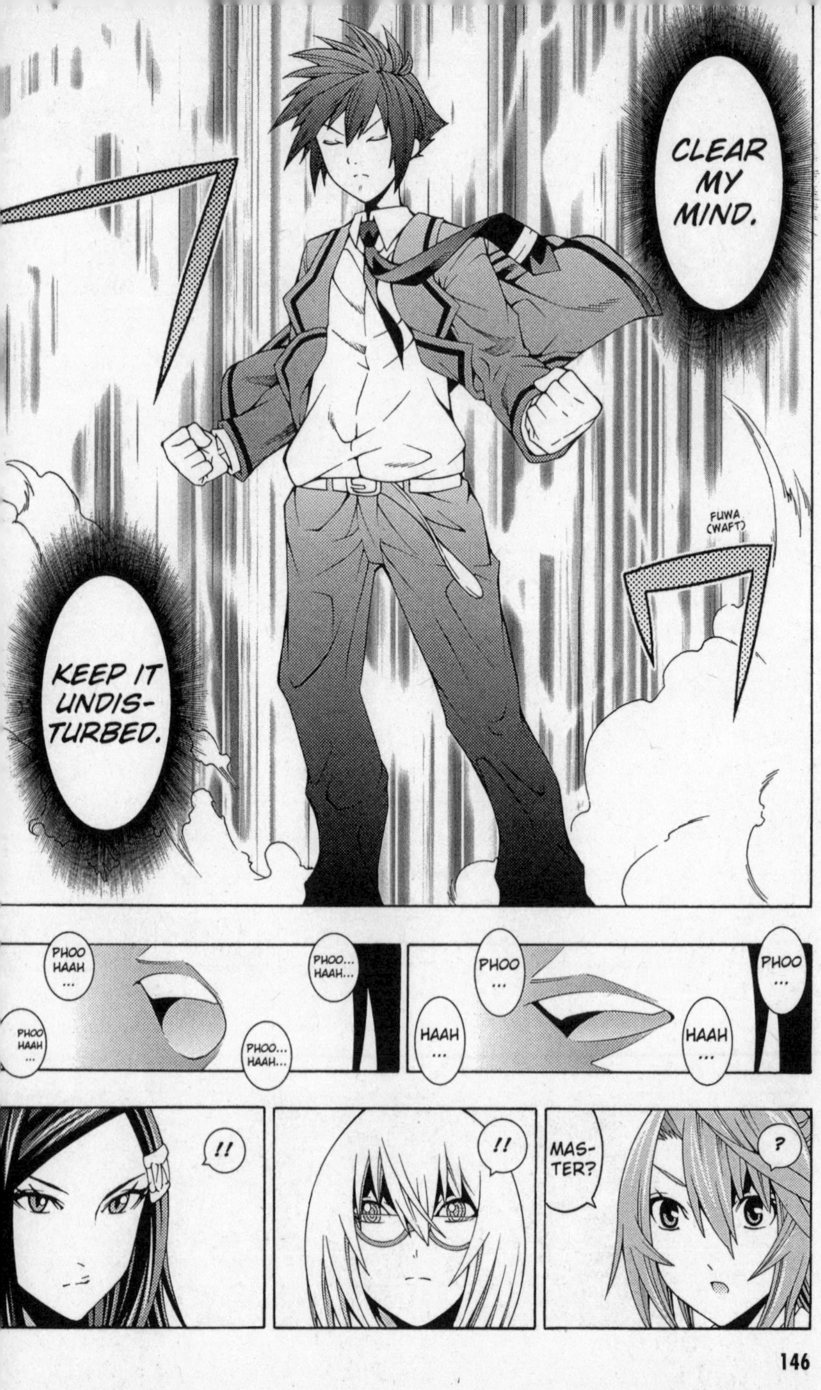
CLEAR MY MIND.
FUWA (WAFT)
KEEP IT UNDISTURBED.
PHOO...
PHOO...
HAAH...
HAAH...
PHOO... HAAH...
PHOO HAAH...
PHOO... HAAH...
PHOO HAAH...
?
MASTER?
!!
!!

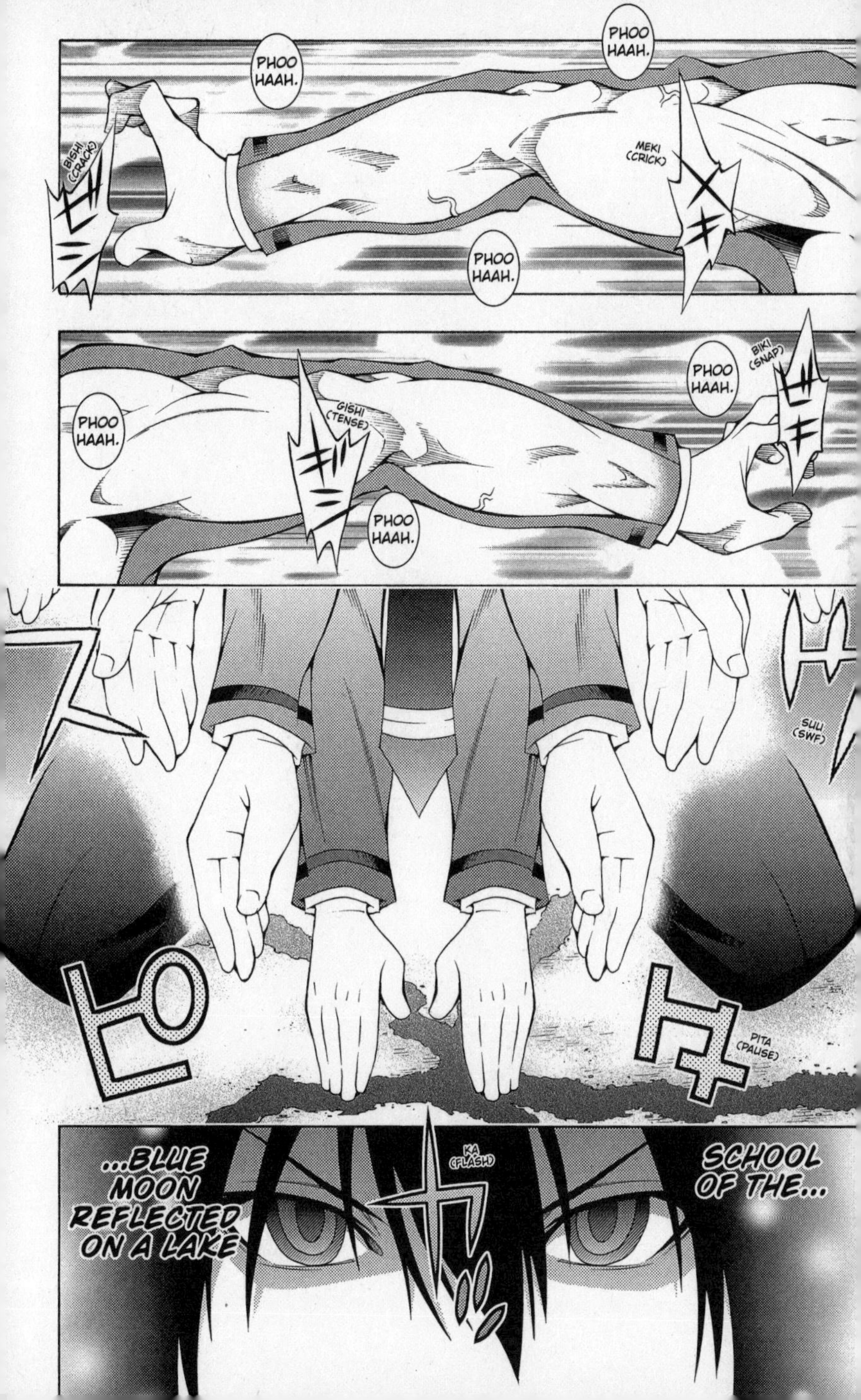
PHOO HAAH.
MEKI (CRICK)
PHOO HAAH.
PHOO HAAH.
BISHI (CRACK)
BIKI (SNAP)
PHOO HAAH.
GISHI (TENSE)
PHOO HAAH.
PHOO HAAH.
SUU (SWF)
PITA (PAUSE)
SCHOOL OF THE...
KA (FLASH)
...BLUE MOON REFLECTED ON A LAKE

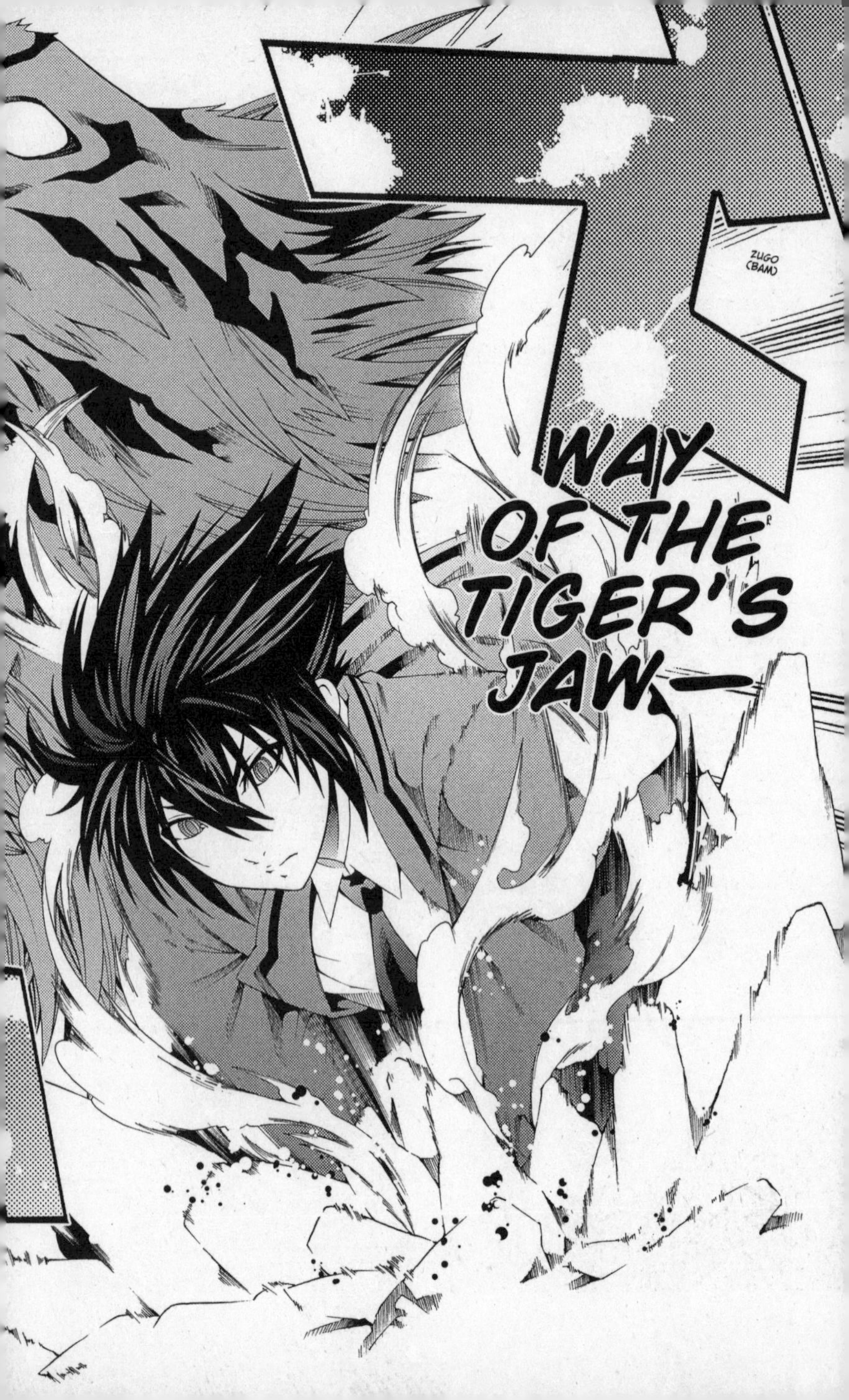
ZUGO
(BAM)
WAY OF THE TIGER'S JAW—

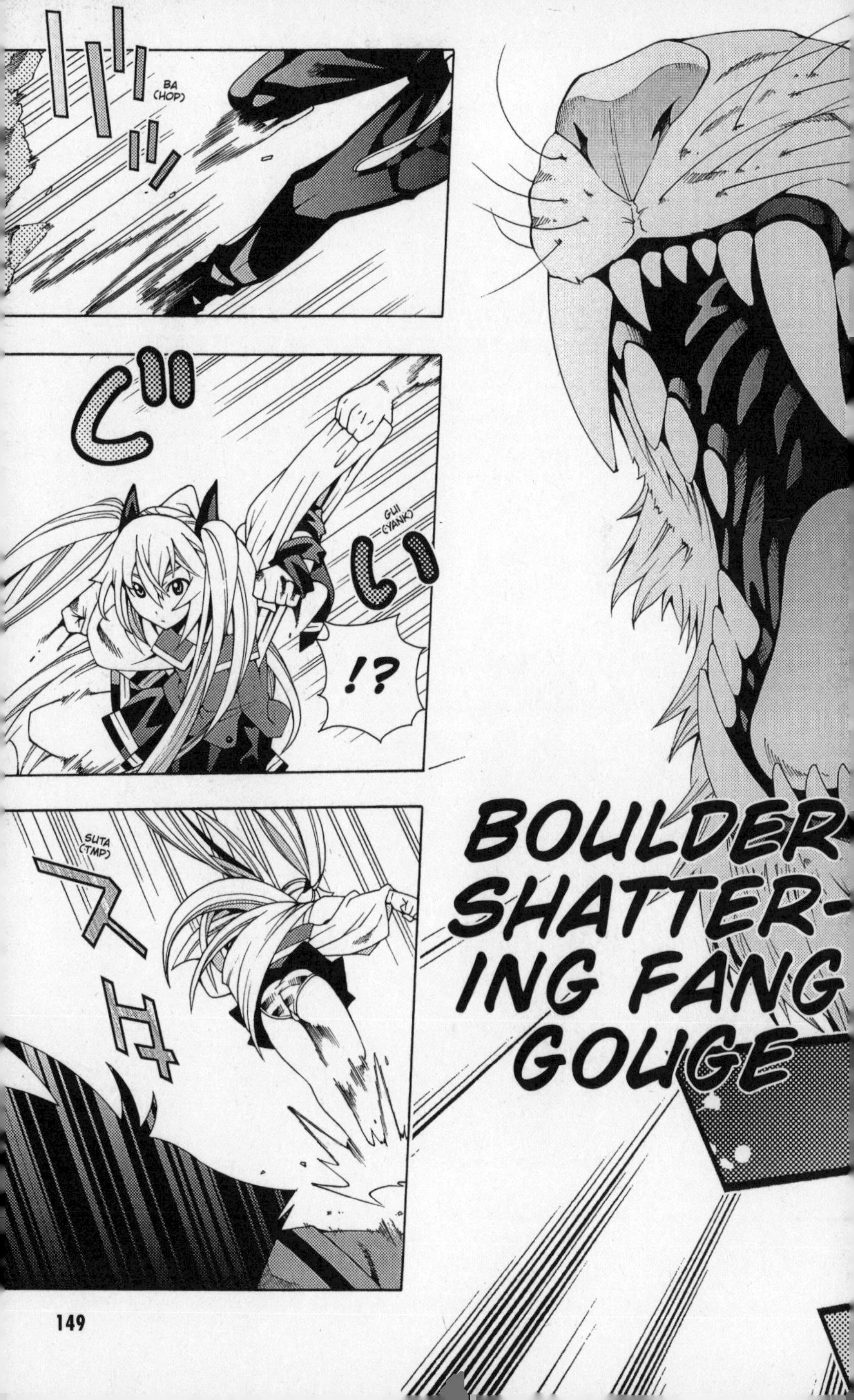
BOULDER SHATTER-ING FANG GOUGE
BA (HOP)
GUI (YANK)
!?
SUTA (TMP)

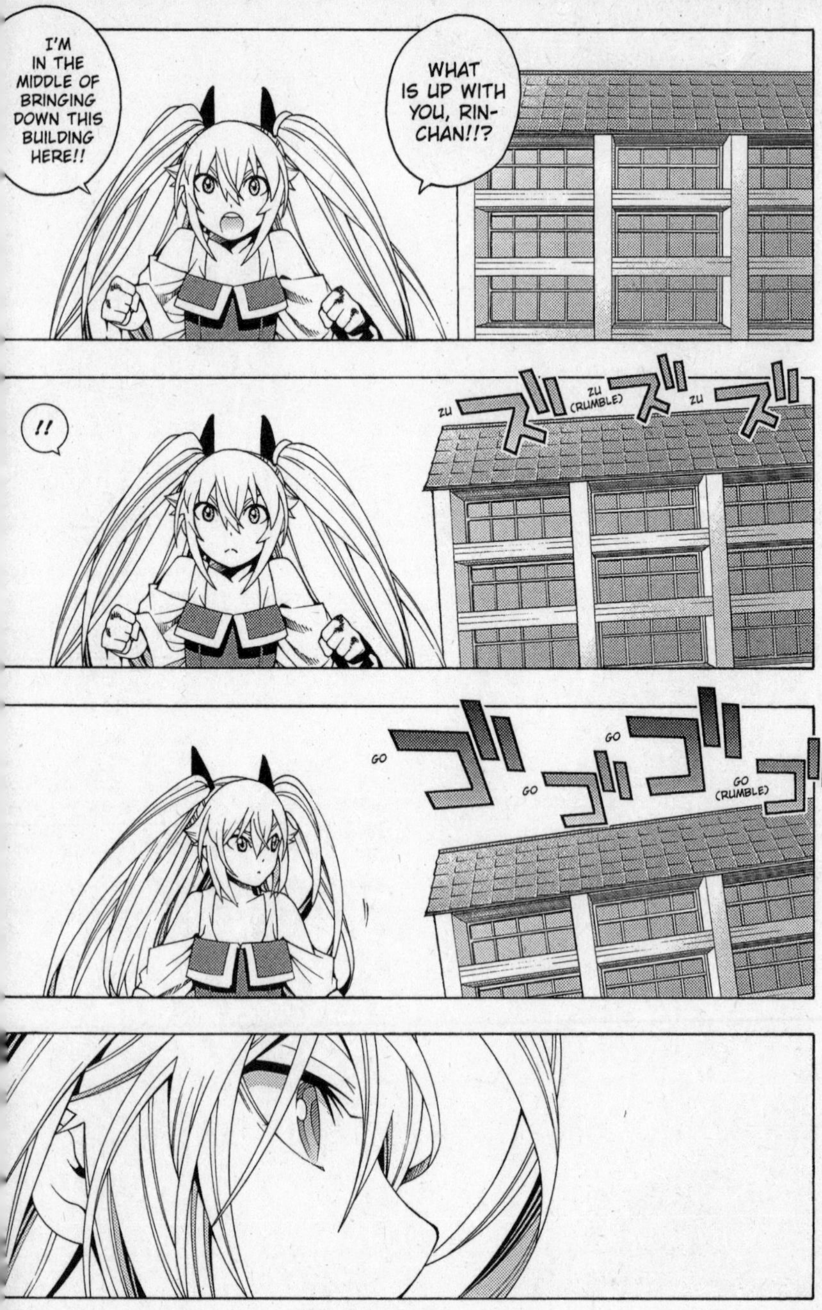
WHAT IS UP WITH YOU, RIN-CHAN!!?
I'M IN THE MIDDLE OF BRINGING DOWN THIS BUILDING HERE!!
ZU
ZU (RUMBLE)
ZU
!!
GO (RUMBLE)
GO
GO
GO

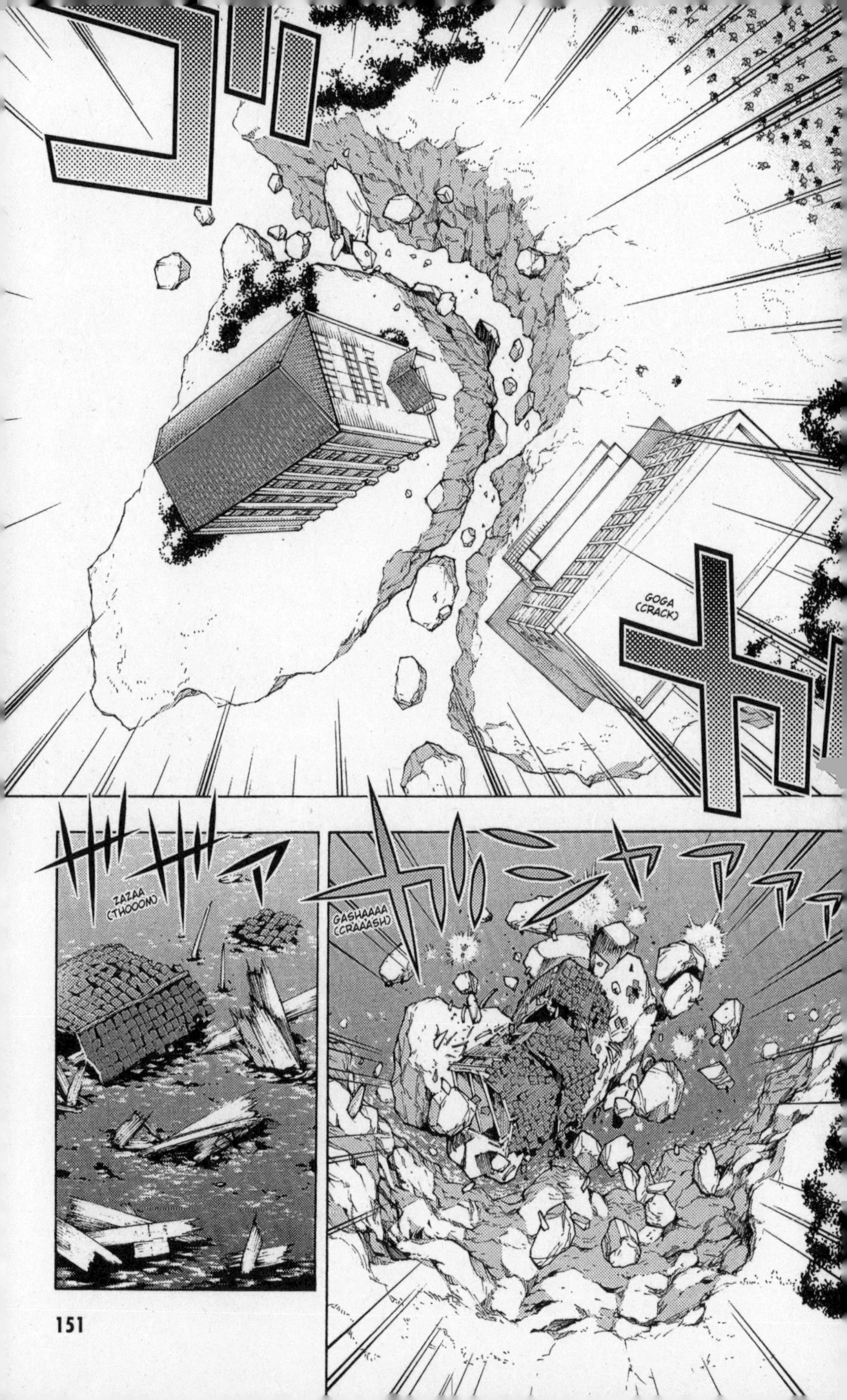
GOGA
(CRACK)
GASHAAAA
(CRAAASH)
ZAZAA
(THOOOM)

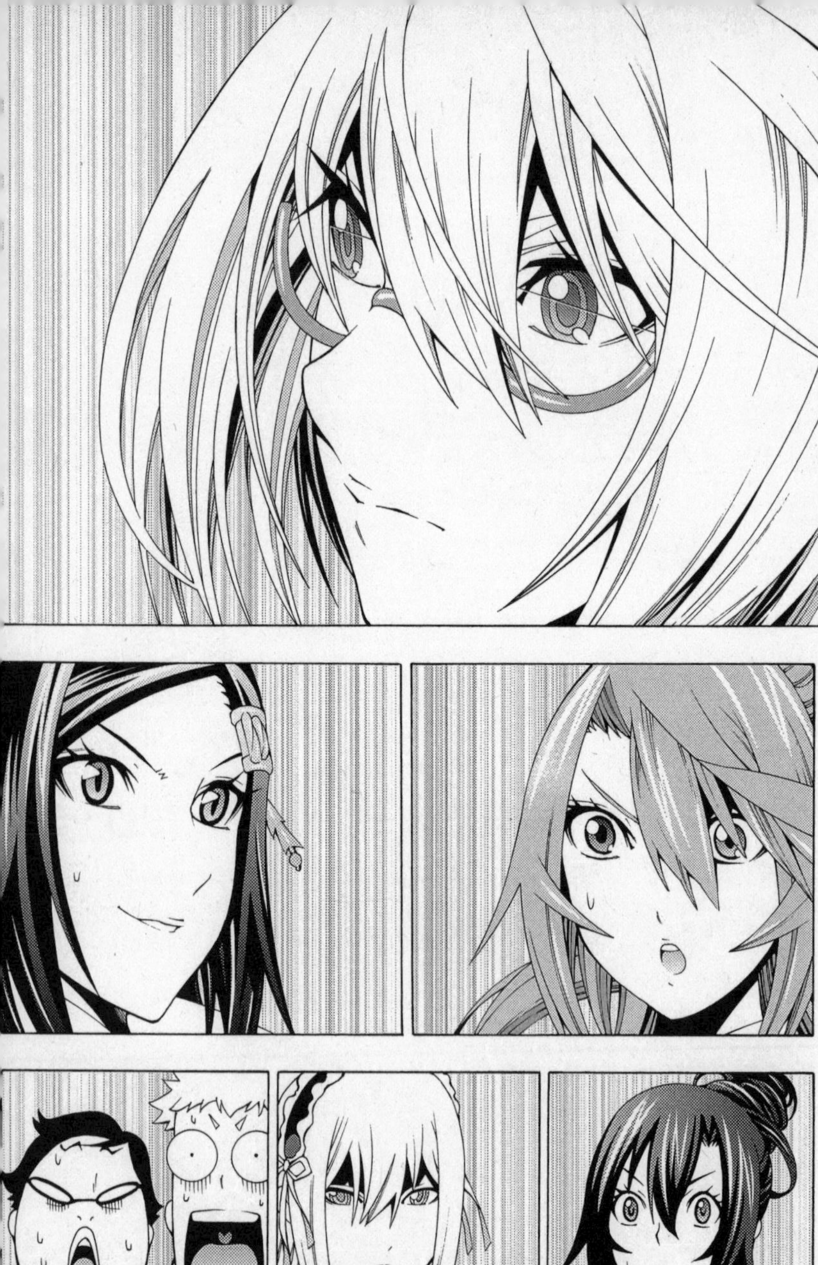

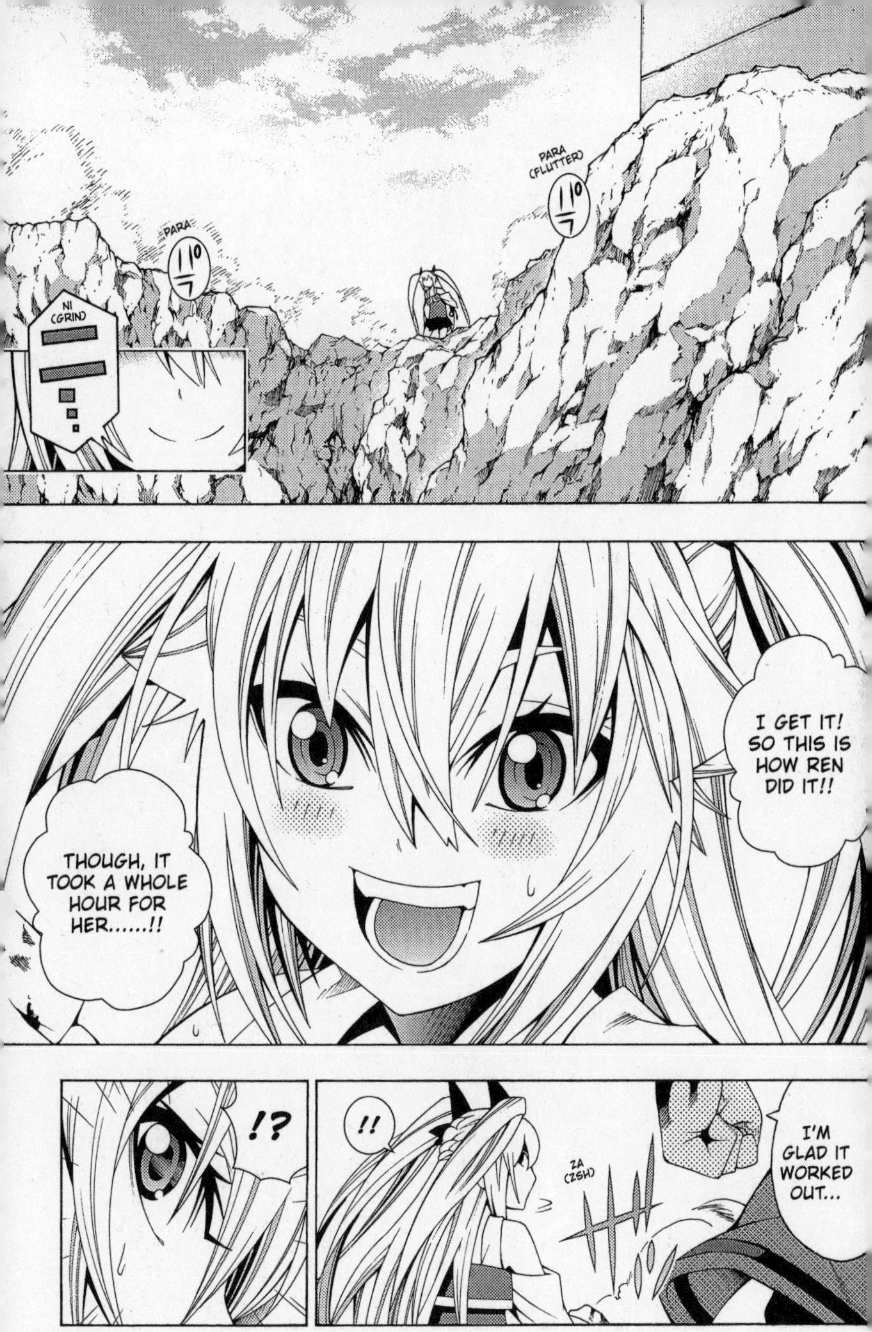
PARA (FLUTTER)
PARA
NI (GRIN)
I GET IT! SO THIS IS HOW REN DID IT!!
THOUGH, IT TOOK A WHOLE HOUR FOR HER......!!
I'M GLAD IT WORKED OUT...
ZA (ZSH)
!!
!?

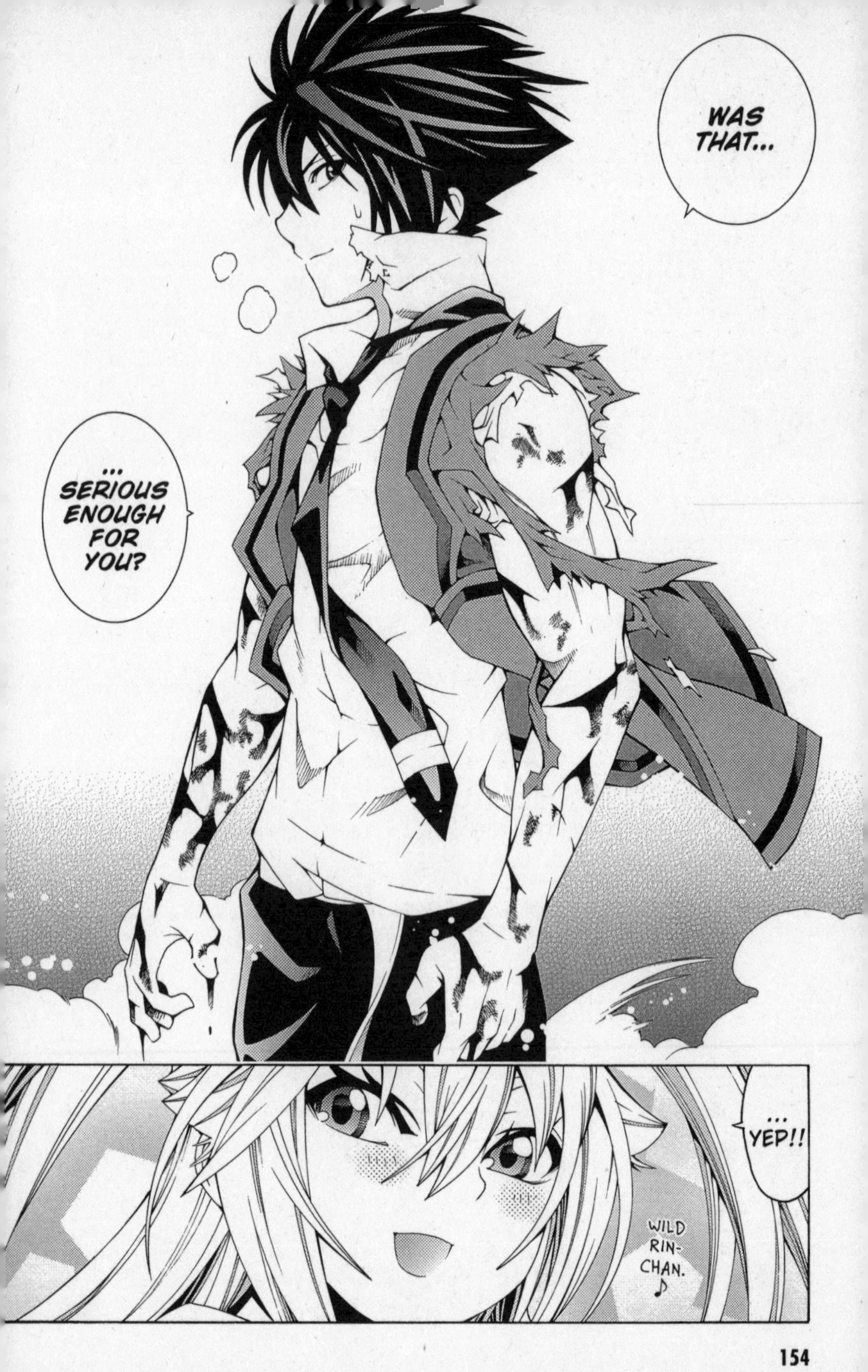
WAS THAT...
...SERIOUS ENOUGH FOR YOU?
...YEP!!
WILD RIN-CHAN. ♪

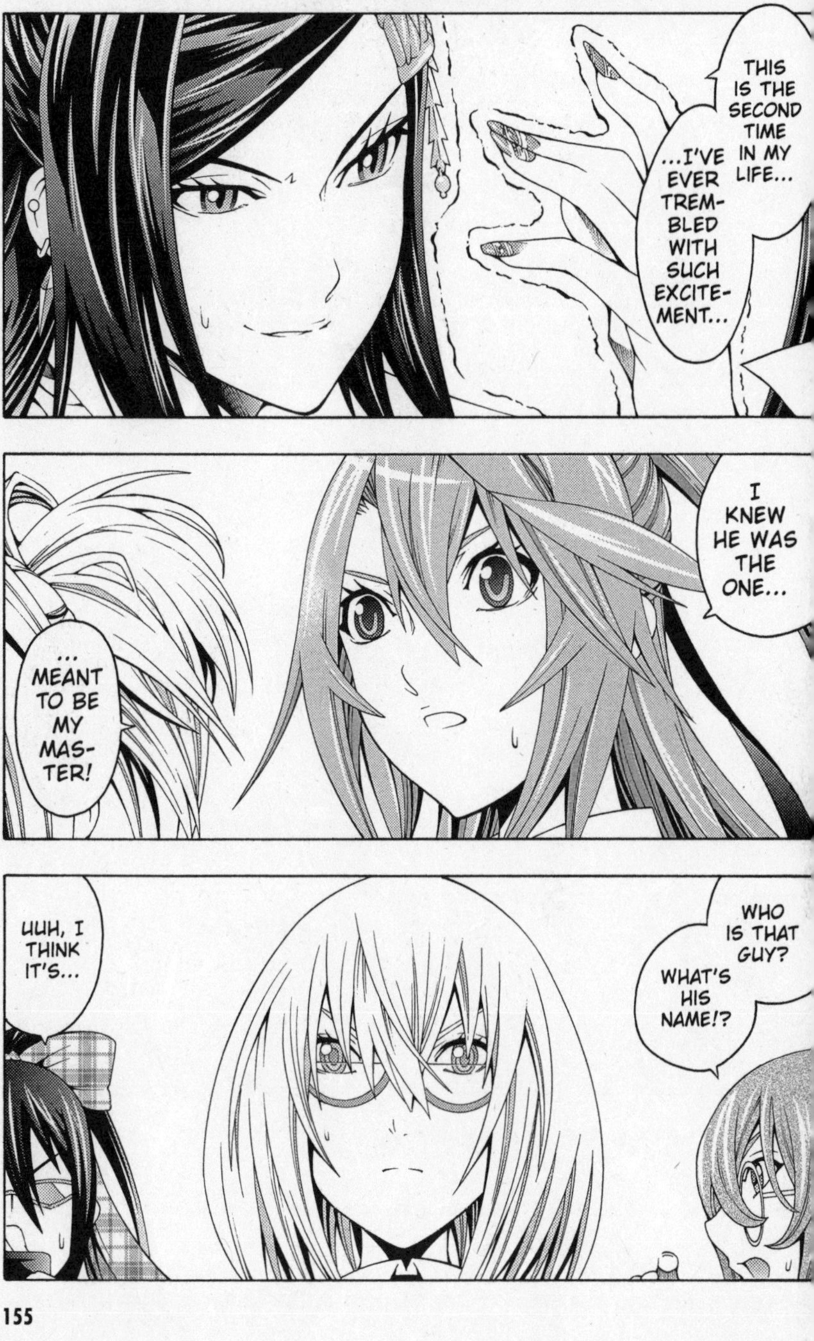
THIS IS THE SECOND TIME IN MY LIFE...
...I'VE EVER TREMBLED WITH SUCH EXCITEMENT...
I KNEW HE WAS THE ONE...
... MEANT TO BE MY MASTER!
WHO IS THAT GUY? WHAT'S HIS NAME!?
UUH, I THINK IT'S...

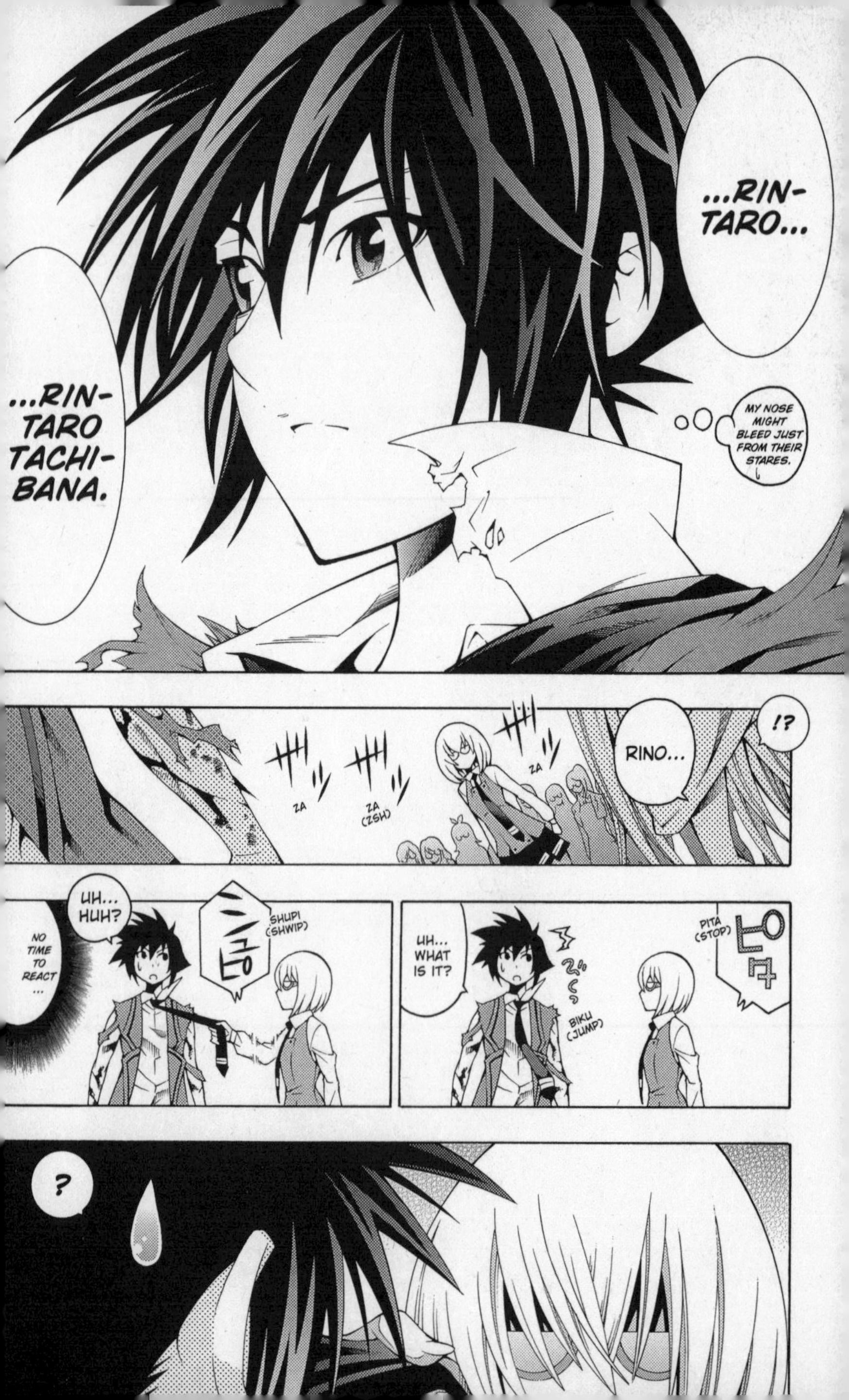
...RIN-TARO...
MY NOSE MIGHT BLEED JUST FROM THEIR STARES.
...RIN-TARO TACHI-BANA.
!?
RINO...
ZA
ZA (ZSH)
ZA
PITA (STOP)
UH... WHAT IS IT?
BIKU (JUMP)
SHUPI (SHWIP)
UH... HUH?
NO TIME TO REACT...
?

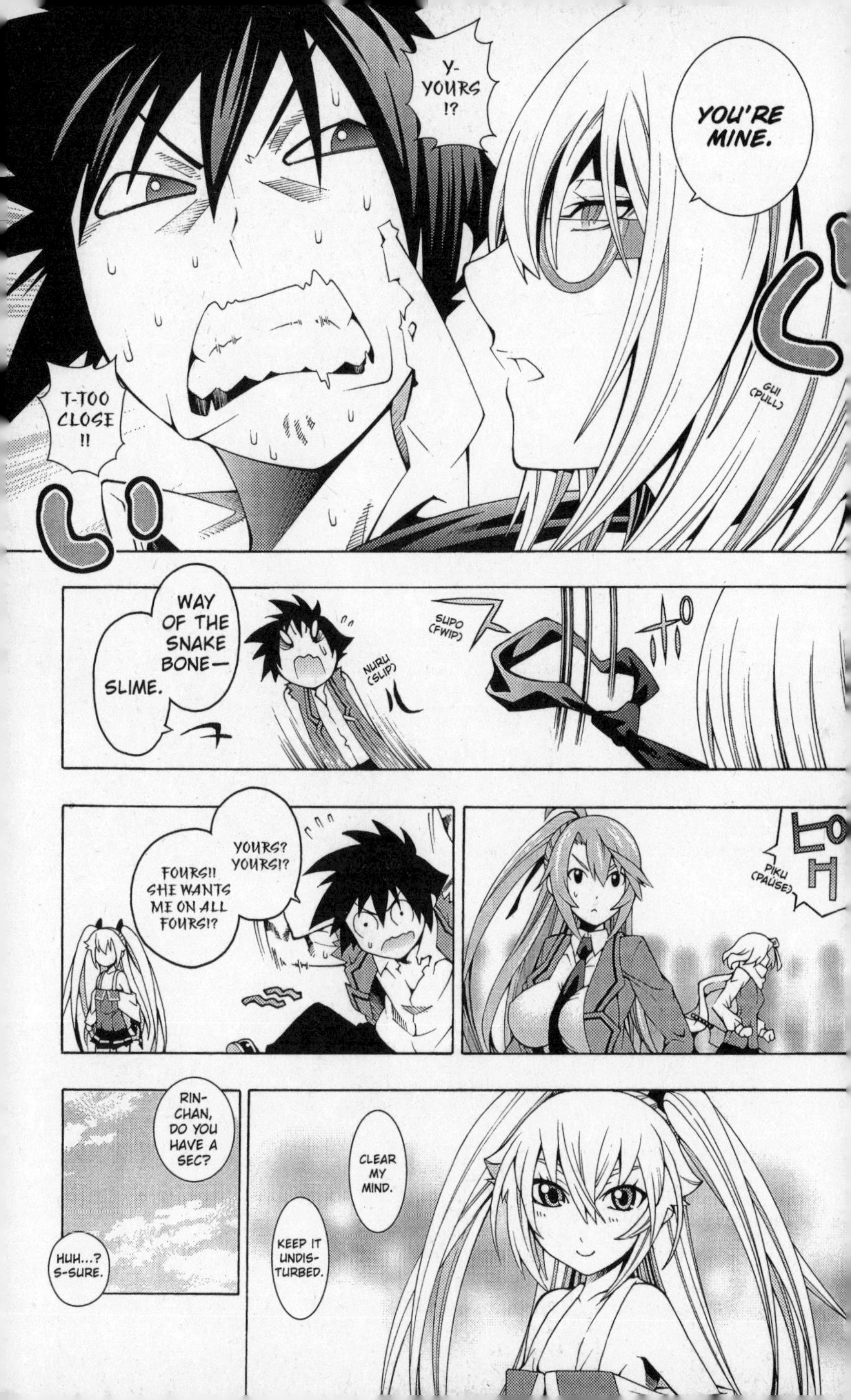
YOU'RE MINE.
Y-YOURS!?
GUI (PULL)
T-TOO CLOSE!!
SUPO (FWIP)
NURU (SLIP)
WAY OF THE SNAKE BONE—SLIME.
PIKU (PAUSE)
YOURS? YOURS!?
FOURS!! SHE WANTS ME ON ALL FOURS!?
CLEAR MY MIND.
KEEP IT UNDISTURBED.
RIN-CHAN, DO YOU HAVE A SEC?
HUH...? S-SURE.

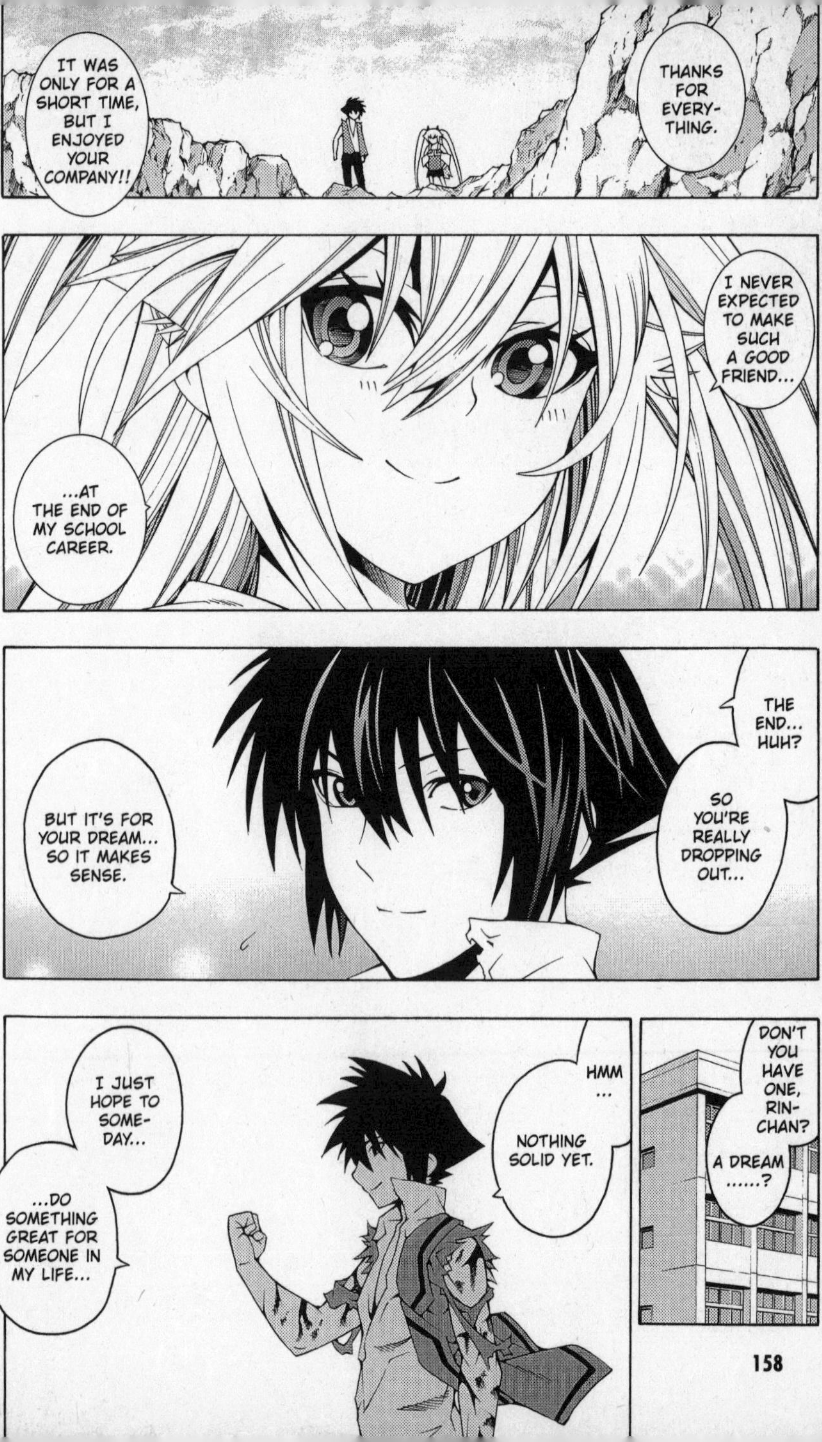
THANKS FOR EVERY-THING.
IT WAS ONLY FOR A SHORT TIME, BUT I ENJOYED YOUR COMPANY!!
I NEVER EXPECTED TO MAKE SUCH A GOOD FRIEND...
...AT THE END OF MY SCHOOL CAREER.
THE END... HUH?
SO YOU'RE REALLY DROPPING OUT...
BUT IT'S FOR YOUR DREAM... SO IT MAKES SENSE.
DON'T YOU HAVE ONE, RIN-CHAN?
A DREAM ......?
HMM ...
NOTHING SOLID YET.
I JUST HOPE TO SOME-DAY...
...DO SOMETHING GREAT FOR SOMEONE IN MY LIFE...

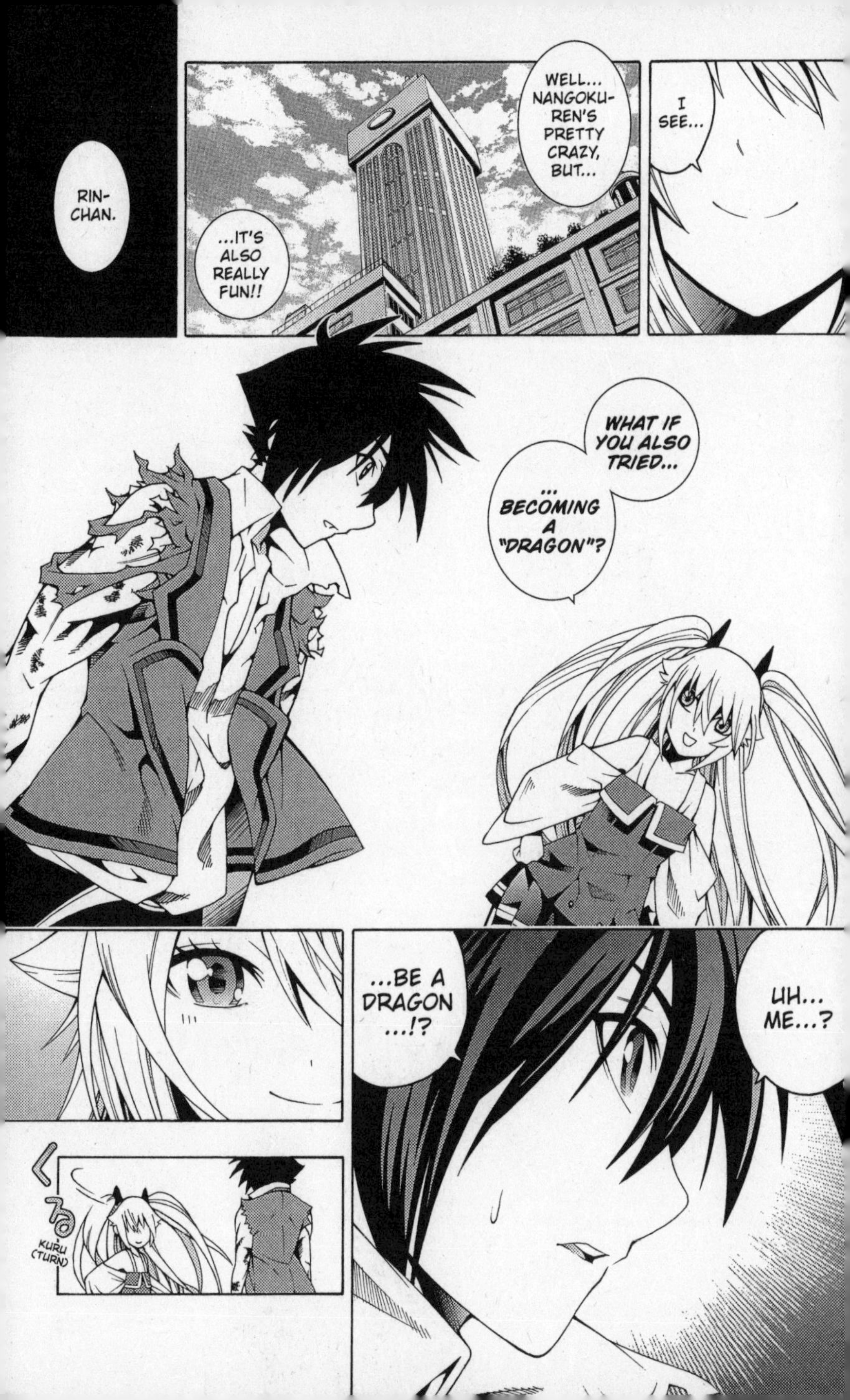
I SEE...
WELL... NANGOKU-REN'S PRETTY CRAZY, BUT...
...IT'S ALSO REALLY FUN!!
RIN-CHAN.
WHAT IF YOU ALSO TRIED...
... BECOMING A "DRAGON"?
UH... ME...?
...BE A DRAGON ...!?
くる
KURU (TURN)

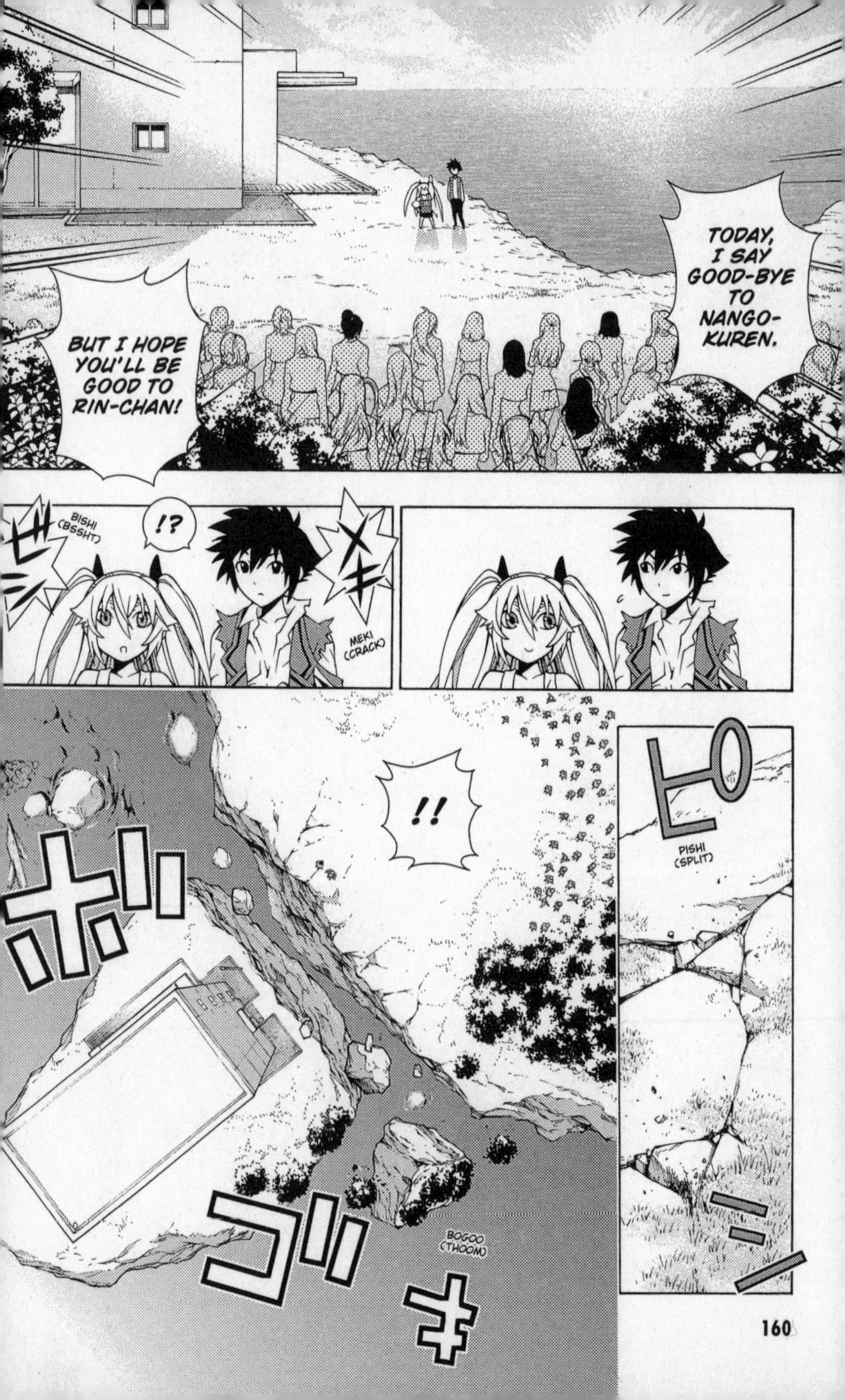

TODAY, I SAY GOOD-BYE TO NANGO-KUREN.
BUT I HOPE YOU'LL BE GOOD TO RIN-CHAN!
MEKI (CRACK)
!?
BISHI (BSSHT)
PISHI (SPLIT)
!!
BOGOO (THOOM)

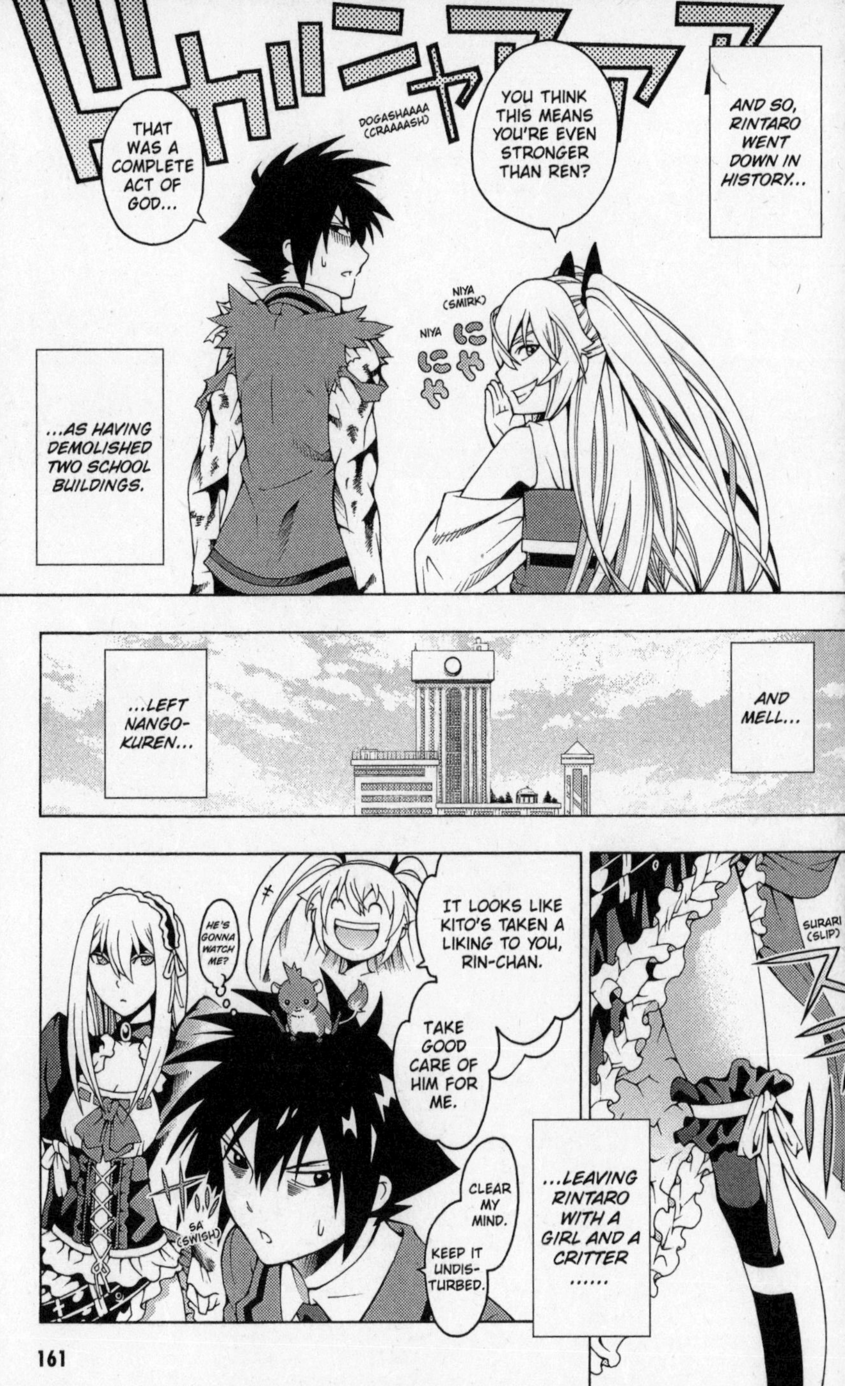
DOGASHAAAA (CRAAAASH)
AND SO, RINTARO WENT DOWN IN HISTORY...
YOU THINK THIS MEANS YOU'RE EVEN STRONGER THAN REN?
THAT WAS A COMPLETE ACT OF GOD...
NIYA (SMIRK)
NIYA にやにや
...AS HAVING DEMOLISHED TWO SCHOOL BUILDINGS.
AND MELL...
...LEFT NANGO-KUREN...
SURARI (SLIP)
IT LOOKS LIKE KITO'S TAKEN A LIKING TO YOU, RIN-CHAN.
TAKE GOOD CARE OF HIM FOR ME.
HE'S GONNA WATCH ME?
...LEAVING RINTARO WITH A GIRL AND A CRITTER ......
CLEAR MY MIND.
KEEP IT UNDISTURBED.
SA (SWISH)

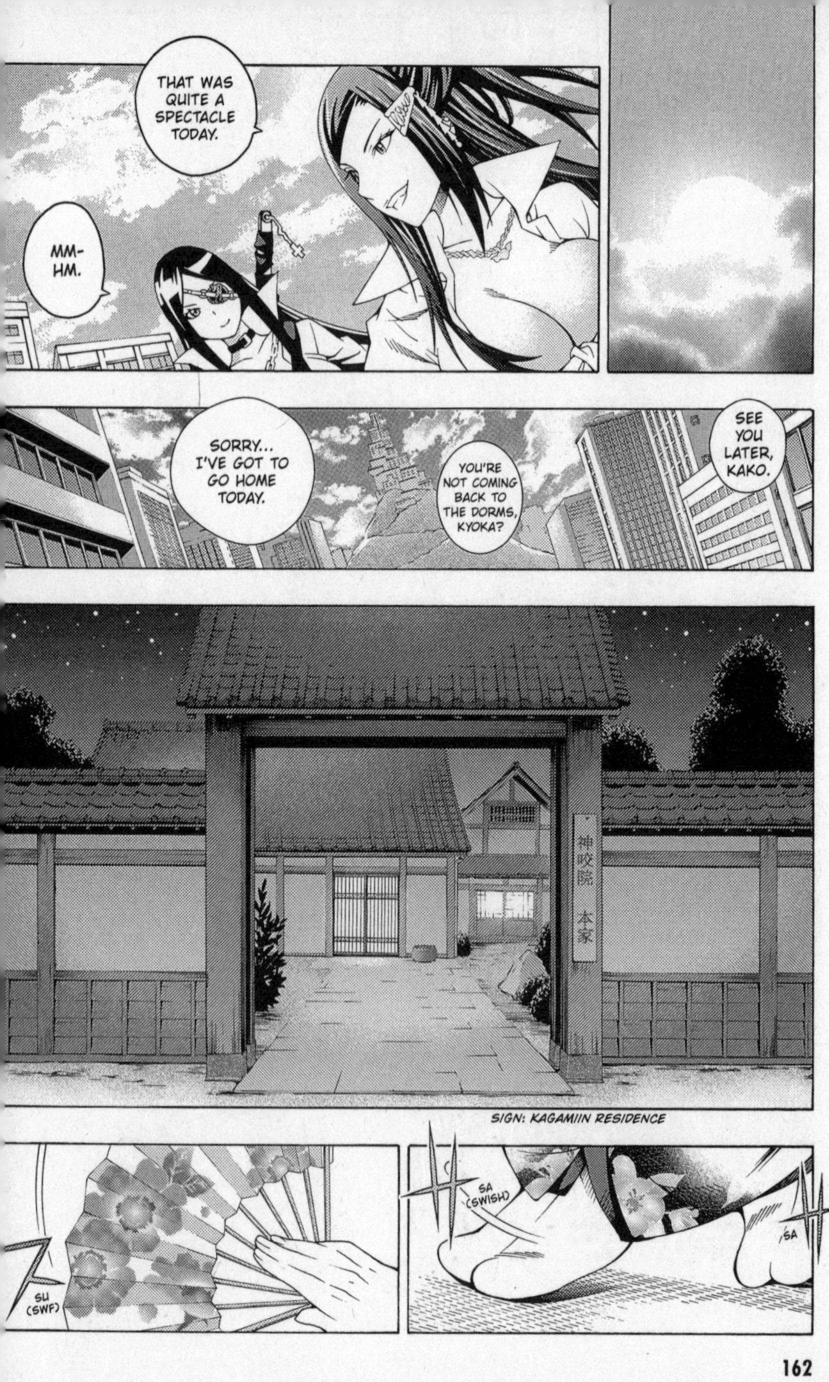
THAT WAS QUITE A SPECTACLE TODAY.
MM-HM.
SEE YOU LATER, KAKO.
YOU'RE NOT COMING BACK TO THE DORMS, KYOKA?
SORRY... I'VE GOT TO GO HOME TODAY.
神咬院 本家
SIGN: KAGAMIIN RESIDENCE
SA (SWISH)
SA
SU (SWF)

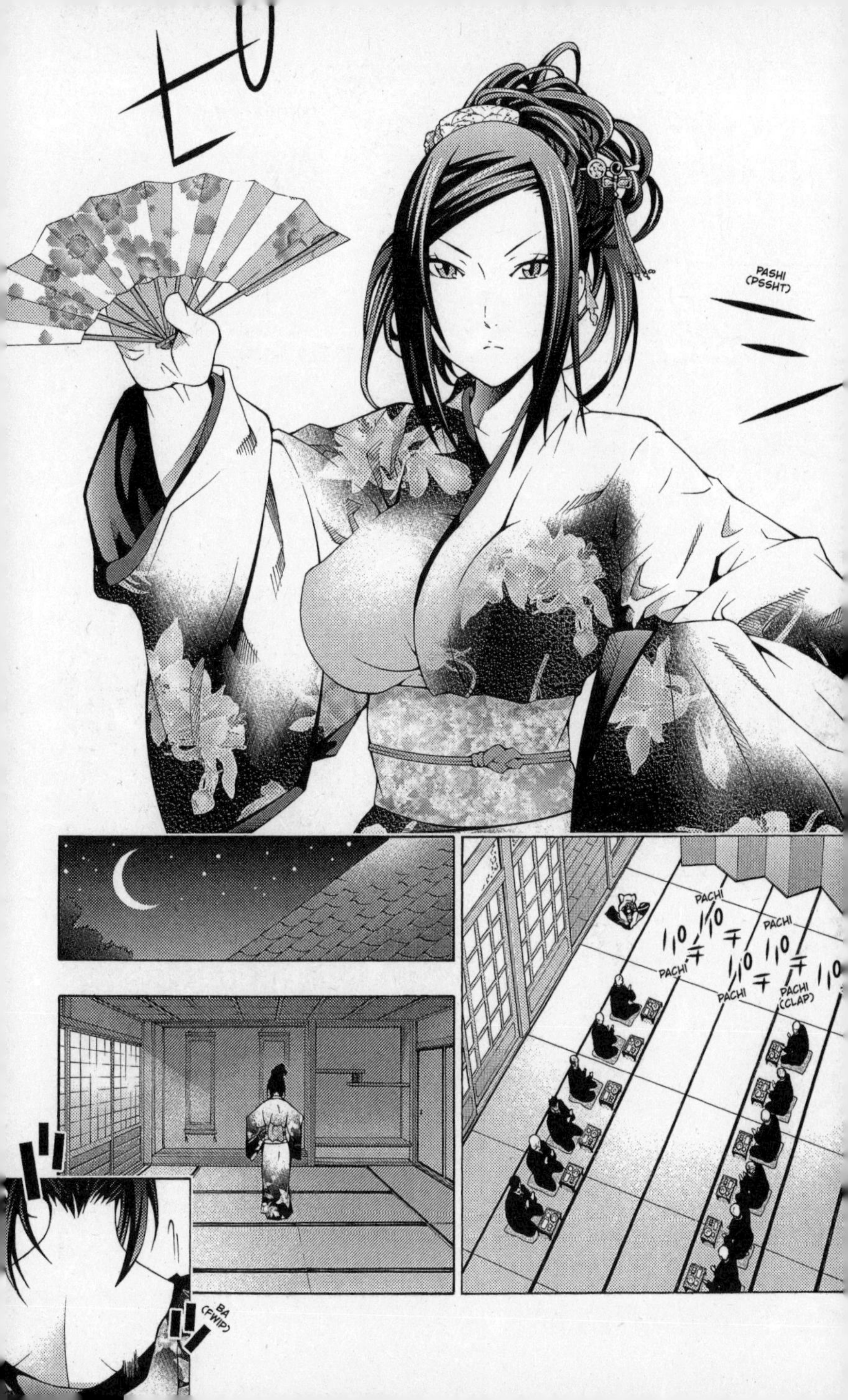
PASHI (PSSHT)
PACHI
PACHI
PACHI
PACHI
PACHI (CLAP)
BA (FWIP)

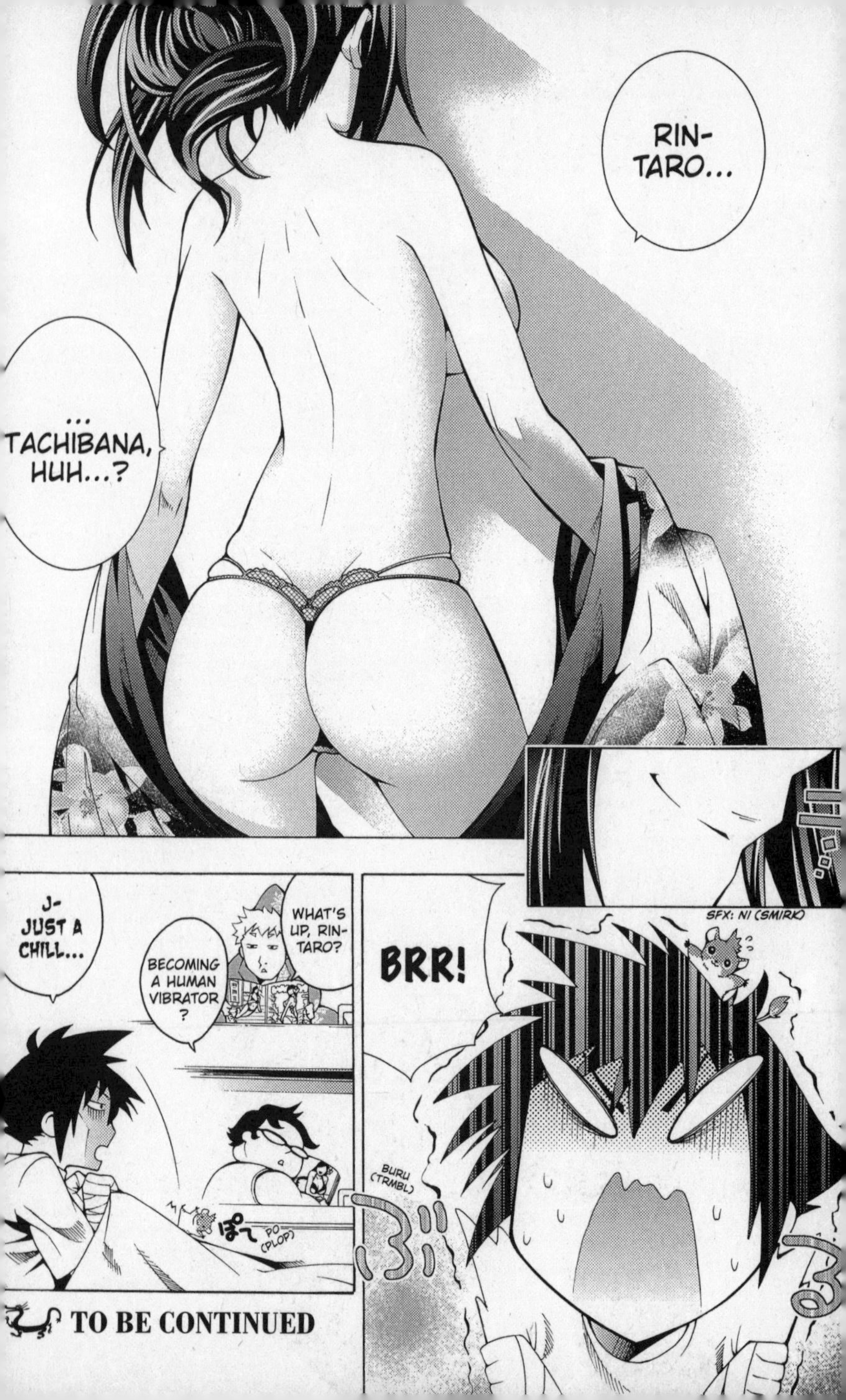
RIN-TARO...
... TACHIBANA, HUH...?
SFX: NI (SMIRK)
BRR!
BURU (TRMBL)
WHAT'S UP, RIN-TARO?
BECOMING A HUMAN VIBRATOR?
J- JUST A CHILL...
PO (PLOP)
TO BE CONTINUED

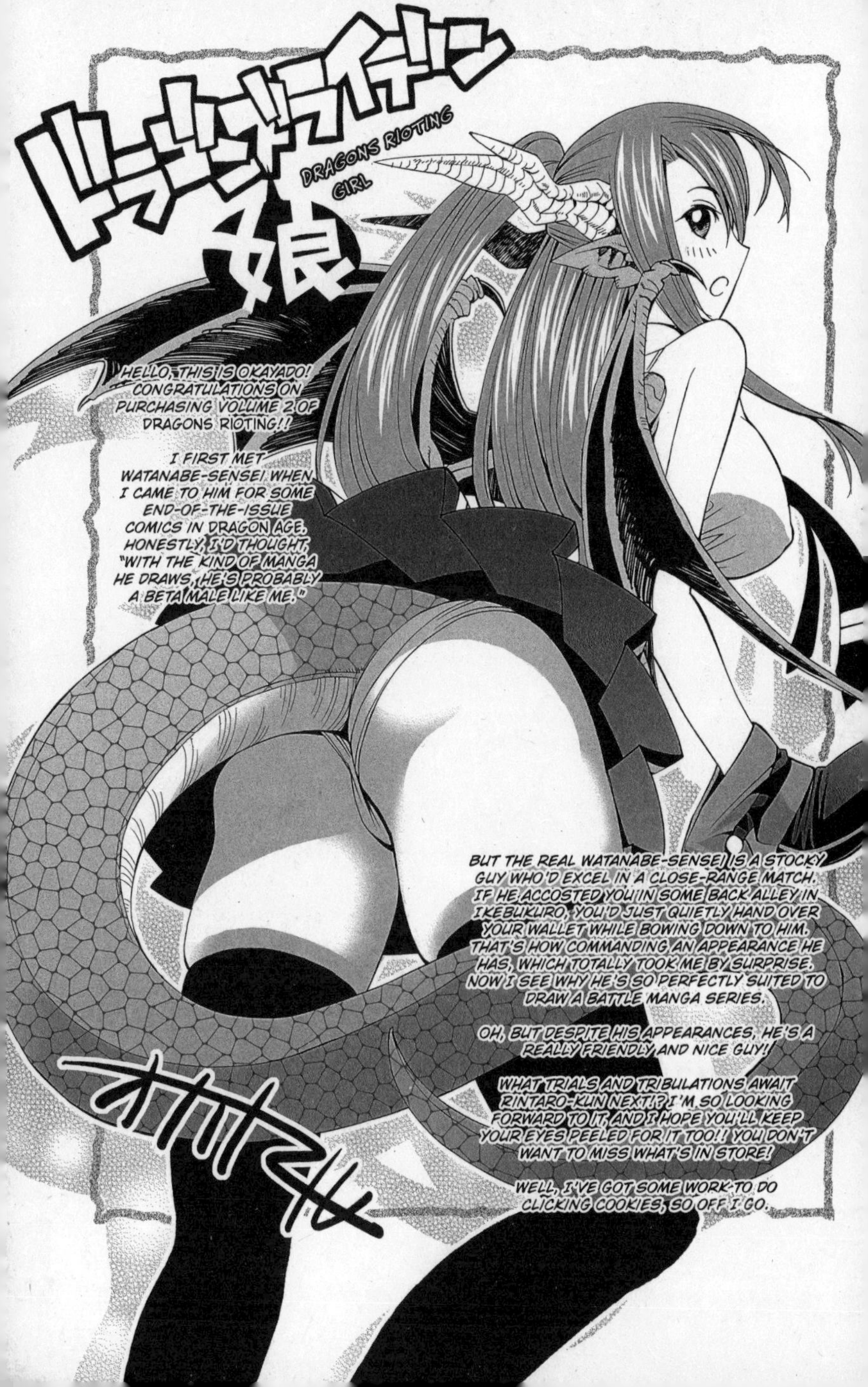
DRAGONS RIOTING GIRL
HELLO, THIS IS OKAYADO! CONGRATULATIONS ON PURCHASING VOLUME 2 OF DRAGONS RIOTING!!
I FIRST MET WATANABE-SENSEI WHEN I CAME TO HIM FOR SOME END-OF-THE-ISSUE COMICS IN DRAGON AGE. HONESTLY, I'D THOUGHT, "WITH THE KIND OF MANGA HE DRAWS, HE'S PROBABLY A BETA MALE LIKE ME."
BUT THE REAL WATANABE-SENSEI IS A STOCKY GUY WHO'D EXCEL IN A CLOSE-RANGE MATCH. IF HE ACCOSTED YOU IN SOME BACK ALLEY IN IKEBUKURO, YOU'D JUST QUIETLY HAND OVER YOUR WALLET WHILE BOWING DOWN TO HIM. THAT'S HOW COMMANDING AN APPEARANCE HE HAS, WHICH TOTALLY TOOK ME BY SURPRISE. NOW I SEE WHY HE'S SO PERFECTLY SUITED TO DRAW A BATTLE MANGA SERIES.
OH, BUT DESPITE HIS APPEARANCES, HE'S A REALLY FRIENDLY AND NICE GUY!
WHAT TRIALS AND TRIBULATIONS AWAIT RINTARO-KUN NEXT!? I'M SO LOOKING FORWARD TO IT, AND I HOPE YOU'LL KEEP YOUR EYES PEELED FOR IT TOO!! YOU DON'T WANT TO MISS WHAT'S IN STORE!
WELL, I'VE GOT SOME WORK TO DO CLICKING COOKIES, SO OFF I GO.

DRAGONS RIOTING ❷
TSUYOSHI WATANABE

Translation: Christine Dashiell

Lettering: Anthony Quintessenza

This book is a work of fiction. Names, characters, places, and incidents are the product of the author's imagination or are used fictitiously. Any resemblance to actual events, locales, or persons, living or dead, is coincidental.

DRAGONS RIOTING Volume 2
© TSUYOSHI WATANABE 2013
Edited by FUJIMISHOBO
First published in Japan in 2013 by KADOKAWA CORPORATION, Tokyo.
English translation rights arranged with KADOKAWA CORPORATION, Tokyo, through TUTTLE-MORI AGENCY, INC., Tokyo.

Translation © 2016 Hachette Book Group, Inc.

Yen Press
Hachette Book Group
1290 Avenue of the Americas
New York, NY 10104

www.HachetteBookGroup.com
www.YenPress.com

s name

hat are

10 9 8 7 6 5 4 3 2 1

BVG

Printed in the United States of America